Convergences:
Inventories of the Present

Edward W. Said, General Editor

The Decline and Fall of the Lettered City

LATIN AMERICA IN THE COLD WAR

JEAN FRANCO

HARVARD UNIVERSITY PRESS

Cambridge, Massachusetts, and London, England   2002

Copyright © 2002 by the President and Fellows of Harvard College
All rights reserved
Printed in the United States of America

Library of Congress Cataloging-in-Publication Data

Franco, Jean.
    The decline and fall of the lettered city : Latin America in the Cold War / Jean Franco.
       p. cm.—(Convergences : inventories of the present)
    Includes bibliographical references and index.
    ISBN 0-674-00752-2 (cloth : alk. paper)—ISBN 0-674-00842-1 (paper : alk. paper)
    1. Latin American literature—20th century—History and criticism.   2. Literature and
society—Latin America.   3. Latin America—Civilization—1948–   I. Title.
II. Convergences (Cambridge, Mass.)

PQ7081 .F637 2002
860.9'98'09045—dc21   2001051659

For Alexis

Contents

Introduction

This border place no longer exists.

MICHAEL HARDT AND ANTONIO NEGRI, *Empire*[1]

In 1953 I sailed to Central America on a Dutch merchant ship that reached Santiago de Cuba a few days after the attack led by Fidel Castro on the Moncada barracks. We found the shops closed and the whole town in mourning. I was on my way to Guatemala and was living there when the Arbenz government was overthrown by a mercenary army subsidized by the United States. From one day to the next the city became a hostile territory—friends had taken refuge in embassies; there was no longer news on the radio, only marimba music; and at night the curfew confined us to the house. What I remember most vividly about that time was not the emptiness of defeat but the poet Alaíde Foppa de Solórzano reading her poems during the curfew, an experience that was to leave a trace in everything I have written, especially in this book. Literature is a protagonist in this drama of loss and dislocation not only because it articulated the utopian but also because it is implicated in its demise. That is why what began as a book on the Cold War and culture developed into an exploration of a postwar battlefield from which many of the old landmarks seem like ghostly remnants.

The United States staged its cultural interventions during the Cold War as a defense of freedom against censorship, while on an altogether different plane, in what was pitched as a war of "values," the Soviet Union defended a realism in which the "real" was defined as class struggle and "peace" became a political tactic. As far as the

United States was concerned, there was a distinct advantage when the autonomy of art and the freedom of the artist could be pitted against programmatic realism. The appeal to Latin Americans dangled by front organizations, such as the Congress for Cultural Freedom, was not only freedom but inclusion in "universal" culture, although this disguised a not-so-subtle attack on national, ethnic, and local cultures, which were denigrated as aberrant, as merely provincial, or as idiosyncratic. This gave the project a rather more frontally avowed intention than the aesthetic modernisms of Europe and the United States, the power of which, in Fredric Jameson's words, "was, during the cold war and in the period of their North American canonization, displaced and invested in essentially anti-political forms of academic aestheticism."[2] In Latin America, on the other hand, the literary high ground was claimed by "apolitical" writers, most of whom were outside the academy.

There are, therefore, significant differences between the withdrawal of the U.S. intelligentsia from "committed" art in the 1940s and the split that occurred in Latin America between the public commitment of writers and their writing. In the United States, modernism became institutionalized in the Cold War years, when the focus was on the "spiritual critique" of literature. In Latin America it was a time of acerbic polemics and debate as writers' hitherto untested claims of commitment were challenged by publics whose imaginations were fired by armed struggle and revolution. All kinds of aesthetic and political projects now appeared possible—the aesthetic utopias of modernism and the historical avant-garde, the notion of pure art and pure literature, participatory theater, liberation from capitalism.

But the continent was also a battlefield of another kind as both the United States and the Soviet Union carried on covert activities to influence the hearts and minds of Latin Americans. Thus abstract universalism and freedom were values disseminated by CIA-funded journals against the universal teleology of revolution, behind which lurked the Soviet national project. As I suggest in the first two chapters, there is more to this than conspiracy theory. In the United States itself, the turn from public art to abstract expressionism, from a politicized avant-garde to a depoliticized avant-garde art, from realist to experimental writing (a turn that was never absolute or all-embracing), was based on claims for artistic autonomy.[3] In Latin America, on the other hand, one serious effect of deploying art and literature in the service of the great powers was a devaluation of literature itself and ultimately of writers' ethical claims. Cold War pragmatics overrode the very values that literature ostensibly espoused; at the same time, culture was being remapped and the prestige of writers undermined by the rapidly changing field invaded and structured by mass communications. Meanwhile, the "universal," defined as Western values, proved to be as counterfeit as the teleological assumptions that underwrote the universalism of the communist Left. Artistic freedom became subsumed under the tendentious "freedom" posited by the Cold War warriors while the ideal city of workers was annexed by the Soviet empire.

It can be argued that the Cold War in Latin America actually began with the Cuban revolution, although the 1954 intervention in Guatemala served as a prelude. The Cuban and the Nicaraguan revolutions appeared to spring organically from their own national past and appealed to the long-standing program of national liberation that would allow Latin American countries to develop their own style of modernization in liberated territories, freed from the taints of past corruption and materialism. A tradition of catholic anticapitalism wedded to a notion of "good" use value against evil exchange mobilized not only Che Guevara's nonmaterial incentives and Ernesto Cardenal's community of Solentiname but also the antimaterialism of the militant avant-garde movements. This was the period when conceptual artists were throwing money into the Seine and when Abbie Hoffman threw dollar bills into the New York Stock Exchange. "Money is the alienated *ability of mankind,*" wrote Marx in an early essay, but in the 1960s it was money and exchange as such that came under suspicion, a suspicion that threaded politics with art and surfaced in literary texts, art happenings, and political movements from the Tupamaros to the Sendero Luminoso.[4] The alternative community was imagined as the pure antithesis to the miseries of the real nation, to market-driven capitalism and bureaucratic communism alike. But the idealized austerity of the guerrilla and the idealized simplicity of the peasant could not be reconciled with the exuberance and excess of the aesthetic, nor with the status of the writer as hero. This would be the essence of the drama that unfolded not only in Cuba but also among insurgent groups throughout Latin America as literature became subordinated to warfare. The military metaphor of the avant-garde reached a limit when Cuba, in its self-appointed role as Third World liberator, pressed supporters into service that was no longer metaphoric. The literary avant-garde could not be transformed into a vanguard for many reasons, not the least being a masculinist bias that brought about an exodus of gay writers from Cuba. In Chapter 3 I examine the often conflicting utopian projects that were tested by the *realpolitik* of siege economy and war.

Conspiracy theories that only take into account North American intervention can never account for a writer's disaffection from left-wing cultural politics, for that disaffection was in many cases a tacit rejection of the rigidity of Soviet-inspired aesthetics. As I argue in Chapter 2, socialist realism in Latin America always came up against realities of race, of underdevelopment and the legacy of colonialism that were not containable in its narrow structure. It was poetry rather than the realist novel that narrated Latin America's fragmented history as an epic adventure with the poet, not the politician, as prophet.

The extent of the conflict of competing universals can only be understood in the context of societies in which literature conferred status and relative independence on writers who were not only vociferous critics but had, in the 1960s, substantially redefined their traditional pedagogical role. Poets and novelists influenced the way literature was read, history understood, and language valued. Jorge Luis Borges, Carlos Fuentes, Octavio Paz, Lezama Lima, García Márquez, Vargas Llosa, Julio Cortázar, Augusto Roa Bastos, and José María Arguedas—the list could be longer—introduced theories of reading and understanding to elucidate not only their own work but also that of their forerunners and contemporaries. They created canons and produced a corpus of criticism that included essays, monographs, speeches, and journalism, that provided a serious evaluation of contemporary culture, and that revamped literary genealogy in a way that transgressed narrow national boundaries. In his essay on the new Latin American novel, Carlos Fuentes described the work of his contemporaries as a healthy break with the language of power.[5] In *Don Quixote or the Critique of Reading,* he ascribed to Cervantes's novel a crucial role in the secularization of society, drawing parallels between Cervantes's time and his own: "As if he foresaw all the dirty tricks of servile literary naturalism, Cervantes destroys the illusion of literature as a mere copy of reality and creates a literary reality far more powerful and difficult to grapple with: the reality of a novel in its existence at all levels of the critique of reading."[6] Mario Vargas Llosa described literature as a permanent insurrection and the author as one who commits deicide.[7] Julio Cortázar resurrected surrealism from the graveyard, while inserting theories of writing into his novel *Rayuela (Hopscotch)*.[8] Borges's entire work is an allegory of reading. Octavio Paz not only reinterpreted the history of the avant-garde in Europe as a poetics of disenchantment but also wrote on a range of poetic theory, on Lévi-Strauss, and on Indian culture—the fruit of his years in Delhi, where he served as Mexican ambassador.[9] Furthermore, a substantial group of writers—Miguel Angel Asturias, José María Arguedas, Augusto Roa Bastos, Darcy Ribeiro, and Alejo Carpentier—undertook ethnographic study as well as literary explorations into the linguistic and racial heterogeneity of the continent. The point I am making is that for two decades, writers were more important arbiters of taste, especially among the younger generation, than critics or academics and more important monitors of political correctness than politicians. The presence of students and young people at readings, in conferences and even mass meetings at which writers pronounced on politics, revolution, and literature—as a result of a growing upwardly mobile university population—brought into visibility social actors, many of them recent immigrants into the city, and a young generation of readers impatient for change. The physical presence of this public heightened the rhetoric of polarized Cold War politics.

Responding to these demographic changes, writers self-confidently instigated the public to read as "contemporaries of the rest of the world." Indeed, the development of a critical consciousness was a political task. A plethora of little magazines debated Hegel, Gramsci, Fanon, and Sartre.[10] But if "demystification," "engagement," and "liberation" were key words of the early 1960s, so was "modernization," in which project art and literature became pioneers. Referring to the opening of the Di Tella Institute in Buenos Aires in 1963, one journal commented that "the modern world is now available to everybody."[11] To many writers this access to the modern world felt like a massive prison break out of the confining teleology that placed Latin American culture as well as its economic development "downstream" from the West.

That teleology had been reflected in the preface to Anderson Imbert's influential book *Historia de la literatura hispanoamericana (History of Spanish American Literature)*, which was published in 1953 and in whose preface the author sorrowfully acknowledged that "our contributions to international literature are minimal" (and this despite the success of Borges and the emergence onto the literary scene of Juan Rulfo and Juan Carlos Onetti). In his view, only a handful of Latin American writers could compare to those of Europe and among them there was not a single novelist. "In general," he complained, "we are afflicted with improvisation, disorder, with the fragmentary and the impure." No doubt bearing in mind Wellek and Warren's definition of imaginative literature—"organization, personal expression, realization and exploitation of the medium, lack of practical purpose, and of course, fictionality"[12]—Anderson Imbert was dismayed at having to include what he termed "excess verbiage" *(farrago)* in his survey.[13] Julio Cortázar's fictional character Morelli in the novel *Rayuela,* on the other hand, makes no such apology. The past is past. He does not look to a history of Latin American culture that could only seem aberrant when judged against the criterion of European cultural history, but addresses himself to the future. Even though writers and painters "are on the margins of the superficial time of their generation," he writes, "it is within another time frame where everything attains the condition of a figuration *(figura),* where everything can be evaluated as a sign and not as a theme for description, that they are exploring a form of writing that may appear alien or antagonistic to their contemporaries and to their history but that nevertheless includes these, explains them, and in the final analysis leads them toward a transcendence at the end of which is the human being."[14] For Morelli, writing is an allegorical and secular project whose goal is the fully human. More important, Cortázar moves literature into this other space where it cannot be considered "underdeveloped" and where it is out of the reach of either abstract universalism or crude referentiality.

This appeal to the transcendence of literature did not mean an abdication of moral leadership; on the contrary, the outsider status claimed by writers gave them a critical space, independent of the state. Thus Vargas Llosa, on receiving the Rómulo Gallegos prize from the Venezuelan government, declared that "literature is fire"; Cortázar participated in the Russell tribunals on human rights; and García Márquez used the Nobel prize ceremony to appeal for an end to Latin America's solitude, an appeal that may seem ironic in the context of globalization. Such sweeping claims could be advanced because these writers enjoyed a transnational status, thanks to the translation of their novels. If I speak of these writers as if "they" formed a cohesive group (which of course they did not), it is only because I want to stress their reliance on the still valid romantic symbol of authorship beyond which was the great black oblivion. But though the writers of the 1960s considered themselves Latin Americans, they were for the most part firmly situated within their respective nations, and the autonomy of the literary work mirrored the ideal of the autonomous nation that was to be restored to the people from whom it had been confiscated.[15]

Nicola Miller argued with some justification that "Spanish American intellectuals defined themselves in terms set by the state, whether they supported or opposed it."[16] She tends to think that the influence of intellectuals has been exaggerated, but because she does not take literary texts into account, she misses the fact that fiction and poetry left their mark on political thinking—García Márquez's Macondo only needed to be mentioned for people to understand that it was a fantasy of a liberated territory. Borges's work has been a rich resource for sociologists, political scientists, and cultural critics, the best known example being Foucault's gig on "The Chinese Encyclopedia" at the beginning of *The Order of Things*. Asturias's Gaspar Ilóm, the protagonist of his novel *Men of Maize,* was adopted as a nickname by the *guerrilla.* Subcomandante Marcos of the Zapatista insurgents in the state of Chiapas quotes Eduardo Galeano and often refers to literary texts.

The prestige of literature derived, in part, from the alternative realities it represented. In the 1960s and 1970s, literature became the mirror in which the antithesis to the real state was reflected. In the writing of García Márquez, Juan Rulfo, and Roa Bastos we come upon different versions of this antistate in confrontation with the despotic and patriarchal state imagined as territory and male body. Roa Bastos's novel *I, the Supreme,* with its lengthy account of the decay of the despotic body, the threat of the feminine, and the translation of life into history and body into language, is the most exhaustive exploration of the discursive limits of the patriarchal state whose integrity rests on exclusion, especially the exclusion of the mortal body that surreptitiously enacts its revenge. Though based on the rule of Dr. Francia in nineteenth-century Paraguay, the novel speaks to more recent military dictatorships that portrayed themselves as the cure for a "body" invaded by the virus and bacteria of communism.

In the 1960s, the nation-state was still the vehicle for development and modernization, in which enterprise literature had a considerable stake. In an essay on "the 'boom' novel and the Cold War," Neil Larsen, after identifying the 1960s boom as a form of Latin American modernism, asked whether the elevation of modernism to a hegemonic position obeys, "if only indirectly, a Cold War political logic?"[17] His answer is that the boom marked a political disengagement and a retreat from historical and social realism. Certainly the literary texts are often at odds with the more forthright public pronouncements of their authors. Yet I do not consider this a failure of political nerve nor a retreat; rather, I attribute it to the difference between reductionist public rhetoric and the complexity of fiction in which writers explored the foundering not only of national autonomy but also of the autonomy of the text. The political and the literary institution of the nation-state mirrored each other. In the chapters on "peripheral fantasies," I argue that many novels of the boom not only track the power of certain fantasies (of liberation, of enterprise, of community) that politics and literature held in common but also come up against their limits. The always masculine protagonists of the boom novels, in their attempts to dream up an economically workable society freed from outside control, encounter the specter of the excluded (especially the feminine) as well as the unhappy consequences of identifying the human exclusively with the domination of nature. Yet to transcend these limits would have meant the collapse of their enterprise itself. The final chapters of *One Hundred Years of Solitude* register the breakdown of the male fantasy in dramatic fashion with the invasion of ants, the death of Amaranta Úrsula, and the reduction of the Buendía enterprise to the solitary task of deciphering. Rather than a retreat from a revolutionary project that García Márquez never seems to have seriously entertained, the novel is the fantasy of a society based on kinship; Macondo aspires to be a "cold" society—to use Lévi-Strauss's term for societies whose mechanisms are conservationist rather than geared to change. The change that comes from the outside is a degeneration.

For many writers of the boom generation, history was a cycle of failed experiments, for their novels reenact the inevitable foundering of those other booms—of rubber or coffee, of bananas or mining—that left a landscape marked by the monuments of failure. Despite their espousal of modernity they were as haunted as their predeces-

sors by the specter of anachronism, by the fact that they were thinking what others had done before them in Europe or North America.
Where they differ from their predecessors is that now the costs as well
as the achievements of modernity are apparent. For the Uruguayan
Juan Carlos Onetti and the Colombian Álvaro Mutis (whose writing
is discussed in Chapter 5), it is progress that is spectral, an unsustain-
able illusion that cannot even inspire belief. Their novels explore the
breakdown of hegemony at the point where the subject himself is no
longer able to believe in achievement as an ultimate good. Efforts at
individual enterprise not only occur in the void, given the absence of
an autonomous and truly independent nation, but more than anything they are staged at the moment when people no longer believe the
fantasy of progress and development but act as if they do. Indeed, by
grouping the three chapters on the novels of the boom under the
rubric "peripheral fantasies," I underscore the deep sense of alienation that comes from being off-center: the "marriage of nostalgia
and hope" on the one hand and "the feeling of provincialism and
isolation" on the other.[18] Certainly the common *topoi* of the novels I
discuss in Chapters 4 and 5—the burial of the unhonored dead, the
passage into oblivion, and the foundering of individual enterprise—
reflect both the desire of the periphery for recognition and the deep
sense of futility at the inability to overcome the constitutive exclusion
of Latin America from the universal. Onetti's novels, in particular,
register the collapse not only of development but also of the belief
in development as the reigning economic ideology of the 1960s and
1970s.[19]

In this secular wasteland, popular culture increasingly came to
promise a vigorous native regeneration as well as the possibility of a
new kind of class and racial synthesis that magical realism salvaged
from the grim realities of exploitation and discrimination. Although
now little more than a commercial slogan, magical realism was deeply
implicated in the racial question, codifying racial difference as magic
and the marginalized indigenous both as remedy and poison. In
Chapter 6, I trace the racial roots of magic, its deployment in the service of Latin American specificity (but dependent on the clichéd car-
tography that separates "rational" Europe from the nonrational rest),
and finally, in a deterritorializing move, the capture of "magic" by
Borges and Onetti in the service of the secular reenchantment of literature. Magic is here dislodged from its source in popular religion and

associated with the power to inspire unanchored belief. Borges thus becomes a key figure in the deterritorialization or abstraction that characterizes the postmodern.

Yet popular culture did succeed in breaching the walls of what Ángel Rama termed "the lettered city"; through this breach, indigenous languages and cultures entered into productive contact with lettered culture.[20] Describing this as "transculturation," a term he adapted from the Cuban anthropologist Fernando Ortiz, Rama argued that the writing of José María Arguedas, who was bilingual in Quechua and Spanish, exemplified the potentiality of a cultural counterpoint in which one culture did not dominate the other. As John Beverley rightly pointed out, "[t]he idea of transculturation expresses in both Ortiz and Rama a *fantasy* of class, gender and racial reconciliation."[21] However, fantasy cannot simply be dismissed but must be "traversed," that is to say, worked through before it is suspended. Arguedas dramatically represents that breach of limits that García Márquez was unable to entertain. Brought up in the sierra and frequently left by his father in the care of indigenous villagers, he was, unlike the Lima intelligentsia, bicultural and bilingual. He was also both an ethnographer and a writer of fiction. In a famous put-down, Cortázar labeled him as "provincial," an astonishingly uncharitable judgment, no doubt inspired by the Peruvian author's deep commitment to the culture of so-called traditional societies that offended Cortázar's urban sensibilities. Yet curiously enough both Arguedas's and Cortázar's writing represents, albeit in very different ways, the "invasion" of the literary text by the "noise" from outside.

In Arguedas's final novel, *El zorro de arriba y el zorro de abajo (The Fox Above and the Fox Below),* the narrative account of highland emigration to a coastal community industrialized by the fish meal industry is interrupted by Arguedas's own comments on his impending suicide, on literary criticism, on his personal life, and on his childhood in the sierra. The novel thus enacts the sundering of literature from the project of modernization. Interestingly, his critic, Julio Cortázar in his *Libro de Manuel (A Manual for Manuel)* made a similar if even more radical break with genre boundaries. His novel is intersected with news flashes that give accounts of urban guerrilla activities and human rights violations and is backed up by speculations on literature, music, the news, and everyday life. Clearly the autonomy of the literary text on which the modernist project had been based and within which national projects had been contained was by now irreparably damaged.

The reference to "cultural revolution" in the book's third part is thus partly ironic, for radical change for most people came about not through armed struggle but from unanticipated changes, as media and the new information economy were consolidated at the height of a demographic explosion that transformed Latin America from a mainly peasant society to an urban society. Although these changes affected some parts of the continent more than others, the effects of mass culture disseminated by the media had a considerable impact on the intelligentsia, for whom the printed book was no longer the emblem of cultural literacy. In José Donoso's novel *Curfew,* the death of the widow of a famous writer (Neruda) occurs at a moment when a new charismatic figure emerges—that of the popular singer—marking the fact that it was now mass culture that created celebrity. The printed book, once the instrument for acquiring cultural capital, now encountered powerful rivals in radio and television. This was especially true in times of economic crisis, as in Mexico in the mid-1980s, when the price of books became exorbitant, halting what Carlos Monsiváis and José Emilio Pacheco termed "democratization from below." Along with Elena Poniatowska, these writers felt that the crisis was so acute as to call for civic action on behalf of the right to read.[22] But this was only the beginning. In many parts of the continent, the Cold War turned into the "dirty war" on communism (broadly defined as any movement that hindered capitalist expansion), culminating in a "second Cold War"—a term used to describe the civil wars in Central America—and military repression in the Southern Cone[23] that were the overture to the global changes in power relations of the 1970s and 1980s.

The secular and republican project of nationhood, born of the Enlightenment and monumentalized in Latin American cities, was over. The city, once imagined as the *polis,* had long been an image of repression and confusion, either a panopticon surveyed by the all-seeing eye of a dictator as in the Guatemala City of Miguel Ángel Asturias's *El señor presidente,* or as internally corrupted like the Lima of Mario Vargas Llosa's *Conversation in the Cathedral.* "Who fucked up Peru?" is the question asked by the novel, and the answer lies in a social body in which classes are bound together by a deadly network of favors and lies. Alongside this sense of disillusionment with the republican ideal, a number of violent incidents occurred that materially destroyed its monuments—incidents such as the tank attack on the Palace of Justice in Bogotá in which guerrillas were holding captive the justices of the supreme court; the destruction of the Moneda Palace in Chile during the military coup against Salvador Allende (1973); the attack on demonstrators in the Plaza de Tres Culturas in Tlatelolco (1968); the emptying of the Plaza de Mayo by the military government of Argentina; and the Guatemalan army's attack on the Spanish embassy. Though unrelated, these events struck at the heart of the republican ideal—the system of justice, the unity of the nation, the presidential system, and the right of asylum. These were acts of profound disrespect on the part of the military, one of the pillars of the republican state.

Drawn into the deadly logic of the Cold War, the military of the Southern Cone and Central America became engaged in a war on communism that would not only destroy civil society but also facilitate the transition from welfare states to the porous neoliberal state by removing certain obstacles—the bargaining power of workers, the dreams of a liberated society. This epochal change was brutal. Repression, censorship, and forced exile ended the utopian dreams of writers and projects of literature and art as agents of "salvation and redemption." Insofar as military governments represented their regimes as essential to the crusade against communism, they were certainly participants in the Cold War; what makes the Latin American situation so distinct is that those same military governments left older structures, both cultural and political, in fragments. Terms such as "identity," "responsibility," "nation," "the future," "history"—even "Latin American"—had to be rethought.

The emphasis on information and surveillance during the military dictatorships encouraged the emergence of a professional intelligentsia whose education was practical—less classical and more technological. These professionals were acutely aware of participating in the information revolution. Jean-François Lyotard has argued that "knowledge in the form of an informational commodity indispensable to productive power is already, and will continue to be, a major—perhaps *the* major—stake in the worldwide competition for power."[24] But in Latin America, the informational commodity was to be productive in a sinister way. The agents of change, at least in the Southern Cone, were the very military governments for whom information came by way of torture and repression. Theirs was a war not only on communism but also on all forms of dissidence including socialists, hippies, women, gay men, and children who became the "homo sacer," the dispensable noncitizens.[25]

The scale of repression, particularly in Argentina, left profound scars on cultural life. The secular project initiated by the Enlightenment reached its culmination in the disenchanted world of these technologically advanced repressive states. When people found themselves looking for unmarked graves and attempting to identify their children or parents from piles of bones, they confronted the twisted nature of late capitalism's logic in which individual human life, especially in the Third World, is of little moment. Andreas Huyssen discussed the "discourse of the end of utopia" in his book *Twilight Memories* and made the interesting suggestion that utopia has not disappeared. Rather "the transformation of temporality in utopian discourse, the shift from anticipation and the future to memory and the past, manifests itself quite strongly in German literary developments since the 1960s."[26] A similar reflection could apply to the Southern Cone, for there is a very marked difference between the novelists of the boom generation and their recurrent tropes of ruin, funeral, and mourning that I discuss in Chapter 4, and a postboom generation's turn from history to memory. But although there are parallels with the post-Holocaust concerns in Germany, the experience of disappearance especially in Argentine gave a different inflection to historical trauma, leaving scars that official policies of amnesia could not erase.

Meanwhile processes of production had changed and it was not long before the discipline imposed by the military became incompatible with the global economy that demanded freedom of movement, the development of technical skills, and internalized regulations in place of externally imposed discipline. It also demanded the reorganization of the state whose functions now included "political mediation with respect to global hegemonic powers, bargaining with respect to transnational corporations, redistribution of incomes according to biopolitical needs within in own territories" while "the traditional idea of counter-power and the idea of resistance against modern sovereignty in general [became] less and less possible."[27] In the market-driven neoliberal states of the 1990s, the intelligentsia would find it difficult to reimagine forms of resistance for they could no longer assume a position as sharpshooter from the outside. The separation between inside and outside the state was now as obsolete as the simple binary alternatives of the Cold War itself.

The military governments used language in such a way as to create a dialect of euphemisms, which could be used to mask their control of behavior by fear. But even in countries that did not experience military repression, modernization and migration into the cities brought about major changes to everyday life and hence to national and self-identities. New urban subcultures were not bound to ideal models of an authentic national character And the demographic explosion was such that older forms of community were greatly strained when they did not altogether break down. The tramps, vagabonds, and lay-abouts that had long stood for some unspeakable abyss of humanity now made their disturbing and sometimes seductive presence felt in the social context of the street, acting as an interruption of civility, a breach of decorum. In the 1950s and early 1960s, the Brazilian writer Clarice Lispector had already been haunted by these figures on the margin who threatened the personhood of the lettered. When, in the 1970s, the Chilean writer Diamela Eltit kissed a vagabond in front of the video camera, the act marked a recognition that the margin was now in the center. It also drew attention to the stubborn intransigence of race and gender differences that could not be overcome simply by pedagogy or social reform but needed, rather than passive surrendering to the other, a leap over the dualisms of Hegelian philosophy in order to take risks.[28] Furthermore, in the new regime, the responsibility for being a force for integration could no longer be displaced onto the nation, especially when acting in one's own best interests had become a universal law. The comfortable promises exemplified in the Sandinista electoral slogan "Everything will get Better" could no longer persuade anybody when the nation was revealed to be a multiplicity of scarred tissues—of unmet demands of women, the indigenous, the poor, of gay men, lesbians, and transvestites.

The Cold War certainly defeated communism in Latin America. Whether it can be seen as a triumph of capitalism and democracy is less certain, for neoliberalism has favored new transnational elites who are no more democratic or egalitarian than the old. As one commentator put it, "[P]hysical coercion through military and police force is replaced by economic coercion, as the threat of deprivation, poverty and hunger forces people to make certain decisions and take certain actions. Their apparently 'free' choices are, in fact, coerced by structures and by groups who control those structures."[29]

The time lag between past atrocities—the overthrow of Arbenz, the overthrow of Allende, the invasion of the Dominican Republic, the dirty wars and Operation Condor, the war against Noriega— has given a phantasmagoric cast to the immediate past. The time lag means that news only "breaks" when there is no longer danger of a spontaneous revolt. Television news is particularly insidious in this regard, for there is rarely a video clip that corresponds to what is happening unless it is the unreal flash of stealth missiles, which, however, can never show what is happening on the ground. But expository journalism in Latin America is still dangerous and the list of slain journalists is a long one. Journalists are routinely killed in Colombia; they were killed in Guatemala during the violence there and in Mexico during the drug wars. Because journalism is often regarded as a craft rather than an art, it is seldom counted as a factor in the cultural field. Yet who can forget Alma Guillermoprieto wading rivers to find out what happened in Mozote, El Salvador, or Susan Meiseles's photographs of bodies in San Salvador? In contrast, think of the "cover stories"—the kidnapping of Noriega in Panama, the invasion of Grenada, the military's account of Allende's presidency, the perverse use of death camp prisoners by Admiral Massera to produce "information," and the "belated" emergence of the "truth" when the events themselves have receded into the distant past and can no longer disturb us in the same way. The full consideration of all this is beyond the scope of this book, but the violent underpinnings of the so-called transition to democracy are the main concern of the final chapters.

Indeed, the shift from projects of national autonomy to military repression and from repression to respectability in the eyes of the United States through the restoration of democracy (defined usually as voting) not only destroyed but exposed in that very process of destruction the multiple "invisibilities" on which the lettered city had been founded—certainly the invisibility of women but also the invisibility of entire nations like Panama, the invisibility of peoples—the dark-skinned Argentinians, the low-class Chileans, the indigenous of Peru and Guatemala and Mexico. Cortázar's short story *Apocalypse in Solentiname,* based on Somoza's bombing of the "liberated territory" of Solentiname in Nicaragua, which had been founded by the poet Ernesto Cardenal, can be taken as an epitaph for the destruction of older ideals of community and also of the bounded territory of the literary. What invades Cortázar's study is the political violence that had been excluded from the happy souvenir photographs he had taken.

But by the 1980s, the situation was even more grave since the very concepts around which older debates had circulated—concepts of national and Latin American identity, modernization, and emancipation—seemed inapplicable in a globalized world. Knowledge itself came under scrutiny even as universities were being reorganized to accommodate what had hitherto been excluded. Latin American studies, whether pursued in the United States or in Latin America, underwent self-criticism that ranged from critical questioning of U.S. hegemony in the continent to the implications of exclusion and marginalization in the literary canon.[30]

Literature confronted its own exclusions, though often in an oblique fashion. In Chapter 8 I comment on the fantasies that accrue to marginalized men and women and the confrontation with the low that are often eroticized. The testimony of the Guatemalan Indian woman Rigoberta Menchú is an unavoidable illustration of the power of the margins; it has had repercussions beyond the borders of Latin America, unleashing in the U.S. academy and in the press conservative hostility because of the threat to the canon (and hence to the imagined community of Western culture). It also motivated self-examination among Latin Americanists who, however progressive they might think themselves, could not help but be involved in furthering the hegemony of the North, a fact that did not escape Subcomandante Marcos of the Zapatista movement, who blamed the "mental laboratories" of foreign universities for historical amnesia.[31] The track of Menchú's life from south to north, its penetration of fortress America, is itself a symptom of the unanticipated effects and contradictions of globalization.

The contemporary narrative of globalization as purveyed by the World Bank and by official circles in Europe and the United States is a narrative of development fantasized as a journey into prosperity. Seen from Latin America, the outcome is not so certain and the pauperization of those left behind hardly makes for a heartening "story." The stigmatized bodies of those marked for death in the drug wars and in urban violence reveal the other side of the globalization narrative.

In Chapter 9, I discuss urban chronicles from Colombia, Venezuela, and Mexico that record the devastation that occurs when traditional codes of masculinity are articulated with "the generally accepted values of an individualistic society."[32] There is a strong link between consumerism and the death drive among the young men of the underclass for whom "the crisis in masculinity" is more than a slogan, and for whom the past of conquest and repression culminates not in redemption but in social suicide. Apparently "senseless" violence explodes out of the mix of the individualism of contemporary capitalism and the void left by the suppression of alternatives.

Though some of the chapters in the book suggest a chronological sequence from Cold War to neoliberalism, in fact they are traversed by different temporalities. The historical narrative can no longer be viewed as a continuum when archaic codes latch onto modern consumption and when gender and ethnic differences are stripped of their historical load and deployed as lightweight actors in the marketplace. Yet history and memory have never been so important or contested, for amnesia is more than ever the condition of modern society. Even if we grant that amnesia is a necessary condition for action, the question of what is cast aside becomes crucial.

The literature I discuss in Chapter 10 engages the uncertainty of memory and the inexpressibility of horror, especially in the Southern Cone and Central America. Here the politics of memory is linked to legal and judicial redress, to keeping memory alive through commemoration and monuments. Literature has an ambiguous position especially now that it is firmly installed in the marketplace. Situated within a spectrum that extends from entertainment to philosophical reflection, at one extreme literature flirts with the marketability of torture and at the other with the often fragile links between personal and collective memory. Yet between those extremes there is also literature that balances psychoanalysis and philosophy to find ways of representing trauma.

Even so, the marketing of literature and the reduced space for experimental writing has inevitably brought it into crisis, a crisis that can no longer be met by appealing to some pure outside. In the final chapter, I examine the shift in contemporary criticism from "revolution" and "liberation" to Deleuzian "lines of flight," to Benjaminian weak messianism, and to the work of mourning. What had once been the secular project of literature is now resignified in semireligious language that seems intended as a safeguard against its dissolution into the more general categories of performance, poetics, and the aesthetic.

Redemocratization on neoliberal terms has had an uneven effect on culture. During what is often called "the transition to democracy," grassroots movements of women, gays and lesbians, transvestites, the indigenous, and Afro-Americans reinvigorated the political and cultural scene. One critic enthusiastically forecast the dawn of an era of great women's writing in Latin America.[33] The anthology ¿Entiendes? ("the first of its kind"), which collected Latin American and Spanish queer writing, not only gave witness to the presence of queer theory in the academy but situated it in a broader context of activism and gender theory.[34] During the same period, indigenous peoples were organizing internationally, and in 1994 the Zapatistas emerged from the Lacandon jungle to announce not only the first rebellion against neoliberalism but also to speak in indigenous tongues, making it clear that Mexico was a multicultural society.[35] But despite hard-won political gains by these movements, they have also come up against limitations imposed not by direct oppression but by the conditions under which they have been forced to negotiate.[36] And though a wave of literature based on the specific experiences of these minorities seems to have no end, this literature often markets a bland version of difference. In a discussion with Ernesto Laclau and Slavoj Žižek, Judith Butler understandably asked, "[W]hy does resistance appear in a form that is so easily coopted by the opposition?"[37] Or to put it another way, what happens when any resistance can be marketed as entertainment? In the final chapter, I review examples of cultural critique and of art practices that expose strategies of containment, as well as examples of the politics of translation as it works against the geopolitics of domination. These are not intended to propose solutions but rather should be seen as reenactments in new circumstances of demands for the not-yet-realized universal.

PART ONE

Conflicting Universals

CHAPTER ONE

Killing Them Softly: The Cold War and Culture

Atravesamos unos tiempos calamitosos
imposible hablar sin incurrir en delito de contradicción
imposible callar sin hacerse cómplice del Pentágono.

These are disastrous times
you can't speak without committing the crime of contradiction
you can't hold your tongue without becoming an accomplice of the
Pentagon.

NICANOR PARRA, "TIEMPOS MODERNOS"

In the early 1960s I was traveling from Paris to Le Touquet airport (a journey that at the time was a cheap way to get from Paris to London) and reading *The Death of Artemio Cruz,* a novel by the Mexican writer Carlos Fuentes. The man sitting opposite me introduced himself as Mr. Brown and asked if I realized that the author whose book I was reading was a communist. I told Mr. Brown, or whatever his name was, that this was not apparent from the novel, which seemed to me to have more to do with the corruption of the ideals of the Mexican Revolution than with communism. Having identified me as a naive leftist, Mr. Brown then launched into a zealous account of his own work. He had been attached to the American Embassy in Mexico, which he claimed had done a marvelous job subsidizing the translations of American books to provide a healthy alternative to authors like Fuentes. The encounter troubled me. If Carlos Fuentes, who at that time still seemed to be waiting for Mexico's bourgeois revolution, was to be labeled a communist, then so was almost everybody I knew. What surprised me was not so much the paranoid belief that any deviation from the world of conservative U.S. was a bad thing—after all, I had followed the McCarthy hearings from England and had personally witnessed the end of the Arbenz government in Guatemala—but rather the belated realization that the Cold War had placed its icy paw on Latin American culture.

In the period immediately following World War II, the "world" as far as the United States was concerned was, above all, Europe—a Europe whose culture had to be defended against Soviet influence. Cold War politics had already been put in place during the war, and by its end the assertion of cultural leadership had been translated into aggressive policy, although there were contradictions between the stated U.S. mission as a redeemer nation defending freedom and the vast web of domestic and foreign surveillance.[1] The founding of the CIA in 1947 added a powerful institution for gathering information, counterinsurgency, and fighting a war "with ideas instead of bombs," a policy that embraced covert propaganda, covertly funded university research, subsidized publications, and even the defense of particular cultural values, especially an abstract universalism that disqualified the "provincial" (which is to say cultures rooted in heterogeneous local traditions).[2]

The hemispheric policy of the United States in the postwar years was based on the view that "a reformed capitalist system would protect the liberties and enhance the lives of North and South Americans. It would also keep Latin America open for U.S. traders and investors."[3] But there was no Marshall Plan for Latin America, primarily because it did not seem in danger of becoming communist but also perhaps because large corporations and private empires such as that of the Rockefellers and the United Fruit Company were making "policy" in the region, which not unnaturally provoked resentment. On a visit to the southern hemisphere, Dos Passos, by then a Cold War warrior, registered the fact that anger against the United States was providing recruiting material for the communist party. One of his hosts told him, "We read about the Marshall Plan for Europe, but when the Communists tell us it is imperialism we tend to believe them."[4] Yet during the 1940s the Communist Party was outlawed in many countries of Latin America and was certainly not likely to take power. In fact what the United States labeled as communist were often populist nationalist regimes—Perón in Argentina and eventually Arbenz in Guatemala.[5]

The CIA-financed invasion of Guatemala in 1954 that overturned the democratically elected government of Jacobo Arbenz, who had threatened to nationalize the United Fruit Company's plantations and break its economic hold over the country, showed exactly how far the United States was willing to go in identifying communism with any attack on the business interests of its citizens. But it also unleashed a monster. Anticommunism became an alibi for slaughter, torture, and censorship—often in the name of "stability" in opposition to "chaos." Nation-states were euphemistically identified as "friendly" or "unfriendly," terms that Jeane Kirkpatrick would later use in her notorious attempt to distinguish "authoritarian" from "totalitarian" regimes.[6]

Nelson Rockefeller's views on the hemisphere, on the surface at least, were more constructive. Believing that the United States had more to gain from economic prosperity than from immiseration, he used his immense business interests in order to pursue a policy of re-formed capitalism, urging that "if the United States is to maintain its security and its political and economic hemisphere position it must take economic measures at once to secure economic prosperity in Central and South America, and to establish this prosperity in the frame of hemispheric cooperation and dependence."[7] Rockefeller's vast interests in Latin America in effect made him one of the few poli-ticians, before the Alliance for Progress was set in motion, to propose a project for Latin America designed to reform the infrastructure and avert revolution. As Coordinator of the Office of Hemispheric Affairs during World War II, he fashioned an apparently benevolent form of imperialism, one that was "the ultimate expression of the Good Neighbor policy."[8] He also developed a formidable propaganda ma-chine. As one critic observed, "[A]long with the doctor there goes the industrial technician and engineer, the radio script-writer, the public relations expert, the artist, the poet and the movie actor."[9] His office was responsible for films, movies, and newsreels sent to Latin Amer-ica. The press division "saturated Latin America with news and fea-ture stories, locking in about 1,200 newspaper publishers who were dependent on subsidized CIAA (Office of Coordination of Inter-American Affairs) shipments of scarce newsprint on U.S. flagships. Nelson even published his own monthly magazine, aptly entitled *En Guardia* with a circulation of 80,000 by the summer of 1941."[10] His office also sponsored local radio programs and beamed short-wave radio programs all over the continent.

According to some of Rockefeller's critics, "he had launched the cold war before it had even been declared, fusing hemispheric unity against the Soviets at the Pan American Conference in 1945 and that year's founding conference of the United Nations. His success in laying the legal foundation for a regional military pact paved the way for the Organization of American States (OAS), for the North Atlantic Treaty Organization (NATO), and for the Southeast Asia Treaty Organization (SEATO), which became the raison d'être for the war in Vietnam."[11] And while the Rockefeller Foundation's Humanities Division was defending high culture, the Office of Hemispheric Affairs was encouraging the production of films such as *Down Argentine Way* and *That Night in Rio*.[12]

Rockefeller was also a force to be reckoned with in the institutions of high culture. He was elected to the board of the Museum of Modern Art in 1932 and gave support to the Mexican muralists before the scandal erupted over Diego Rivera's mural for the Rockefeller Center in which the artist included a portrait of Lenin,[13] after which his influence contributed to the shift from "New Deal realism" to the "institutional enshrinement of abstract expressionism."[14] He collected "primitive art," much of which is now in the Metropolitan Museum of Art in New York. The Museum of Modern Art—his "mother's museum"—was instrumental in sending many exhibitions of contemporary American painting to Latin America.[15] But perhaps Nelson Rockefeller's most innovative move was his use of Disney as informal ambassador to the countries south of the border, and the use of cartoons and documentary films to get across the U.S. program of modernization.

Animating Latin America

Nelson Rockefeller was one of the first politicians to understand the potential of American mass culture as a form of velvet persuasion, and in wartime Hollywood he had found ready allies for his propaganda machine. During the 1930s, Hollywood had already exploited the differences between the "Latin" and the red-blooded American. Films such as *Flying Down to Rio* pitted the pragmatic, common sense of the north against the incompetent south. "All your army and navy will not stop me from marrying you," the hero tells Dolores del Rio. In one B movie after another, James Cagney or Ronald Reagan or some other Hollywood hero of the day saved the banana plantation from the idiocy of the locals.[16] Wartime policy, however, demanded more diplomatic treatment. The Rockefeller office issued a memorandum that proposed using Disney-type animation to win over the hearts and minds of Latin Americans to the Allied cause. The memorandum described animation as a "magical medium" and underlined the importance of "[b]eautiful and reverent scenes in which The Christ of the Andes is seen in the background, or a huge Cross fills the sky; or more subtly, when the voice, the music, and the artists' style of painting suggests a religious atmosphere . . . as when we see the Spirit of Pan-America or of Victory, standing behind our weapons." It was also suggested that the credit lines should mention local scholars in order to facilitate first of all "the acceptance of certain films throughout all of South America. Second, it would be flattering. Third, it would provide a plausible and publicity-wise pretext for getting certain anti-American old gentlemen to make their first trip to U.S.A., and thus get their eyes opened."[17] This condescending view of old-fashioned Latin American intellectuals susceptible to flattery and easily bedazzled would resurface during the Cold War with the founding of Latin American committees of the Congress for Cultural Freedom.

As Coordinator of Inter-American Affairs, Rockefeller oversaw a vast media program that included American newsreels; his office provided trucks and projectors so that they could be shown throughout Latin America. The motion picture division was headed by John Hay Whitney, who "wanted Hollywood to fulfill the "ideal of Inter-American unity" by producing more films on relevant Latin American themes and by refraining from stories that would irritate the republics of the south."[18] Rockefeller's office also recruited a group of Hollywood personalities—Orson Welles, Daryl Zanuck, Carmen Miranda, and Walt Disney—to promote "good neighbor" relations. For Orson Welles, the experience of working in Brazil would be highly problematic, as he ironically became increasingly drawn toward a culture he could not altogether grasp or understand. For Disney, on the other hand, it was a positive turning point. His studio produced about twenty educational shorts and three films—*South of the Border, Saludos amigos,* and *The Three Caballeros*—the last of which, though ridiculed, was a box office success. Embroiled in a dispute with the cartoonists' union and politically suspect because he had appeared with Lindburgh at America First rallies that opposed U.S. entry into the war, Disney was happy to escape to Latin America on a goodwill mission.

Saludos amigos is an episodic travelogue in which the journey of Donald Duck and "el grupo" (the artists and technicians) is illustrated with cute animation and infantile stories—a watercolor of Brazil, the story of El gaucho Goofy, and the tale of the little mail plane that successfully flies across the dangerous Andes. Braving storms and danger, the plane returns to Chile from Mendoza carrying the mail, which turns out to be a tourist postcard.[19] This was a Latin America that people could live with, a place of picturesque customs that could be captured on film and artisan products that could be taken home and put on display. Disney saw Latin America as a potentially unspoiled reserve for tourism.[20] In the Argentine episode, an American cowboy is shown taking refuge on a U.S. mountain peak from a forest of billboards and oil rigs. He is then whisked to Argentina, transformed into a gaucho in a pristine pampa where he dances with his horse as the female partner before returning to his home. Latin America is here offered as a frontier culture and a fantasy land that can be experienced and then left behind.

In *Saludos amigos,* Disney revealed the magic of animation that he would later develop in *The Three Caballeros* and *Fantasia.* In one of the episodes, "Acuarela do Brasil," a painter's brush sketches in landscapes that then become animated scenes. Donald's Brazilian guide, Joe Carioca, is first drawn in Donald's sketchbook and then begins to move to a samba rhythm using his umbrella as a flute and Donald's hat as an accordion. This power of metamorphosis later carried to extraordinary lengths in *The Three Caballeros* is as self-reflexive as any modernist art. Indeed, the very term "animation" suggests the breathing of life into the inanimate and the almost mythic power that this implies.

Saludos amigos was little more than a sketch for *The Three Caballeros,* which mixes real actors and animated characters and pedagogy with the libidinal economy, presenting the southern hemisphere as a pleasure garden. In the opening sequence, Donald Duck receives a box of presents from Latin American friends on his birthday, Friday the thirteenth. Out of the first package comes a reel of film, called *Aves raras* (Rare Birds), that establishes the attractive exoticism of the subject matter in the Disney manner—by converting the rare birds into "characters." A paternalistic voice-over situates the audience in the position of school children. Each episode is unpacked in this way. After several desultory episodes, including a story about a gauchito and his magic donkey, doubtless designed to dispel any anxiety over the fact that Argentina was now ruled by Perón and his "descamisados," Donald opens the packages from Brazil and Mexico. Out of the first comes his Brazilian "amigo," the parrot and gadabout dandy, Joe Carioca, a figure who manages to conflate two stereotypes—the insouciant Latin American and the mimic—particularly apt (or unfortunate) stereotypes given the accusation that Latin America parroted metropolitan manners. The third "amigo," the mariachi bird, emerges out of the Mexican package.[21]

Arthur Freed of the MGM studio had drawn attention to the fact that Latin music was crossing frontiers: "[H]emispheric solidarity, good neighborliness and the like is only a background reason for the flood of South American features . . . The actual reason is South American music. Swing music which has held the center stage for five or six years is now passing out and the rhumba stuff is jumping into the number one position in American taste."[22] And the Brazilian and Mexican sequences of Disney's film exploit this taste. The Mexican episode includes an Agustín Lara song sung in English, the hat dance, the *jarabe tapatío,* and Christmas songs, thus reproducing more or less the repertoire of the Baile Folklórico of Mexico, which, as García Canclini has pointed out, turned regional music into a national repertoire.[23] Disney took this further, translating the national repertoire into international folklore.

Some critics were outraged by the Mexican sequence, in which Donald and his friends fly over an Acapulco beach where "real"—that is, nonanimated girls—are sunbathing. Blindfolded and teased by a group of girls, he tears off the blindfold and chases them in a kind of erotic fury until his two friends pull him back into the studio. The *New Yorker,* in particular, commented on the episode's bad taste and the fact that "a sequence involving the duck, the young lady, and a long alley of animated cactus plants would probably be considered suggestive in a less innocent medium."[24]

Snatched away from the real beach, Donald has to content himself with a photograph of Mexico City by night, which metamorphoses into the image of a beautiful girl singing "You Belong to My Heart." The seductive Latin woman was a standard character in Hollywood films but Disney's version turns the north–south relation into an abstract erotic encounter with Donald feminized in comparison with the Latin characters. This love affair between feminized North America and Latin America is harmlessly expressed through photographic production. The episode underscores the difference between the pleasure of the flesh and the pleasure of representation. Cupid's arrows speed from Donald Duck to the girl, but the miracle of animation sublimates what otherwise would get out of hand while underscoring the power of the cinematic apparatus to create fantasy. Julianne Burton remarks that "[b]ecause cartoon figures inhabit a world beyond materiality, beyond mortality, beyond conventionality, cartoons can also be the site of unbridled expressions of the individual and collective unconscious, defying norms of propriety as well as physics . . . Cartoons in this sense can be understood as a kind of dream's dreaming, the unconscious of the unconscious."[25] *The Three Caballeros* ends in a wild, orgasmic outburst of exploding fireworks and flowers that turn into lips. Donald is sent flying into the air, and descends in bemused fashion covered with a serape and flanked by his two friends.

It is easy to ridicule Disney, but it must be borne in mind that he was a great technical innovator who had a very clearly defined sense that the animated cartoon should be a caricature of life and action. Its purpose, he said, "was to picture on the screen things that have run through the imagination of the audience—to bring to life dream-fantasies and imaginative fancies that we have all thought of during our lives or have pictured in various forms during our lives." President Eisenhower sent him a telegram acknowledging his "genius as a creator of folklore."[26] But Disney was not so much bringing to life universal dream-fantasies as inventing them. *The Three Caballeros* was a celebration of the pleasure principle freed from ethical considerations and responsibility, and most important of all, abstracted from a context while the technical innovation underscored the industrial superiority of the United States. *The Three Caballeros* heralded things to come. But it also invites speculation on the very idea of "animation"—giving soul and life to an inanimate object, a drawing, or a sketch on a piece of paper. The animated cartoon vies with the real and forecasts the power of the simulacrum that today draws millions of Latin Americans to Disneyland and Disneyworld.[27]

In the early 1950s, the U.S. government organized a mobile motion-picture unit that toured the state of Veracruz with the blessing and active participation of the governor, Ángel Carvajal.[28] The Motion Picture Division of the Office of the Coordinator of Inter-American Affairs sponsored a highly sophisticated program that included the modernization of the Mexican film industry and produced films for specific audiences it wished to influence. The extensive showing of films produced and distributed by the United States Information Agency (USIA) in the provinces and the rural areas of Mexico required, of course, local collaboration. This is, indeed, the weak link in anticolonial arguments, since on many different occasions and in many parts of Latin America such technological improvements were welcomed by sectors of the population.[29] It could also be argued, however, that this complicity was encouraged by the "negative case scenario" that was applied towards Argentina. During World War II, the supply of film stock to that country had been blocked because of U.S. hostility toward Perón, which had dire results for the Argentinian film industry.[30]

Phantom Debates

While these events at the level of popular culture may have gone unnoticed by the intelligentsia, "high" culture too was drawn into the culture war. Soviet influence had reached its height in the 1930s in the "proletarian moment" in U.S. literature, in the social protest literature of Latin America, and the "engaged literature" written during the Spanish Civil War; in the 1940s and 1950s these were eclipsed by a buoyant American triumphalism casting itself as "universal." The Third World was not yet much of an issue, especially given an early setback of a meeting of the Congress for Cultural Freedom in India, where it failed to convince Indian intellectuals of the urgency of attacking communism. But Latin America, though not deemed particularly important at this stage, was certainly not overlooked by the United States. Writing in 1975, Warren Dean calculated that in twenty-five years of operation, the USIA translation program had been responsible for publishing nearly 22,000 editions totaling 175 million copies, many of which were targeted for Latin America. Though the program itself was not clandestine in the usual sense (Dean called it "furtive"), there was no acknowledgment in the publications that the translations had been subsidized by the U.S. government. Yet the agency not only directly subsidized the writing of books such as Jay Mallin's *The Truth about the Dominican Republic,* a defense of the indefensible U.S. intervention of 1965, but also unloaded an immense amount of rubbish onto a largely unsuspecting public. Warren Dean summed up its propaganda aim succinctly: "[T]he intent of the book publishing program is to make influential foreigners more receptive to the assumptions of U.S. foreign policy, and to do so in ways that will not be recognized as originating with the U.S. government."[31] Yet other publications, for instance *Reader's Digest,* or *Selecciones* as it was known in Spanish, sought to justify in a more straightforward fashion U.S. interventions and carried on its own anticommunist crusade.[32]

The line between cultural criticism and propaganda was decisively crossed with the founding in 1950 of the American Committee for Cultural Freedom and the Congress for Cultural Freedom (the latter founded by Michael Josselson, formerly an officer in the Office of Strategic Services, and Melvin J. Lasky who had earlier served in the American Information Service and as editor of *Der Monat*). The sponsors of the first meeting held in West Berlin in 1950 included persons of diverse persuasions, among them Eleanor Roosevelt, Upton Sinclair, G. A. Borgese, A. J. Ayer, Walter Reuther, Suzanne Labin, and Dr. Hans Thirring. Among the most active supporters were such militant ex- and anticommunists as Arthur Koestler, Franz Borkenau, Melvin Lasky, Sidney Hook, James Burnham, James T. Farrell, and Arthur Schlesinger Jr.[33] The Communist Information Bureau (Cominform) had been founded in 1947 and backed a number of front organizations including the World Peace Council, the World Federation of Trade Unions, and the International Union of Students. Widespread fear of atomic war gave impetus to the peace movement that recruited many prominent intellectuals—among them Joliot Curie, Louis Aragon, Paul Éluard, and several Latin Americans including Jorge Amado, Pablo Neruda, and Nicolás Guillén. An international meeting of the Partisans of Peace was held in Paris in 1949.[34] Given this division of the globe, nonalignment was difficult. You chose one side or the other.[35]

With a view to putting the Congress for Cultural Freedom "on the map" and countering the pro-Soviet peace congress for which Picasso designed his peace dove, an ambitious Paris Festival, funded by the CIA, was organized in 1952 and featured opera, ballet, and literary debates. An exhibition entitled "The Twentieth Century Work of Art" also held in Paris was intended to demonstrate that art needed free-dom in order to flourish.[36] Given the difficulties of publication in the Soviet Union, this certainly turned out to be the winning card. Soviet cultural politics resembled nothing so much as a gaggle of chefs vying to see which unpalatable dish their followers would swallow (see Chap. 2). But the line between art and politics had already been crossed and the International Organization Division of the CIA was now involved in promoting particular kinds of culture—a culture that would be described as international, free, not bounded by national or regional ties, and apparently autonomous and covertly funded.[37]

For at least one of its apologists, the problem was not so much the CIA funding of the Congress for Cultural Freedom but the fact that it was covert. "It is one of the ironies of the story that the CIA gave its support secretly, conspiratorially, and believed that it could not—as to this day it does not—claim credit for one of its more imaginative and successful decisions."[38] Imaginative it might have been, but this extension of covert activities into the cultural field and the suspicions that it aroused fed a climate of paranoia and conspiracy on both sides and ultimately undermined the very values that were supposed to be defended. Nothing was outside the conflict, neither artistic values nor literary criticism. Though never incorporated into Cold War scholar-ship as thoroughly as were the sciences, area studies, and the social sciences, literary criticism was not immune from the fears and anxi-eties of the period.[39]

The recruitment of intellectuals as representatives of the freedom defined by the United States compromised the values of independence they supposedly embraced, particularly as ex-communists among them seemed intent on destroying liberalism. Poets and writers re-cruited to the cause of freedom were sometimes aware of the contra-dictions of their involvement in propaganda. For example, the poet and critic Allen Tate, who had long viewed industrial society whether in America or Europe as a disaster,[40] became a spokesman for the Congress for Cultural Freedom although it conflicted with his belief that the responsibility of the poet is "to write poems, and not to gad about using the rumor of his verse, as I am now doing, as the excuse to appear on platforms and to view with alarm."[41] This testy state-ment made in a Congress-sponsored lecture seems to indicate a cer-tain amount of discomfort with his role. Tate's argument in the two lectures that he gave for the Congress—"The Man of Letters in the

Modern World" and "To whom is the Poet Responsible"—was that the man of letters must defend the purity of language; the responsibility of the poet was "the mastery of a disciplined language which will not shun the full report of the reality conveyed to him by his awareness."[42] The poet who maintained that ends do not justify shoddy means was promoting, consciously or not, a hidden agenda. No amount of awareness on the part of the poet could possibly allow him "the full report of reality" at a time of secrecy and covert activity. The anticommunist platform of the early years was modified in 1958 when the Congress began to pursue an apparently more eclectic policy in the interests of winning over more supporters.

One activity of the Congress for Cultural Freedom eventually gained it notoriety. Beginning in 1953 it sponsored a number of journals that were funded by the CIA through front organizations. The most prestigious was *Encounter* magazine, edited from London by Stephen Spender and Irving Kristol, later by Spender and Melvin Lasky (after 1958) and by Frank Kermode, whose memoires *Not Entitled,* published in 1995, reflect the bitterness of the duped.[43] *Cuadernos por la libertad de la cultura,* the Congress-sponsored journal founded in 1953 for Spain and Latin America, was edited by Julián Gorkin (or Gómez as he was originally called), a former member of the Spanish Communist Party and of Comintern, and later a member of the Partido Obrero de Unificación Marxista (POUM) during the Spanish Civil War before becoming an equally convinced anticommunist. The choice of a Spaniard as editor was dictated by the Cold War concern for Europe, but as the years went by it was Latin America that claimed attention and the humanist facade of *Cuadernos* was frequently roiled by U.S. policy in the hemisphere. Very soon the journal found itself navigating turbulent waters. Faced with the prevailing anti-Americanism and with unjustifiable U.S. political and military interventions in Latin America, the journal's cover of Hispanic humanism became less and less plausible.[44] Gorkin had initially recruited prominent intellectuals such as Rómulo Gallegos, Jorge Mañach, and Gilberto Freyre, and had compiled a list of political figures the journal was prepared to support—including Juan Bosch, Raúl Haya de la Torre, and even Fidel Castro (in the days before he took power).

The first issue of *Cuadernos* in May 1953 included a number of articles by disillusioned leftists such as Ignacio Silone.[45] While its criticism of totalitarianism seemed unimpeachable, little was said about encroachments of freedom in the U.S. sphere of influence though the support for "friendly dictators" and the investigations into "un-American activities" were hardly a secret.

Gorkin was something of a cynic. When Guatemala was invaded by U.S.-backed rebels and the elected government overthrown, he wrote that Guatemala had entered into the great universal drama of our century, "that of communism and anticommunism." Why then, he asked, had Latin Americans denigrated Castillo Armas as the new caudillo "struggling against the democratic legality represented by Arbenz" rather than greeting him as a liberator who had "freed his country from a communist dictatorship"? Gorkin went on, rightly, to conclude that Latin Americans saw, beyond Castillo Armas, "the United Fruit and the Department of State and the military dictators of Nicaragua, Santo Domingo and Venezuela,"[46] while making the serious and unjustifiable charge that Arbenz—controlled by the communists—had initiated a reign of terror. He concluded that Latin American anti-imperialism and anti-caudillismo had obscured the clear danger of communism. The fact that the leaders of the Arbenz government took refuge in embassies after his overthrow showed that "they could not count on the masses." Gorkin did not mention the fact that the masses were unarmed and that the army had defected to the rebels with devastating long-term results for that embattled country, in which peace was only declared in 1997. The very perversity of Gorkin's argument was symptomatic of the problems of defending unfreedom as freedom.

In Latin America, any cultural policy promoted by the United States was bound to be received with suspicion that the essays published in *Cuadernos* did little to allay. Windy disquisitions on pseudo-problems, an emphasis on the hegemony of Spanish culture, and attempts to canonize the older generation (Germán Arciniegas, Salvador de Madariaga) were scarcely likely to influence a younger generation who felt stifled by limitations on what could be published and who found themselves confronting repression and censorship by U.S-supported governments. Not surprisingly few younger writers could be found to contribute to *Cuadernos* or to support the branches of the Congress for Cultural Freedom in Argentina, Chile, Mexico, Peru, Uruguay, Colombia, and Brazil,[47] although there were contributions from Jorge Luis Borges, Octavio Paz, and Alejandra Pizarnik.

In 1953, a Continental Congress of Culture in Santiago de Chile revealed that the problem of "freedom" in the hemisphere was a thorny
one.[48] Organized by well-known communists and communist sympathizers, notably Pablo Neruda and Jorge Amado, the Chilean government (the very government that Gorkin had praised for its love of
liberty) tried to stop the Soviet delegation from attending and then accused the communist journal *El Siglo* of organizing a conspiracy—
which caused the paper to be closed down for ten days. Some U.S. del-
egates were denied permission to attend the conference. One of the
resolutions of the Congress exhorted the governments of America "to
eliminate the obstacles that impede the free exercise of culture," thus
taking a page from *Cuadernos*.[49] To confuse matters yet further, the
Cuadernos correspondent accused the conference organizers of con-
cealing the political motives behind the shield of culture—which was
precisely the aim of the CIA-funded journals. Nor did the McCarthy
hearings help the cause of freedom, since the measures taken against
communism were comparable to those used by the enemy.[50]

To help the journal overcome its unpopularity in Latin America,
readers were urged to start national organizations and distribute
Cuadernos and *Preuves*. Beginning with its third issue, *Cuadernos* included a statement of its aims on the back cover that attacked "those
political and economic doctrines that pretend to exclusively deter-
mine the meaning of liberty," while stating that "indifference and
neutrality towards such a menace (of communism) is equivalent to be-
traying basic human values and an abdication of the free spirit."

In 1958, with Cuba in crisis, *Cuadernos* became somewhat critical
of U.S. policies. Jorge Mañach wrote, "Washington sees in the Latin
American Republics an extension of the rearguard in the struggle
against communism. This concept has managed to stifle all casuistic
[by this he may have meant subtly argued] and specific policies towards the said republics, at least in the sense of solidarity with more
democratic and genuine interests of its peoples. What interests the
United States above all is that these republics have "anti-communist"
governments however arbitrary and abusive they may be in other
ways."[51] Mañach also praised the heroism of the guerrillas of the Sierra Madre. In 1959, the Cuban writers, professors, and journalists
who were members of the Congress wrote expressing their "jubilation
at the end of tyranny and the return of freedom" to their country.
"Our sympathy and support are with the revolutionary forces that are

fighting in this decisive hour for complete victory, so that freedom of thought, as well as all the other rights and dignities of the Cuban people may be fully respected and wholly realized."[52]

But the fate of *Cuadernos* was sealed. In 1963 Gorkin was replaced as editor by a Latin American. The new editor, Germán Arciniegas, was a Colombian of the older generation, editor of an anthology of Latin American literature *The Green Continent*, and a founding member of the Congress for Cultural Freedom. The change was too little and too late, however. After making a feeble protest against the U.S. invasion of the Dominican Republic in 1964, *Cuadernos* stopped publication in June 1965.

The Cultural Gold Standard

The bait that *Cuadernos* offered to Latin American writers was a readership outside the boundaries of their national communities. Their work was published in the same journal as "world" writers such as Thomas Mann, Benedetto Croce, and Upton Sinclair. Not only this but the prestige of having one's work published in Paris, a city that for Latin Americans had always stood for the enlightened metropolis, was an added incentive, though one that had a price. In the view of its editor, culture must transcend the nation and region of origin in order to become "universal." The apparently unimpeachable notion that culture was universal and literature was autonomous was, in fact, a commonplace widely promoted within the U.S. academy. René Wellek and Austin Warren's influential *Theory of Literature* held that Western civilization was a seamless whole and that the role of literature was fidelity to itself.[53] But the presumption of universality as the gold standard for culture was a handy way of downgrading the cultures of emergent nationalisms. In a typical instance, Michel Collinet pontificated that "[n]ationalism should not be anything more that a transitory moment in the transformation of autocratic societies into democratic societies."[54]

The idea that the "universal" transcends the national dislocates it from its older meaning of a common destiny for all mankind, whether understood eschatologically as by Christianity or in terms of post-Enlightenment secular progress as in Comtian positivism or in the Marxist sense of a universal class. It lacks even the power of the "concrete universal" of new criticism. For the contributors to *Cuadernos,* the universal was a cultural concept that anticipated "globalization" and "internationalism" while retaining a notion of quality that would eventually be lost when the political and economic agenda overrode questions of taste. Even more serious, given the heterogeneity of Latin America, the universal became a handy alibi that allowed U.S. cultural hegemony to be passed off as a continuation of the legacy of Western culture. And given the bias towards Spanish contributors, Latin Americans may well have detected traces of the old imperial discourses that had also claimed universality.

But why was national culture viewed with such suspicion? Jorge Castañeda has observed that, in the years before the Cuban revolution, opposition in Latin America was articulated either by the Communist Party (outlawed in Brazil, Chile, and several other countries at the beginning of the Cold War) or by a populist nationalism whose program he summed up as "a redistribution of income through the incorporation of the popular masses—above all, the urban working classes—into the political system, a central role for the state in economic and social policy, and a constant invocation of the nation and its sovereignty in discourse."[55] In the 1940s and early 1950s, Perón had epitomized a populist nationalism that had a strong appeal throughout Latin America. The "universalism" of *Cuadernos* was a response to the proliferation of populist nationalist discourses and to the obsessive debates among the intelligentsia over national identity. For these latter the nation was still the institution that, in its reformed or postrevolutionary phase, was seen as the vehicle of social justice and the administrator of a more egalitarian and cultured society. Throughout Latin America and especially in the decades between 1930 and 1950 (the year that saw the publication of Octavio Paz's *The Labyrinth of Solitude*), there was a proliferation of books analyzing national character. These national soul searchings were usually based on analogies between the nation and the individual body/psyche/organism/soul, and generally were meant to address the question "Why hasn't Mexico/Argentina/Chile/Bolivia/etc. developed into a modern industrialized nation?"—to which there was a multiplicity of answers, not to mention a whole array of recipes for that development suggested by Latin American specialists north of the border.[56] Among the intelligentsia, national autonomy—political and cultural—had a powerful appeal that *Cuadernos* could not ignore, for it was allied to the secular foundations of post-Enlightenment knowledge. The journal's response was to declare cultural and political nationalism an understandable reaction to colonialism and semicolonialism, while arguing that the nation was an intermediary stage, "a transition toward the universal with all its rights."[57] This espousal of abstract universalism as a "higher stage" of development is now a cliché, as can be seen from museum catalogs that continuously underline the fact that the paintings or sculptures "transcend" specific experiences; it is the good housekeeping seal placed on a cultural product—the guarantee that however exotic a culture might appear, it is translatable into the dominant canon. In the journal's first editorial Gorkin wrote, "Our CUADERNOS aspires to gather and translate the universal into our language but also and especially to gather up and canalize the rich and varied expressions of the Latin American spirit in the direction of the universal . . . The New World has much to say and much to judge: we offer to translate and reflect it."[58]

What constituted the universal was, of course, established by the metropolis and disseminated through schooling in such a way that what was culturally specific to Europe was passed off as common to all. No wonder that Frantz Fanon's *Black Skin, White Masks* came as a culture shock. But the Congress for Cultural Freedom went further, insisting that not only the culture of the Americas was European, but that it was now under attack and must be defended. As Gorkin also wrote, "Except for some minorities who cultivated *indigenismo* to the extreme and were liable to fall into the strangest and even picturesque aberrations, few Iberoamerican intellectuals and artists fail to recognize their great educational debt to European culture. They therefore consider this culture as their patrimony. And they have never ignored their realization that it must be defended."[59] By a sleight of hand, the universal was thus identified with the goals of the Congress for Cultural Freedom and the rich heterogeneity of Latin America was to be filtered through Europe.

Although *indigenismo*—a term applied to nonindigenous accounts of native American cultures—has been properly criticized because it claims to "give voice" to the indigenous, the hostility of *Cuadernos* to such trends stemmed not from the perils of interpreting the indigenous from the standpoint of European-educated intellectuals, but from what Natalio González (ex-president of Paraguay, a country the majority of whose population speaks *guaraní*) described as the "disconcerting imbalance" these cultures produced.[60] The Spanish critic

Salvador de Madariaga dismissed indigenous cultures as being "of purely archaic interest." He argued that human evolution followed European norms, that two traditions—the Socratic and the Christian—predominated and, he hoped, would continue to do so. "Today more than ever, when both traditions are threatened especially in Iberoamerica, it is important that the close union, determined by blood and culture between Iberian America and Europe should remain strong."[61] Writing on "Western influence and Latin American Creative Work," Roberto Giusti later defined Latin American intellectual culture as that which has letters as its principle medium and is "essentially Western."[62] Given this outlook, it is interesting that *Cuadernos* could not quite avoid bringing up the question of the indigenous and the national from time to time.[63] The journal even cautiously acknowledged a tradition of national literatures.[64] In general, however, what was not considered universal was described as "folkloric" or provincial.

In an appeal for the end of the cultural Cold War, Carlos Fuentes would argue that it made no sense to think of the universal and the national as somehow in opposition. In doing so he revealed how far the *Cuadernos* position was from that of a younger generation of writers, many of whom were in 1959 celebrating the fact that Cuba had become the first "liberated" territory of Latin America.

Cheated Utopian Fantasies

The successful Cuban Revolution drastically changed the cultural scene because, for a few years at least, it achieved what *Cuadernos* had failed to do—mobilizing writers across national borders, publishing younger writers, and gaining the support and admiration of intellectuals ranging from Sartre to Sontag. Anti-imperialism and not Western culture set the agenda. Besides, following the Bandung Conference[65] the world had acquired a new political geography, one in which there were not only two superpowers but nonaligned nations. Newly decolonized and liberated nations clearly saw the fact of their emancipation from colonialism or neocolonialism as an essential first step from which other policies might follow. After attending the Belgrade Conference of nonaligned nations, Carlos Fuentes wrote, "With its vanguard action, the Cuban Revolution has opened a path so that in the future our countries may overcome the unilateral pressure that the United States exercises through the Panamerican system."[66] After visiting Cuba, which he described in the Mexican journal *Política* as "the first liberated territory of Latin America," Fuentes enthusiastically supported the Cuban Revolution as well as the short-lived Mexican Movement of National Liberation. Always impressionable, he would soon revise his opinion of Cuba. Nevertheless his words convey the mood of eagerly awaited change that was prevalent in the early 1960s. Clearly a counter-offensive had to be launched.

After closing down *Cuadernos,* the Congress for Cultural Freedom looked for a new and less-compromised platform for Latin America. The London-based *Encounter* stepped temporarily into the breach with a special issue, "Rediscovering Latin America," published in 1965 and written for the most part in the condescending tone that the British used for colonials. Its assistant editor John Mander contributed an overview of the continent based on only a two-week tour, and outlined the terms for Latin America's invitation to what Alfonso Reyes called "the banquet of civilization." On the basis of his rapid travel through the region, Mander published no less than two books analyzing the Latin American situation.[67] Though embracing noninterventionism in its editorial, the essays included in this issue of *Encounter* repeatedly underscored Latin America's cosmopolitanism and its place within Western civilization. In a series of vignettes of Mexico City, Lima, Panama, Caracas, and Buenos Aires, Mander quoted an unnamed Mexican as saying "all our traditions are Spanish"; in Panama, he noted that the Negro "is open to Western civilization" while the Indian is tightly withdrawn, and in Bogotá that "you feel here how profoundly 'European' Latin America has remained—much more so than the United States." Mander concluded that Latin America "has many hopeless aspirations, but being 'European' need not be one of them: it is not an aspiration but a fact."[68] The trick was not to deny that Latin America is *American* but, as in the case of the United States, to incorporate it into the "West." What is distinctly Latin American is futile utopianism. Thus, in Buenos Aires, Mander discovered that "the melancholy of Argentina . . . is not the melancholy of the Old World; it is a New World melancholy born of cheated utopian fantasies and ideals" (p. 14).

Those cheated utopian fantasies constituted a real threat, as the 1969 Rockefeller Report on the Americas would make clear with its warning that "development" would also inevitably bring about a "revolution of rising expectations."[69] Mander's bland solution was to welcome Latin America into the Western "family of nations," for "if we can persuade the peoples of the 'other America' that we see them as an integral part of that complex common fate, that peculiar enterprise known as Western civilization, they may still respond" (p. 14). The problem was that "Western civilization" had become identified with a corporate capitalism whose values were not those of a humanist culture.

The International Style: Preparing for Globalization

The Canadian critic Serge Guilbaut has documented the rise of a new kind of avant-garde in the 1940s, one centered in New York that had little in common with the historic avant-garde. Skirting the perils of "illusionist" art and mass culture, the U.S. abstract expressionists found themselves coinciding "fairly closely with the ideology that came to dominate American political life after the 1948 presidential elections." This was the "new liberalism" set forth by Schlesinger in *The Vital Center,* an ideology that "barricaded itself behind an elementary anti-communism and centered on a notion of freedom. Artistic freedom and experimentation became central to Abstract Expressionist art."[70] The language of this avant-garde imbued American technical virtuosity with global significance. Indeed as early as 1943, on the occasion of the third annual exhibition of the Federation of American Painters and Sculptors, Mark Rothko and Adolph Gottlieb attacked American isolationism and asserted that "it is time for us to accept cultural values on a truly global plane."[71] What "global" meant in this context was not only communicating through symbols and myth the "timelessness" of art, but also an internationalism that radiated outward from the United States. Abstract expressionism emerged at a time when New Deal patronage was replaced by corporate sponsorship and when the Museum of Modern Art was assuming cultural leadership. The values it espoused—"freedom," "artistic autonomy," and "the international style"—were represented as a higher form of art than national, local, or overtly political art. It is not surprising to find in the 1965 issue of *Encounter* cited earlier an essay on the "International Style" by art critic Lawrence Alloway, who wrote that "an advantage of international art, as it exists today, is that in the absence of verbal cues and aids, we can face any painting in a known style, with a framework which we share, at least, in part, with the artist. The artist, as he shapes and inhabits the work, is more accessible in internationally viable art than he is in exotic, local art, where the shared culture, without which contact cannot take place, is unknown to strangers."[72] The language here is staggeringly blatant. International art is "internationally viable" in so far as it is in a "known style." But what does this mean if not that the art is more marketable?

Alloway looked forward to a further stage of development when there might be an "analysis and discussion of these artists, free of the continental allegiance to which they are at present bound." The author quoted with approval Enrique Castro Cid, who had refused to exhibit his paintings in the exhibition entitled "Magnet: New York" because he wished to exhibit in New York "as an artist, and not as a national," and concluded that "[p]resumably this attitude will spread, with the increase of critical self-consciousness in Latin America, and it is a reminder that national and continental shows, patriotic or paternal, are interim stages in the development of anybody's art." It is interesting that "critical self-consciousness" is invariably understood to transcend the local and the national. For Alloway the "advantage" (for whom?) of international art is "the absence of verbal cues and aids." The whole language of this criticism, especially in its use of euphemisms ("the artist is more accessible," "internationally viable art"), cannot quite conceal the sales pitch. Abstraction is "higher" than figuration, the transnational superior to the national. A new hierarchy of values is created that filters out the dross of social commitment, referentiality, intentionality. Although the rewards of this kind of accessibility were considerable, it is too easy to dismiss it as opportunist.

It is true that artists who worked in the "international style" were rewarded with fellowships, shows in New York and Paris, and booming prices but it also coincided with a time when young artists in Latin America were eager to branch out in new directions. In Mexico, for example, the figurative art of the muralist movement, the first Latin American art movement to have a major influence north of their borders, had become routinized; and although it was by no means the only artistic tendency in Mexico, it was by the 1940s and 1950s far too institutionalized. The powerful cultural cacique and muralist David Alfaro Siqueiros was quick to register the souring of attitudes toward his own work, although having taken part in a frustrated assassination attempt on the life of Trotsky, he could hardly have been surprised when André Breton, a Trotsky sympathizer, objected to a Paris exhibition of Mexican art he organized on the grounds that "Siqueiros's hands were stained with blood." Though Siqueiros defended himself, the exhibition that was to have gone from Paris to Stockholm and then to New York ran into trouble. The New York organizers wanted to show only the pre-Hispanic, colonial, and popular arts, excluding modern art. When Siqueiros refused, the exhibition was canceled. "We were no longer the healthiest, most youthful and most powerful force in the art world. Our work could no longer be shown in the Metropolitan Museum," he wrote.[73] In his view, McCarthyism and U.S imperialism explained the fact that "[o]ur art has been completely sabotaged in the United States" (p. 163). Yet while Cold War politics had certainly invaded art criticism, conspiracy theory alone cannot account for a marked change of taste that took place in the 1960s and 1970s, and the enthusiasm of artists and their admittedly elite publics for technical innovation.

When the twenty-year-old José Luis Cuevas cast a stone against muralism in 1956, it was in the form of an open letter—"Against the Cactus Curtain" and "Against Nationalism and Conformism"[74]—in which he traced the fictitious development of "Juan," an aspiring artist who loses all inventiveness by conforming to the muralist canon. Cuevas affirmed that "[a]gainst that Mexico—banal, limited, provincially nationalist, of reduced aspirations, fearful of the foreign because unsure of itself—against that Mexico I protest." Cuevas is, of course, not an abstract painter; but in his search for the archetypical his drawings and paintings of prostitutes, the dying, and the mad could not have been further from the social art of Siqueiros and Rivera.[75] Cuevas was not espousing a dubious universalism; rather he was attacking populist nationalism as detrimental to artistic experiment and to marginal sensibility. In fact Mexico, even during the high noon of muralism, was open to an immense variety of influences and tendencies, thanks to the arrival of Spanish and European refugees, the visit of André Breton in 1938, the growing importance of New York as an artistic center, and the emergence of a vanguard of younger painters who experimented in a variety of styles. But although some art critics have detected conspiracy in the discrediting of the muralist's public art,[76] it is difficult to separate the change in public taste (which in the art world was, after all, an elite taste) and the younger artists' desire to break with stereotypes.[77] They were striving not for "accessibility" but rather for access.

The art critic Marta Traba in a survey of the art scene in Latin America in the 1960s and early 1970s noted that a number of artists had gravitated to New York but denied that they had succumbed to the values of a technological society.[78] Borges's often-quoted statement that the Argentinian cultural tradition is "all of Western culture" and that "we have a right to this tradition, greater than that which the inhabitants of one or another Western nation might have" removes Argentinian cultural tradition from its position downstream from Western culture and makes it into the crossroads where all kinds of hybrids can flourish.[79] Octavio Paz would argue less convincingly that "there is no Argentine, Chilean or Mexican literature, only literature in one language (sic); Latin America, even though underdeveloped, is an integral part of the West."[80] Denying that the economic notion of underdevelopment could be applied to culture, Paz claimed that existentially Mexicans and Latin Americans are now contemporaries of the rest of the world. José Donoso wrote of the "asphyxiation" of Latin American writers who, before the 1960s, communicated only with their "parish."[81] Vargas Llosa would ruminate on the solitary fate of unrecognized Peruvian writers like Oquendo de Amat;[82] and Carlos Fuentes—who originally had wanted to record Mexican reality as a kind of *comédie humaine*—was forced to recognize that the writer even in an "underdeveloped" country could not close himself off from artistic developments in the rest of the world.[83] It is not difficult to understand these attitudes. Artists and writers were claiming virtual space uncontaminated by Cold War antagonisms.

From the Universal to the Cosmopolitan

This space was immediately occupied by another Cold War warrior. *Mundo Nuevo* was funded first by the Congress for Cultural Freedom, which in 1966 reorganized its Latin American branches into the Paris-based Instituto Latinoamericano de Relaciones Internacionales (ILARI);[84] it later was funded by the Ford Foundation.[85] The first issue of *Mundo Nuevo,* which appeared in July 1965, was not only much more engaged with literature than its predecessor *Cuadernos* but presented itself as a forum for dialogue and discussion. The editor was

Emir Rodríguez Monegal, a Uruguayan critic who had edited the literary pages of the influential Uruguayan journal *Marcha* between 1943 and 1945 and again from 1950 to 1957. A fierce defender of Borges, an aficionado of Anglo-Saxon literature, and an opponent to the politicization of art, he believed himself to be a missionary for the new wave of Latin American literature. His personal rivalry with Ángel Rama, a rivalry that went back to the 1940s, was immediately inflated and exaggerated by Cold War binarisms.[86]

Mundo Nuevo made no apology for being based in Paris. The first editorial stated that its aim was "to situate Latin American culture in a context that is both international and contemporary. It will attempt to initiate a dialogue that transcends the familiar limitations of nationalism, political parties (whether national or international), and literary and artistic cabals. *Mundo Nuevo* will not submit to the rules of an anachronistic game that has tried to reduce all Latin American culture to irreconcilable group rivalries and has prevented the fertile circulation of opposing ideas and points of view."[87] This claim was somewhat disingenuous given the fact that *Mundo Nuevo* had been founded expressly to counter Cuban influence. All the same, the journal did succeed in attracting writers—Carlos Fuentes, José Donoso Augusto Roa Bastos, Cabrera Infante, Octavio Paz, and younger writers such as the Mexican writer Gustavo Sainz. Some prominent writers—Vargas Llosa and Julio Cortázar—initially refused to collaborate, and others—García Márquez and Roa Bastos among them—came to regret their collaboration when the journal was shown to have received indirect funding from the CIA. After only twenty-five issues, and after the revelations in *Ramparts,* the decision was taken by the funding organization to move the journal to Buenos Aires and Rodríguez Monegal resigned as editor. An anonymous declaration in the August-September issue of 1968 announced that the journal would now concentrate on themes rather than on authors, specifically on the "the central problems of Latin America," problems that were certainly not literary. The move to Buenos Aires was to prove disastrous for the journal; it was not only boycotted by the Argentine intelligentsia but the move was made during a particularly turbulent period of censorship and repression that preceded the return of General Perón.

An interesting shift is discernible between *Cuadernos* and *Mundo Nuevo,* a shift from the universal (identified with Western culture) to an altogether different value—that of cosmopolitanism. The main achievement of *Mundo Nuevo* during its Paris period was the visibility it afforded to the new generations of Latin American novelists who were now part of a far-reaching brotherhood that also included North American writers such as William Burroughs and Edward Albee. Rodríguez Monegal was skillful in slipping in reviews and references even to the writing of those who did not collaborate with the journal, often using personal reminiscences to give the impression of being at the center of a rapidly developing avant-garde.[88] He even compared the new novelists to the "lost generation" of American writers and represented himself as their Maecenas.

Mundo Nuevo was intended as a response to the Cuban Revolution's hold on the imagination of younger writers and to the influence of the Cuban journal *Casa de las Américas,* which was widely distributed in defiance of the censorship that prevailed in many Latin American countries. *Casa de las Américas* celebrated the liberation struggles of the Third World, the Black Power movement in the United States, the heroic guerrilla, and the tradition of Latin American anti-imperialism epitomized by Martí. It awarded literary prizes in the categories of the novel, poetry, the essay, and the short story, which were then published and distributed throughout Latin America. Attractively illustrated, *Casa de las Américas* responded to the long-standing dream of the avant-garde to close the gap between life and art and to foster intellectual commitment to the cause of emancipation; it situated Latin America as an ally of other Third World nations in the struggle against imperialism. It represented a new cultural geography, one whose center had drastically shifted from Europe.

In the face of this challenge, *Mundo Nuevo* not only tried to represent itself as having made a clear break with *Cuadernos*—"the new"—but took a conciliatory position invoking "a living culture, projected towards the future, without frontiers, free of dogma and fanatical enslavements."[89] To be sure the international success of the Latin American writers in the early 1960s made a difference, and a strength of the journal was its support of the significantly named "boom" of the Latin American novel. *Mundo Nuevo* attempted to register, as *Cuadernos* had not, Latin American specificity within an international culture. The fact that the journal received funds from the CIA may thus be less interesting than the cultural policy of its editor.

Emir Rodríguez Monegal was very much the heart of the enterprise, not only contributing interviews and articles but also notes on congresses he had attended and on cultural debates. He was intensely critical of the national identity debate, and in an interview with Severo Sarduy in which the latter spoke of "cubanidad," Rodríguez Monegal replied, "In parenthesis I have to say that after having suffered Argentinidad, and Mexicanidad for years, this Cubanidad, as a word and not, of course, as a concept irritates my ear a little."[90] His affirmation that almost all of the great Latin American writers had lived outside their own countries was in sharp contrast to the views of Haydée Santamaría, director of *Casa de las Américas,* who disapproved of Latin American writers living in Europe. When the Guatemalan writer Miguel Ángel Asturias won the Nobel prize for literature, Rodríguez Monegal appended an oblique criticism ("Universalism of Miguel Ángel Asturias") and made reference to Borges as a writer whose work was "less rooted in the teluric or rooted in a more Europeanized and less instinctive *tellus* than that of Guatemala."[91] While not participating in the rabid anticommunism of the time and even occasionally criticizing the blunders of U.S. Cold War policy, Monegal was quick to pounce on the often rhetorical gestures of the Cubans and their supporters—for instance, the attack on Pablo Neruda for attending a PEN club meeting in New York and the withdrawal by pro-Cuban writers from a meeting of the Community of Writers in Mexico in 1967 because writers on the Left "could not belong to the same community as pro-imperialist writers."[92]

As a critic, Rodríguez Monegal may have felt closest to the New Critics and their apparently apolitical stance, but his main interest during his editorship of *Mundo Nuevo* was unquestionably the promotion of Latin American novelists, hence his interest in their reception in Europe and the United States. Reporting on the meeting of the PEN club in New York in June 1966 at which there was a dramatic confrontation between Neruda and the Soviet defector Tarsis, he was critical of this introduction of Cold War hostilities into what he regarded as a purely cultural event and clearly supported Carlos Fuentes's view that the meeting was "the burial of the Cold War in literature." "Isolation and lack of cultural communication only serve international tyranny of which they are the useless relics," he wrote.[93] What he valued is best summed up in his introduction to an interview with Borges. "In the well-known phrase 'Latin American writer'

Borges put the accent on the word 'writer.' Those who in Latin America had trafficked in local color, in the teluric and indigenismo, in nationality as a safe-conduct for bad literature, were suddenly contradicted by this young man who had not forgotten that his grandmother was English, nor that he had learned German in Switzerland, that his country . . . was a flood plain, a land where for centuries people speaking very different tongues intermingled."[94] Literature, he argued, is not *primarily* a social document, but fiction, poetry and thought, and above all language. "Borges, rootless and cosmopolitan, represented literary value at its purest."

But how does the language of literature attain this purity? Borges's fictions exemplified the ideal of literary autonomy. Yet the perfection of those fictions may have been at the price of a feeling of betrayal and treachery to home and to lineage.[95] The irony is that *Mundo Nuevo,* was, whether its editor liked it or not, implicated in the cultural war whose existence he was eventually forced to acknowledge. When *Encounter, Mundo Nuevo,* and several other journals were accused of receiving funding from the CIA, he bitterly recognized that "the CIA and the corrupt of other persuasions can pay intellectuals without their knowing it. What they cannot do is buy them."[96] This was also the line taken by the editors of *Encounter.* But as Thomas Braden's well-known account of the CIA put it, the idea was to "legitimate existing organizations; disguise the extent of American interest; protect the integrity of the organization by not requiring it to support every aspect of official American policy."[97] Unlike Spender who acknowledged that intellectuals were being used for "concealed government propaganda," Rodríguez Monegal went on insisting that the journal was independent. In May 1967, in a note to the reader, he emphasized that *Mundo Nuevo*

> is not the organ of any government or party, of any group or sect, of any religious or political persuasion, but rather a journal that is edited solely according to the decisions of its editor who is the only person responsible for choosing the material it publishes. The link between *Mundo Nuevo* and ILARI (Instituto Latinoamericano de Relaciones Internacionales) is purely functional; through the said Institute the journal receives money only from the Ford Foundation: nobody imposes on its readers or collaborators national or international slogans; it does not entertain dogmas of any color nor does it formulate policies for others. This is a journal of dialogue.[98]

But even though the link between the front organization and the CIA was "functional," its general purpose—that of weaning influential intellectuals away from Cuban influence—had been served. Whether Rodríguez Monegal "knew" it or not, this is what the journal defended and represented.

In the August 1967 issue, in a further attempt at clarification, Rodríguez Monegal published a lengthy explanation and defense that included the revelations published in the *New York Times* and *Ramparts* magazine that the Congress for Cultural Freedom and *Encounter* and other journals had received funding from the CIA. Although he now acknowledged that he had been misled, he also maintained that "whatever the source of the funding, the journal had maintained its independence." Recognizing that the CIA had indeed manipulated organizations during the Cold War, the editor cobbled together a defense whose very casuistry reflected the sense of betrayal. Arguing that because the Cold War was over and the CIA no longer had any use for independent intellectuals, they had become a nuisance best thrown aside. What better way to dispose of them than to let it be known that they had been indirectly funded and that they had therefore been "agents." Thus, he concluded "the CIA doesn't even need to take the trouble to finish them off. In the ranks of their rivals they will find not only willing executioners but executioners who have been in training over a long period. The operation could not be more brilliant."[99] What is astonishing about this tortured exculpation is that its narrative structure comes right out of a Le Carré novel, where the good independent agent is always thwarted by the bad bureaucracies of both sides. Rodríguez Monegal described the independent intellectual as a sharpshooter *(francotirador)* betrayed by bureaucrats. "The worthiness of the cause of the independent intellectual is not and never has been in question in the contemporary world. This crisis only proves even more the need to defend this every day at whatever cost and against all enemies. Now the struggle begins anew." In a farewell note, he would claim that the journal had never strayed from aesthetic and political objectivity.[100]

But there was a deeper problem—that of literary valuation. Rodríguez Monegal would caustically insist that the "boom" in Latin American writing (a word that was tainted by its association with the marketplace) had nothing to do with "the eloquent publicity campaign of publishing houses, or the manipulations of Latin American and/or international communism, or the cultural activities of the CIA."[101] In a lecture in Caracas given shortly after the revelations of CIA funding, he tackled the question of literary valuation, stressing the enormous diversity of projects that had been included under the rubric of the "boom." He distinguished between four groups of novelists: early innovators, for example, Borges, Carpentier, Asturias; the generation represented by Guimarâes Rosa, Cortázar, and Rulfo, who invented new narrative forms; a third generation that included Clarice Lispector, José Donoso, Carlos Fuentes, Gabriel García Márquez, and Cabrera Infante, whose attention turned not only to form but also to the creative possibilities of language; and the youngest generation, for whom the medium is the message and that included Nestor Sánchez, Manuel Puig, and Severo Sarduy. Like all categories these are open to question. What is interesting about them is not so much their heuristic potential as their ascending hierarchy that puts a totally diverse group (Sánchez, Puig, and Sarduy) at the highest level of abstraction and hence creativity. Yet in the same lecture, Rodríguez Monegal introduced a relativism that undermines evaluation. The critic cannot divest himself or herself of all prejudice. The trick is to acknowledge this prejudice even at the cost of introducing relativity into judgment. His conclusion that "[l]iterature must first of all be literature. And criticism criticism"[102] seems merely to beg the question. Who dictates what is literature in the first place? What institutions (including the CIA) participate in shaping tastes and taboos? If the purpose is to include Latin American writers in a canon that also includes Faulkner, Proust, and Alain Robbe Grillet, this canon is not shown to have any ground more substantial than taste. Nor was CIA funding simply a technical problem. Its (albeit clandestine) approval underpinned cultural projects that were disarticulated from projects of national liberation and the democratization of culture, and contributed to the elevation of the writer to heroic stature.[103]

Mundo Nuevo paid scant attention to two significant developments of the late 1960s: the emergence of "Third World" literature and the growing influence of the market on the publication and distribution of literature.[104] Almost the only article published in *Mundo Nuevo* that dealt with Third World culture was a commentary on negritude in the wake of the first World Festival of Negro Arts held in Dakar in April 1966. The author, Clarival do Prado Valladares, held up Brazil as a humanistic solution to racial problems in contrast to the potentially segregationist implications of negritude, a view that idealized Brazil in a way that would not be tenable in the light of contemporary research.[105]

The second development during the 1960s that went practically ignored by the journal was the growth and influence of the culture industry, a topic that was of increasing concern to critics in Latin America. Always sensitive to changes in fashion, Carlos Fuentes had just completed his appropriately named novel *A Change of Skin,* which switches abruptly between an existential narrative describing an actual journey to Puebla and a journey in memory of two couples that ends in a cataclysmic happening. He had quickly registered the arrival on the scene of youth culture and his reaction was to attempt to appropriate it.[106] Fascinated by pop and camp, Fuentes also realized that the intrusion of American pop culture into the feudal structures of Mexico fundamentally changed the position of the writer, who could no longer pontificate from the privileged position of the lettered. The repertoire of mass culture was there for everyone; it was destroying the distinction between high and low culture and replacing it with diversified markets. In an interview with Rodríguez Monegal, he confessed as much: "No sir, we no longer have Parnassus of the spirit nor Arcadias of good taste: we are up to our necks in the rat race, we are submerged like any gringo or Frenchman in the world of competition and status symbols, the world of neon lights and Sears-Roebuck and washing machines, the films of James Bond and Campbell soup cans."[107] In other words, Fuentes extended an ambiguous welcome to consumer culture. Responding to the cultural climate, Fuentes's "change of skin" was a recognition that success and quality were not necessarily in harmony. While the Left wanted to replace literature with politics, and idealistically thought it possible to resist the influence of market, the defenders of cultural freedom welcomed the apparently democratic culture of the marketplace while wishing to retain their privilege as trendsetters, something that would soon prove impossible.

The Conservative Turn

That art should be universal and the writer free were the two principles of both *Cuadernos* and *Mundo Nuevo,* although neither of these principles was examined in any depth. It would fall to the poet and essayist Octavio Paz and to the Peruvian novelist Mario Vargas Llosa to attempt their elucidation, which in both cases involved self-justification. Although neither of them could be described as ever having been part of the Left, both shifted from a commitment to certain broadly leftist notions of social justice to conservative positions, which in the case of Vargas Llosa became a fully fledged defense of neoliberalism. Indeed, it is tempting to see this turn as similar to that of the New York intellectuals who from being revolutionaries came to endorse American capital.[108] The public embracing of views that were anathema to the Left helped to give conservative intellectuals "permission to speak," for instance in the pages of the journals *Plural* and *Vuelta,* of which Paz was editor. Paz and Vargas Llosa were both powerful political and cultural essayists, and both used television to extend their influence.[109] They found themselves in the uneasy position of claiming to be outside or on the margins of the state while holding considerable power within its institutions. Each made a clear separation of their literary writing from their political essays.

Octavio Paz was a child of the Mexican Revolution, during which time his father acted as legal representative for the Zapatistas. As a youth, Paz participated in the congress of antifascist writers in Spain during that country's civil war and later spent time in Yucatan, where he would write about the conditions of the indigenous peasantry working in the henequen plantations.[110] But in the 1940s, Paz developed a poetics and a theory of poetry that turned it into the remedy, the healer of disenchanted and alienated modernity. Initially critical of surrealism, he met André Breton in Paris after World War II and was drawn both to Breton's poetics and his anticommunism. Of course this is also the stance chosen by many U.S. intellectuals who liked to see themselves as rebels, as swimming against the tide. When some of his political writing was collected under the title *Tiempo nublado (Cloudy Weather)*, it was published in the same year by the same publishing house as was another "weather" book—a collection of Vargas Llosa's essays entitled *Contra viento y marea* (literally, *Against Wind and Tide*).[111]

In the case of both writers, the conservative position, not to mention the positive embrace of neoliberal policies, was a crystallization of convictions already present in their early work that had hardened in the face of attacks they suffered from the Left. In 1943, Paz was criticized by Neruda for a lack of political commitment and, in response, charged that the Chilean's "literature was contaminated by politics and his politics by literature." Finding the situation in Mexico intolerable, Paz then spent several years abroad in the United States and France.[112] Vargas Llosa came under attack by the Cuban journal *Casa de las Américas* for not spending the money he had been awarded for the Rómulo Gallegos prize on a political cause. His breach with Cuba, however, was widened by the Padilla affair (see Chap. 3).

In re-editing his poetry, Paz often modified or excised autobiographical references as well as traces of earlier socially committed poetry.[113] But this process of purification and abstraction was consistent with a poetics that endowed poetry with the status of a religion, with an ethics and even a politics. Poetry is a heretical religion in the tradition of the gnostics and the mystics, and promises a true revolution, one that will heal the divided self. Paz closed his essay *Children of the Mire* with the ringing assertion that "the time has come to build an Ethics and a Politics upon the Poetics of the now. Politics ceases to be a construction of the future; its mission is to make the present habitable."[114] In both his poetry and his essays, the copulative verb "is" resolves all differences: and in the image, everything can be transformed into everything else. "Hombre, árbol de imagenes, / palabras que son flores que son frutos que son actos" ("Man, tree of images / words that are flowers, that are fruit, that are acts").[115] The poetic suprapersonal involves a cleansing of the accidental in the spirit of the mystics. The title of his collection of poems, *Libertad bajo palabra,* which can be translated as *Out on Parole* or *Freedom Thanks to the Word,* while suggesting that there are some constraints to freedom, nevertheless makes "the word" its source.

For Paz, poetry that has no need of "theology, priest, mission or apostles" is always a transgression.[116] And because he is beyond any ideology, the poet is uniquely placed to envision "a new man and a new society in which inspiration and reason, rational and irrational forces, love and society, the collective and the individual might be realized";[117] poetry is one of the few resources for transcending the self and "encountering what is deep and primordial."[118] In his essays on poetry, especially *El arco y la lira,* Paz put poetry outside exchange value and outside history: "poetry has not yet been incarnated in history, the poetic experience is a state of exception."[119]

In its very abstractness, Paz's writing seeks to transcend the polarities of the Cold War. In his essay on the Mexican character, *El laberinto de la soledad (The Labyrinth of Solitude),* he had claimed that the differences between East and West are more superficial than those that separate modern civilization from those of the past. There is no struggle between two civilizations, only a division within civilization itself. All human beings experience birth as a trauma, but though this traumatic separation accounts for human solitude, it also produces the desire for communion that is momentarily realized in love. In love, in myth, and in the temporary communion of the fiesta, the antagonists—life and death—are fused. Myth—"masked, hidden, concealed—appears in all acts of our lives and intervenes decisively in our History; it opens the doors to communion." In an astonishing conclusion to this essay that anticipates "the end of history" thesis, though with a somewhat different inflection, Paz speaks of modern *fiestas* as an expression of the hope that "society will recover its original liberty and man his primitive purity. Then History will stop. Time (doubt, the enforced choice between good and evil) will no longer tear us apart. The kingdom of the present, of perpetual communion will return; reality will throw off its masks and we will finally know it and know our fellow creatures."[120] It goes without saying that in this scheme of things the female is always the "other"—the desired object that allows the individual to lose himself, to heal the primary division.

But if poetry is out of the reach of politics, the poet is not. During the course of his career, Paz published numerous political essays. Over the years, he constructed a figure of the poet beyond base materiality and licensed to pronounce on all kinds of issues even if from the margins, for as "a man of conscience he serves language. But he only serves it when he puts it into question: modern literature is above all the critique of language."[121] But in his political criticism, while disclaiming expertise, Paz adopted an omniscient view of politics in Mexico, Eastern and Western Europe, China, and the Americas, which he characterizes as different but related failures.[122] In *The Labyrinth of Solitude* and in *Postdata* (1970), published in English in 1972 as *The Other Mexico: Critique of the Pyramid*, Paz drew on psychology to argue that societies take refuge behind a mask that conceals universality; it acts as a shield, a wall—a symbol-covered surface. "Mexican-ness is no more than another example, another variety, of the changing, identical, single, plural creature that each is, all are, none is. Man, men: perpetual oscillation."[123] He was thus able to claim the uniqueness of the Mexican character without letting go of the universal.

The utopian vision of community that poetry promises is not incompatible, in Paz's view, with the need for critical consciousness. But it can be argued that although he criticized the bureaucracies of Eastern Europe and the welfare states, including that of Mexico, he overlooked the fact that a new kind of state—the neoliberal state—was coming into existence. This is the "democratic" state that sustains the illusion that the free market is the agent of regulation and change and that the apparatuses of the state are there simply to negotiate between citizens when, in effect, the cards are stacked against the poorer classes. In 1990, the year that he received the Nobel prize, Paz represented Mexico at a major exhibition of Mexican art shown in the United States and sponsored by the head of the media conglomerate Televisa and Mexican private enterprises. This was also the year when the North American Free Trade Association (NAFTA) was being negotiated. In the introductory essay to the exhibit's catalogue, which is also a masterly synthesis of Mexican art from pre-Columbian times, Paz stressed the function of Mexico as the mediator between north and south thus tacitly endorsing the politics of NAFTA.[124] He seems never to have recognized the iron hand in the libertarian glove.

A Fish in the Water

This ambiguity of being against the state while within it goes even deeper in the case of Mario Vargas Llosa, who, while starting from premises very different from those of Paz, became the vociferous defender of the neoliberal view of the state. This is not so surprising, however, if we take into account that even though he supported armed struggle and the Cuban Revolution, many of Vargas Llosa's novels have protagonists whose entrepreneurial spirit is stifled by want of opportunity and by society's corruption.[125] He devoted a good deal of energy to developing a theory of literature (in his case, the novel) and establishing a position as an independent critic not only of letters but of contemporary politics. After the break with Cuba (see Chap. 3) and his opposition to the Peruvian military government that was supported by some on the Left, he rapidly became a critic first of the state's intervention into cultural affairs and finally, when he stood as candidate for the presidency of Peru, a campaigner on behalf of the free market economy and a fierce opponent of what he called "statism." While Paz claimed poetry as the heretical religion, Vargas Llosa considers the novel to be a form of blasphemy, and the novelist a Lucifer who supplants God by imagining a world different from God's creation.[126] According to this view, the writer is inevitably opposed to the status quo, a "perpetual wet blanket" even in postrevolutionary societies such as Cuba. Indeed, in the improbable case that a society completely overcome its contradictions, literature would be superfluous.[127] "Demons" and "lies" have an important role in his theory of fiction. Both are positive terms: "demons" stand for the writer's unconscious and "lies" for the freedom of the imagination.[128]

Unlike Paz who excised autobiographical elements from his poetry, Vargas Llosa constantly makes use of them in his novels, even referring to his first and second wives by their real names.[129] The relation with his father who left home to live with another woman and who apparently was cold and unsympathetic seems to have been fundamental in creating his sense of being at one and the same time a rebel against paternal authority and yet a more responsible person than his progenitor, an attitude that is also reflected in his politics. This and his marriage to his aunt Julia, whom he later divorced to marry his cousin Patricia, have become part of his personal mythology. It is a mythology that enables him to present himself as his father's accuser while at the same time transgressing convention by marrying an older woman who was a distant relative; it is also a mythology that informs his later political persona as both conformist and conservative rebel—the Newt Gingrich of Peru, a rebel against statism and champion of hegemonic capitalism and the free market against prevailing leftist opinion, a defender of democracy and a reluctant leader of the *Movimiento Libertad*. In an article on the informal economy published in the *New York Times,* he described himself as "revitalized and cheered" by the black market that flourished in poor neighborhoods of Peru.[130] He documented his defeat in the presidential elections in the appropriately titled book *El pez en el agua (A Fish in the Water).*[131] Here he turned the tables on the Left by describing it as out of date and still defending lost causes, while representing himself as an oasis of sanity in an irrational world. But his defeat in the presidential race also owed something to a factor he has been reluctant to confront directly—namely, the racial question. He traces his own genealogy to the *conquistadores,* and during childhood and adolescence had little knowledge of the indigenous areas of his country. After his defeat in the presidential elections, he successfully applied for Spanish citizenship.

Thus it is not surprising that the most uncomfortable event in Vargas Llosa's political career was his appointment in 1983 to a commission to investigate the murder of eight journalists in the indigenous community of Uchuraccay in the Andes. The commission concluded that the villagers had killed the journalists after mistaking them for members of the guerrilla movement *Sendero Luminoso,* and Vargas Llosa would take a great deal of care to defend the commission's conclusion as the truth. But what is most significant about the event is that he seemed so unaware that evidence gathered from quechua speakers, whose words were translated, might be unreliable. Even more significant was his suggestion that unnamable primitive rituals were practiced by the villagers, a suggestion that he turned into fodder for his novel *Lituma en los Andes.*[132] Vargas Llosa once wrote that the greatest demonstration that a society is an open society, "in the meaning that Karl Popper gave to that term, is that fiction and history co-exist, autonomous and different without invading or usurping each other's domains and functions."[133] Like Paz, however, he uses that separation to affirm his authority to speak as one outside the political game and, hence, supposedly more trustworthy.

Both Paz and Vargas Llosa found themselves defending freedom in a way that escalated into libertarianism. Their opposition to the state—which they conceived either as the welfare state or as the bureaucratic Stalinist state—led them to overlook the fact that neoliberalism also functions within the framework of the state and has its own systems of control. The logic of "freedom" as defined in the trenches of the Cold War became indistinguishable from the freedom of the marketplace.

CHAPTER TWO

Communist Manifestos

He was *our* lion and the nation did not have the money to buy another one.

JOSÉ DONOSO, *CURFEW*[1]

I sat at a matinee showing of *Il Postino* in New York, listening to a full house laughing sympathetically as the communist defied the local mafia. I thought that communism must indeed be dead. "Freely adapted" from Antonio Skármeta's novel *Ardiente paciencia (Burning Patience)*,[2] the film (a Franco-Italian coproduction) transposes the novel's characters and events from Chile to Italy in the 1950s and has the poet Pablo Neruda teaching a postman poetic language so that he can woo a beautiful barmaid. In 1950 Neruda was indeed living in Europe, so the transposition is plausible. The novel on which the film is based, however was set in a far more eventful time of Chilean history—the period between 1969 when Neruda was nominated presidential candidate of the Communist Party (and then withdrew in order to support Salvador Allende) and his death in 1973 a few days after Pinochet's successful coup overthrew the elected government. In both the film and the novel, the postman, Mario, craves the power of poetry so that he can win his Beatrice, and Neruda is the great celebrity that he was in reality.

In the film, Neruda is shown craving the Nobel prize and winning the Lenin prize; in the novel he is awarded the Nobel prize. In the novel he is old and sick; in the film he has embarked on a new love affair with Matilde Urrutia (whom he met in 1950 and eventually would marry). Skármeta had dedicated *Burning Patience* to Matilde, making her the source of Neruda's inspiration and "through him, that of his humble plagiarists." Woman as muse. Beatriz/Matilde. Though the film sticks closely enough to events in Neruda's life, politics have been reduced to a plot device. Out of admiration for Neruda, the postman joins the Communist Party and is killed in a demonstration just before the birth of his son. In a nostalgic ending, Neruda and Matilde return to the village years after Mario's death. His widow plays them the recordings that Mario had made of the sound of waves on the beach and the sound of the beating heart of the yet unborn son, recordings that he had planned to send to Neruda. In both the novel and the film, the postman is allowed no real talent as a poet; he is only someone who records, who uses technical reproduction. The working man is no rival to the successful poet who had climbed to stardom because of his gift. Romance provides the momentum for this story, which in the film deprives the women of any role but that of muse, and it is Matilde who utters the most revealing words. Examining the photograph of Neruda at the wedding of Mario and Beatriz, she says "But I'm not in it"; and indeed she is not, and neither in a way is the postman's wife Beatriz. They are phantoms of the male imagination, unintentionally reflecting the archaic gender relations that prevailed on the Chilean Left.[3]

Matilde Urrutia did tell her own story, after a fashion, in a memoir entitled *Mi vida junto a Pablo Neruda (My Life with Pablo Neruda),*[4] which opens with the military coup of 1973, when Neruda was dying of cancer. Most of the memoir is a flashback account of their clandestine romance that began in 1950 when he was living with Delia del Carril and still married (as he had been since 1930) to María Antonieta Haagenar. Matilde's story is in the tradition of a "true romance" and tells of their secret meetings, their marriage, and their journeys in Europe, the East, and in Latin America. The story ends pathetically in postcoup Chile.

My Life with Pablo Neruda is interesting if only for its political ingenuousness. Indeed, before the agony of Neruda's last days, politics hardly comes into the story except for occasional commentaries on the "goodness" and the unaffected simplicity of the people. The poet who was the poster boy of the communist Left exists in this memoir primarily as a romantic lover, a writer of love poems—the genre that made his reputation. Why must Marxism, which had such a profound influence on generations of Latin American intellectuals, be sweetened in this way?

Speaking of the contributions of Marxism to cultural studies, Stuart Hall commented on "the resounding silences, the great evasions of Marxism—the things that Marx did not talk about or seem to understand which were our privileged object of study: culture, ideology, language, the symbolic. These were always-already, instead, the things which had imprisoned Marxism as a mode of thought, as an activity of critical practice—its orthodoxy, its doctrinal character, its determinism, its reductionism, its immutable law of history, its status as a metanarrative."[5] To those silences and evasions, we might add the Communist Party's transformation of the subtleties of Marx into slogans and the sublation of the national interests of the Soviet Union into a universal creed. Marx's refined understanding of the ironies of history were lost. Transposed to Latin America, Marxism as administered by Communist Parties and directed by the "actually existing" regime of the Soviet Union passed external political decisions off as rationality. Jorge Castañeda has stated that the original sin of Marxism was its "congenitally alien character in Latin America," pointing out that several Latin American Communist Parties were founded by foreigners.[6] But this is not surprising given that "internationalism" is embedded in Marxist theory, and certainly the earliest years of the expression of Marxism in Latin America had yet to be entirely governed by Soviet imperial policy. Add to this the fact that Marx's work is often badly translated and crudely digested.

The popularity of the Communist Parties in Latin America probably reached a peak in the early 1950s when the Brazilian party claimed a membership of over 1 million. Marxism attracted the intelligentsia because it offered a rational explanation of inequality and the goal of liberation from imperialism, both formal and informal. Anti-imperialism proved to be the strongest lure, and was responsible for recruiting many artists and writers into nationalist and anti-imperialist politics. Diego Rivera, who had been a member of the central committee of the Mexican Communist Party before his expulsion in 1929, and who was later a friend and admirer of Trotsky, rejoined the party in 1952. His wife, Frida Kahlo, painted a miniature head of Stalin. Her personal diary was filled not only with declarations of love for Diego but also with assurances of her faith in the Communist Party: "I am a communist being," she wrote. "I clearly understand the materialist dialectics of Marx, Engels, Lenin, Stalin, Mao Tse . . . I love them as pillars of the new communist world."[7] Whether she truly understood dialectical materialism remains a moot question, but there is no doubt as to her sentiments. One of her last public appearances was at a protest meeting against the CIA-engineered overthrow of Guatemalan president Jacobo Arbenz, who had been labeled a communist sympathizer. When she died shortly afterward, members of the Communist Party stood guard around the coffin in Bellas Artes, provoking a scandal that caused the resignation of the director Andrés Iduarte.[8]

The Egyptian economist Samir Amin once remarked on the fact that the shortcomings of the Soviet system were less important to many Third World intellectuals than its opposition to the West. Third World peoples were skeptical about Western democracy. "We saw every day how such democracy was systematically denied our peoples and how Western diplomacy only sought democracy when it was in its tactical interests to do so."[9] Carlos Fuentes made a similar point in his introduction to the diary of Frida Kahlo. "Perhaps Frida and Diego (Rivera) overestimated the promise of Soviet communism. They did not underestimate the threat of U.S. imperialism."[10] In any case, Communist Parties in Latin America and their sympathizers cannot easily be fitted into the U.S. State Department's kit for profiling communists. For in addition to witnessing the indignity, not to mention the injustice, of U.S. interventions in the region, they were faced with daily demonstrations of rank abuses of power in their own countries, with parodic elections, corruption, and capital flight. After seeing the conditions in which the workers of northern Chile lived, Neruda wrote of the unforgettable faces, the brilliant eyes "like an unquenchable flame that only consumes desert air." There is no reason to doubt that such experiences deeply moved him.[11]

Communism provided a secular narrative that gave purpose and meaning to individual lives. Although accepting communism meant accepting the eventual revolutionary overthrow of the bourgeoisie, in practice this was not an imminent possibility. In fact, the Communist Parties of Latin America pursued a popular front policy in the postwar period. In the words of Jorge Castañeda, their "long-term objective remained a national, democratic revolution, agrarian reform, and an alliance with the middle-classes and the national bourgeoisie. But now the principle enemy was once again imperialism, reduced to its barest expression, the government of the United States."[12] This oversimplification would lead to problems when party members were drawn into the more arcane aspects of party politics.

In Mexico, in particular, the problem was complex since the party was never legally recognized and was often persecuted. Yet governments adopted programs that at least rhetorically adhered to anti-imperialist and egalitarian ideas. From its inception, the Mexican Communist Party took great pains to recruit prominent artists and intellectuals, although it had a hard time keeping them in line, as the wavering loyalties of Diego Rivera reveal. The real hardships of militancy were not experienced at this level, however. The Mexican writer José Revueltas, who had begged to join the party when he was still in his teens, was recruited only after his first stint in prison.[13] Self-educated, Revueltas was a militant before he was a writer; he participated in hunger strikes, joined a peasant strike in northern Mexico, was imprisoned on the Islas Marías, and after his release visited Russia. Yet even his enthusiasm flagged when he confronted the sectarianism of a party that prohibited the reading of fiction—especially Gide, Zola, Joyce and Proust—and even Marx's early writings.[14] He himself suffered from party censorship like those writers whose works were "forbidden by the Holy Dogmatic and Stalinist Office."[15] Carlos Monsiváis, who devoted a memorable essay to "martyrs, militants and rememberers *(memoriosos)*," characterized Latin American Stalinism as a mix of martyrdom and extreme dogmatism. "Persecuted by the police, beaten, tortured, assassinated, their bodies thrown into ravines and back streets, the militants waited patiently, believing themselves to be in control of events, hated deviations, and insisted on uncontaminated purity. Without political power, they claimed a monopoly of moral behavior."[16]

In a sympathetic account of Revueltas's long march through a variety of left-wing splinter organizations and his political resurrection and apotheosis during the student demonstrations of 1968, Carlos Monsiváis argued that even at that late date there was no historical understanding of a party in which the experience of martyrdom "was wasted in internal struggles, persecutions, trials (in absentia), and violent changes of direction." And this was not only the experience of the Mexican party but was repeated throughout Latin America. Especially in the 1920s and 1930s, party members were supposed to have an inner conviction and wholeness of purpose that was rarely to be found in real life. At the same time, the qualities admired in the militant—devotion to the cause, singleness of purpose—were often transmuted into rigidity and intolerance of any deviation. Defying the stubborn class divisions of Latin America, the Communist Party gave working-class and peasant militants a political education and a confident understanding of the world in which they lived. Militancy infused purpose into their lives even when they found themselves caught in internecine ideological struggles with their own comrades.

The experience of Miguel Mármol, the Salvadoran communist who miraculously escaped death by execution in 1932 and whose memoirs were transcribed in Prague by the poet Roque Dalton (himself to become a tragic victim of internal ideological disputes),[17] is an eloquent record of the paranoid suspicion that prevailed especially when the party had to work underground, but it is also a tribute to the sense of *enlightenment* that Marxism provided; militants knew that, once they had learned to eradicate petty bourgeois deviations, truth and full consciousness were within the grasp of party members. People who could never have aspired to a higher education were trained and educated by the party; some of them, like Mármol, were sent for schooling to Moscow. To be sure this was a rudimentary political education. In his introduction to the memoir, Roque Dalton not only recognized the fact that Mármol's version of Marxism was simplistic but argued that one had to understand, in the case of El Salvador, "the chaotic, embryonic, backward—underdeveloped—nature of Salvadoran culture, even in its role as an object of study in the process by which our country's militants acquire revolutionary consciousness."[18]

The Soviet Union's use of national Communist Parties as extensions of its foreign policy led to tortuous and frankly incredible changes of political direction, one of the worst examples being the attempt to justify the Soviet-German pact of 1940 after years of anti-Nazi activity by the Soviets. In Mexico, too, there were several spectacular examples of the long arm of Soviet foreign policy. In 1935 Evelio Vadillo, a Mexican militant and friend of José Revueltas, disappeared for twenty years in Soviet prison camps, a case that became one of the central themes of Revueltas's 1964 novel *Los errores (The Errors)*.[19] The far-reaching hand of the Soviet Union was also felt with the arrival of Trotsky in Mexico in 1937. The painter, David Alfaro Siqueiros, took part in an unsuccessful attack on Trotsky's house in Coyoacán and it was Neruda, then Chilean consul in Mexico who eventually secured a visa for Chile that allowed him to escape imprisonment.

Literature by disillusioned party members proliferated in the postwar years. In Mexico, however, Revueltas's novel *Los errores,* which documented the internal struggles of the party in the 1930s, was barely reviewed. The silence had less to do with the quality of Revueltas's writing, which was uneven, than with a tacit agreement that the events it described were still too controversial. Or perhaps it was difficult, given Mexican nationalism, to acknowledge that working-class struggles had been determined by nazism and communism, two doctrines foreign to the country. Criticism of the party among left-wing intellectuals even at this stage was all too readily seen as treachery or as ceding to imperialism.

The events narrated in *Los errores* take place at the beginning of Lázaro Cárdenas's presidency (1934–1940), a particularly sacrosanct moment in Mexican mythology because Cárdenas was widely regarded as the president who saved the ideals of the revolution. With characteristic pig-headed obstinacy the party had initially opposed his presidency, though this is incidental to the novel, which focuses on the struggle between the sinarquistas (a protofascist party) and members of the Communist Party during the early years of his presidency and in which the Mexican participants were chess pieces in the international policies of the Soviet Union and Germany. In one of the more bizarre moments in the novel that underscores the similarities between crime and clandestine politics, a pimp robs a pawnshop by smuggling a dwarf into the store in a guitar case.

Revueltas often found it difficult to match the coherence of theory with narrative coherence (given that he wrote in a realist style). He also tended to make rigid distinctions between intellect and body, reason and instinct, so that the "consciousness" of his characters is often at the mercy of instinct, self-interest, and lust for power. Beginning with his first novel *Los muros de agua (Walls of Water)* and culminating with *El apando (The Payoff)*, imprisonment is a powerful trope in Revueltas's fiction, a "wall" that blocks not only physical but intellectual freedom. For the truth is that Revueltas knew a world that other writers of his time did not, and this included Neruda, to whom *The Payoff* is dedicated. Having spent time not only in Islas Marías prison but also in the notorious Mexico City prison Lucumberri that now houses the national archive, he knew about violence, drug-addiction, prison lore, escape plans, and murder.[20] He also knew that Marxist theory had gotten lost in a labyrinth of calcified verbiage.

In *Los errores* the extent of Revueltas's bitter disillusionment is explicit. One of the characters is an intellectual who, after being expelled from the party (as was Revueltas), reflects on the disassociation of language from experience. Expressions like "petty bourgeois theoretician alienated *from* the masses," "objectively counter-revolutionary attitudes," "deviation from the principles," "antiparty spirit," and "influences foreign to the working class" acquired in the mouths of comrades "a frightening dimension" as they were expelled from the jaws "by the lever of that impersonal, neutral hole whose dogmatism was already a compact and immovable second nature." Henceforth, he made it his mission to revise Marxism, writing theoretical treatises and throwing himself enthusiastically into the 1968 Mexican student strike that culminated in the massacre of Tlatelolco. After Tlatelolco, Revueltas was arrested and sent to Lucumberri prison where he was to spend four years and where he was one of the victims of an organized attack by common criminals against the political prisoners. Visiting him in prison in 1970, I found him sitting on a patch of grass between the cell blocks reading Isaac Deutscher's biography of Stalin. He had also been composing notes, essays, and commentaries on Marxist theory and had come to the conclusion that "the twentieth century has not existed"—meaning that the century that many had seen as the fulfillment of eighteenth-century utopian socialism and of nineteenth-century scientific socialism had witnessed only the sterile confrontation of the great powers and the threat of nuclear war.[21] Actually existing socialism had become alienated, converted into the repressive and imperialist Soviet state, and only the revival of critical consciousness within socialism could restore its integrity.

The heavy toll exacted by the party on the faithful militant is also poignantly described in Elena Poniatowksa's novel *Tinísima*.[22] The author spent ten years researching and interviewing for this book, which reconstructs the life of the photographer Tina Modotti, who came to Mexico as Weston's model and mistress in the 1920s and became a part of Mexico's small bohemian circles. She was recruited to the Communist Party after falling in love with the Cuban communist Julio Antonio Mella, who was assassinated in her presence early in 1929. Modotti was arrested the following year when communists were being blamed for an attempted assassination of President Ortiz Rubio. After her expulsion from Mexico, she took refuge in Berlin and eventually in Moscow where she lived with Vittorio Vidali, a fellow Italian refugee and communist militant, and worked for *Socorro Rojo* (Red Aid). She undertook perilous clandestine missions to

Spain, Germany, and Vienna, missions that were doubly dangerous because of the paranoia that prevailed in Moscow and that put party members in constant risk of denunciation and worse. In 1935 Vidali and Modotti were sent to Spain, and during the civil war she worked as a nurse in a hospital. At the end of the war, both of them returned to do party work in Mexico, Modotti now carrying a Spanish passport in the name of Carmen Ruiz Sánchez.

Poniatowska's fictionalized biography is a valiant attempt to account for sacrifice and duty to a cause without falling into Cold War accusation and counter-accusation. Nevertheless, the author has trouble accounting for the passion that compelled this ravishing and admired beauty to accept the degradation of working in the service of Soviet bureaucracy, a degradation that included justifications of the Moscow trials, denunciations, humiliating self-criticism, and putting "the cause before her own desires." In Poniatowska's telling of the story, Modotti's subservience resembles nothing so much as Christian abnegation. The ultimate irony was that this once celebrated beauty and talented photographer was to end her life in anonymity to the point that, on her return to Mexico, friends no longer recognized her as Tina Modotti. Like *Il Postino's* Beatriz, Modotti is not in the photograph. But whereas Beatriz was still the invisible muse, Tina had even lost this questionable status.

Though coming from a very different background, the account of the Mexican Communist Party given by Benita Galeana in her autobiography tells a similar story. In her introduction to a translation of the memoir, Elena Poniatowska links Galeana to the tradition of strong Mexican women, and indeed, Benita was proud of beating up on men. She was also something of a trickster. She was recruited into the party in the early 1930s by her husband and for a time it gave her a sense of purpose and even stability. Semiliterate when she joined, she would confess later that the party did not offer her much in the way of political education nor recognition. "I've gone to jail fifty-eight times for the struggle. I've suffered hunger, privations, persecutions. I have almost gone blind and I've risked my life many times for the Party. But to this day, they haven't bothered themselves for me."[23]

There was a considerable difference between those, like Galeana and Tina Modotti, who battled in the trenches for the Communist Party during the 1930s and the writers and artists who rose to prominence during and after World War II, when the party had abandoned its divisive "class against class" policy.[24] At this time party membership increased, particularly in Italy and France, countries that were still magnets for Latin Americans. It was this success that hardened U.S. anticommunism, turning it into the central obsession of the postwar years, an obsession that had immediate repercussions in Latin America. It proved all to easy for repressive regimes to win the favor of the United States by using anticommunism as the justification for their repression of dissent. The brunt of this repression was borne by militants for whom imprisonment became a badge of honor, a proof of commitment. The novelist Manuel Otero Silva was imprisoned in Venezuela; Pablo Neruda escaped arrest by crossing the Andes after President González Videla outlawed the Communist Party; the Puerto Rican writer José Luis González sought refuge in Mexico where he lived for seventeen years. But there were also considerable advantages for the favored few who became internationally known. Neruda and Jorge Amado, both of whom attended the huge peace rally organized in Paris in 1949, found themselves sharing the platform with the cream of the Left's intelligentsia—Paul Éluard, Louis Aragon, Joliot Curie, and Pratolini. This visibility gave them an international public. Neruda's poems were translated into all the European languages as well as into Armenian, Japanese, and Chinese. His "Canto a Stalingrad" even appeared in Yiddish in Mexico. Neruda and Nicolás Guillén read their poetry to eager audiences around the world and, indeed, it can be argued that the presence of such partisan publics had a considerable effect on the rhetoric of their poetry. During the immediate postwar period, Jorge Amado's novels were serialized in *L'Humanité,* providing him with the French readership that Latin American writers had always dreamed of.

Monumental Representations

In Latin America, joining the Communist Party was one way of getting close to that elusive entity—the "people." In regions with high levels of illiteracy, a corrupt upper class, and severe exploitation, many writers felt the need to get beyond the unavoidable privilege that literacy gave them and to find ways of addressing workers and peasants. Although Marxist literary theory began to have some purchase during the 1970s, when it was mediated through French theory, at the beginning of the Cold War most artists and writers who joined the party interpreted their role as "voicing" the class struggle and predicting the ultimate victory of the proletariat. Benefiting from the strength of the party in the postwar years and its anti-imperialist program, writers were able to address a public of sympathizers. At the very moment when muralism, that ambitious experiment in public art, came under severe criticism, writers were trying to overcome class barriers.

Mexican muralism had influenced painting not only in many parts of Latin America but also in the United States, where it helped inspire the public art of the New Deal. It had created a tradition of public art that would become a model for Cuba, for Sandinista Nicaragua, and for the Chicano movement in California.[25] If there was one achievement of muralism that transcended the value of individual works, it was that it took painting out of the museum and into public space. This democratizing move was eventually undermined by the stereotyped images that covered public buildings. Whether these images constituted "realism" is a moot point, for realism is not simply figurative painting but figurative painting with a message, or at least this is how David Alfaro Siqueiros saw it. In a 1967 essay on the Mexican movement as "the new path for realism," he argued that realism and public art could guide the masses toward the future.[26] With his usual intemperance he dismissed vanguard painters, including some of the most famous and fashionable Europeans, claiming that they had been imposed on the public by fraud on the part of galleries and critics. He accused the younger generation of escapism and hysteria that he darkly attributed to sexual problems.[27]

Siqueiros favored monumentalism. His paintings often depict huge figures that reach out of the wall or the canvas toward the viewer in gestures of suffering or liberation. *New Democracy* in the Palace of Fine Arts shows a female Jacobin breaking her chains in an act of liberation. Breasts thrust forward into the viewer's face, she seems to be in the throes of orgasmic ecstasy and joy in a supreme moment that seems to have less to do with the "new democracy" of the title than with the exultation of release. Siqueiros's paintings that depict the power of the human race, the potential to harness science and overcome enslavement to nature, are situated in an enlightenment narrative of progress and modernization and of the artist as demiurge, producing the work of art out of brute material. They work best when they produce the effect of estrangement and of the grotesque, as do the two powerful paintings *Ethnography* (1939) and *Echo of a Scream* (1937) that are now in the Museum of Modern Art, both of which can be described as allegorical. *Ethnography* shows the body of an Indian wearing a pleated shirt and a straw hat with his face covered by a rigid and terrifying Olmec mask that erases his humanity.

Siqueiros's polemical defense of realism had, of course, much to do with the Cold War and the contrived alignment of the avant-garde in opposition to realism, which forced him to defend his own idiosyncratic version of the latter. But ultimately his theory and practice ran aground for reasons that had little to do with aesthetics and more with the muralists' ambiguous relations both to the Mexican state and to the art market. In his 1965 essay on realism, Siqueiros would argue that the rich bought his easel paintings only *after* he had painted them, while others painted directly *for* the rich, a distinction that may not always be apparent in the paintings themselves, especially in the portraits.[28]

Postrevolutionary Mexico was unusual in Latin America for the extent of state patronage of the arts.[29] Artists and writers were recruited to the project of building a hegemony based on nationalist premises and on a concept of nation that institutionally incorporated distinct social groups—workers, peasants, the army—and that was even prepared to accommodate "revolutionaries" such as Diego Rivera.[30] In a 1922 manifesto, the Syndicate of Technical Workers, Painters and Sculptors to which the muralists belonged had described their aesthetic aim as being "to socialize artistic expression and wipe out bourgeois individualism,"[31] an aim that, by the 1950s would already seem impossibly utopian in a Mexico engaged in capitalist modernization. By 1965, when Siqueiros wrote his defense of realism, the assertion that the state was committed to revolutionary change and social justice was frankly unbelievable. It took a certain amount of cynicism to accept state patronage while attempting to claim oppositional space. As Carlos Monsiváis has argued, muralism in the postwar years had become jaded. On the occasion of Siqueiros's funeral he wrote, "Today as the last of them (the muralists) dies, the myth of the Past is heroically enthroned. Men like gods have allowed the monumentalism of public art that is also the life of the State, of a State that declares itself the image and likeness of the murals, an identical plastic and revolutionary task."[32] This is a damning criticism since it alleges that what Siqueiros had deemed revolutionary (the monumental qualities) is hegemonic and reflected rather than questioned the monolithic Mexican state. The muralist whose "irresponsibility" led him to be expelled more than once from the party of which he had once been secretary, and who had once led an armed attack on Trotsky's house, became quite cozy with the representatives of the state, with Presidents López Mateos, Díaz Ordaz, and Luis Echeverría.[33] The contradiction that Siqueiros would not openly acknowledge perhaps explains why, especially in his later years, he often destroyed murals and restarted them. Monumental art (unless parodic like Botero's paintings) tends to produce icons—figures that are venerated as sacred and therefore leave no room for a disparity of interpretations. Monumentalism reinforces the cult of the artist, turning art into a kind of pedagogy and the public into obedient pupils.

Mexico was a special case, for in no other country was state patronage so crucial to the development of a movement nor have the competing claims of abstractionism and figurative painting been so keenly debated. In the Palace of Fine Arts a mural by the "nonpolitical" Tamayo shares space with murals by Siqueiros and Rivera, and an abstract mosaic by Carlos Mérida was commissioned for the Social Security Building. But what helped to dislodge muralism's virtual monopoly of state patronage was the very modernization that the state was promoting. The opening of private galleries gave space to artists who did not believe, as Siqueiros believed, that muralism was "the only road."[34] The famous attack that José Luis Cuevas launched in 1956 against the "cactus curtain" that shielded Mexican art from contemporary developments was not only a criticism of the muralists but of Mexican provincialism—"vulgar, limited, provincially nationalist, restricted, fearful of the foreigner and unsure of itself."[35]

The Vicissitudes of Realism

The literature of social protest never achieved the influential status of the muralist movement, although the so-called novels of the land held a certain exotic fascination for European and North American readers. In the introduction to *The Green Continent* (1944), an anthology of Latin American writing in English translation, the editor Germán Arciniegas (who was later to belong to the Congress for Cultural Freedom and was never a member of the Left) wrote, "Writers . . . in their attempt to portray the human tragedy in its full depth, tend to elect such primitive and violent aspects of life as yet remain,"—thus constituting the primitive as an object of curiosity to the "modern" reader.[36]

During the "proletarian moment" of the 1930s, writers had attempted to interpret the proletariat in Latin American terms, substituting the Indian or the plantation worker for the industrialized proletariat. The most successful of the proletarian novelists was Bernard Traven, a mysterious German refugee whose well-wrought novels of repression and resistance were translated into successful films during the golden age of Mexican cinema. John Huston adapted and directed Traven's *The Treasure of the Sierra Madre* with Humphrey Bogart and Walter Huston in leading roles. Traven's mapping of the class struggle onto the racially diverse constituencies of Yucatan *(The Rebellion of the Hanged)* and the province of Veracruz *(The Treasure of the Sierra Madre)* represented one possible way of writing a socialist-realist novel adapted to a region in which the peasantry predominated.[37]

While little is known of Traven, who seems to have delighted in making a mystery of himself, the vicissitudes of the Brazilian novelist Jorge Amado are particularly well-documented. With the legalization of the Communist Party in 1945, he became directly engaged in Cold War polemics. Like Neruda, he would become an elected official—in his case, a federal deputy representing the state of São Paulo. In his literary work, Amado emphasized "the education of the people, popular enlightenment, a stress on our problems, and also technical and formal exploration in order to give the content of our art a pure and simple form closer and more accessible to the great mass of people who are avid for culture."[38] Infused with cultural nationalism, grafted onto a narrative of dispossession and exploitation, Amado's trilogy *Os subterrâneos da liberdade (Freedom Underground)* depicts the tension between utopian vision, heroic narrative, and political correctness. It reflects the presence and power of the "people," a term that in Cold War politics replaces "the proletariat" so that it includes peasants in alliance with professionals and the intelligentsia. Orson Welles, who was sent to Brazil under the sponsorship of Nelson Rockefeller's Good Neighbor policy at a time when Amado's reputation as a novelist was at its highest, was clearly deeply influenced by him and he returned to the United States with footage reflecting the epic narrative then favored by Amado. The story of a group of rafters who make the journey from Bahia to Rio could well have been scripted by Amado himself.[39] But Amado's public also extended far beyond Brazil, thanks to the international peace network set up by Communist Parties throughout the world. Amado received the Stalin Peace Prize in 1951, and wrote a book *O mundo da paz (The World of Peace)* intended to combat the misrepresentation of communism in the capitalist press.[40]

Amado's optimism that the party allowed him freedom to write would undergo a profound change after the Second Congress of Writers in the Soviet Union denounced the cult of personality, which led to a reassessment of his realist aesthetic.[41] The militant or subaltern protagonist of his earlier novels was deposed. The first novel written in his lighter style was *Gabriela cravo y canela (Gabriela Clove and Cinnamon)*.[42] It became a best-seller of unprecedented proportions and, until the publication of *One Hundred Years of Solitude* in 1967, held the record for copies sold in Brazil. Not long after its publication, Amado was elected to the Brazilian Academy of Letters, an event that marked his transformation from maverick to grand old man of letters.

Amado made an honest assessment of Stalinism after the 1956 Soviet Writers Congress and the suppression of the Hungarian uprising. He also radically transformed himself from a political novelist into the acclaimed popular author of *Gabriela* and became one of the principle publicists for Bahia's tourist attractions. One of the most interesting and ambiguous records of this transformation is his novel *Dona Flor e seus dois maridos (Dona Flor and her Two Husbands)*, adapted for the cinema by Bruno Barreto in 1978 and remade by Hollywood as *Kiss Me Goodbye* (1982).[43]

It is the sexual politics of this novel that vividly (impudently) illustrates the turn from a masculine heroic narrative favored by socialist realism to a woman-centered narrative that celebrates pleasure and the sensual. Dona Flor's first husband is a pleasure-loving libertine, the second a staid pharmacist. In the film, the first husband is seen in the opening shots from behind, his hips moving frenetically as, dressed in drag, he participates in the Carnival. He dies of a heart attack but returns as a ghost and continues to pleasure Dona Flor inventively during her respectable but sexually boring second marriage, in which the husband placidly has her assume the missionary position. The focus on the anus as the source of pleasure and the butt as the erotic zone par excellence is more explicit in the film than in the novel, although both make the point that prudent heterosexual copulation decreed by social custom cannot suppress private fantasy of unbridled enjoyment. Yet the enjoyment is in Dona Flor's imagination. By splitting her persona to accommodate both the pleasure of fantasy and the solid comforts of respectability, Amado subtly suggests his own accommodation. Dona Flor is able to live happily both as a knowing performer of bourgeois morality and as a transgressor in imagination. As Amado's own career illustrates, you can have your cake and eat it too, conform publicly and transgress in the virtual realm of fiction.

Neruda, Amado's companion in many public appearances, also underwent a shift of persona in the 1950s when he began his clandestine love affair with Matilde Urrutia in defiance of the sexual orthodoxy that tended to prevail on the communist Left. And in his case too, there was a retreat from public poetry to love poetry and a poetry that celebrated the sensual pleasures of everyday life.

The Epic Version

It was not the realist novel but poetry that came to represent the utopian hopes of the communist Left. There is a strong tradition of visionary poetry in Spanish in which the poet assumes the role of prophet and seer. *Countersong to Walt Whitman* by the Dominican poet Pedro Mir, published in Guatemala in 1952, and *Canto General* by Pablo Neruda, composed during the 1940s and published in 1950, brought together Marxism's utopian vision, an aesthetic manifesto, and anti-imperialist polemic with a national and continental narrative.[44] Two decades later and in the wake of the Cuban Revolution, Ernesto Cardenal's *El estrecho dudoso (The Doubtful Strait)*[45] and Nicolás Guillén's *El diario que a diario (The Daily Daily)*,[46] both published in 1972, fragmented the totalizing enlightenment narrative of liberation and brought this particular corpus to a close.

The poems by Mir and Neruda are situated in the polarized discourse of Cold War imperialism. *Countersong to Walt Whitman*, written after the publication of Neruda's *Canto General* and clearly influenced by it, laments the broken promise of the United States, which has failed to live up to its democratic potential:

> (O Walt Whitman, of tattered beard!)
> what about the fallen faces, what about the silenced tongues,
> what about the defeated guts and the ruined arteries.)

> You will not find
> > ever again
> > > The flawless sound
> of the word.

Although *Countersong* alludes to many tenets of Marxism—the belief that work is the formative principle of the (always male) subject, for example, and faith in the revolutionary potential of the exploited—and predicts the future ending of class struggle, it is Latin America and the Dominican Republic and not Europe that are to be the theaters for revolution. Mir addresses America as a plural subject whose peoples will redeem the entire hemisphere, a claim frequently made since the late nineteenth century—from the prophetic writing of José Martí to the vanguard slogans of the Cuban revolutionaries.

Neruda's *Canto General* is not only a more ambitious poem than Mir's but also a more elusive one. The poem is not a continuous narrative but rather a combination of diary and encyclopedia, a virtuoso display of inventive metaphors, a version of world history, an account of personal conversion; it includes "letters" to friends and moving descriptions of landscape. It is a poem about friendship and hatred, about loneliness and community; a utopian poem, a protest against repression; a national and universal history, and a history of the Chilean Communist Party. Its Marxism is messianic rather than scientific; and its forms of address and speech genres embrace polemical accusation, fraternal salutations, and even appeals, promises, and threats to potentially hostile readers (for example, those in the United States). The poet sometimes assumes the voice of the dead; sometimes there is omniscient narration, at others the sublime contemplation of untrammeled nature. Like his rival and ultimately his enemy, Octavio Paz, Neruda was striving for a poetry of communion that might heal the fragmented modern subject. But whereas for Paz poetry became a form of individual transcendence, for Neruda transcendence of the merely mortal was to be found in community.

Canto General is very much a work in progress reflecting its composition over a ten-year period during which its author went from being a sympathizer to becoming an active member of the Communist Party.[47] The paradox is that although the poem aspires to monumentality it is composed of fragments, divisions, and discontinuities, held together by a poetic voice that is itself ventriloquist—sometimes shamanistic, at other times comradely, prophetic, solipsistic.

In his excellent reading of the poem, Enrique Mario Santí makes a case for understanding the political in the poem not in terms of the "pious theme of social conscience" or by appealing to such "platitudes as 'empathy' and 'solidarity,'" as critical tradition has in fact done." For Santí what counts as political is the poem's subversion of the Western tradition to which it is clearly indebted and its embrace of the "interpretive risks of exile." Santí is not able to dispense with Marxism altogether in his reading of the poem but he reads its biblical language as "pointing up the textuality of his Marxist politics." Santí perceptively notes that the poem circles around the theme of conversion and prophecy, which is rehearsed in several different forms.[48] Few people would deny the messianic strand of Marxist thought—the majority of Revueltas's novels have biblical titles—and the prophetic is undoubtedly the dominant strategy of Neruda's poem although it is also deeply rooted in romantic tradition, especially that of Whitman's *Leaves of Grass* and Hugo's *La légende des siècles.* But the "platitudes" that Santí points out are difficult to dismiss because, as he wrote the poem, Neruda not only found himself responding to different publics but increasingly attended to writing poetry that was to be performed before a sympathetic audience. This is not a trivial matter. There is a difference between poetry that is meant to be read aloud and poetry that is also a visual image (the poetry of Mallarmé, of Vallejo's *Trilce,* some of Octavio Paz's poems). Although some of Neruda's earlier poems were clearly meant for recitation, the experience of reading his verse to workers at union and party meetings and his delight in these readings is reflected in the rhetoric of the poem, which constantly evokes the presence of these publics.[49] The readings not only renewed faith in poetry as a civic and public form of address, but brought the unlettered into the circle of literature. In this respect the poet had an advantage over the novelist. He could draw on vital traditions of popular poetry, such as the *décima,* as well as on such familiar oral forms as oratory, sermon, and litany. The "platitudes" reflect a counterhegemonic common ground between writer and public.

The translation into print of the devices of orality are especially effective in the second canto of the poem, "The Heights of Macchu Picchu"—the poet's invocation of the dead builders of that Incan fortress. It includes the cadence of prayer, litany, and the solemnity of funeral oration as the poet addresses the dead in a shamanistic appropriation of their power:

> Give me silence, water, hope.
> Give me struggle, iron, volcanoes.
> Cling to my body like magnets.
> Hasten to my veins and to my mouth.
> Speak through my words and my blood. (42)

The words would be echoed in the poem of another communist writer, Aimé Césaire's *Cahier d'un retour au pays natal,* for he too would promise "ma bouche será la bouche des malheurs qui n'ont pas de bouche" ("My mouth will be the mouth of misfortunes that have no mouth").[50] But what is particularly interesting in "The Heights of Macchu Pichu" is that it is not only Catholic or Christian ritual that is evoked but also shamanism, a religion that communicates with the dead and calls on them to possess the living. The amnesia of the historical record is countered by this embodiment of the forces of the past.

Contemporary distrust of universalizing narratives and representations tends to make readers wary of this claim to speak for the dead. But the heroic "I" of the romantic tradition that unproblematically represented the voiceless did not seem in any way inappropriate in the 1950s. In Neruda's case, it was an essential aspect of his poetics and his contact with a public in readings, in political campaigns, and strike meetings where barriers of class were overcome. Through the party, he entered into communion with others:

> When I joined hands with my people
> and went to combat with the entire sea:
> when I abandoned my solitude and put
> my pride in the museum, my vanity in the
> attic with broken-down carriages,
> when I became party with other men, when
> the metal of purity was organized,
> then evil came and said: "Hit
> them hard, let them rot in jail!"
> But now it was too late, and the movement
> of man, my party
> is the invincible springtime, hard
> beneath the earth, when it was hope
> and common fruit for the future. (390–391)

The party offered him a "permanence" beyond his mortal life: "You have made me indestructible because with / you I do not end in myself" (399).

It is difficult at this date to imagine the fervor of that particular political culture. In 1951, I was fortunate to hear Neruda read the ninth canto of his poem, "Let the Woodcutter Awake," in the patio of the Florentine palazzo that was the headquarters of the Italian trade union organization. Many in the audience were party members or sympathizers and they roared in appreciation as they identified the names of familiar enemies and heroes—Lincoln, America, Stalin— and sensed the counterpoint of vituperation and eulogy. For them it was an emotional occasion, a moment in which their partisanship could be unequivocally declared:

> Stalingrad, your steely voice surges,
> floor by floor hope's reborn
> like a collective house
> and there's a new tremor on the march
> teaching,
> singing
> and building. (262–263)

Neruda's portrayal of Stalin as a watchful father, a portrait that seems to come straight out of the film *Stalingrad,* may be hard to swallow now that we have the benefit of hindsight. Yet not to recognize it would mean leaving out of consideration the extent to which the Cold War left its mark on literature, here specifically in the narrative mode of this section of the poem with its third-person narrator and its overt message:

> In three rooms of the old Kremlin
> lives a man named Joseph Stalin.
> His bedroom light is turned off late.
> The world and his country allow him no rest.
> Other heroes have given birth to a nation,
> he helped to conceive his as well,
> to build it and defend it.
> His immense country is, then, part of himself
> and he cannot rest because it's never at rest. (264)

What is most striking about these lines is not so much that Neruda was blind to Stalinism, which was an essential condition for remaining within the party, but rather what they say about Neruda's paternalistic politics. Stalin is represented as father of his country, a father who both conceived and gave birth to the nation and whose body is one with it. This is an apt description of what Gilles Deleuze and Félix

Guattari called "the despotic state" in which all signs are inscribed on the despot's body,[51] although Neruda certainly did not intend any critical judgment. Indeed, so uncritical is he that he countenances aggression:

> And from the laboratory covered with vines
> the unleashed atom will also set forth
> toward your proud cities. (269)

This is where the prophetic voice turns sinister, for the freeing of the destructive force of the atom must haunt any future society however idealistic. The language of threat is both curious and disingenuous. The camouflaged Soviet laboratory, "covered with vines," also covers something more threatening—namely, nature unbound. "Unleashed," the atom sets off on a journey of destruction. By this sleight of hand, atomic destruction is attributed to nature and the death of cities can be presented in biblical fashion as justifiable retribution. Pre-Chernobyl of course. But this is also a rather odd comment on the Enlightenment story of humankind's liberation from nature, since this liberation occurs not through revolution but through a technical advance that is harnessed to all-too-perverse ends. Such indiscriminate slaughter would have involved the innocent as well as the guilty, and would have endangered the earth itself. Neruda's words resonate with the apocalyptic threat of Cold War "diplomacy."

Though the *Canto General* aspires to prophesy the future, the vision is anachronistic. The "workers" or the "people" addressed in his poem belong to a preindustrial or semiindustrial era, like the builders of Macchu Picchu:

> Behold me from the depths of the earth,
> laborer, weaver, silent herdsman:
> tamer of the tutelary guanacos:
> mason of the defied scaffold:
> bearer of the Andean tears:
> jeweler with your fingers crushed:
> tiller trembling in the seed:
> potter spilt in your clay:
> bring to the cup of this new life, brothers,
> all your timeless buried sorrows. (41)

These Incan workers are not very different from the modern workers he addresses in the poem who belong to an era before the conveyer belt and Taylorization. They tend to work with their hands and to enter into direct contact with the material world:

> I write for the people, even though they cannot
> read my poetry with their rustic eyes.
> The moment will come in which a line, the air
> that stirred my life, will reach their ears,
> and then the farmer will raise his eyes,
> the miner will smile breaking stones,
> the brakeman will wipe his brow,
> the fisherman will see clearly the glow
> of a quivering fish that will burn his hands,
> the mechanic, clean, recently washed,
> smelling of soap, will see my poems,
> and perhaps they will say: "He was a friend." (393)

These verses tell us a great deal about Neruda's Marxism with its emphasis on fraternity, on the conception of work as a masculine activity, as a "trade" or skill. Though he writes of miners and metalworkers, the very fact that he describes "the people" as having "rustic eyes" links all workers to the purity of the countryside and to nature.

For Neruda nature and work are inseparable. In a poem written after *Canto General,* "Carta para que me manden madera" ("A Letter Ordering Wood"), the newly sawn wood of the forest evokes the essentially pure and complementary relation of humans and nature.[52] And when he addresses the "fallen" United States in "Let the Woodcutter Awake," lost purity can be recovered through the spirit of Lincoln, the dormant woodcutter who must "come with his ax / and his wooden plate / to eat with the peasants" (269). Cutting wood is an innocent relation with nature, not yet darkened by the notion of ecological destruction. It not only exemplifies the benign in our use of nature (like Lincoln's wooden plates) but belongs to the *topos* of use against exchange that will surface again in postrevolutionary Cuba and Nicaragua.

Neruda's poetic narrative is constructed as a series of antinomies. The most basic of these is construction (and the attendant semantic field of unity, association, community, bonding, and "patria") and, conversely, destruction (solitude, fragmentation, and entropy). These are disseminated throughout the three "geographical" and historical narratives that make up the poem—the poem of Chile, the poem of Latin America (the common history of conquest and tyranny), and the poem of the world divided by the Cold War, which becomes the explicit and partisan address of "Let the Woodcutter Awake." The tropes of construction and destruction recur not only throughout the *Canto General* but also throughout Neruda's other poetry—in his love poems, in landscape poems—sometimes playfully, at other times tragically. They are also marshaled into two autobiographical narratives, one in which construction and destruction are linked to experiences of early childhood. In an autobiographical essay he described how the wooden houses in southern Chile, where he grew up, "burned like match boxes. Perhaps my earliest memory is of myself seated on some blankets in front of our house that was burning for the second or third time."[53] In his later years he would enjoy building and buying houses, filling them with his collections of books, sea-shells, ship's prows, and art.

In the *Canto General* he had envisaged a city built by workers. In the later poems a more private person emerges, one whose poetry increasingly and directly addresses his love of domesticity and everyday life, his love of the pristine natural landscape, the sea, the icescapes of Antarctica, the stones of Chile. This personal narrative is present in his early poems, but there it is interwoven with accounts of solitude and anomie before he was redeemed during the 1950s by the fraternity of the party and later by his love affair with Matilde, which he declared in the love poems *Los versos del capitán (The Captain's Verses),* published under a pseudonym. In these private poems, the tropes of *Alturas de Machu Picchu* recur in a new context, and once again they reiterate the narrative of a sterile existence that is redeemed not by community but by his love affair:

> Before I loved you, love, nothing belonged to me.
> I went to and fro along streets, between things
> . . . everything belonged to others and to no one.
> Until your beauty and poverty
> Showered gifts on autumn.[54]

Doesn't "everything belonged to others and to no one" betray a certain lack that the party had not filled? Why does "love" in these poems have the same redemptive function as the "party" in the *Canto General?* There is a marked withdrawal in these poems into the private world and domesticity.

Neruda constructed his own poetic and living persona as a simple and ingenuous man of the people, a people's poet who disclaims any knowledge of the dirty world of *realpolitik*. This strategic naïvité was later deployed to justify his political blindness. But as Emir Rodríguez Monegal has pointed out in a biography of the poet, Neruda was active politically from 1936 onwards, that is, even before he joined the party in 1945. He was a member of the Chilean Popular Front (1937); a communist senator (1945); public accuser of the Chilean president Gabriel González Videla; political fugitive and underground militant.[55] He was present at the World Peace Congress held in Paris in 1949 and became a delegate of the Congreso Mundial de Partidarios para la Paz, traveling throughout Europe and to the East on behalf of the peace campaign. He won the Stalin prize in 1950. In 1952 he was on the jury for the international peace awards and participated in the Continental Congress of Culture, which took place in May 1953 in Santiago. He appeared at countless rallies and meetings in Chile and in Europe. And in 1969, just a few years before his death, Neruda was the Communist Party's candidate for president of the republic, withdrawing only when the party allied itself with the socialists to support Salvador Allende.

Quite apart from these well-publicized activities, Neruda also swam in the muddier waters of party politics, although in his memoirs he often equivocated about the extent of his knowledge and involvement. On Siqueiros's assault on Trotsky's bunker, he commented, "Someone had sent him on an armed raid of Trotsky's home,"[56] without clarifying that the "someone" could only have been Stalin or one of his representatives. Neruda seemed unwilling to acknowledge that Siqueiros had engaged in a dubious escapade or that he had abetted a felon. "During clandestine sorties from jail and conversations on every topic, Siqueiros and I planned his final deliverance. On a visa I personally affixed to his passport, he traveled to Chile with his wife, Angélica Arenal." There are many indications that Neruda had a far more detailed grasp of politics than he admitted to publicly. For instance, he was the intermediary chosen to convince the Brazilian communist Luis Carlos Prestes to change his mind when Prestes was urging that the Argentine Communist Party should not oppose Perón.[57] Certainly the CIA was aware of his activities and in 1964 campaigned to prevent his being awarded the Nobel prize.[58]

In a revealing passage in the his memoirs, Neruda contrasted his reactions to the changes in the Soviet Union and those of Jorge Amado, with whom he traveled to China and whom he found "edgy and depressed." "We are old friends, we have shared years of exile, we had always been united by a common conviction and hope. But I believe that I have been less sectarian than he: my nature and my Chilean temperament inclined me toward an understanding of others. Jorge, on the other hand, had always been inflexible" (234).

The tribulations of Amado are documented earlier in this chapter. For him the Communist Party was the vehicle of economic emancipation and the great party of national unity.[59] Amado had participated in many discussions of party aesthetics and had attended the 1954 meeting of the Soviet Writers Union. In 1956, along with other Brazilian writers, he spoke up for far-reaching discussion, "especially of the personality cult among us, our enormous errors, and the absurdities of every kind, and the dehumanization. Because of this there has been an asphyxiation of thought and action."[60] In contrast to this serious confrontation with Stalinism, Neruda claimed that his "Chilean temperament" had always made him more tolerant of others, a strange admission given his vituperative attacks on avant-garde poets and political "traitors." One cannot help wondering whether his prophetic vision had failed him here. In any event, the revelations of the personality cult and Stalinism are described as bringing about a rebirth of faith, "cleansed of darkness and terror"; now they could "continue the journey with a firm grip on the truth." Neruda acknowledged no change in his own work but described Amado's transformation as one that altered the whole course of his writing, for he had now divested his work "of the direct political character that had marked it until then. As if the epicure in him had suddenly come into the open, he threw himself into writing his best books, beginning with *Gabriela Clove and Cinnamon,* a masterpiece brimming with sensuality and joy" (235)—an interesting comment since it attributes to Amado a change that affected his own writing.

Neruda was too much a public figure, too closely identified with Chile's Communist Party—which had a strong and respectable tradition—to leave it. But he did weakly acknowledge, "I had contributed my share to the personality cult. . . In those days Stalin seemed to us the conqueror who had crushed Hitler's armies, the savior of all humanity. The deterioration of his character was a mysterious process, still an enigma for many of us" (237). Yet Stalinism was scarcely "a mysterious process." The deterioration had begun long before World

War II and, far from being enigmatic, it was built into the structure of the Soviet state, whose policy of autocratic industrialization and hierarchical bureaucratic structure—euphemistically referred to as "democratic centralism"—became a successful war machine but, as it turned out, a poor engine of social justice. Because the Cold War had exacerbated the division between social justice and democracy, tending to put them on opposite sides of the fence, there was on the one side a tendency to see democracy as a sham and on the other a tendency to disregard justice. Because of Neruda's self-representation as a "simple" poet, he was able to avoid discussion of these issues. And, as his memoirs show, he had considerable stake in preserving his public persona.

The memoirs cannot be taken at face value, however. Edited by his widow Matilde Urrutia and his friend, the Venezuelan writer Manuel Otero Silva, their outsider hands seemed to have sutured many gaps in the story. The memoirs open with a disclaimer: "Many of the things I remember have blurred as I recalled them, they have crumbled to dust, like irreparably shattered glass." Would the poet Neruda have used such a clumsy mixture of cliché and metaphor? Had the memories crumbled to dust or were there episodes that needed explanation yet could not be fully revealed?

Although Neruda claimed that the memoir writer "re-creates for us with special attention to detail,"[61] this does not turn out to be the case, for, except in the descriptions of his early years that he had already published in different versions, Neruda's observations scarcely rise above generalizations and cliché. This is particularly true of his recollections of the East. Unlike Octavio Paz who, as ambassador to India in the 1960s, took an interest in Indian literature and philosophy, Neruda's residence during the prewar years as consul in Rangoon and Ceylon and Singapore left few cultural traces. He remembered them primarily for his loneliness and for the perhaps self-imposed isolation from these cultures. The memoirs hardly make much of a distinction between Asian countries so that it is sometimes difficult to tell whether he is referring to his time in Rangoon, Singapore, or Batavia. All are situated in an "Orient" whose religions he found repulsive and whose people he viewed primarily as victims. Candidly, he remarked that "the Orient struck me as a large hapless human family, leaving no room in my conscience for its rites and gods. I don't believe, then, that my poetry during this period reflected anything but the loneliness of an outsider transplanted to a violent, alien world" (84).

A few paragraphs later, he claimed that his religion had become "the street" (86) and that the English had marginalized him for consorting with the natives. "I had not come to the Orient to spend my life with transient colonizers but with the ancient spirit of that world, with the large hapless human family." The repetition of "hapless" (Spanish—*una gran familia desventurada*) to describe the peoples of the Orient reveals an underlying lack of curiosity. Like countless other displaced Westerners, he only seems able to find the way "deep into the soul and life of the people" through a woman. "I lost my heart to a native girl,"—a native girl who, however, was Eurasian and "dressed like an Englishwoman." "But in the privacy of her home, which I soon shared, she shed those clothes and that name to wear her dazzling sarong and her secret Burmese name." Neruda seemed to be finding his way "deep into the soul" of colonial mimesis without, however, showing much curiosity as to its functioning. His claim to be privy to the native reality behind the Eurasian clothing does not seem to have led him to more than a superficial understanding. The most striking evocation of his relationship with this Eurasian mistress, Josie Bliss, is the moment of parting when she threw herself at his feet, an act of self-abasement that, in others, might have given rise to some self-criticism.

The gaps in the memoirs are many, the most blatant being Neruda's reference to his first marriage. "My solitude became even deeper. I decided to get married. I had met a creole—to be exact a Dutch girl with a few drops of Malay blood—and I became very fond of her. She was a tall, gentle girl and knew nothing of the world of art and letters." The Dutch girl whom Neruda married is "not in the photograph" for, when it comes to writing of her, he or his editors relied not on his memories but on a description of this wife written by his biographer, Margarita Aguirre, who could only have got the material from Neruda himself! It is this obliqueness that make these pages an anthology of publicly acceptable material rather than an autobiography. The memoirs represent the public and authorized narrative that reveal little that is not already known. But while the reluctance to write of private affairs such as his first marriage is understandable, it is the political reticence that is the more striking.

It is interesting that when José Donoso cast a retrospective glance over the era in his novel *Curfew*, he made the central event, not the death of Neruda just after Pinochet's coup but the funeral of Matilde and the wake in a house from which the roars of a moth-eaten lion in the Santiago zoo can be heard. The aged lion transported from its native habitat roaring in the background is associated with Matilde's "lion's mane" and the lion rug that had decorated Neruda's apartment in Paris. But the caged beast is also like the wild genius transplanted into the petty resentments and political maneuvering of Santiago. What is being buried in Donoso's novel is not so much Matilde as the past, and that past includes the Communist Party, its rhetoric, its fellow travelers as well as its opponents. Although Matilde had requested a Catholic mass at her funeral, intrigue would prevent its being celebrated. But these intrigues between the claims of the party and those of Matilde herself are eclipsed by the arrival of a new celebrity, Mañungo, the 1960s folk singer who returned from exile in Paris with his son and who, after witnessing the brutality of the military regime, decides to stay and fight. The plot of Donoso's novel is creaky but it is an interesting reflection on the struggle of the secular religion of Marxism and Catholicism over the burial of the widow. It also marks a historical transition, for even as the mourners gather for the funeral the poet's celebrity is eclipsed by that of the popular singer, whose fame registers a shift in cultural politics from literary lions to pop stars.[62]

Both Siqueiros and Neruda, two of the most prominent communist intellectuals in the continent, seem to belong to an end rather than a beginning. With them, the myth of the poet and artist as demiurge and as public figure reached the point where it could be carried no further. The year 1956 was significant for them both. It was the year that José Luis Cuevas denounced the "cactus curtain" of national culture and initiated the polemic against Siqueiros. For Neruda, 1956 was the year he published his "New Elemental Odes"—poems that celebrate a turn from public poet to the bard of everyday life, although he remained loyal to the party.[63]

Nineteen fifty-six was a significant year for other reasons. In his anthology *Marxism and Aesthetics,* published in Mexico in 1970, the Spanish exile Adolfo Sánchez Vázquez claims that this was the year when the rigid mold of Marxist aesthetics was broken.[64] His anthology embraced conflicting tendencies in Marxist aesthetics from Marx to Plekanov, from Brecht to Fanon, as well as the contribution of Latin America and the Third World to contemporary theoretical debates. In his scheme of things, the period 1932–1956 was one of mistaken rigidity from which Marxism had now become liberated. Though the anthology was clearly intended for a Spanish-speaking public, it failed to take into account the significant difference between what counted as Marxist aesthetics in Latin America and in Europe. Even the editor's retrospective dismissal of 1932 to 1956 is flawed from a Latin American point of view, for during this so-called black period of socialist realism there were inventive departures from the European script. Jorge Amado and Bernard Traven wrote realist novels that introduced questions of ethnicity as well as of class,[65] and other Latin American writers—among them César Vallejo, Nicolás Guillén, Pedro Mir, and Pablo Neruda—composed poems that would certainly never have taken the form they did had they not been propelled by the visionary strain of Marxism. It was also during this "black period" that the muralists painted some of their finest monumental art, an art that is a radical departure from the sentimental idealism of Soviet art. None of this, however, seems to have counted as theory. By the time the anthology was published this periodization had some authority, for there was a new kid on the block. It was to the writers associated with Cuba that Sánchez Vázquez looked for the Latin American contribution to Marxist theory, and his anthology included essays by Lisandro Otero (secretary of the Cuban Union of Writers) and Roberto Fernández Retamar (literary director of Casa de las Américas). In the section on "art and politics," the novelist Julio Cortázar nudges shoulders with Fidel Castro and Che Guevara.

What is perhaps most significant about the anthology is the representation of the period 1932–1956 as one of monolithic rigidity.[66] Sánchez Vázquez argued that the doctrinaire realism that had prevailed between Zhdanov's declarations of 1932 and the Twentieth Congress of the Soviet Communist Party in 1956 had marginalized valuable avant-garde and modernist practices. What he failed to say is that Latin America was too heterogeneous a continent to be contained by one particular version of the aesthetic and that many avowedly communist writers and artists never followed the Zhdanov model.

The paradox of the Communist Parties was always the incompatibility between egalitarian goals and party hierarchy, between the desire to eliminate social injustice and the perpetuation of patriarchal structures. The universal class of Marxism was now represented by the Soviet Union, whose national interest was paramount and left no space for the particular and the regional. "International" communism that would potentially have made members citizens of the world was, in fact, both a hierarchy and an empire.

CHAPTER THREE

Liberated Territories

The "liberated territory" was a powerful fantasy of the Cold War period, a hope of liberation that would turn first Cuba, then Nicaragua, and finally Chile into political and cultural showcases that bore the burden of high expectations. Cuba and Nicaragua in particular inherited a baggage of aspirations from the historical avant-garde—the need to redistribute cultural capital, a valorization of the new and the unchartered, the belief that culture must be committed to the cause of social justice and change, and the expectation that, in a postrevolutionary society, human beings would shake off the cobwebs of alienation and corruption. Che Guevara's nonmaterial incentives and Ernesto Cardenal's experimental community of Solentiname in Nicaragua along with many guerrilla groups shared this common view of a humanity degraded by money and submission to market values.[1] What I want to explore is how this austere discourse structured cultural practices and eventually came between the alliance of the avant-garde with the political vanguard.

Cuba: The Avant-Garde Meets the Vanguard

In the nearly four decades that have passed since Che Guevara became Minister of Economy in Cuba's postrevolutionary government, capitalism has triumphed, socialism is discredited, the nation-state is an agent of the global economy, and the Left in many countries is now part of a coalition, sharing power with conservative parties or accepting aspects of the conservative agenda.[2] The besieged Zapatista movement is urging justice rather than revolution for the indigenous of Chiapas.

Small wonder that in Wim Wenders's film *Buena Vista Social Club* (1999), Cuba basks in the sepia tones of nostalgia. The portraits of Che, like such slogans as "The revolution is eternal," are as outdated as the elaborate colonial baroque salon in which gymnasts and dancers train. Wonderful as they are, the aged musicians "rediscovered" by Ry Cooder speak, play, and sing across a temporal distance that avoids any mention of what has passed in between. Most telling of all, the musicians receive their overdue accolade in Carnegie Hall, in the middle of a city always on the move that is light years away from Havana—once in the vanguard but is now apparently (at least in the filmmaker's eyes) at a standstill, mired in nostalgia.[3] Yet after the film's release, aged Cuban musicians were invited to perform in concerts around the world, as if the past had now acquired value over the present.

But along with this nostalgic view of Havana in decay, there is another image of the city as the Sodom and Gomorrah of the Caribbean. This particular narrative has an interesting genealogy. It belongs to a long-standing critique that identifies luxury with degeneration, the Old World with corruption and the New with the pristine; it is a view that goes back to the church's hostility to usury and the missionary church's idealization of the indigenous. Although I am not claiming a continuity between Catholic anticapitalism and certain readings of Marx, the two are analogous in their project of purifying society in order to restore the true value of human life. Further, the old topos of city versus country was given a new twist when, in the first years of the Cuban Revolution, people were discouraged from living in Havana and encouraged to live in the healthy countryside. Prostitutes were reeducated, casinos closed, private enterprise squeezed out. Discipline rather than pleasure became the order of the day.

It is hard to backtrack and discover the moment when armed struggle was not an idle project, when the liberation of territories from neocolonialism was regarded as realistic, and when in the face of corrupt judicial systems and politics, violent action was seen as necessary by the young, especially the young male. Even though armed struggle in Latin America did not begin with the Cuban Revolution and not all guerrilla movements have been aided by Cuba, it was Cuba that made revolution part of the immediate agenda for political action and affirmed armed struggle as the only way to bring about change.[4] There was no need to wait for the magical conjuncture of mass workers' movement and the crisis of the bourgeois state that Communist Parties hoped for. Besides, there was the widespread belief that capitalism was rotting on the tree, that it could not last.[5]

The guerrilla movements drew the intelligentsia and the middle class into their ranks. Jorge Castañeda calculated that 64 percent of those who died as a result of counterinsurgency repression were intellectual workers, many of whom must have been students[6] who wanted to purge themselves of the original sin of being middle-class intellectuals. Indeed, Che Guevara never confused intellectual work with revolutionary struggle and declared that "there are no artists of great authority who also have great revolutionary authority. The party members should take this task into their hands and seek to achieve the main objective: to educate the people."[7] Personal experience of the armed struggle was the motor of transformation that created the new man: "[T]his type of struggle gives us the opportunity to transform ourselves into revolutionaries, the highest point of human evolution," Guevara stated.[8] Thus not only was the enforced austerity of the *guerrillero* difficult to reconcile with the sensuality of art, militancy became the true test of the authentic intellectual.[9]

Although the 1968 Cultural Congress of Havana emphasized the role of intellectuals in the revolution, the "call" *("llamamiento")* from Havana was for them to "intensify the struggle against imperialism by assuming the role that corresponded to them in the struggle for the liberation of the people," which included joining a party and if need be participating in armed struggle.[10] What is striking, however, is that the call for responsibility was most often addressed to intellectuals but not, as the Uruguayan writer Mario Benedetti pointed out, directed with the same urgency toward workers, technicians, or sportsmen.[11] I remember Mario Vargas Llosa addressing a meeting in Cuzco in 1968 and being asked why he didn't take to the hills, rifle in hand, as if this were the only possible role for him. Rereading the Cuban journals of the 1960s, the anxiety surrounding the term "intellectual" is palpable: foreign intellectuals' support for the revolution was critical to its success, even as the domestic intellectual was being reined in. Yet at the 1961 Cultural Congress of Havana, Fidel Castro would acknowledge that intellectuals frequently "raised the flag that the political vanguard had let fall."[12]

Perhaps for this reason, some writers became critical of their own vocation. The Argentine writer Rodolfo Walsh, who joined the *montoneros,* would resolve the incompatible claims of politics and literature by abandoning literature.[13] A poem by the Peruvian poet Antonio Cisneros eloquently voices the frustration. He recalls a meeting in Paris, in the Rue Sommerard, with an old friend now converted to Maoism, whose asceticism the poet is ultimately unable to share:

> But my gods are weak & I doubted.
> And the young stallions were lost behind walls
> & he did not return that night to the hotel on Sommerard Street
> Obstinate & slow gods, trained to gnaw at my liver every
> morning.
> Their faces are dark, ignorant of revelation.[14]

Cisneros's poems say a great deal not only about the doubts but also about the attraction of revolutionary politics for Latin Americans, as well as for North Americans and Europeans, who at first found in Cuba the freedom to innovate and experiment that was missing in other socialist states.[15] Jean-Paul Sartre, at that time one of the most famous intellectuals in the world, visited the island with Simone de Beauvoir and reportedly told Alejo Carpentier, "c'est une révolution qui n'enmerde pas." He wrote that "for the first time in our lives, we were witnessing happiness that had been attained by violence."[16]

At the helm of "the first liberated territory of the Americas," the postrevolutionary Cuban government pursued heteronomous projects of national autonomy and social justice and experimented in autochthonous forms of modernization and socialism. Che introduced nonmaterial incentives to boost production, a project that was more remarkable for its idealism than for its results. In the cultural field, Fidel's 1960 promise to university students—"Everything within the Revolution; nothing outside the Revolution"—was widely but erroneously taken to have opened a space for divergent movements and opinions. However, the terrain of intellectual discussion was dominated by recycled male intellectuals. Although the literacy campaign of 1961 offered students, many of whom were women, a practical form of participation in the revolution, it would be hard to name a single woman who, in the 1960s, made a significant contribution to postrevolutionary thinking (Haydée Santamaría and Wilma Espín held political positions but this is not the same thing). The most prominent black intellectuals were the poet Nicolás Guillén, who had made his reputation before the Cuban Revolution, and the exiled Haitian René Depestre.[17]

Batista's Havana had been a louche, Mafia-run gambling joint with a tourist sex trade and a rough way of treating political opponents whose bodies, particularly after the Fidelistas had established themselves in the Sierra Madre, were likely to be fished out of the harbor. The spin-off was a vibrant night life—the music of Beny Moré, the Aragón orchestra, Elena Burke—and the most sophisticated culture industry in Latin America. *Selecciones de Readers Digest* was published in Havana, and Cuba was the first country to produce radio soap opera (and later television soap opera). The first radio soap opera, *The Right to Be Born ("El derecho de nacer")*, was a runaway success throughout Latin America. But schooling was poor and there was much illiteracy (though less than many other Latin American countries), which restricted the environment for high culture so much so that writers were often forced to subsidize the publication of their own books.

The new government acted quickly to found the National Press in 1960, whose first published book was *Don Quijote;* its press run of 150,000 copies was considerable for that time. The National Press was replaced in 1962 by the Cuban National Publishing House, whose divisions published scientific and educational books, children's books, as well as literature. Readership expanded as a result of the successful literacy campaign in 1961. New cultural institutions were founded, including the Union of Writers and Artists which published its own journal, and Casa de las Américas, a meeting house for Latin American artists and writers—both of them under the aegis first of the Instituto del Libro and later under that of the Ministry of Culture.[18] The Union of Writers and Artists published Cuban writers and was one of many institutions (including the armed forces) that organized competitions for literary prizes. The Casa de las Américas gave annual awards to unpublished works by Latin American writers and distributed the prize-winning books throughout Europe and countries of Latin America that were free of censorship.[19]

The revolution's emphasis on youth was promising. The short-lived journal *Lunes de Revolución,* published from 1958 to 1961 and edited initially by Guillermo Cabrera Infante and Pablo Armando Fernández, not only aligned younger writers of many different persuasions with the revolution but gave them a public in the intense early days of the new government.[20] *Caimán barbudo* (founded in 1966) and *Juventud rebelde* both privileged youth as the uncontaminated bearers of a new spirit.[21] The journal *Casa de las Américas* had an innovative and attractive design, and although it reflected particular political interests—the year of the heroic guerrilla, Che, black power, May 1968—it also included a great deal of literary criticism, fiction, and poetry that was not simply another articulation of immediate political strategies. In 1967 its editor Roberto Fernández Retamar would optimistically affirm that Cuba, now that the revolution had been won and after a short period of struggle with sectarianism, could engage in the construction of a new culture.[22]

But it wasn't long before signs of the institutionalization of the revolution became apparent. *Lunes de Revolución* was closed down in 1961. A documentary film about Havana night life entitled *P.M.*, made in part by Cabrera Infante, was never shown.[23] Antonio Arrufat was dismissed as editor of *Casa de las Américas,* to be replaced by Roberto Fernández Retamar. The writer Virgilio Piñera was briefly imprisoned for homosexuality. The independent publishing house *El Puente,* which published writers who were not interested in committed literature, lasted only until 1965 and by this date several writers, among them Guillermo Cabrera Infante, Severo Sarduy, and Calvert Casey, were living abroad. The latter, a Cuban-American writer of short stories, killed himself in Rome. On her second visit to Cuba Simone de Beauvoir noted that the honeymoon of the revolution was over: "less gaiety, less freedom, but much progress on certain fronts."[24] García Márquez, who worked for a short period in Havana for the Cuban press agency *Prensa libre,* reportedly resigned because even in those early days, he had felt that the agency was becoming influenced by Soviet-style bureaucrats—although down to the present he cultivates a personal friendship with Fidel.[25] After 1968 more stringent government control began to be applied.[26]

Building a new society required discipline, not irony; hard work, not a freewheeling bohemian style. The alliance between the political vanguard and an avant-garde that saw itself as a cultural guerrilla was bound to become strained, although the incompatibilities were at first obscured by the word "revolution," which signified armed struggle (and hence sacrifice and discipline), and later by participation in building the new society—that is to say, wholesale class war on the one hand and, on the other, cooperation and community. When the term "revolution" migrated into art and literature, it could allude to content or rhetorical claims of political correctness, or to a writer's definition of the new and the experimental. It was the latter that first irritated the newly institutionalized Cuban intellectuals.

The Union of Cuban Writers had little tolerance for the literary avant-garde. In an open letter to the Mexican writer Emmanuel Carballo, published in 1966, the secretary of the Union of Cuban Writers, Lisandro Otero, wrote, "Some writers of the bourgeoisie believe that literature is a perennial form of insurrection, of nonconformity, of rebellion. They believe that literature only exists where there is a lack of reverence, sarcasm and protest."[27] In the same year, he wrote, "Rebellion, of this sort, has no place in a post-revolutionary society; conformity, consent and using freedom to accept the revolution are the attitudes of the revolutionary writer."[28] The fine line between letting a thousand flowers bloom and weed-eradication was about to be crossed.

As for the old bohemian Havana—"the seamy, exciting city, booming with casinos, nightclubs and whorehouses,"[29] vividly depicted in Cabrera Infante's novel *Tres tristes tigres (Three Trapped Tigers)*[30]—it was about to change its face. A policy of favoring the countryside over the city and a gradually tightening austerity would be exacerbated by the U.S. blockade, though the sensual Cuban culture, especially its popular culture, proved irrepressible. The city grew shabby. The stigma of degeneracy was applied to prostitutes (who were reeducated) and to homosexuals, some of whom were imprisoned and later, in 1965, sent to disciplinary camps—the Unidad Militar de Ayuda a la Producción (UMAP). Others made a discreet exit to Europe and the United States.[31]

While the Afro-American cult "santería" was discouraged as an archaic practice, it was less easy to suppress the annual carnival, although in 1969 it was postponed because all hands were needed for the sugar harvest. The government's assumption of control of the celebration, however, was a significant development. Since colonial times the carnival had been the expression of abundance, sensuality, and excess, a mass spectacle of dance and celebration in which the Afro-Caribbean took over. Transformed from a religious to a secular event, it is now held around July 26, the date of Fidel's failed attack on the Moncada barracks in Santiago in 1953, and is administered by local assemblies and through them by the national government. Rather like the Rose Bowl parade in Pasadena, carnival floats are forms of propaganda. As Randy Martin argued, "the state is putting itself on display. The Ministry of Light Industry, the Provincial Direction of Culture, of Gastronomy, and of Sewers and Storm Drains join forces with a host of others in what amounts to an inventory of institutions, mass organizations, and the teams of musicians and dancers."[32]

If the carnival staged abundance, so in a different way did the congresses of writers and artists. Since Cuba was the focus of worldwide attention during the 1960s, hitherto neglected poets and novelists found themselves visited by other writers from around the world and invited to have their work translated into other languages and published in the many new journals. Anthologies of Cuban literature in translation quickly began to appear[33] and Latin American writers who flocked to Havana, particularly in the early 1960s, lavished praise on the revolution's cultural achievements. Susan Sontag wrote the introduction to a book of Cuban posters.[34] Cuban film attracted the attention of Europe and U.S. film critics. In an article published in 1967 before he became disaffected, Mario Vargas Llosa spoke of the gains in education and the publication of authors such as Joyce, Proust, Faulkner, Kafka, and Robbe-Grillet, stating that Cuban political culture had not yet been vitiated by a spirit of sectarianism and dogmatism. "In Cuba there has been no 'aesthetic dirigisme,' the manifestations that occurred in inept bureaucrats were quickly suppressed."[35] He would later change this assessment.

Yet this proliferation of creativity was tempered by the insistence on austerity. Lisandro Otero, for example, editor of the journal *Revolución y cultura (R-C)*, answered a question put to him by *Juventud Rebelde* about his journal's poor paper quality and graphic design by stating that it was "an exercise of austerity in the midst of our present graphic voluptuousness."[36] The last phrase may well have been directed at the flashier *Casa de las Américas*. On the musical front, the new song movement—"nueva trova"—with its plaintive tone and the stripped-down style of conversational poetry tended to be favored over the exuberance and excess that had marked popular culture.

In 1967, the journal *R-C* announced its intention "to overcome the obstacles left by colonial ideology."[37] Far more cheaply produced than the journal *Casa de las Américas,* *R-C* was also more blunt in its statement of cultural policy. After the Mexican Revolution, the muralists had described themselves as cultural workers and chosen the machete as their icon; *R-C* redefined artists as workers and wanted to put them to work in the cane fields. In its first issue, Carlos Rafael Rodríguez—a long-standing member of the Communist Party and still influential today, though he has modified his position—stressed in an address to the art school the importance of manual labor, especially agricultural work that would make "our future artists stronger, their feeling of responsibility to the rest of the society clearer, and what society expects of them more evident."[38] Skating uneasily between the need for professional training and political exigencies, Rodríguez approved of those young people who were willing "to offer their lives in any part of the world where people are struggling for independence," while on the other hand he emphasized the need for professional training that included "elements of modern technique from a scientific point of view."[39] The speech closed with a tribute to exemplary individuals—Martí; Camilo Torres, the revolutionary priest who had recently been killed in Colombia; Antonio Mella, the Cuban student leader who was assassinated in Mexico in 1929; and Fausto Díaz. The violent deaths of these heroes clearly underscored that the revolution's slogan, "Patria o Muerte" ("Fatherland or Death") was to be taken seriously.

Art students were naturally interested in hearing something more than piety and promises. Rodríguez's lengthy response to their concerns is interesting not for its theoretical depth—it does not get much beyond platitudes: "the relative autonomy of the superstructure," etc.—but rather for what is declared "decadent." The "peludos," the long-haired hippy protestors were all very well in the United States and not to be confused with "homosexuality and decadence," but in Cuba long hair and sandals were deemed inappropriate. "In Cuba, sandals and homosexuality go together because most sandals are on the feet of homosexuals and it's natural that those things provoke a hostile attitude in the population."[40] Thus while acknowledging that it is alright for Cubans to want to dress in more modern fashion ("though this should conform to the spirit and morals of our society"), homosexuals are plainly destined to be sent "off the field" (to translate the title of a volume of poems by Heberto Padilla that, as I describe below, was strongly attacked) and, indeed, as Nestor Almendros's film *Improper Conduct* demonstrated, many chose to leave during the exodus from Mariel in 1980. Vagrancy became a suspect category and this made unemployed gay men particularly susceptible to being rounded up and sent to camps where they were greeted with the slogan "Work makes men."

The influence of "rigid party men" that de Beauvoir had already detected in the early 1960s was criticized in 1967 by J. M. Cohen in a postscript to his introduction to the Penguin collection *New Cuban Writing*. He wrote that "the liberal cultural group is finding it harder to defend itself against the rigid party men whose prejudices against uncommitted writing, aestheticism, homosexuality etc. have made the lives of some of the younger writers increasingly difficult. One can only hope that this tendency will soon be reversed."[41]

In 1968, "the year of the heroic guerrilla," the prize-winning poems of Heberto Padilla, *Fuera del juego (Sent Off the Field)*, were published with an introduction that censured them because the poems were not deemed to be "within the revolution," a criticism that was poorly received by many writers hitherto friendly to Cuba. Padilla's imprisonment on March 20, 1971, later commuted to house arrest and public confession, showed how quickly censure could escalate into repression.[42] In his public confession, Padilla stated that one of his sins had been to think that he could "vegetate like a parasite in the shelter of the revolution and . . . cultivate literary popularity abroad, at the expense of the revolution and aided by its enemies." Padilla had lived for a time in Eastern Europe and the Soviet Union, and his Soviet-style confession was the last straw for many supporters. In 1980 he left Cuba for the United States where he founded the literary journal *Linden Lane*.

In effect the Padilla affair not only revealed that Cuba was losing ground in the propaganda war but cracked open what some had taken as a natural link between the revolution and avant-garde writing (even though Padilla's poetry was hardly experimental), making it clear that whatever Cuba's achievement in the realm of public education and the democratization of school and culture, the marriage of aesthetics to revolutionary politics was a difficult one.[43] Indeed, the vituperative polemical exchange in the Caracas daily *El Universal* between Reinaldo Arenas, who left Cuba during the 1980 Mariel exodus, and one of Latin America's most respected critics, Ángel Rama, demonstrated not only the impossibility of dialogue on the Cuban question but the degeneration of argument into insult and accusation. The dispute was especially ironic since Rama had himself been criticized by the Cubans.[44] Arenas, author of a highly codified novel based on the memoirs of the Mexican friar Servando Teresa de Mier, who was imprisoned by the Inquisition, had himself been imprisoned.[45] His provocative and transgressive behavior was very much in the spirit of the old bohemian avant-garde. His contribution to a *Casa de las Américas* questionnaire on literature and revolution is typically caustic; he stated that "the revolution was not yet mature enough to have a literary, philosophical or moral formation,"[46] and he coupled Martí with Lezama Lima as examples of "relevant" writers. In his autobiography *Before Night Falls,* written in the United States, Arenas takes pleasure in recounting his sexual adventures with members of the armed forces or other representatives of officialdom, suggesting that public homophobia is the complementary side of private guilt-ridden homoeroticism.[47] Indeed Brad Epps has argued that Arenas's criticism of the revolution "is intricately intertwined with the revolution's criticism of 'people like him.' And people like Arenas are, in the rhetoric of the regime, decadent, frivolous, and dangerous narcissistic pleasure-seekers."[48]

Less publicized than the Padilla case or Arenas's defection was the situation of writers who were marginalized or ignored, especially gay writers whose way of life seems to have run a real danger but who preferred to stay in Cuba. Virgilio Piñera was a particularly striking case. Before the Cuban Revolution he had published a translation of the Marquis de Sade and a novel, *La carne de René* (1952), whose representation of masculinity would have been considered subversive at that time in almost any society. The novel, whose title is a play on "carne" as flesh and meat, takes on the whole apparatus of Catholic devotion and rejection of the body. Che Guevara's anger at finding a copy of Piñera's plays in the Cuban embassy in Algiers underscores the fragile nature of "masculinity" and the danger represented even by a writer whose weapon was silence.[49] The persecution of gay men and women can only be explained on the grounds of the considerable investment of the revolutionary leaders in masculinity as a positive value, but this investment also turned gay writers into a critical opposition even when they desisted from open criticism. Thus while Alejo Carpentier, whose novels leave traditional gender categories unchallenged, was given a long leash, José Lezama Lima, a central figure in the prerevolutionary avant-garde and a Catholic, was marginalized. His novel *Paradiso* with its openly homoerotic episodes was reluctantly published in Cuba and then appeared in a corrected edition in Mexico.[50] *Paradiso* could scarcely be held up as a model of revolutionary writing not only because of the homoerotic episodes but because Lezama's aesthetic embraces Christian notions of resurrection and charity quite alien to the secular project of revolution.[51] The revolution's emphasis on "masculine" virtue is clearly what made homosexuality so transgressive, but it was not until the 1990s that this began to be timidly acknowledged, notably in Gutiérrez Alea's widely distributed film *Strawberries and Chocolate,* which pits a straight party man against a gay man and forces the former into recognizing his suppressed emotions. Released after the exodus from Mariel, the film has been criticized for containing its gay narrative within safe boundaries.[52]

Inside/Out, Outside/In

Although the difficulty of cultural exchange in the blockaded country was alleviated by frequent congresses and by the invitations extended to foreign writers, especially Latin Americans, many of whom spent extended periods in Cuba, lines were soon drawn between those who were "inside" the revolution and those who were outside. In 1966 the best known Latin American poet of the Left, Pablo Neruda (whose poetry was much admired by Che Guevara's wife), received an open letter from Cuban writers that criticized him for attending the PEN conference in New York (perhaps an indirect stab at the Communist Party of which Neruda was a member). The Beat writer Allen Ginsberg was expelled from the island. In 1969 Mario Vargas Llosa was criticized for spending the money he won from the Rómulo Gallegos prize on himself instead of giving it to a worthy cause, a precedent set by García Márquez, who presented his winnings to the banned MAS party of Venezuela. An invitation extended to the Chilean poet, Nicanor Parra to be on the jury of the Casa de las Américas prize was withdrawn because he attended a reception at the White House. This policy of proscription reached absurd heights in 1969 when Haydée Santamaría advised juries to award literary prizes to Latin American writers who lived in their own countries and not those who lived abroad.[53]

With the benefit of hindsight, García Márquez noted that the unconditional defense of Cuba defined the Latin American *intelectual de izquierda.*

> And the Cubans, through their own mechanisms, determined who complied with this solidarity, and who did not, taking advantage of the situation that prevailed for many intellectuals in their countries. The second tier intellectuals, without opportunities in their own lands, found a way of acquiring power. Entire pilgrimages of second-rate intellectuals wended their way to Havana with the purpose of displacing the frontline intellectuals from their position of leadership.[54]

This is a cynical view for not every supporter of the revolution was a "second tier" opportunist and there were many who hoped that Cuba might break through the logjam of underdevelopment to usher in an era of Latin American socialism and a new kind of egalitarian culture and experimentation in the arts. Yet even the well-disposed were criticized if they wavered in their unconditional support for the revolution.

It was not, however, the freedom of the intellectual that the Cuban government chose to debate but "responsibility." This was one of the central questions discussed at the Congress of Havana in early January 1968. The congress—attended by five hundred intellectuals, writers, and artists from the Americas, Europe, Africa, and Asia—attempted to define the specific role of the artist in societies that were both underdeveloped and in the process of revolution. Inevitably there was a certain amount of self-recrimination as intellectuals described themselves as complicitous with dominant ideologies or as co-opted.[55] Their alternative course was to align themselves with the struggle in those societies and to point the finger of responsibility at the intellectuals of what Fernández Retamar called the "underdeveloping world" who, he claimed, had stolen cultural capital from Third World countries.[56] The unacknowledged problem with their definition of the artist's role was that it was enough merely to belong to the Third World to be deemed "responsible," and responsibility was linked exclusively to armed struggle and not to the more pressing matter (as far as Cuba was concerned) of citizenship.

Notwithstanding the anti-intellectual bias of official Cuba, such discussions tended to underscore the privileged position of the intellectual, although the idea of an artistic vanguard was frowned on. *El Caimán barbudo,* a journal whose first editor, Jesús Díaz, called "dissonant" rather than "dissident," irritated the authorities and the editorial board was changed. *Pensamiento Crítico* a journal of the philosophy department of Havana University was closed down in 1970.[57] The reduced space for artistic experiment and criticism made it difficult to establish a criteria for evaluating what counted as culture in a revolutionary society, especially as the Padilla incident described above made it clear that the space even for mild irony did not exist.[58] The censure of Padilla on the grounds that he had not thrown himself behind the revolution and his *mea culpa* after a period of imprisonment widened the gap between Cubans, their unconditional supporters, and some increasingly critical former supporters. In 1970 Vargas Llosa wrote an acerbic critique of Fidel Castro's support of the Soviet intervention in Czechoslavakia[59] and this was followed in 1971 by his resignation from the editorial committee of *Casa de las Américas*. "How times have changed," he wrote in a letter to Haydée Santamaría. "I remember very well the night we spent with him (Fidel) four years ago when he willingly listened to observations and criticisms made by us 'foreign intellectuals' whom he now calls 'canalla.'"[60] In a letter addressed to Fidel protesting the Padilla affair that was signed by a group of Spanish and Latin American intellectuals (but not by García Márquez and Julio Cortázar), these signatories declared that it recalled "the most sordid episodes of the Stalinist era."[61]

That pragmatism triumphed over good intentions can be attributed in part to the *realpolitik* of the Cold War. Political expediency was cast as "revolutionary," as became clear in polemical exchanges over literature and revolution among the Colombian Oscar Collazos, who was then employed by Casa de las Américas, Julio Cortázar, and Mario Vargas Llosa. Collazos's complaints reflected the opinions of the then director of Casa de las Américas, Haydée Santamaría, who was critical of what she called "cosmopolitanism." While frequently citing Roland Barthes, Collazos criticized Latin American writers' sense of inferiority in comparison with Europe. But Collazos was unable to produce a convincing account of literature's connection to revolution; indeed, at one point he argued for the speeches of Fidel Castro as literary models. The best he could offer by way of explanation of the creative process is that the writer is "impregnated" by reality and that creation is a "desembarazo" (that is, either a release from a burden or from the burden of pregnancy)—as if there were some natural connection between environment and writing. But more disturbing than Collazos's sloppy argument was the narrow and superficial criteria for discriminating between revolutionary and nonrevolutionary art. As Cortázar argued in his reply, Collazos's barely disguised defense of orthodox realism failed to account for writing that challenges received notions of "reality," nor could he allow for experiment. Vargas Llosa, for his part, accused Collazos of not understanding the novels he criticized nor understanding that criticism is as necessary in postrevolutionary societies as in any other.[62]

What this polemic helped clarify was that "evaluation" and "discrimination" of literary works could not be made on the grounds of political correctness alone without seriously undermining the institution of literature itself. For this reason, the Cuban experience could not set the agenda for other countries. And eventually within Cuba it was seen as counterproductive, to the point that even Fidel amended his earlier distinction between "inside" the revolution and "outside," declaring that the rationale for socialism "is to maximize human capacity, human possibilities and to elevate to the utmost, creative freedom not only of form but also of content."[63] In fact, the Cuban government was forced to reinvent the economic and political goals of revolution, most notably during the 1980s when, after a period of encouraging market reforms and some free enterprise, there followed the period of "rectification." Fidel's interest in "creative freedom" was expressed during a battle against the corruption of the bureaucracy when there was a perceived need for more initiative from the grass roots.[64]

A definitive history of the Cuban years has still to be written. Certainly disaffection would be a central theme of such a history, a disaffection that gradually extended to the most persistent supporters and one that was thoroughly exploited by those hostile to Cuba. Many of those who left or were expelled were not only among the country's most talented writers but in some cases—for instance, Jesús Díaz—had been the poster boys of revolutionary literature.[65] There was also a wide gulf between the achievement of universal or near-universal literacy and the sophisticated public demanded by writers. Many Cuban writers inside and outside Cuba—among them Cabrera Infante, Alejo Carpentier, José Lezama Lima, and Severo Sarduy—never held an egalitarian view of literature. On the contrary, they delighted in recondite literary and cultural allusions, in the privilege that literature afforded them.[66]

In evaluating cultural policies, Cubans from the island tend to speak of a number of different stages. The years between 1971 and 1976, when there was considerable censorship, are known as the "Grey Years"; the years after 1990, when the effects of the blockade severely curtailed some activities, are known as the "Special Period." While the enforced austerity of these later years has not killed off some of the vitality of Cuban culture, its practitioners grapple with the problem of isolation on the one hand and the lure of the tourist and global market on the other. The problems debated in the 1960s—responsibility and revolution—have altogether faded from view, giving way to discussions of democracy and civil society by the younger generations of writers and artists who no longer feel bound to politically correct positions.[67] And with the passing of time, the growing influence of the media, and the foundering of the political system, the importance once attached to the opinions of writers has diminished.

In a balanced account of the Cuban situation published in 1997, Ambrosio Fornet wondered whether "the conscious ethic of austerity and solidarity will, as a result of this crisis, yield to the temptations of a consumer society and the melancholy allure of skepticism and frivolousness. Will it be possible to avoid a grotesque pirouette whereby *comunista* turns into *consumista* and the hope of improving and developing the revolutionary project is frustrated once and for all?"[68] The question is still an open one and it would be imprudent to rush to judgment. But clearly what was brought to a close during the first decades of the Cuban Revolution was any belief that the avant-garde and the revolutionary vanguard could share the same terrain. Indeed, it would be in Paris and not in Cuba that one of its most innovative writers and a gay man, Severo Sarduy, would find his particular utopian space.

Weakened by the blockade, by emigration, and by poverty, Cuba could not maintain its exemplary status. The project of revolutionary art and literature—motivated to a large extent by the need for a more egalitarian culture and the need for solidarity and support—was hardly likely to come into being in conditions of censorship. Print and written culture in the past had formed a cultural barrier—a gated community or an unwelcome division, depending on how you looked at it. The revolutionary guerrilla had seemed to offer a practical way of crossing that boundary by joining up with the people and eventually forming a more egalitarian society. But for many reasons, the path of the guerrilla, exemplified by Che Guevara, was not only impossible for most people to follow but, after his death in 1967, his image became monumentalized as the martyr figure.[69] Perhaps the most interesting postscript to the project for a revolutionary art is that the visual arts underwent their own "boom" in the 1980s, although as the art critic, Osvaldo Sánchez suggested, the form it took—"anthropological, mythical, and religious—was due undoubtedly to a loss of faith, to the spiritual ruin of revolutionary thinking."[70]

A more attainable project was the democratization of culture, in the first place through the successful literacy campaign and also through film, television, and grassroots theater projects such as the Teatro Escambray (founded in 1968) and the Teatro Mirón of Matanzas. The Teatro Escambray actively engaged in combating peasant opposition to the state regulation of land. Like similar theater projects in other countries of Latin America, the group drew on local knowledge and local customs in order to create the conditions for dialogue with the community.[71] The Cuban film industry, on the other hand, had barely existed before the revolution but developed rapidly thanks to a group of talented and largely self-taught directors.[72] Its educational potential was recognized with the foundation of the Instituto Cubano de Arte e Industria Cinematográficas (ICAIC), which sent mobile cinemas around the island, trained new directors, and organized a yearly film festival.

Because films had to be made with scarce resources, Cuban cinema was seen as an example of austerity in contrast to the consumerism of the North, which gave credence to the notion that there was a distinctive form of Third World film. Indeed, the director Julio García Espinosa argued for "imperfect cinema" that took no account of quality or tecnique.[73] For a time Cuban films—*Portrait of Teresa, Lucia, A Certain Way*—received close critical attention internationally especially for their frank treatment of gender politics.

But the Cuban film that attracted most attention was Gutiérrez Alea's *Memories of Underdevelopment* (1968, shown in New York in 1973). Peter Schjeldal, the *New York Times* film critic, speculated that the film might breach the barriers of the Cold War. Such hopes were short-lived, however, for in 1974 Alea was refused a visa to enter the United States to receive the prize from the National Association of Cinema Critics. Infused with Cold War logic, the film is set in the early days of the revolution and is based on the novel by Edmundo

Desnoes.[74] Both novel and film are ambiguous enough to have invited very different responses. The film explores the difficulties and contradictions facing a young intellectual of the middle class as he watches his wife, family, and friends leave the island, while he himself stays behind, an outcast and an observer who cannot commit himself to the revolution. As a counterpoint to his introspection, documentary clips, newsreels, and tape-recorded speeches register the historical change from which the protagonist tries to defend himself. Julianne Burton, commenting on the use of "collage," called it "an implacable criticism of false consciousness."[75] Yet, in the context of postrevolutionary Cuba, *Memories of Underdevelopment* can also be seen as an expression of the fear of the rise of new social classes that the revolution privileged to the detriment of the old-style intellectual. The intellectual, alienated from his social class is displaced by a predatory lower class that the film does nothing to idealize. The dilemma of the intellectual is highlighted when the protagonist picks up a girl from a lower-class family, sleeps with her, and is then denounced and entrapped for sexually harassing her. Instead of liberating the individual, sex is a form of manipulation—a theme rather more explicitly developed in the James Bond novels and other Cold War pop fiction. But what the film makes devastatingly clear is that the choice is between exile and comfort or austerity and home, between discipline and the guilty pleasure of trying on his wife's flamboyant dresses. What the revolution excluded was identified with exile and the bourgeois lifestyles of the past. The ending is framed by the Cuban missile crisis, which weights the choice as a moral one in favor of patriotism, though it is also dictated by fear of atomic war.

Gutiérrez Alea's aim had been to apply Brechtian estrangement to cinema, which he felt should shock spectators out of their passivity; he was disconcerted, however, when the film was viewed in the United States as a criticism of Cuba.[76] He attributes the different ways of seeing the film to the different locations (First and Third World) of the spectators. While inverting the values of "inside" and "outside," the film remains within the binary framework of Cold War politics.

Cuba in the Narrative of Decolonization

The Third World is the imagined community of the Cold War period, when newly decolonized nations in Asia and Africa sought alternative forms of national development to those of the polarized great powers. Promulgated at the Bandung Conference of 1955 by already constituted states,[77] included under the rubric "Third World" were both populist nationalist and socialist countries. The effect was to suppress differences among those nations, allying quite disparate forces in the struggle against imperialism. Third Worldism justified Cuba's participation in revolutionary struggles in Latin America and in Africa, and accounts for the confidence placed in a projected alliance of postcolonial and postrevolutionary nations, which, however, never came to fruition. That Cuba considered itself in the vanguard of such an alliance was demonstrated during Che's clandestine and frustrating guerrilla war in the Congo.[78] That Cuba was also the avant-garde of anticolonial (or postcolonial?) cultural politics was the claim of Roberto Fernández Retamar's *Calibán,* published in 1971.[79]

On the surface *Calibán* refers back to a famous precedent—José Enrique Rodó's *Ariel,* which was written in 1900 in the wake of the Spanish–American War and Theodore Roosevelt's proclamation of U.S. ascendancy in the hemisphere. Indeed, much of Fernández Retamar's essay is devoted to a genealogy of Latin American writers and thinkers who are evaluated according to their political alignment for or against the North. Rodó had implicitly identified the materialist North with Caliban, but claimed that Latin America was the direct heir to the classical values of beauty and harmony. The wise teacher Prospero, in a manner that is reminiscent of Matthew Arnold's appeal to sweetness and light, enjoins his young male students to guard the spirit of Ariel and the ideal of classical beauty so the coming meritocracy might avoid crass materialism. Rodó was a citizen of Uruguay, a country that had exterminated its indigenous population, so it is not surprising that considerations of race, gender, and heterogeneity were not allowed to disrupt this idyll, which clearly appealed to the intelligentsia who cast themselves in the role of Ariel. On the other hand, the Caliban of Shakespeare's *The Tempest* provided a handy emblem for the formerly colonized. In foregrounding Caliban over Ariel (in opposition to Ernest Renan and Rodó), Fernández Retamar effected what might seem to be a fruitful inversion, grounding the exceptionality of Latin America in *mestizaje,* its racial mixture that constitutes both its unity and its difference. Like Caliban, he argued, Latin Americans are forced to speak in the language of the conquerors (although this argument ignores that language can also be contested). Tracing the identification of Caliban with Carib and cannibal and associating the name with the popular masses, Retamar asked "what is our history, what is our culture, if not the history and culture of Caliban?" He thus equated "us" (Latin America) with the masses. This proves to be an awkward elision and can only be explained on the grounds that there are different arguments running throughout the essay.

The first argument is that "there is no Ariel–Caliban polarity: both are slaves in the hands of Prospero, the foreign magician. But Caliban is the rude and unconquerable master of the island, while Ariel, a creature of the air, although also a child of the isle, is the intellectual." Overlooking the fact that Shakespeare's Caliban claims "the island's mine, by Sycorax, my mother," acknowledging a "natural right" that comes through maternal heritage, Fernández Retamar sought to give both the intellectual and the militant a role in the anticolonial struggle. At other points in the essay, however, Caliban is identified with the intellectual. Prospero represents the European and Yankee university and Caliban the Latin American university. What separates the Calibanesque intellectuals from the traitors also varies; sometimes they are spokespersons for the exploited like Martí, critics of the United States like Rodó, or champions of a native culture that does not slavishly imitate Europe. Clearly, if *Calibán* initiated a debate at all, it was one that only involved intellectuals.

The essay is also a Cold War document in which political positions are coded as cultural values. This accounts for Fernández Retamar's lengthy but otherwise puzzling attacks on Carlos Fuentes and on Borges, whose work is said to be a painful testimony of a class "on its way out." Only if the literary intelligentsia are taken as crucial mediators who need to be brought back to the fold do these particular attacks have any meaning. Fernández Retamar would himself confirm this, for in the postscript to the essay's English translation published in 1989, he wrote, "*Calibán* stemmed from a particular, and difficult, situation for my country and myself, and it should be read with that situation in mind." This critical situation was the defection of the intelligentsia both as a result of Cuban cultural policy that privileged the militant over the intelligentsia, but also as a result of the U.S. intervention in the cultural wars as the champion of innovation and modernity. *Calibán* was written, after all, not in 1961 at a moment when the cultural and the political avant-garde were momentarily reconciled, but in 1971, under altogether different circumstances. By the

late 1960s, what had at first seemed like generous eclecticism had nar-
rowed into political expediency. The U.S. boycott and Cuba's conse-
quent economic dependency on the Soviet Union affected political,
economic, and cultural life. Cuba's cultural relations were increasingly with Eastern Europe and the Soviet Union.

Of course here I have the benefit of hindsight, for matters looked
very different to me and to many other people in the early 1970s. But
even on its own terms, *Calibán* is an elusive document, using the figures of Caliban, Prospero, and Ariel as shifting allegories of domination and emancipation that do not quite hide the fact that Cold War
parameters control the argument. That the Cold War brought existing
socialist states into crisis is obvious; it was also a violent birthing of
the New World Order in which culture wars mimed the global struggle. Fernández Retamar claimed for Cuba a vanguard position in this
struggle, which he described as that of a Latin American family,
"numbering 200 million brothers and sisters" and part of "another
even larger vanguard, a planetary vanguard—that of the socialist
countries." The problem was that what bound those 200 million
brothers and sisters was the signifier "Third World," not the economic and financial network that would characterize the New World
Order.

In the postscript to *Calibán*, Fernández Retamar named the enemy
as "the CIA funded journal *Mundo Nuevo,*" which had "challenged
the hegemony of the revolutionary position in Latin American intellectual work" from "behind the facade of modernity." These loaded
words should make it clear that *Calibán* has an encoded message.
Growing criticism of Cuba had as much to do with the damaging
aftermath of the Padilla affair as with the impact of *Mundo Nuevo*.
The Mariel stampede a decade later, which anticipated the mass walk
out of East Germany, demonstrated that the sacrifice of civil liberties
could not work if there were not considerable material incentives.
Furthermore, by the mid-1970s, many intellectuals were no longer attracted to the austerity of the guerrilla nor appeared to have any
hopes of a Latin American revolution. Even earlier, during the 1968
student demonstrations in Europe and the Americas, when the face of
Che Guevara was seen on banners and on sweatshirts, the struggle
was often over the rigidity of the education system and, in the case of
Mexico, for civil liberties. Carlos Fuentes who was in Paris and not in
Mexico City during the 1968 demonstrations, proclaimed the student

protest there as "the first revolution in the center," and stated that "thanks to France we can understand and be understood," and with these words definitely discounted Cuba's vanguard position.[80] The remark measured the immense ideological distance between 1960 and 1968.

The Cold War transposed the narrative of decolonization into another register since many of the new African nations aligned themselves with the Soviet Union, thus Fernández Retamar's "planetary vanguard" of socialist countries included some very disparate and perhaps incompatible interpretations of what socialism might be. Written not long after Cuba's interventions in Latin America and the Congo, the essay was an attempt to place Cuba strategically in the discourse of decolonization. *Calibán* signals, according to Edward Said, "a profoundly important ideological debate at the heart of the cultural effort to decolonize, an effort at the restoration of community and repossession of culture that goes on long after the political establishment of independent nation-states."[81] Gayatri Chakravorty Spivak, on the other hand, believes it to signal an impossibility. "In Latin American space, one of the things that cannot be narrativized is decolonization, as the Ariel–Caliban debate and today's intimate involvement with the U.S. have clearly articulated for us."[82] But in fact, there was never truly an Ariel–Caliban *debate* unless you can have a debate over an interval of seventy years. Independence *was* narrativized, however, albeit by reproducing the European fantasy of the autonomous nation-state. Clearly in settler colonies, like those of Latin America, decolonization did not occur with the withdrawal of the colonizer. What happened after independence from Spain was informal economic colonization by European powers and finally North American economic ascendancy, an event that is accurately registered in Conrad's *Nostromo*. The Mexican Revolution, Guatemala, Chile, Cuba, and Nicaragua represent disrupted attempts at emancipation from neocolonialism, narrativized in the United States as failures of socialism or as communist plots. But *Calibán* is too vague and contradictory to be Cuba's *18th Brumaire*.

The essay did appeal to some U.S. dissidents who were seeking redemption for the imperialist sins of their own country. Indeed, this search for outside saviors was something of a tradition ever since the Mexican Revolution that drew dozens of U.S. intellectuals, writers, and artists south of the border. For the dissidents, Latin America constituted a space not only of chaos and irresponsibility—the tropic zone uneasily bordering the U.S. south—but also as an alternative to American values, and even as a salutary stimulus to self-criticism.[83] In his introduction to the English translation of Fernández Retamar's essay, Fredric Jameson writes that "inasmuch as it acknowledges the Other it [*Calibán*] also serves as a more chastening form of self-knowledge,"[84] a self-knowledge that would come to fruition in solidarity movements as well as in Latin American studies within the United States.[85]

Revolutionary Nostalgia

In my adult lifetime, Cuba has gone from representing the revolutionary vanguard to evoking nostalgia for the lost revolutionary ideal, exemplified in the two photographs of Che Guevara that have been endlessly reproduced. In the first of these—the photograph of the dead Che Guevara—a life is caught at the very moment when it ceases to be life. Che was executed in the town of Higueras in Bolivia in 1967 and his body transported by plane to Vallegrande where it was washed and dressed and placed on view in a laundry room. The Bolivian army wanted to transmit the message to the world that a dangerous guerrilla and his cause were dead. But the photograph aroused quite different reactions in many viewers, who saw it as the image of a martyr. In an article written soon after the event, the English critic John Berger compared the photograph to two famous paintings—Mantegna's *Descent from the Cross* and Rembrandt's *Anatomy Lesson*—to explain its unusual power,[86] although the photographer, the Bolivian stringer Freddy Alborta, had never seen these paintings and by his own account was thinking only of the technical difficulty of photographing in a crowded room and of how he could lend dignity to the scene.[87] But whatever the photographer's intention, the photograph gave rise to an intense postmortem mythology. According to one of Che's recent biographers, Paco Taibo II, the image evoked the story of death, redemption, and resurrection. "Drawn by these ghosts," he wrote, "the Vallegrande campesinos paraded in front of the body, in single file, in awesome silence. That night, candles for Che were lit for the first time in the small holdings around the town. A saint was being born, a secular saint of the poor." Several biographies of Che evoke the sense of his haunting spirit to account for the extraordinary persistance of his image.[88]

In one of Hollywood's more benevolent attempts to film the guerrilla wars of the 1960s and 1970s, Roger Spottiswoode's *Under Fire,* made after the Sandinista victory in Nicaragua in 1979 and released in 1983, is also haunted by Che Guevara. The hero of the film is a photographer, Russell (played by Nick Nolte), and it opens with a series of his black and white still shots of a war in the Chad. The focus of the story, which need not be told in detail here, is the photograph Russell takes of a dead guerrilla leader, Rafael, whose death, were it to be publicly known, would deliver a devastating blow to the Sandinista cause. Russell, who has come to sympathize with the guerrillas, shoots the photograph with the dead Rafael propped up between two *guerrilleros*, his eyes opened as if he were alive and holding a newspaper with a report of his death, which the photograph is intended to refute. What is most interesting in the movie is the power attributed to photography. When some of Russell's photographs of the guerrilla camp are stolen they are used by the army for identification, which leads to summary executions. The photographer earns redemption, however, when he photographs the army's execution of a U.S. anchorman.[89] Photography in this film does not simply record history, but makes it. "I have other awards," Russell remarks at one point to demonstrate that he doesn't need one more trophy, but his woman friend Claire replies, "You haven't won a war." In a curious twist, the success of the Sandinista revolution is attributed to what on the one hand is the deception of photography, which can make the dead look alive, and on the other to its value as a witness, without examining what it is about photography that allows it to be both.

It is quite likely that the film was inspired by the photograph of the dead Che, whose open eyes seem to gaze obliquely at the spectator. That pose, however, turns out to have been fortuitous, imposed by the circumstance of the occasion. Che's eyes are open because the Bolivian military needed to identify the corpse, which is photographed to confirm the fact that the dangerous *guerrillero* was dead. In a striking installation by the Argentine artist, Leandro Katz, the photograph enters into a play of images juxtaposed with the conflicting accounts of Che's death that underscore not the icon but rather its multiple meanings. The conflicting accounts Katz came upon led him to embark on a series of chronologies—a compilation of microhistorical events narrated from different points of view ideologically at odds with one another. The chronology is not only a summary of the many accounts of the Bolivian campaign but also intersects with other narratives and representations. Far from attempting to suture these stories into a single narrative, Katz's installation raises questions of identification and falsification, of the state's use of photography, and the guerrilla's use of nicknames, false identities, and codes. It is as if the corpse is a focal point of conflicting discourses and desires.

The most widely disseminated photograph of Che is quite different. It was snapped by the Italian photojournalist Alberto Korda at a rally in Havana when Che appeared momentarily on the platform, wearing his beret with the commandant's star and looking into the distance. It is this photograph that has become the much-reproduced icon. Jorge Castañeda even speaks of the "prestancia crística" of Che—his aura or charisma as an anointed one. The photograph has been reproduced on watches, pins, scarves, and mugs as well as on banners at soccer games and demonstrations, in mass meetings of Venezuela's populist president Chávez, and in the Plaza de la Revolución in Havana, where it hung beside an image of Christ during the pope's visit.

The Argentine artist Liliana Porter in her installations *The Simulacrum* and *Untitled*—acrylic, silk-screen collage on paper—illustrates what happens to cultural icons in the marketplace. She transfers the Korda image of Che onto a dessert dish that is placed between several kitsch ornaments—Donald Duck, Mickey Mouse, and a ceramic dancing woman of the kind sold in gift shops. She thus reverses the auratic, showing an image trivialized by its reproduction. In *Untitled* the Korda photograph is reproduced in a vertical sequence of three, with the smallest reproduction at the top and the largest at the bottom and out of focus. Mickey Mouse stands in front of the dish on which the image of Che is transposed. In an interview Porter stated that the "souvenir of Cuba" would not have existed, if Che Guevara had not existed. "In order for that banal object to exist, a lot of things must have happened, and the only one that is rescued is the stereotyped image which is transformed into a souvenir which is an ornament. This is the dramatic thing—the painting makes a statement about the passage of time and its consequences. The drama lies in the inapprehensibility of reality, in its impenetrability, in the banality of meaning, in the empty space, in the emptiness of meaning."[90] In *Untitled* Che's face is blurred and out of focus—defaced—and hence cannot serve as a mirror of identity. Possibly the defacement reflects the misrecognition of women and gay men for whom there can be no identification with the warrior hero. But in Porter's installation it is also consumer culture that appropriates and destroys the auratic, and the heroic image undergoes a mutation of meaning when it becomes an ornament that is ultimately shelved alongside pop figures (like Mickey Mouse) for which there is no human referent.

Castañeda in his biography observed that "Che Guevara did not end up in a mausoleum or pharaonic square but on T-shirts, Swatches and beer mugs. The sixties of which he was so emblematic did not alter the fundamental economic and political structures of the societies the young revolted against, but had their impact relegated to the more intangible confines of power and society." "Che Guevara is a cultural icon today largely because the era he typified left cultural tracks more than political ones."[91] Those cultural tracks are the crossroads of a globalization that cannot control its supplementary effects. But whereas in the rest of the world the icon is used to signify anything from teenage defiance to rebellion, in present-day Cuba, where the concern is with survival rather than revolution, Che both stands for an irrecoverable political past and is constantly evoked to revitalize energies in the present. Fidel castigated shoddiness and mediocrity as the negation of "Che's ideas, his revolutionary thought, his style, his spirit, and his example."[92]

Religious and Secular Anticapitalism

The Sandinistas who formed a government in Nicaragua after overthrowing Somoza in 1978 inaugurated a cultural policy that was strongly influenced by the Catholic intelligentsia and by liberation theology but also, according to some observers, by poetry. In *Literature and Politics in the Central American Revolutions,* John Beverley and Marc Zimmerman maintained that "literature has been in Central American not only a means of politics but a model for it."[93] They argued that the Sandinistas developed a counterculture "maintained in the schools, churches and small journals during the lowest ebb of the movement" and that this would "come in the 1970s to redefine the whole sphere of literature, so that even non-Marxist and nonrevolutionary writers were coopted or reread in relation to the insurrectionary project of the Frente."[94] If this argument has any validity, it means that Nicaragua followed a trajectory radically different from that of Cuba, one that had its foundation in cultural institutions. Certainly Nicaragua brought together, as Cuba did not, the poetics of the avant-garde with the vanguardism of the revolution and the messian-ism of liberation theology, while also benefiting from the Cuban expe-rience, notably in grassroots theater.[95]

What drew these divergent projects into an alliance was their iden-tification of capitalism with human degradation. The Catholic dis-trust of usury and the avant-garde distrust of commerce were fused in the revolutionary messianism of the poet Ernesto Cardenal, who became minister of culture in the Sandinista government. While Cardenal's political strategy changed over the years from a nonviolent opposition to dictatorship to embracing the armed struggle, he always identified money with the degradation of humanity. Published in 1966 and drawing on citations from the chronicles of the conquest of Cen-tral America and Nicaragua, his collection *El estrecho dudoso (The Doubtful Straits)* documents the blind obsession of the Spaniards with the gold and the precious stones that were valued by the indige-nous tribes only for their aesthetic value. In *Homenaje a los indios americanos (Homage to the American Indians* (1972), he used cita-tions from indigenous denunciations of the money economy. "With money came taxes / and the first beggars appeared with the Col-ony."[96] While recognizing that the pre-Columbian Inca regime per-mitted no opposition, Cardenal lamented the passing of a civilization in which religion and the economy formed a seamless whole. His poem *"Apocalipsis"* ends with a vision of a new planet in which the species is no longer composed of individuals but is a single organ-ism.[97]

A participant in the failed rebellion of 1953 against Somoza and an admirer of Thomas Merton, which led to a brief period in the Trappist monastery at Gethsemene, Kentucky, Cardenal was ordained as a priest in Colombia at the height of the influence of liberation the-ology and at a time when many poets of the Americas shared his antimaterialist aesthetic.[98] In 1967, he announced his decision to found a community among the fishermen and peasants of the San Juan River in southern Nicaragua, a region remote enough from the Somoza government and its national guard. Drawing on a long tradi-tion of Catholic anticapitalism, the community was intended as the very antithesis of capitalism—as the pure against the impure, the aes-thetic against the instrumental, unalienated labor as against alienated labor. The project seemed particularly quixotic given the cruel nature of Somoza's government. In a decade of communes and liberated territories, Cardenal's community—Solentiname—was distinguished by its religious and artistic character and by its absolute negation of the Somozan state. It was, in other words, what Foucault once called a "heterotopia" and the latter-day incarnation of many such experimental communities from the Dominican and the Jesuit missions to the anarchist and Tolstoyan communes.

Financed by Cardenal's royalties and by the sale of artisan products, Solentiname was founded on the premise that the aesthetic was not merely for a privileged class.[99] It attempted to realize *before the revolution* a society in which art could be practiced by everyone. But it was also a community with a religious vocation. There were daily readings of the Bible and of political works—"The Declaration of Havana," "The Thought of Camilo Torres," "Salvador Allende's Speech in the National Stadium of Santiago," and "Marx and the Bible" by Porfirio Miranda. In one of his commentaries Cardenal said, "the New Testament is against the rich. The New Testament says that he who has two tunics should give one to the person who does not have any and this is socialism."

While Cardenal admired the writing of Thomas Merton, Martí, Ezra Pound, and William Carlos Williams,[100] he also believed that poetry "should have a message and a teaching on the life of our peoples." He once stated, "I don't believe in literature for the sake of literature. Literature and art ought to contribute to future society, to the new man of whom Saint Paul spoke and the new man of whom Che spoke.[101] Solentiname was intended as the culmination of the historical avant-garde's dream of fusing art and everyday life, while reflecting at the same time liberation theology's view of the poor as the agents of history.

In Cardenal's poetry the language is shorn of metaphorical glitter in favor of a plain style, reflecting the bias against metaphor, which is identified with "exchange" and hence with the abstraction from the material. In his reading of Cardenal's poetry, Greg Dawes describes how the poet arrived at his view of "objective reality" from the mid-1960s onward, during which he published *El estrecho dudoso* (1966), *Homenaje a los indios americanos* (1969), and *Canto Nacional* (1973).[102] He describes the first two of these collections as an attempt to present the history of the oppressed in a narrative rather than a poetic form. But the difference between narrative and poetry may in fact be difficult to sustain; instead it is more productive to think of differ-

ent aesthetic responses that include contemplation, wit, and irony—
especially the irony of hindsight that Cardenal used to such good effect in *El estrecho dudoso.*

Following the victory of the Sandinista government and Cardenal's
appointment as minister of culture, he began to create nationwide poetry workshops.[103] The goal of both Cardenal and the director of the
workshops, Mayra Jiménez, was to democratize poetry, which meant
not only the democratization of writing but also lessons in reading
and appreciating complex poetry.[104] When the Ministry of Culture
was abolished in 1988, one of the complaints against Cardenal was
that the program of the workshops was too rigid, too imitative of his
own poetics in eschewing metaphor.

> El lago calmo.
> Nosotros dos de pesca
> El bote rompe la tranquilidad del lago
> con su pequeñas olas.
> Llegamos al sitio donde íbamos a pescar.[105]

> [The lake becalmed
> The two of us fishing
> The boat breaks the lake's calm
> with its little waves
> we arrive at the place where we were going to fish.]

This is not to deny that many of the scenes described are evocative
or delightful, but there is also the suspicion that they correspond to a
particular view of innocence and simplicity. Even poems that describe
combat have a wistful, static tone. Yet in oral poetry from other parts
of Latin America, the "simple" people delight in punning, in language
games and inventive metaphor.

Cardenal is a visionary for whom history unfolds within the escha-
tological narrative of Christianity. He came to the priesthood at the
height of the influence of liberation theology, when priests worked for
the "definitive appearance of God as the absolute future of man"—
to quote Father Elacurría, a Jesuit priest murdered in El Salvador.[106]
This prophetic tone was reflected in the community meetings in
Solentiname before its destruction by Somoza in retaliation for the
participation of some of its members in the armed struggle, to which
Cardenal lent his support. Reconstituted during the Sandinista government, the Solentiname community and their visitors applied the

Bible to politics and everyday life in their weekly discussions. Che Guevara was compared to Jesus Christ, and special revolutionary consciousness was attributed to Christians. "Christians know through the gospels where the revolution is going, and what the goal of love is. And Christ is now revealing that secret hidden from the beginning of the world here to this little group in Solentiname."[107] This revolutionary thinking did not, however, extend to women's reproductive rights. In one of the discussions, birth control and family planning were described as a U.S. conspiracy.[108]

Solentiname was not the only story. After the Sandinista victory, cultural brigades went into the countryside and popular culture centers opened all over the country. The Movimiento de Animación Cultural Rural (The Movement to Promote Rural Culture) organized by Alan Bolt González included the Nixtayolero theater group that performed throughout Nicaragua, though it eventually came to criticize Sandinista policy.[109]

In a well-known book on the avant-garde, Peter Burger argued on the basis of European movements that "the intention of the historical avant-garde movements was defined as the destruction of art as an institution set off from the praxis of life."[110] For some this meant the destruction of the old society—the old Adam—and the creation of territories liberated from the evils of capitalism. But in the real world where no territory was completely isolated, the democratization of art did not always conform to the exigencies of the postrevolutionary state. On a visit to Nicaragua with a delegation of university teachers in 1981, I visited Cardenal who was then minister of culture. His staff had gone off to help with the coffee harvest, and in the corner of the office of this most peaceful and idealistic of men was a rifle in case he needed to defend himself. In both Cuba and Nicaragua, efforts to translate avant-garde theory into practice ran into difficulties as these societies came up against the realities of war and economic hardship.

Permanent Revolution

Avant-garde tactics of provocation had targeted bourgeois society, or at least bourgeois society imagined in the late nineteenth and early twentieth century as complacent, pragmatic, and insensitive. Yet such tactics were greeted with hostility by Cuba, and in Chile, during the Popular Unity party of Salvador Allende, the poet Nicanor Parra's parodic verse was hardly welcomed with enthusiasm.[111] However, for a brief period in the late 1960s and early 1970s, the political and artistic avant-garde fused in urban guerrilla movements, and nowhere in more spectacular fashion than in Uruguay. Founded in 1962, the Uruguayan Tupamaro guerrilla movement staged revolutionary actions and political spectacles. They organized a funeral procession complete with mourners in order to smuggle arms into the town of Pando, where they briefly took over official buildings. As Luis Camnitzer commented, this "set the tone for other theatrical stagings in which Montevideo and its inhabitants played the script written by the guerrilla 'actors.'"[112] In Argentina, the First National Movement of Avant-Garde Art mounted a counterinformation operation "to create a parallel subversive culture which wears out the official cultural machinery."[113] Their exhibition "Tucumán arde" ("Tucumán Burns") countered the idealized representation of Tucumán in official publicity with photographs and statistics showing the dirty truth of poverty and exploitation. It was shown in the General Workers Union buildings in Rosario and Buenos Aires, although official pressure forced the union to close the exhibition, after which some members of the group joined the armed struggle.

The convergence of revolutionary action and avant-garde provocation was not lost on the Argentine writer Julio Cortázar. He described his novel *Libro de Manuel (Manual for Manuel)* as an attempt to "achieve a convergence of contemporary history with pure literature."[114] Set in Paris among a group of young people known as "la Joda" ("the Fuckers"), it is an encyclopedia that charts the meeting of armed struggle and avant-garde happenings. Its effectiveness, however, depends on the reader's acceptance of conspiracy and violence as the overriding global regime that can only be opposed by conspiracy and violence. La Joda is bonded by friendship and sexual relationships and its members communicate in coded languages or private jokes. Such groups often make their appearance in Cortázar's novels and short stories and suggest that he envisaged them as imaginary substitutes for a public sphere that no longer had any material existence. The novel is also imbued with the same distrust of material incentives that is central to the thinking of Che Guevara and Ernesto Cardenal. In the preface, Cortázar wrote that what counted was affirmation: "man's erotic and playful thirst, his liberation from taboos, his claim for dignity shared in a world already free from this daily horizon of fangs (comillos) and dollars."[115]

Using a collage of newspaper cuttings to chart the everyday violence of the state and various acts of resistance, the novel fuses the personal and the political and juxtaposes the language of journalism with the inventions of the Joda, who progress from creating anti-consumerist happenings in cinemas to conspiring against corporate power. Yet their sexual politics—orgasm as liberation—betrays the masculinist blindness of both the avant-garde and vanguard, a blindness that would later be explored in Manuel Puig's *The Kiss of the Spider Woman*.[116] The Joda's opposition to the corporate state left no room for civil society and limited resistance to a group that is ignorant of its own sexist bias. *A Manual for Manuel* reflects the logic of revolution without socialism, of rebellion without a state, while reflecting the archaic gender politics that bedeviled the revolutionary endeavors of the time.

PART TWO

Peripheral Fantasies

CHAPTER FOUR

Antistates

Constellations of meaning accrue around powerful cadavers. In Mexico, they are still looking for the bones of the last Aztec emperor Cuauhtémoc, who was hanged by Cortés. The dismembered body of Tupac Amaru II in Peru inspires utopian belief in a new social body.[1] In some instances the state attempts to stifle the threats from the afterlife by seeing that the corpse disappears, although the effect may be the opposite of the one intended. In many countries of Latin America, cadavers have been spirited away, found, and reburied. The body of Che Guevara, photographed with his eyes open for the purpose of identification and put on display for journalists in Vallegrande, Bolivia, was secretly buried, "rediscovered," and buried once more in Cuba. Sometimes bodies circulate like the kula ring of Triborian islanders. The corpse of Eva Perón conserved in all its cosmetic splendor by a Spanish embalmer, Dr. Ara, disappeared after the fall of Perón from the trade union headquarters where it was on display and was held by the military who inexplicably did not destroy it. In fact it traveled to various locations in Buenos Aires and the military officer, Moor Koenig, who was in charge of it became so obsessed with the "Sleeping Lady," as she was called, that he had to be sent away from Buenos Aires to a post in Patagonia. In 1957 the body was buried with the name María Maggi on the tomb in a Milan cemetery, and only reidentified as Eva Perón just before Perón's return to Argentina in 1971, when it was reburied. During its disappearance, the guerrilla group *Los montoneros* kidnapped the body of General Aramburu as a bargaining chip for the return of Evita's body. A largely fictional but partly true account of Evita's postmortem nomadism was written by Tomás Eloy Martínez in his novel *Santa Evita,* which vividly depicts the power of this afterlife even on the very people who wanted it to disappear.[2]

In the 1980s, visiting the Recoleta cemetery in Buenos Aires, I was surprised to see a man dodging in an out among the tombstones and gesturing in my direction. I thought of Moosbrugger in *A Man without Qualities* but he turned out to be neither a flasher nor a murderer but a man earning an honest penny by showing tourists the mausoleum of the Duarte family where Evita had finally been laid to rest. Foucault included cemeteries and brothels in his account of heterotopias—spaces that are not utopian but are "other" spaces within our system.[3] But Eva Duarte's tomb is an altogether different matter, for it is the burial place not only of a charismatic woman but of all kinds of ideal projects of nationhood.

Though the voices of the dishonored dead or those who have disappeared are suppressed in official discourse and even obliterated from the historical record, they invade the polis through myth and legend, and are evoked by the landscape. For history and memory seem to run along different lines—the first preserved by means of documentation, monuments, national holidays and commemorations, the second by means of oral tradition and popular culture.[4] Local tradition often preserved the repressed of official history that interred whatever interfered with the integrity of its narrative. Thus the conquerors buried indigenous civilizations, and the independent republics attempted to bury the viceroyalties under a torrent of words that has never smothered the hauntings, the legends, and the alternative ceremonies that are the mark of loss and that surface in popular culture.

The disappearance of a dangerous body results in a haunting; its presence, on the other hand, invites a ceremonial send-off. The funeral wake is a passage; indeed, a rite of passage from life to the virtual. The very word "wake" in English ("vigilia" in Spanish) suggests the anteroom of memory, when there is still a "cuerpo presente" (a bodily presence). One of the great works of the twentieth century, James Joyce's *Finnegan's Wake,* is keened over the body of Ireland but an Ireland (and a Western world) that comes vigorously alive in the process, garbled, heterogeneous, stripped of its classical profile. The wake is both festivity and mourning, and the funeral feast a moment of horror and hilarity. The presence of the corpse as a spur to the memory and imagination before forgetfulness sets in acquires a particular pathos and significance when it is not an official body. In this case the funeral wake restores significance to certain insignificant and deviant lives that have come to represent the antistate.

The Anticapitalist State

The state offered an ambiguous face in Latin America—being the agent of modernization yet dependent, bearing the hope of national autonomy while practicing exclusions and repression. Intellectuals were ambiguously situated, participating in state power and standing in opposition to it, and their fictional writing often traces the limits beyond which the state's determination of what amounts to truth and justice is dissipated or nullified. The Argentine critic Josefina Ludmer has identified crime (delito) as the topos that both marks and challenges such limits.[5] But, there also persists the topos of an antistate, a world turned upside down in which the excluded and the marginalized move to the center. So the Puerto Rican writer Edgardo Rodríguez Juliá, in *La noche oscura del Niño Avilés (The Dark Night of Child Avilés)*, envisions a black revolt that installs an uninhibited society, the mirror opposite of Puerto Rico's colonial structure. Black Puerto Rico, which according to José Luis González had been "forgotten" in the histories of the island, is re-imagined in this novel as a rebel community and an inverted pyramid.[6] Parodying the language of the chronicles of conquest and settlement, the partisan narrators relate their versions of the struggle between the Bishop Trespalacios and the rebel leader, Obatalá, whose followers engage in all those licentious activities censored by the church.

In José Donoso's novel *El obsceno pájaro de la noche (The Obscene Bird of Night)*, the antistate is figured as a half-ruined convent and orphanage that harbors the detritus of the patriarchal order—old women, old newspapers, orphans, and Mudito, the doorkeeper whose body has been raided by the hegemonic power. The narrative of the aristocratic Azcoitía family (whose name, like that of many of the Chilean elite, suggests they may be descended from Basque immigrants) depends on legitimate descent, although this has had to be manipulated and reinvented given the uncertainty of paternity. In any system that depends on true paternity, women are the weak link and the legitimacy of such a dubious aristocracy is always in question, liable to be subverted because of infidelity or infertility while the fertility of the lower orders is always a threat to them. The ur-narrative of the Azcoitía family is shrouded in mystery since the ancestor covered the possible sin of his daughter behind a cloak. In Donoso's novel, it is not only women but also the low body that transgresses the integrity of legitimating narratives. Old women, servants, and nurses hoard the detritus—nail parings, snot, discarded sanitary napkins—and perhaps, according to Mudito, use this filth to reconstitute something like "a negative plate, not only of their patrons from whom they've robbed this rubbish, but of the entire world" (p. 65). The doorkeeper of the refuge, Mudito, had once been the writer Umberto Peñaloza, who had failed to get recognition from the Azcoitías who plundered his body and converted him into the silent figure of Mudito in order to keep itself intact. Having been subjected to their bizarre experiments, Mudito contrives an elaborate plot to father a child by one of the orphans, the daughter of a murderer, and pass it off as an Azcoitía heir.

Between these low and high bodies, there is, however, another body—that of the *imbunche* of Chilean folklore. The *imbunche* is a kidnapped body all of whose orifices have been sewn up. It is not so much a body without organs, in the sense that Gilles Deleuze and Felix Guattari give to this term,[7] as a body without senses, something like a literary corpus or the novel *The Obscene Bird of Night* itself. The anti-state of rejects turns Mudito into the *imbunche*, his orifices sewn up by an old woman who, after warming herself at a fire, leaves him as a package to be swept into the river by the wind. Authorship is either a captive of the state or subsides into the anonymity of popular culture.

The Despotic Body: Failed Legitimation

The despotic state is imagined as a body that absorbs all other bodies in its ideal and immortal representation. Resistance and opposition is often imagined as occurring in remote areas or in marginal topographies. Much of Gabriel García Márquez's writing is concerned with those premodern bodies that confound state reason and that often occupy geographical territories that the state has not codified. Such territories constitute a kind of primitive socius as against the modern state and are "virgin territories"—sometimes quite literally so, for they may be founded by a virgin matriarch.

In an early article written for a Barranquilla newspaper, García Márquez describes his visit to a hospital where he comes across a native of La Sierpe who claims that a monkey is growing in his stomach. La Sierpe is a region situated in the middle of a swamp, bonded by a foundational legend that tells of the beautiful and virginal woman, La Marquesa, with magical powers over nature and over her own life. The inhabitants still preserve the customs of the Spanish conquerors from whom they are descended ("se enamoran como católicos y españoles" ["they fall in love like Catholics and Spaniards]").[8] From the pregnant man García Márquez learns the story of the Marquesa, a powerful and magical woman who can choose when to die. When that choice is made, she has her cattle trample around her deathbed until they create an impassible swamp. Her enormous wealth is buried in the middle of the swamp under a golden melon tree. The pregnant man claims to have reached the buried treasure after an incredible feat of navigation through a sea of aquatic flowers, uncanny odors, and the fantastic noise of parrots, monkeys, and marsh hens. Strange winged animals with the heads and beaks of birds and pelicans with metallic plumage flew around the raft. But within sight of the melon tree the traveler, "the only man who had dared to set foot on the territory of legend," turned back; on land, his foot begins to swell—a sure sign that he is a liar.

Traditional storytelling with its penchant for exaggeration and the marvelous defies factual reporting, but this lost colonial wealth in García Márquez's account can be transmuted into cultural capital. The burial or loss of treasure marks the disjunction between the colonial past and the republic, between primitive accumulation that is never turned into capital and its passage into myth. Many of García Márquez's lifelong obsessions are evident in this tale—the journey into a zone of legend, the powers of persuasion that allow the witness and storyteller to pass off the counterfactual, and finally that lost historical moment that can only be reconstructed as myth. If myth flourishes on absence and scarcity, what does literature gain by its appropriation if not nostalgia for a past that one would not want to inhabit?

Lack and nostalgia are recycled in many forms throughout García Márquez's work. In "The story of Eréndira and Her Wicked Grandmother," the remote heroic legend of conquest has degenerated on the lawless frontiers; wealth is accumulated through Eréndira's body for she has been prostituted by her grandmother in order to repay for a house that had burnt down through her negligence. Eréndira's sexual labor is commuted into the gold ingots that the grandmother wears around her waist. After Ulysses, son of diamond smugglers, kills the grandmother to free Eréndira, she escapes taking the treasure with her.[9] The wealth of the Marquesa and of Eréndira is a form of primitive accumulation but, in each case, the male is left with the fantasy that fills the void left by the sequestered riches, while the woman (as nature or territory) is the source of production. The story can be read as the story of the exploitation and ultimately the exhaustion of natural resources, a theme that recurs throughout the Colombian author's work.

In "Big Mama's Funeral," García Márquez again describes a remote territory ruled by a virgin matriarch. Jungle, swamp, cattle ranches, and plantations constitute her immense body which is a virginal body overcoded by sexual difference. Men fight and are sexually promiscuous, while women are prudish.[10] This sex-gender system is generated by the territorial body that has a longer span than human mortality but cannot reproduce itself (nature is exhaustible). The death of Big Mama brings this regime to an end and prepares the way for the deterritorialized nation-state that overcodes the tribal and prenational socius.[11] The disjunction between the old territorial community and the modern state is not the result of revolution but is a natural process. In this allegory, the colonial period (that which now survives in oral tradition) is imagined as a land whose mythic wealth can now only be remembered by the storyteller who must pass on his knowledge "before the historians arrive."

For García Márquez, the Spanish colonial empire is a great machine for the production of the marvelous. The secular republic, on the other hand, faces the problem of legitimacy since it cannot claim divine or natural right and has difficulty securing the belief that is necessary for the hegemonic narrative. In one of his stories, "Blacamán the Good: Miracle Worker," a magician who had practiced his arts during the viceroyalty, embalming dead viceroys so skillfully that they could go on ruling after death, roams the fairgrounds after Independence doing simple sleight-of-hand tricks. The magician's name, Blacamán, is commonly used by popular street performers in Latin

America, but it is also a distortion of "black man" and might refer to the fact that African-Americans were often associated with magic and witchcraft. Once Spanish colonial rule comes to an end, however, his magic no longer works.[12] After Independence and during an invasion of the American marines (the allegorical figure for foreign intervention), Blacamán flees across a desert with his apprentice. Tortured by hunger and thirst, his magic fails him and his apprentice subdues and mocks him by flinging a rabbit at him. The power of the Spanish colony had derived from the immortal body of the state incarnated in its placeholder, the mortal viceroy. The power of the new state apparently derives from its power to reproduce itself "naturally" (like the rabbit), though in fact this is no more than a act of legerdemain. Dominated by the apprentice who now proclaims himself "Blacamán the Good," the former master is stigmatized as "Blacamán the Bad" and is reduced to performing as a fairground magician until his miraculous snake-bite lotion fails to cure him and he dies. Blacamán the Good whose wealth comes from the sale of natural resources is not only the new ruler but his "magic" is of a more contemporary variety. A conspicuous consumer with a fleet of Cadillacs, he has Blacamán the Bad (and with him the past) buried in a mausoleum so that his lamentations can be heard by the populace. The despotic modern state allows the past to lament in order to confirm that it was worse than the present.

Writing of Venezuela in the years following the dictatorship of Vicente Gómez, Fernando Coronil argued that the spirit of the dictator lives on despite the state's attempts to suppress its founding father. "When today Gómez's spirit is invoked in his mausoleum or incorporated in a *materia* (spiritual medium) and speaks to followers in the mountain of Sorte, the authority of his words is inseparable from the long-buried foundations of his power as representative of the nation's two bodies" (that is, the material wealth and his role as representative of the people).[13]

García Márquez often represents the two bodies as the body of woman (nature) and the body of the magician/patriarch (the state). In his novel *The Autumn of the Patriarch,* the recourse to magic by the secular state is relentlessly parodied. The patriarch of the title tries to reenchant his power by claiming that he was born of a virgin mother. On the death of his birth mother, a bird catcher and prostitute, he has her embalmed body paraded through the republic as if she were a saint and a miracle worker who could make mules procreate. In a description that recalls his earlier chronicle of La Sierpe, in which a herd of cattle create a swamp around the Marquesa's death bed, the crowds that gather for the funeral are compared to a torrent of fearless oxen whose hooves devastate everything in their way and create such a stampede that the noise could be heard even in the presidential palace. But the patriarch's attempt to create legend is thwarted by empirical investigation first by the papal nuncio, who is ignominiously expelled for discovering the truth, and then by another emissary, an Eritrean who is assassinated as he rides over the mountain. In a brilliant pastiche, Gárcia Márquez describes the emissary's mule falling down the mountainside and plunging to its death through a geography that is also a series of national cliches that have been embalmed in scholastic geography, history, and literary texts:

> From the mountain tops with their perpetual snows, through successive and simultaneous climates of the weather charts, from the precipices and the tiny springs of the great navigable rivers, over the escarpments on which the learned professors of botanical expeditions had climbed on the back of the Indians to gather their secret botanical collections, down beyond the plateau of wild magnolias where sheep whose warm wool gives us clothing and protection were grazing, down to the mansions of the coffee plantations with their paper garlands and their solitary, endlessly ailing inhabitants and the perpetual noise of turbulent rivers where the torrid zone begins and where at nightfall you can smell the pestilential scent of the dead carcasses and the treacherous killings, down through the cocoa plantation with their everlasting leaves and colored flowers and bay fruits whose seeds are used as the principle ingredient in the production of chocolate and the motionless sun and the burning dust and the different kinds of cucumber and the sad skinny cows of the Atlantic, down through the only charity school for two hundred miles around and the final landing of the still living mule which exploded like a succulent guava fruit among the banana leaves and chickens.[14]

What García Márquez describes here is not only the fall of the mule but the fall of language into secular knowledge. For the mule falls through references to romantic fiction (the endlessly ailing inhabitants of the mansions), to school geography text books (the great navigable rivers), through scientific naming, and the realpolitik of political repression—in other words he falls from a theocentric culture into a nineteenth-century encyclopedia.[15] What García Márquez demonstrates is a process of secular disenchantment in which literature is complicit. This is a topic that is most fully developed in *One Hundred Years of Solitude,* where the very act of deciphering the tribal history of the Buendía family is also the moment of their extinction. In García Márquez's writing, the antistate is not envisaged in a utopian future but in a rapidly disappearing past.[16]

García Márquez's later novels—*Love in the Time of Cholera, The General in his Labyrinth, Of Love and Other Demons*—are situated in this fallen world. In *Of Love and Other Demons,* in particular, the place that fantasy reimagines is a cruel universe, one that cannot be reenchanted.[17] In García Márquez's early writing, a primordial maternal body of the state had been succeeded by the despotic male state against which he imagined the antistate of Macondo. From *Love in the Time of Cholera* onwards, the antistate became less utopian and the allegorical structure increasingly difficult to maintain. When he came to write his novel on Bolívar, *The General in his Labyrinth,* what interested him was not the projection of the historical figure as an allegory of the republic but rather the reverse, the peeling away of the cosmetics of legend and of history to reveal the individual beneath.[18]

The Body of the Secular State

Augusto Roa Bastos's extraordinarily rich novel *I, the Supreme* takes the fiction of the "king's body" to the limit of dissolution. Based on the life of Dr. Francia, the nineteenth-century Paraguayan ruler who transformed the Paraguayan republic into an autonomous state by cutting it off from European trade and commerce, the novel fuses the idea of the liberated territory with the "I" of post-Enlightenment individualism. The fiction of an autonomous subject and the fiction of the autonomous state cannot preserve the boundaries intact, since those boundaries are, indeed, fictional and constituted as a masculine subject. Though this is a novel set in the nineteenth century, the representation of an autonomous state, figured as an anticapitalist state outside the system of mercantile exchange, resonates with the projects of both the avant-garde and with Che Guevara's nonmaterial incentives.

The novel opens with a handwritten lampoon: "I order that on my death my corpse be decapitated, the head placed on a stake for ten days in the Plaza de la República where the population shall be summoned by the sound of ringing bells. All my civil and military servants will be hanged. Their bodies will be buried in fields outside the city gates without a cross or mark to preserve the memory of their names. At the end of the said period I order that my remains be burned and the ashes thrown to the river."[19] The proclamation orders the disposition of the head and body of "Supreme I. Dictator of the Republic," as if the immortal state body can go on giving orders after the death of the mortal dictator. It also decrees ignominy and amnesia to be the fate of those whom the republic would bury and forget, in words that recall Creon's condemnation of Polynices in Sophocles' *Antigone*. Writing that, supposedly, speaks to posterity will become another form of burial against which the plural Dr. Francias of the novel uselessly rage.

In the closing pages, *Tenebrio Obscurus* like a giant fly devours the image of Francia leaving no trace of him—the innumerable eyes of posterity, like the images in the eye of a fly, are multiplied so that there is no one true image. Those eyes, "devour my image, nor do I distinguish the one who is wrapped in the black cape lined in scarlet" (p. 453). This "other" image "wrapped in the black cape" is the one handed down to posterity by the two British travelers, the brothers Robertson, whose travel diary was one of the most sensational accounts of the Francia regime. The Robertsons, eager to open trade with Latin America in the aftermath of Independence, found themselves blocked, frustrated, and humiliated by Francia's determination to keep Paraguay free of the contamination of trade.[20] Educated by Jesuits, Francia inherited their anticapitalist ethos and guarded his liberated territory which he ruled in paternalistic fashion, an enlightened head on an illiterate body. However, as Francia foresees at the beginning of the novel, posterity will not view him in a favorable light for "the chimera has occupied the place of my person."

The duplication of Dr. Francia as an enigmatic personality and the public image of Latin American eccentricity was constructed by hostile critics on whose accounts Thomas Carlyle based his portrait published in *Miscellaneous Essays*.[21] How is it, asked Carlyle, that Latin American heroes such as Bolívar and San Martín should not have acquired the universal fame of Hannibal and Washington? Why, in other words, are Latin Americans so invisible? Carlyle, himself a critic of industrial society, pictured Francia as a hero of the Enlightenment, keeping alive the "rush light of knowledge" in the wilds of Latin America. What is lacking, he believed, was some genius of writing in

Paraguay to make known this prodigy. But it would be over a century before this "genius of writing" appeared in the person of Roa Bastos, who far from subscribing to the heroic version that Carlyle wanted, presented a Dr. Francia as a pastiche of historical discourses, "misplaced" ideas, and patriarchal power that the despotic state (Dr. Francia) literally "dictates" to his secretary without any certainty that his spoken words can be accurately translated into writing, let alone put into practice.[22] Indeed, striving for national autonomy, Francia's state confronts the Hydra-headed "magic" of capitalism.

The novel's varied discourses—internal monologue, edict, the harangue, memoirs, "the perpetual circular," and polemic—slip between truth founded on the spoken word and the instability of the written word, between emission and dissemination, between the referent and virtuality. Deleuze and Guattari described the despotic machine and representation as one in which "the voice no longer sings but dictates, decrees; the graphy no longer dances, it cease to animate bodies, but is set into writing on tablets, stones, and books; the eye sets itself to reading."[23] It is the beginning of a deterritorialized state. But Francia comes to power at the very moment when one form of despotic state succeeded another, when the divine right of the viceregal state was replaced by the "enlightened" despot, whose power is knowledge and who must reinvent the magic of the state. Like García Márquez's patriarch, he must first create a legitimating genealogy. In Francia's case this involves "killing" his natural father in order to establish the autogenesis of the Supreme I: "The Supreme is that which is by nature. He never recalls another, only the image of State, of Nation, of People, of Fatherland" (p. 64). In his mythic version a tiger is said to have killed his father and thereafter Francia is born. "I closed my eyes and was born." His autogenesis is described as follows, "In one gulp I drank my own questions, I sucked on my own milk, taken from my frontal lobes"("Bebí de un sorbo mis propias preguntas. Mamé mi propia leche, ordeñada de mis senos frontales") (p. 309). In yet another version of autogenesis, Hero, formerly the viceroy's dog and now owned by the Robertson brothers, ruminates on the possibility of several sexes, while concluding that man is the only reasonable sex. "How is it possible that we have only one progenitor and only one mother. Can't one be born of oneself?" (pp. 132–133).

Although as an abstraction of the nation he is superhuman, the mortal Dr. Francia nevertheless confronts not only his own mortality but also that of writing given the possibility of duplication, forgery, imposters, copiers, pretenders. No wonder that the despotic state is a paranoid state. Francia is both written and spoken, both personal and official; and although he (and the state) silence opposition and popular power, that power escapes him precisely because he can never control either orality or writing. Woman is the treacherous destabilizing force, and La Andaluza, a female contraband trader, his nemesis and potential Delilah. "Do you think you're going to strip me of my lion's skin so that the fatal cloth will brush my body with its black magic of monstrual-menstrual blood?" A pirate, she is in his imagination "adrift in that nonexistent space where you coexist with all possible species"(p. 49). Her female odor paralyzes him with nausea. "Lustful, sensual, lubricious, libidinous, salacious, voluptuous, dishonest, shameless, lascivious, fornicatory" (p. 50).

The figure of the king's body founders on mortality, embodied in women and their menstrual flow—"the female moon unbuttons her phases." That is why Francia reserves his love for the Star of the North, the "changeless" ideal but an ideal that does not speak, an ideal that is not unlike those "twinklings of pure mothers, of asexual women relegated to the distance of the nocturnal firmament"—in other words, something like the male fantasies described by Klaus Theweleit.[24] Roa's remarkable novel, though set in the nineteenth century, follows with devastating accuracy the logic of those twentieth-century fantasies of the liberated territory, nonmaterial incentives, and the eternal masculine.

The Illegitimate State

The codification of the nation-state is a process of abstraction (or deterritorialization in the language of Deleuze and Guattari), an abstraction not only at the level of the economic but also the affective and the social. Yet the paternalistic state's legitimacy can never be established without question just as fatherhood (before DNA testing) could not be established with any certainty. The patriarchal allegory carries an unwelcome constellation that includes illegitimacy and incest.

In his essay, "A Metaphor for the End of the World," Julio Ortega emphasized this problem of legitimation.[25] Reading Juan Rulfo's *Pedro Páramo* as a "world turned upside down," he argued that "a dominant patriarchal and authoritarian ideology" based on ancient Hispanic codes of property and legitimacy and traceable to the *Tractatus de Hispanorum Nobilitate* of 1597 has become distorted. "Given the impossibility of a legal discourse or corpus," he wrote, "this turns into arbitrary violence." Thus it is not that there is a vacuum in place of the state but that the codification of affect cannot be transmuted into the social. When in Rulfo's short story the women of Luvina say, "De lo que no sabemos nada es de la madre del Gobierno" ("What we don't know anything about is the mother of the Government"), they put their finger on the problem, for the blood ties of kinship have been overcoded by an abstraction.

Rulfo himself explained, in an interview with Joseph Sommers, that the Jalisco of which he wrote is an area in Mexico from which the indigenous had disappeared[26] and that had been populated by descendants of the conquistadores who were, according to historian Jim Tuck, "clannish, anarchistic and resistant to central authority whether federal, state or local," and thus "traditionally prone to the leadership of *cabecillas*."[27] Jalisco was the scene of the bitter resistance to secularization during the postrevolutionary regime of President Calles, who completed the work of the anticlerical Liberal Reform Movement of the nineteenth century and executed the decrees written into the 1917 constitution, according to which priests were banned from political activity and were not allowed to vote, own property, or teach. In the face of the resistance of the Roman Catholic Church, Calles organized a national church outside the control of the Vatican, a move that provoked the civil wars known as the Cristero Wars.

The first Cristero War, fought violently in Los Altos de Jalisco, ended in 1930 with the massacre of many of the participants, but the regional hostility toward the state persisted and was expressed in sporadic violence aimed particularly against teachers and *agraristas* (those responsible for agrarian reform).[28] The ferocious opposition to centrally organized educational reform and modernization is of course not uncommon in Latin America. What Rulfo captures brilliantly is the *ressentiment*[29] of those who have not reaped the fruits of the conquest and who now must confront the abstraction of the nation state and the despoliation that secularization represented for them.

In Nietzsche's *The Genealogy of Morals,* the *ressentiment* of the defeated slaves accounts for the moral code of Christianity that replaced the old heroic ideal and sapped the natural vitality of human kind, disguising vengeance as morality. In *The Political Unconscious,* Fredric Jameson turns Nietzsche around in a discussion of the novels of George Gissing, arguing for a positive form of *ressentiment*: the "ideologeme" of *ressentiment* even if generated by "bad faith" corrodes the happy acceptance of commodity culture.[30] But in Rulfo's writing *ressentiment* is the bad taste of defeat, the defeat of the illegitimate descendents of the conquistadores who are relegated to the margins of history. It arises from the sedimentation that accumulates from a long history of repression, a history into which the individual is born, just as (s)he is born into the system of language. Far from producing Christian morality, it leads to violence *tout court*. Subordinated males know that the power exercised over them is without legitimacy but can only act on their *ressentiment* in underhand ways through treachery and furtive murder.

In *Pedro Páramo*, what unravels patriarchal and religious hegemony is not only the violence of secularization but also the money economy that "causes all that is solid" to melt into air. With the dissolution of social and family bonds, the senses become disassociated. Sight and hearing convey not only different messages but different time frames. "Hearing," the sense that determines communication in territorialized cultures, has become a dialogue of the dead, a dialogue that is impossible between the living. When the novel's protagonist Juan Preciado goes home to the "motherland," Comala, he is accompanied by a deaf mule driver, Abundio, who no longer speaks because "there was no sense in setting about saying things that he did not hear, that did not sound like anything and in which he didn't find any flavor." "Hearing" and "taste" are in alliance, but they do not belong to the present. Only the past is heard. Or the soundless voices of souls in purgatory. "I began to feel that a crowded murmur was circling around me, like a swarm, until I could hear some words almost emptied of sound, 'Pray for us.' That is what I heard them saying. Then it froze my soul."[31]

In the middle of the novel, Juan Preciado comes upon a place called "Los Confines" (the boundaries) and a mysterious, incestuous brother and sister sitting nakedly in the ruins of a home; they describe themselves as "desviviendo"—literally, "de-living" "And here we are alone." they explain, "De-living for having known just a tiny bit of life." ("tantito de la vida). The diminutive, commonly used in Mexico, minimalizes the importance of an event, staves off realization of catastrophe (a dead man becomes "un muertito") or, in everyday contact, placates impatience with "un momentito." The "tantito" here diminishes the enormity of their crime of incest, committed only because the couple were so alone and yet had to "poblar el pueblo" ("increase the population of the village"). But it is also a sly allusion to the contradictions of Spanish colonial policy ("poblar") which would have been impossible without miscegenation. The word "desvivir" is a powerful reminder that, in a totally secular world, there is a state of negativity, of existential deprivation; on the other hand, if one accepts a Christian view of things, to know life (and sexuality) is to deprive oneself of life; in the case of the incestuous couple, affect has run counter to religious law and social taboo. Like Eve they have eaten of the tree of knowledge. But unlike Adam and Eve, who were clothed on leaving the innocence of paradise, this couple are naked and unprotected and because there is no religion (only a religious institution) and no legitimate social order, they have "nowhere to go." Like lost souls in a Breughel painting they inhabit a house whose roof is broken. "Desvivir" has become the state of the subject in the secular nation state in which progress has come to a halt and religion is outlawed. At this point in the novel, Juan Preciado finds himself deprived of air: "I had to suck in the very air that issued from my mouth, holding it in my hands before it went away" (p. 71). The self-sustaining individual of liberal doctrine cannot in fact sustain himself and is suffocated.

Whence the deprivation? In the first place, there is a disassociation of the senses, already mentioned. What Juan Preciado *sees* in the present is a country in ruins. "Empty carts, grinding up the silence of the roads. Losing themselves in the obscure road of night. And shadows. The echo of shadows." He *sees* a town in ruins: "The windows of the houses open to the sky, revealing the tough stalks of grass. Crumbling walls that showed their wasted adobe." The sense of touch also becomes uncanny, no longer an assurance of material reality, but only of dissolution and death. When Susana San Juan's father sends her down into a mine to look for money, for "ruedas redondas de oro" ("golden round wheels"), she touches the dusty remnant of a skull—possibly that of some greedy conquistador—and it crumbles in her fingers. The jawbone comes off as if it were sugar (an allusion to the sugar skulls that are made for All Souls Night). Here money is directly named as that which distorts the relationship between father and daughter. Forcibly married to the cacique Pedro Páramo, Susana manages to escape through dreams of love and affect, whereas others are condemned to the purgatory of *ressentiment*.

Gilles Deleuze distinguishes between different forms of relating to time—habit, memory, and repetition.[32] Repetition is the absence of an assignable origin. Glossing Bergson, Deleuze distinguishes *Habitus* and *Mnémosyne:* "L'Habitude es la synthèse originaire du temps, qui constitue la vie du présent qui passe; la Mémoire es la synthèse fondamentale du temps, que constitue l'être du passé, (ce qui fait passer le présent)" ("Habit is the original synthesis of time that constitutes the life of the present that is passing; Memory is the fundamental synthesis of time that constitutes the being of the past [what makes the present pass by]"). Repetition, like Nietzsche's "eternal return" or Benjamin's "illumination," is a becoming-active.[33]

In Rulfo's stories, the past is not the immediate past of retention but the reflexive past of representation, particularity as reflected and reproduced by the storyteller, who in many of the stories is the criminal or the accursed, the ancient mariner, the confessee whose denial of responsibility is ironically contrasted to the anonymous stock of "common sense" or nonsense, which is usually circulated and stirred up by women. The criminal's flight, burial, and abdication of responsibility conflicts with the responsibility often embodied in female characters who are not the ones who tell the story. The dead, however deeply buried, can never be entirely discounted for they continue to act on the living. In Rulfo's writing, differential lines are drawn according to conventional gender attributes: violence and love, mobility and immobility, irresponsibility and responsibility. The women often make an ethical choice the storytellers and the diasporic males are incapable of assuming. Affect is bound to a sense of place, though not so much to the hearth as to the place where the dead lead their afterlife.

Rulfo's female characters—Susana San Juan, Dorotea, the women of Luvina, the wife of the revolutionary in "El llano en llamas," ("The Burning Plain"),[34] the women disciples of Anacleto Morones—treasure the tenuous possibility of affect despite the ruin and destruction brought about by war, rivalry, and the abuse of power. This is not a slave morality but an ethics of responsibility that resists the forgetting of the dead. Clinging to their counterfactual knowledge, the female disciples of Anacleto Morones and the women of Luvina believe that there is justice for the dead, affirming in the face of "common sense" that "they live here and we cannot leave them alone."[35]

Rulfo establishes the feminine (which clearly does not simply include women) as the antithesis both to the state and to the *ressentiment* of the antistate; it is a privileged arena on which to stage everyday acts of resistance. Responsibility fills the ethical void left by secularization, which neither violence nor revenge can suture. The feminine is transgressive of dominant codes whether of *caciquismo, bandolerismo,* the church, or the nation. Because it cannot speak directly through the dominant discourse, it must resort to inflection, irony, silence; these are perhaps the only weapons available to marginalized regions in their obstinate struggle against dispossession by the patriarchal state.

The novels of Roa Bastos and Juan Rulfo register that tenuous moment when what had once been imagined as an organic community, as a social body, becomes irrevocably fragmented and no longer representable in a teleological narrative. Is this a substitution for politics, as some critics have claimed, or can it be read as the impasse of a certain politics whose authority is asserted in the name of the father and by means of the exclusion of women? Certainly in all the novels discussed in this chapter, the feminine is both remedy and poison. Roa Bastos's novel is also an oblique reference to one of the recurrent themes of this book—the hostility to exchange in much oppositional thinking—for Dr. Francia's Paraguay was founded on resistance to commerce (also figured as a woman, La Andaluza). In these novelists of the "boom," the figure of woman invariably threatens the male subject's integrity and hence the integrity of the alternative community.

The literature that allegorized the state in this way was a twilight literature, reflecting what was about to become an anachronistic state formation administering a national territory and an antistate that was also figured as a territory, whose powers of resistance seems to have been augmented by their situation on the periphery, by their remoteness from a center.

CHAPTER FIVE

The Black Angel of Lost Time

Nothing else but time in the cabins:
time in the hapless solitary dining room
immobile and visible like a great catastrophe.
Smell of leather and cloth densely worn out,
and onions, and oil and something else,
smell of someone floating in the corners of the boat,
smell of someone nameless
who comes down the steps like a breath of air
who enters corredors with his absent body,
and observes with his eyes that death preserves

NERUDA, "THE GHOST SHIP"[1]

The specter of anachronism was never far from the minds of Latin American writers. If the economy was backward and underdeveloped, if the politics were "immature," did it mean that literature, too, was always trailing metropolitan culture? How could writers reflect their reality while at the same time claim the independence of literature from this reality? Octavio Paz's insistence that, in the modern world, the time gap had closed and Mexicans had become contemporaries with the rest of the world was one way of situating the society and its culture under the umbrella of modernity. On the other hand, in his 1969 essay on the modern Latin American novel, Carlos Fuentes complained of the cultural lag, saying that "the black angel of lost time hovers over Latin American culture and its exciting and perverse process of development, its impatient devouring of stages that were gradually attained in Europe and the United States, its tense marriage of nostalgia and hope. But also the feeling of provincialism and isolation."[2] Not only was this encouraged by the persistent misreadings of

Latin American culture from the metropolitan centers but, if anything, it was accentuated in the 1960s by the pessimistic assessment of Latin America's own social scientists and by the much-read theories of Gunder Frank, which causally connected underdevelopment to the subordination of certain (peripheral) areas of the globe to the development of the "center."[3]

Latin America had, from the conquest onward, been an experimental body on which the developed world showed off its virtuosity. Charles Gould in Conrad's *Nostromo* represented the thousands of European dreamers who saw the continent as an empty canvas on which to sketch their enterprises. For every anticapitalist utopia figured as a liberated territory, there were hundreds of European and American entrepreneurs extracting rubber and copper, planting cotton and coffee, rounding up the cattle, and imposing their own myths on what they saw as a wilderness. Even Byron had wanted to go to Venezuela, attracted by its newness. The "center" gave or withdrew its interest from such places according to the flow of money and commerce. Modernization was simultaneously development and ruin, enterprise and repetitive frustration, as mines and forests were stripped and plantations doomed by the price cycles. In the Cold War climate, however, development also became a way of fighting communism and, as such, was linked to "a problematization of poverty that took place in the years following World War II."[4] The discourse of development tended to homogenize Third World peoples and "assumed a teleology to the extent that it proposes that the 'natives' will sooner or later be reformed; at the same time, however it reproduces endlessly the separation between reformers and those to be reformed."[5]

The novels of the "boom" were written at this time of intense debate over development. With dazzling ingenuity they displayed the very qualities that theories of development found lacking in Third World peoples, while questioning the teleological assumptions of those theories. Although some critics have read these novels as transposing into literature the political agency that the writers lacked, this criticism has the effect of placing literature below activism.[6] Another powerful criticism of the novels of the "boom" is that while claiming modernity and burying tradition, they restored "the very auratic, premodern, quasi-religious quality that these fully modern narrative projects strove to eliminate."[7] While both these criticisms have some basis, they also seem to overlook that some of the literature of the "boom," at least, undermines its own premises. They also overlook the fact that literature can be the handmaid to philosophical reflection by inventing images that are less abstract than philosophical concepts. In this chapter, I examine precisely that privileged author figure in several narratives in which his virtual suicide marks disillusion with the heroic male-dominated Enlightenment narrative.

Haunted Vessels

More than any other image, that of the sea journey charted the time lag between metropolis and periphery. The long weeks at sea measured the distance between the contemporary and the anachronistic, between original and copy, between the metropolitan canon and colonial mimicry. That is why ships become the potent symbols both for the transference of cultural capital and the stagnation of this commerce.

In García Márquez's novel *Love in the Time of Cholera*, ships and boats traffick between colony and metropolis, between capital city and province.[8] Ocean liners take the progressive Dr. Urbino to Europe and back, bringing with him projects of modernization and reform that only exacerbate the difference between the cultivated elite and the masses. His death from a fall from a tree in pursuit of an escaped parrot is a kind of poetic justice. The parrot has a murky Caribbean background and the gift of mimicry. It entertains the maids by imitating and parodying the French songs it hears on the gramophone, freely appropriating elite culture (Third World cultures are always said to "parrot" the metropolis). The parrot engages in creative translation, while the realist painting that woodenly commemorates the death of Dr. Urbino is a caricature. The parrot's creatively shows up the stodginess of the elite's academic culture, yet the novel itself—with its careful alignment of representative characters—is more realist than modernist, while the deployment of anachronistic citation (sentimental romance, nostalgia) seems to undermine the surface narrative of development and progress.

The city in which *Love in the Time of Cholera* is set is a river port as well as a seaport. The riverboats that ply the River Magdalena are castoffs—old steamboats run on the wood from the forests so that they gradually exterminate animal and vegetable life along the riverbanks. At the end of the novel, a riverboat shelters the aged and persistent lovers (Dr. Urbino's widow and Florentino, an employee of the riverboat company), whose separation and reunion structure the plot and who seem destined to travel eternally, protected by the cholera flag that prevents the boat from docking. Although critics often describe the novel as a love story and see the ending as an affirmation of love (a reading that García Márquez has encouraged), a comforting conclusion is hardly possible given the destruction of nature; for the separation of private from public life allows the private (which includes both love and literature) to insulate itself as if unconnected to the devastating consequences of unmonitored capitalism. Such a dark conclusion to a benign novel retrospectively shadows the entire enterprise.

Ghost Ships

In Mario Vargas Llosa's *The Green House,* an army detachment comes across the ruins of a camp that had once been occupied by a group of rubber smugglers. "There was tall grass all around; the stairs had fallen apart, imprisoned by climbing vines, and they were the resting place for stalks and roots, and nests could also be seen on the steps and supports, swollen anthills."[9] In the dislocated chronology of the novel, these recent ruins come before the foundation of the colony, underscoring that destruction is already factored into its history even before that history begins. Progress is illusory from its initiation, giving Schopenhauer's veil of illusion and Mauthner's radical nominalism a certain plausibility in the Latin American context. What might appear in the metropolis to have a convincing air of reality is here a lifeless ruin.

In Juan Carlos Onetti's *The Shipyard,* historical failure is not simply an attribute of a particular culture or civilization but is the support of fantasy.[10] Although fantasy is understood by psychoanalytical criticism to veil that which is lacking in the subject, in Onetti's novel it is a deliberate self-deception.[11]

The shipyard of the title is situated downriver from Santa María, the fictional scene of much of Onetti's writing; like Faulkner, the Uruguayan author invested an invented landscape with a mythic past.[12] In that mythic past, boats were pulled into the shipyard for repairs; in the present, it is a ruin, and for the remaining employees a secular purgatory, inhabited by "souls in torment." Its bleak emptiness forms a contrast to the replete and populated world of the realist novel to which it is a counterpoint. In Thomas Mann's *Buddenbrooks,* for example, the home of the merchant family whose fortune was built on trade reflects the solidity of their accomplishments. "The heavy red damask window-curtains were drawn; stiff, massive sofas in red damask stood ranged against the walls and in each corner stood a tall gilt candelabrum with eight flaming candles, besides those in the silver sconces on the table."[13] Their wealth is displayed in a solid domestic comfort that is the tangible reward for their "thirst for action, for power and success" which makes Thomas long "to force fortune to her knees." When the Buddenbrooks fail, the failure seems to be genetic—the weak southern artistic gene that strikes at the heart of the puritan effort. Even though Mann's novel charts a decline in one family's fortune and ends with a sad dinner party of survivors at which Sesami Weichbrodt raps on the table in a gesture of defiance, it does not mark the end of the world, only of the Buddenbrooks world.

Onetti's shipyard, on the other hand, allows for no such solidity. For the material base is no longer present and neither is the will to overcome nature. Whereas in *Moby Dick,* the *Pequod* left the harbor in what Charles Olson called "the will to overwhelm nature,"[14] in *The Shipyard* it is nature that is aggressive. In Melville's novel, the sailor's relation to nature is technological; the ship is the "mobile replica of an advanced technological society." It is also a cathedral, a church dedicated to the Enlightenment project of dominating nature. In contrast, the characters of *The Shipyard* live among objects that have no value except in imagination. It is a world of pure forms, of abstraction without substance, of matter that has never been observed to grow or come into being but that is always in a state of decay. We are in a place that is old without ever being new. Ships exist only in the dusty records or in the scattered remains abandoned in the shipyard.

Although Onetti denied that he intended the novel as an allegory, saying that the decadence was "real," numerous allegories may be read from its pages.[15] For instance, the shipyard figures in an allegory of redemption and salvation and resembles the characters of the German baroque drama described by Walter Benjamin as empty remnants of a lost world and its values. "Evil as such which it cherished as enduring profundity, exists only in allegory, is nothing other than allegory, and means something different from what it is. It means precisely the non-existence of what it presents. The absolute vices, as exemplified by tyrants and intriguers, are allegories. They are not real, and that which they represent, they possess only in the subjective view of melancholy."[16] *The Shipyard* is allegorical precisely in this sense. It exudes the sadness of the loss of sense, the loss of love, marriage, of industrial development. Characters enact the roles assigned to them but never live up to the archetype.

The shipyard manager, Larsen, a former pimp, is a survivor for whom his job (for which he will never receive a salary) is a last chance that is so improbable that even pretense and self-deception become difficult.[17] Initially he acts out his role as a business manager, and makes a show of dusting off the archives of the abandoned yard and imagining business problems. "This affair of the *Tiba,* and the gringo Chadwick & Son. When such cases arise, when they come to our attention, does the firm just send a letter or do we have an agent in Rosario? I mention Rosario but I mean any port within our sphere of influence."[18] But Larsen's *Tiba* has long disappeared, its fate unknown and "sphere of influence" is nonexistent. The *Tiba* has, in fact, become a form, an abstract sign though one that no longer has value. Yet Larsen goes on speaking of liabilities of long burned out and uninsured vessels and the price of painting the hulk of a boat per square foot in 1947, as if it still mattered. The owner of the shipyard, Petrus, colludes in the fiction, offering Larsen a fictitious salary and putting an arbitrary value on the shipyard, which he estimates is worth 30 million. "And that does not include the enormous appreciation of some of the goods in the last few years; nor does it include many others which can still be salvaged, such as miles of roads which can partly be reconverted to salable land, and the first section of the railway" (p. 26). When Larsen estimates that a rusty truck might have been worth more than fifty thousand "if they had taken care of it, just by putting it under cover" (p. 33), the "if" in this sentence measures the incalculable.

The novel was written at a time when Uruguay's postwar boom based on the meat-packing industry, a boom that had helped to fund a welfare society, was already fading from memory and when the lure of "development" based on industrialization was being offered to Latin America. "Underdevelopment" was to be wiped out by the development of industry, the introduction of new technologies to farming and to industry, and by technical aid administered by experts. "Wherever one looked," wrote Arturo Escobar, "one found the repetitive and omnipresent reality of development: governments designing and implementing ambitious development plans, institutions carrying out development programs in city and countryside alike, experts of all kinds studying underdevelopment and producing theories ad nauseam."[19] Development was based on the premise that the poor nations could "catch up" with the metropolis by repeating their experience. Larsen's attempt to manage the shipyard can be read as the allegory of development, though this is by no means the whole story.

Larsen comes to the shipyard as its savior, the last in a long line of saviors. Its founder, Petrus, the immigrant, is now old and ill. Apart from two clerks, Kunz and Gálvez, there are no employees, no laborers in the shipyard. This is "postwork" society with a vengeance, with only the shell of industry remaining. Thus *The Shipyard* inverts the story of capitalist progress; instead of material gain there is impoverishment and a slow corrosion that begins with the bankrupt owner himself, a German-speaking immigrant whose pillows are inscribed with the ironic motto "Ein Gutes Gewissen ist ein saftes Ruhekissen" ("A good conscience is a soft and peaceful cushion"). Like everyone else in the novel—except for the doctor, Díaz Grey—Petrus lives on illusion, in his case the illusion that he is still a magnate and not a man with a charge of embezzlement hanging over him.

As for Larsen, "the messiah" to this God (the religious allegory is emphasized), he can hardly be described even as a character in the usual sense for he is a bundle of contradictory attributes in desperate need of a project—"watchful, uneasy, implacable and paternal, covertly majestic, determined to lavish promotions and dismissals, needing to believe that all this belonged to him, and needing to surrender himself unreservedly to all this, with the sole purpose of giving it a meaning, a meaning which could be transferred to the years he had left to live, and therefore to his whole life" (p. 35). But the existential project is torn out of its Sartrean context of "real" problems and applied, so to speak, to an industry that is more virtual than real. Further the godlike power ("implacable, paternal, majestic") is a simulacrum of a regime that is never represented as anything but vicarious in the first place. As soon as Larsen begins to shake the dust off the shipyard files, he sees that even in its prime it might have been a shady business, lending a tinge of irony to the motto "A good conscience is a soft and peaceful cushion."

Everything about the shipyard evokes an enterprise that has ground to a halt. Surrounding it are "streets of earth or mud, devoid of vehicle tracks" but "marked at intervals by brand-new lamp posts with their unfulfilled promise of light"; all that is left of the working shipyard is "the incomprehensible cement building, the ramp empty of boats or workmen, the cranes of ancient iron which would certainly have creaked and broken if anyone had tried to make them work" (pp. 13–14). The machines are "paralyzed perhaps forever"; the sheds are full of the "corpses of tools" that rise "toward the roof of the building, stretching, indifferent and dirty, up out of sight, higher than the topmost step of any imaginable stairway"(p. 35). The landscape is littered with old machines. Outside the cabin in which an employee—Gálvez—and his wife live and onto which the helm of a riverboat is attached, Larsen sees among the weeds and puddles "the rusty skeleton of the truck, the low wall of debris, chains, anchors and masts. Erect and with an exaggerated strut, he avoided metal objects without shape or name lying imprisoned in a tangle of wires, and entered the darkness" (p. 64).

Larsen, whose past experience includes running a brothel, knows that the shipyard is his last chance and so tries to endow it with life, at least in his imagination:

> There had been glass panes in the window; twenty or thirty men had bent over desks; each pair of torn wires had once plugged into a telephone; a girl unerringly plugged in and pulled out the jacks on the switchboard ("Petrus, Limited, good morning"): other girls walked seductively to the metal filing cabinets. And the old man made the women wear gray overalls. Perhaps they thought that it was he who forced them to remain unmarried and not give rise to scandal. Three hundred letters a day, at least, were sent off by the boys in the dispatch section. And there at the back, invisible, almost legendary, as old as he was today, confident and tiny, the old man.

But even imagination cannot overcome the skepticism of the two remaining employees, Kunz and Gálvez, who are selling off the rusty remains whose estimated value nobody believes, not even the prospective buyers. Larsen knows that his potential buyers, "the Russians," are filled with doubts, seeing "the anachronistic details, the difference between what they were looking for and what they were offered."

But Larsen, it is suggested, is generic rather than individual. Doctor Díaz Grey (the Marlow figure in many of Onetti's novels, embodying rational skepticism) sees him as a generic type who resembles all the managers who had passed through Puerto Astillero. Superficially they may appear to be different but they are in fact members of a class whose common characteristic is the "poverty or the ostentatious wretchedness of their fantastic, ill-assorted clothes." Larsen simply fits into a preordained role. Indeed, his very gait suggests a performance in which he is not yet comfortable. "He descended the steps awkwardly, feeling unsafe and exposed, trembling excessively when, as he reached the second flight, the walls came to an abrupt end, and the rattling iron steps spiraled down into the void" (p. 33). The Spanish text is even more explicit than the English translation. Larsen is described as "estremeciéndose con exageración" ("shuddering in an exaggerated fashion"), which conveys the theatrical effect as if all Larsen's actions were self-conscious performance. His "implacable and paternal" manner is, after all, nothing but a front for he is only "tolerated, ephemeral, alien" or "impotent and absurdly immobile like a dark-colored insect waiving its legs and antennae in the air filled with legend, seafaring adventures, past labors and winter" (p. 34). The "seafaring adventures" have dissolved along with work and the seasons into a tenuous and now mythic past.

But the plethora of possible historical narratives gives the reader pause. Petrus may represent the economic colonization of Latin America—that is, those Europeans who came to the Southern Cone to supplant the landowning aristocracy in the belief that they would provide the enterprise and know-how that was lacking in the indigenous and in the settler colony. A foreigner of unknown origin (he speaks German), he never manages to acquire the house that had belonged to the aristocratic Latorre family and thus claim succession. Instead their house is turned into a museum, suggesting that in that area (perhaps the Plate region, perhaps Latin America) the historical development from landowning aristocracy to capitalist society has been short-circuited. The shipyard is one more enclave like the mines and plantations, and its owner is never fully integrated into local society. Indeed, Petrus inhabits an isolated house, built on stilts to protect it from floods though it cannot be protected from its inner destruction. Nor can he found a dynasty that will continue his work. His only offspring, his daughter, Angelica Inés, is mentally unbalanced. There is no other class that can supplant him, for class struggle is yet another myth.

When Larsen surveys "metal spare parts in their tombs, the corpulent machines in their mausoleums, the cenotaphs of weed, mud and shadows, lurking-places arranged without a plan," he does not envisage the exploitation of labor so much as the miserable human beings who had worked there—"the proud and stupid willfulness of a workman or the coarseness of a foreman." The fragments left by industrial decay whose origin is never specified—perhaps because in Latin America there is no need to specify—evoke not so much class interest as blind self-interest. On the other hand, the sarcastic and distant observer Dr. Díaz Grey, at one point and perhaps ironically casts Petrus as a benevolent capitalist, ensuring "the future of the legend." "Petrus, our master, watching over us, our needs and our wages, from the cylindrical tower of the palace. It is possible that Petrus might have given it a finishing touch by having a lighthouse built; or we might have found it enough, to embellish and enliven our submission, to contemplate from the promenade along the beach, on fine evenings, the lighted windows like stars, behind which Jeremías Petrus was keeping vigil and governing us" (p. 111).

The impossibility of grounding any project in material reality is what makes it such an insistent reminder that discontinuity is the experience of the Third World subject or perhaps even of the post-Auschwitz subject or the collapse-of-communism subject. Indeed, I see a connection here between Onetti's novel and Chantal Akerman's film *A l'Est*. This video film of Eastern Europe after communism is comprised of images of moving cars in anonymous landscapes and of people waiting in featureless places, often in the grey early hours of morning or at night. The alternating tracking and still camera shots show an Eastern Europe as a place of waiting with no end in view. People wait—wait in lines for buses, sit and wait for trains, wait for customers for some paltry item—all the while their faces revealing a universal skepticism. There will be nothing particularly good at the end of the wait, at least not for these people. What we witness in the film is the human cost of a massive failure.

Onetti's novel narrates not only the collapse of development but the even more devastating collapse of belief in economic development as the reigning ideology of the 1960s and 1970s in Latin America. There had been a widespread belief that a responsible national bourgeoisie could function in the interests of their nations by developing industry, instituting reforms (literacy, better agricultural methods, industrialization) and bringing prosperity. Many people on the Left thought this was the necessary prologue to socialism. Instead, and particularly in the Southern Cone, there was a slow economic decline. In Uruguay it became more and more difficult to pay for the generous social programs instituted by past regimes, and the military eventually took power to stem a rising tide of unrest. But in Onetti's novel, there is no unrest because his characters live the dominant fantasy, knowing that it is fantasy that is necessary in order to maintain some sense of personhood.

For Onetti, narrative history is not so much a narrative of the past as a mythic story concocted to fit into the dominant fiction. The town, Santa María, has a stained statue of its founder Brausen near the prison. The statue had, according to the narrator, been much criticized.

> The matters under dispute were: the poncho, for being northern, the boots, for being Spanish; the jacket, for being military, the profile of the hero, for being Semitic; his face when seen from the front, for being cruel, sardonic and having the eyes too close together; the inclination of his body, for being unhorsemanlike; the horse itself, for being an Arab stallion. And finally, the position of the statue was described as unhistorical and absurd, as it committed the Founder to gallop eternally toward the south, to retreat, as though regretting all he had done, toward the remote plain he had abandoned in order to give us a name and a future.

The founder of Santa María is meant to embody the precarious hybridity and indeed the nonidentity of a nation that had originally, before Independence, simply been known as the "Banda Oriental"—the Eastern Sector. Its adoption of an Indian name, "Uruguay," when the Indians had been wiped out, contributes to the confusion of origins. Like everything else in the novel, Santa María has been "imagined."

Five or six blocks away from the shipyard, the Chamamé bar alludes to a more remote past; a hitching post recalls the pastoral society of the gaucho, the knife fights, and the commerce in leather goods. But the bar has become modernized, a modernization that consists of the addition of "a few tables, chairs and bottles, another lantern in the corner formerly occupied by the hides and which now held a platform for the musicians. And on a vertical joist, another notice: 'It is forbidden to use or carry weapons'—grandiloquent, unnecessary, displayed there as a sop to authority which took the form of a militiaman with corporal's chevrons who tied his horse to a little tree on the corner every evening." It goes without saying that the prohibition of the use of arms is yet another survival from the past. Argentine and Uruguayan identity had been constituted on the basis of the myth of the free gaucho who defied all authority and was always ready to fight, a tradition whose only relic is the absurd notice. The ancient waiter with his Indian features—the high cheekbones—is another reference to this now remote past of Indian wars that have nothing to do with the tame little bar that is protected only by a militiaman who, in homely fashion, tethers his horse to a tree. Such places, however, constitute a kind of destiny. Larsen regards the bar as the "inferno for which he had been destined since the beginning of time, or the one that he had earned, according to one's point of view." In this world, the immigrant Petrus, as Díaz Grey had observed, is the agent who might have enabled a rural and essentially nomadic culture to become a modern urban society; yet, his foothold in native institutions was too precarious. The only modernization is the cosmetic doing over of the Chamamé bar.

But if the dominant fiction is so unpersuasive, does this not lead to a crisis of the subject—in this case, the masculine subject? For inasmuch as fantasy is the support for reality, it also involves belief and identification. Kaja Silverman argued that by withholding our belief in the dominant system, "we at the same time jeopardize all that is variable about our symbolic order."[20] Slavoj Žižek has a different take on this and one that is applicable to Onetti's world: people understand that something is a fiction but they do it just the same. It is not the knowledge that is an illusion but the reality: "they know that their idea of Freedom is masking a particular form of exploitation, but they still continue to follow this idea of Freedom."[21] Larsen is precariously holding together his very personhood by staging belief as a kind of Pascalian wager, but he knows that it is an illusion. For the model of belief is religious, and a dominant ideology or system of belief that would guarantee the workings of the social and economic systems cannot substitute for religion.

One of the essential elements of ideology, at least according to Louis Althusser, is that it seems like common sense or the natural ways of things.[22] But in *The Shipyard* each of the settings of the novel—whether the shipyard, the shack, the summerhouse, or Santa María—is never anything more than a theatrical prop. The shack inhabited by Gálvez and his wife is described as "part of the game, that they had built and were living in with the sole purpose of enacting those scenes which could not be performed in the shipyard" (p. 75). Larsen's bodily movements are deliberately exaggerated, almost parodic. He swaggers and pretends, always conscious that he is participating in farce or at best melodrama in an environment of indifference,—"in-diferencia"—undifferentiated chaos; the only possible heroism under the circumstances is stoic determination "not to be discouraged by solitude, by the uselessly limited space, by the eyes of the tools which had been pierced by the rancorous stalks of the nettles." Spatial boundaries—the shack, the shipyard, Santa María, the summerhouse—are all alike in a state of threatened entropy and any illusion of mastery is undone.

It is therefore with difficulty that anyone in the novel believes in progress and even more difficult for them to believe in salvation in the religious sense, though the name Jeremías Petrus alludes both to the Old Testament prophet and the New Testament disciple. While Larsen professes to see him as the hidden god of his universe, even the hidden god needs believers. Kunz, nominally the "technical manager" of the shipyard, has been "dragged down by the universal skepticism," so that "the prophecies of resurrection uttered every now and then by old Petrus and regularly repeated by Larsen, did not succeed in giving him back his faith" (p. 154). The sense of loss is so complete that when a letter arrives addressed to the General Manager, Kunz seizes on it as a proof of the "reality of a God whom he, Kunz, had blasphemed." But the letter only confirms the general skepticism, for it communicates the news that Petrus is now in jail charged with forging a bond. In a later scene there is a reversal of roles between Petrus (Peter) and Larsen. Faced with the proof that he has forged bonds, Petrus simply goes to sleep. This sublime indifference arouses both Larsen's anger and admiration. First he wants to repudiate him and spit on him, but then kisses him—an ambiguous Judas kiss, part tribute, part betrayal, part *memento mori*. In a fallen world Petrus is a Peter who cannot supply the foundation on which a church can be built.

In this disenchanted state, Christian belief cannot be commuted into secular ethics nor Christian love into a bond. Romance, marriage, birth, the family—on which the social might be founded— are equally illusory. Larsen's farcical betrothal to Petrus's daughter Angélica Inés, who is quite possibly crazy and certainly no longer young, is one more enactment of universal illusion. The meetings with Angélica Inés (who eventually flees from him in fear) are staged in the weed-choked garden of Petrus's house in a *glorieta* (translated as "summerhouse," although "bower" would seem a better translation given the connotations of romance)." The difficult world of the *glorieta,* the only place in the novel where flowers grow, is a halfway stage between the chaos of nature and human achievement, but it is also a stage in the theatrical sense. For Angelica Inés is yet another simulacrum; she is a woman who looks young and virginal but has probably passed childbearing age, although the distant traces of girl-hood still "remained in her blue eyes," in her undeveloped body and "the little velvet bow at her neck" (p. 15). She is described as a "convincing imitation" of a young woman although she carries with her the mustiness of things past; on her face are "recent wrinkles." She is ambiguity itself: neither completely woman (she has no experience of womanhood) nor completely young; psychologically untouched by time but physically marked by time. Her first traumatic memory is of a flood, an accident independent of her own will. Her strange laugh is dissonant but its dissonance is more like madness than youthful joy, and she cannot complete a sentence. Indeed, she too embodies the precariousness of subjectivity that pervades the whole novel. For romance (as a cover for succession and inheritance) and love—are staged in such a manner that they denote not so much feeling as assigned roles. Angélica Inés understands this very well, for she describes the summerhouse as the place where she has to tell lies.

Larsen conducts a more earthly version of romance with the pregnant wife of the employee, Gálvez. The couple live in a dilapidated shack in the ruins of the shipyard, which is yet another stage, the scene of basic survival where Larsen imagines himself helping the woman "carry water, light the fire, prepare the meat and peel potatoes" (p. 128). But this domestic scene is as unconvincing as his betrothal. Gálvez's wife, though still young and beautiful, is unkempt, negligent; she doesn't wash herself or comb her hair, and she dresses in unattractive men's clothes. Rather than a vehicle of life, she is a vehicle of death. Larsen considers her "finished, burnt and arid as a field after a summer fire, deader than my grandmother; and it's not impossible, I'll bet, that what she's carrying is dead, too" (p. 133). As far as he is concerned she is simply a vessel for the foetus—"perhaps she was no longer a person but the recipient of a feeling of curiosity, of expectation" (p. 134). After Gálvez has abandoned her (he commits suicide), the woman gives birth alone in the shack in a scene that fills

Larsen with revulsion. "He saw the woman on the bed, half naked, bleeding, struggling, clutching her head which she was turning from side to side in anguish. He saw her incredibly round belly, her glassy eyes blinking rapidly, and her clenched teeth. Only gradually did he understand and fully absorb the nature of the trap. Trembling with fear and disgust, he left the window and set off for the coast" (p. 188).

One hopes perhaps vainly that Onetti has his tongue in cheek. He is after all the author of *Juntacadáveres (Body Snatcher),* in which Larsen at an earlier stage of his life takes on the running of a brothel in the hope of discovering "a form of perfect prostitution" and who even sacrifices himself for it. But what Onetti seems to be attempting is the separation of the social, the subjective, and the pragmatic aspects of sex and gender. Angélica Inés represents the social bond of matrimonial alliance; Gálvez's wife the dual aspects of sex as lure of the species and as desire. The novel reflects Schopenhauer's view of the human subject, according to which "[w]e pursue our life, however, with great interest and much solicitude as long as possible, as we blow out a soap bubble as long and as large as possible, although we know perfectly well that it will burst."[23] For Schopenhauer, individuation is nothing but a "trap," the self-deception that, apart from the detachment of philosophy—a condition achieved perhaps by Díaz Grey—is the only way to survive. Larsen's dedication to perfect prostitution in *Juntacadáveres* becomes, according to this view, a form of authenticity. Although *The Shipyard* was written before *Juntacadáveres,* the "blind unconscious striving of the will" is more starkly foregrounded in the earlier novel which views life as a "constantly prevented dying, an ever postponed death."[24] Indeed, the blind will of nature is everywhere visible in the industrial landscape now overgrown with weeds—*yuyos* (a word of quichua origin)—whose persistence outlasts human endeavor. "Right from the very the beginning and for all eternity, there was nothing more than the steeply pitched roof, the layers of rust, the tons of metal and the weeds blindly growing and twining around everything" (p. 34). Purpose and consciousness seem to belong to the rancorous and triumphant nettles that have jealously poked through the eyes of the tools and blinded them. Against these forces of nature Larsen's struggle is increasingly ludicrous. Nature is purposive, active, energetic, unpredictable as the river, and, unlike the shipyard and the littered industrial landscape, in constant growth.

This plethora of religious, philosophical, social, literary, and historical allusions can become heavy-handed—for example, in his tour of the shipyard, Larsen sits down in an abandoned and rotting life raft as if to emphasize the hopelessness of salvation. But possibly such obvious allusions are intended to verge on parody. It is as if Onetti is asking the reader to balance the possibility of belief and coherence with the fallen aspect of the world and its fragmentation and degeneration. Like Larsen he wants us to walk across a void. This is why the "romantic" and the melodramatic plots—the projected marriage of Larsen to Angélica Inés that ends in scandal, Gálvez's denunciation of Petrus for issuing a forged bond, and Kunz and Gálvez's conspiracy to sell off anything of value—are transparent devices that do not even deceive their protagonists. Indeed, the forged bond that sends Petrus to prison is one more form of illusion; it is backed up by nothing at all, although it can be used by Kunz and Gálvez as a form of blackmail.

Onetti's deliberate indecisions (which the alternative endings of the novel confirm) can be read as an invitation to recognize the unreliability of fiction. Yet the fact remains that the narrative fragments of character, plot, and description are, like the broken shards of the shipyard, the bits and pieces of prior narratives—narratives constructed from genealogies, narratives of enterprise and romance, all of which, like Petrus, had originated elsewhere. Onetti offers alternative versions of Larsen's death. In the first he takes off on the ferry boat from which he views "the silent collapse of the walls" of the shipyard. "Deaf to the din of the boat, his eager ear could still make out the whisper of moss growing among the piles of bricks and that of rust devouring metal" (p. 189). In the second, after a botched suicide attempt, he also is taken aboard the ferry, where "the hardest thing for him to bear must have been the unmistakable, capricious September air, the first attenuated perfume of spring, which came slipping irresistibly through the cracks of decrepit winter. He breathed it in while licking the blood from his split lip, as the high-sided boat sailed up the river. He died of pneumonia in El Rosario before the end of the week, and in the hospital registers, his real name appears in full." How he dies is, of course, a matter of indifference.

"In the hospital registers, his real name appears in full" but the name is not disclosed to the reader, to whom the "real" is inaccessible. Onetti's novel turns the national problem, identity, and history into phantasmagoria and Larsen's endeavors into a ghostly repetition. What is missing is anything convincing enough to inspire the belief that had been lost with the death of God. Of course this is not only a Latin American problem, but in Latin America it is as if the disaster has happened without any previous stage of achievement. There is nothing left against which the heroic character can be tested.

European travelers had frequently thought of Latin America as an empty landscape, as if the indigenous inhabitants did not exist. Latin American writers sometimes reproduce this situation but often ironically. If the landscape is empty, it is not because it is pristine as on the day of creation but because it is postapocalyptic. Gaviero/Maqueroll, a character invented by the Colombian poet and novelist Álvaro Mutis and the protagonist of several of his novels,[25] continually sets out on futile journeys on decaying ships, traveling upriver to interiors where his goal is never fully realized. In *The Snow of the Admiral*, Gaviero—whose name can be translated as "the Lookout"—sets out on a disastrous journey during which the boat's pilot is killed and the captain hangs himself. When he arrives at his destination, a sawmill, he finds it occupied by troops but the building itself is impenetrable, enigmatic: "I knew I'd never have the chance to meet anyone who lived in this inconceivable building. A vague uneasiness has been taking hold of me, and now I'm trying to write in the diary so I won't look at the floating Gothic marvel of aluminum and glass lit by that morguish light and lulled by the gentle hum of its electric plant." Gaviero is never privy to the secret of what, if anything, is the higher purpose. His projects are devised out of whatever ruin is at hand. "It's all the same, it doesn't matter. What does matter is something else: what we carry inside, the wild propeller that never stops spinning." Unlike Larsen, Gaviero never attempts to believe in anything except in the drive that is independent of the subject.

In *A Beautiful Dying*, the Lookout finds himself in a river port and is engaged as a mule driver to take bits of machinery up to the improbable railroad that is being built in the mountains. The "railway," however, turns out to be a guerrilla camp and the load he is transporting munitions. Captured by the army, he is eventually released and dispatched to safety on a barge. Gaviero inhabits the borders of delinquency as he takes part in these dubious enterprises, in which women also participate as helpers or in order to trade their bodies. But what stands out is that here nationality has become a vague label, something like "blonde" or "cross-eyed." The people he meets are Flemish or Belgian or belong to any number of exotic nationalities who live on the neglected borders of the transnational empire and who seize on incidental opportunities to cash in. His novels anticipate the postnational narratives of a migrant class of technicians and middlemen.

In *Beyond the Pleasure Principle,* Freud describes the compulsion to repeat as both an exercise of mastery over painful episodes and as a manifestation of the death drive.[26] Freud himself admitted that the essay was speculative and that he himself was not quite convinced by it. As Kaja Silverman perceptively observed, Freud "does not sufficiently distinguish it from other kinds of psychic recurrence."[27] Nevertheless both repetition and the death drive are productive ways of looking at the novels I have mentioned, in which the protagonists knowingly repeat not only their own histories of failure but also historical failures. As Lacan pointed out, in finding and repeating the discovery of the object, "it never is the same object which the subject encounters."[28]

Imperial Nostalgia

In the novels I have mentioned, death is the ultimate outcome of the male fantasy. But there is also a certain nostalgia for an older imperial past (or at least for that past viewed as a heroic conquest of nature), now replaced by the global but invisible empire.[29] This nostalgia borders on the parodic in Werner Herzog's film *Fitzcarraldo,* in which imperial nostalgia is staged as cultural enrichment. Filmed in the Amazon jungle, *Fitzcarraldo* traces the feat of the historical protagonist, an Irish adventurer, who towed a ship over a mountain in order to bring opera to the Amazon. Such an enterprise was, in reality, only made possible by the rubber boom and its extraordinary exploitation of native labor, though this is suppressed in the film itself. When Les Blank documented the filming, he revealed that neither the filmmaker nor most of the crew seemed to find anything odd about the fact that, for their reenactment, they deployed a plane, a helicopter, three ancient steamboats, a cast of about 700 extras—including Campa, Machiguenga, Camisea, and Shivancoreni Indians, some prostitutes, flush toilets, cold-water showers and electric generators, and a bulldozer that used 150 gallons of fuel that had to be flown in by light plane and ferried up the river in dugout canoes.[30] All this was mobilized, at great expense, to give the film its air of "authenticity," which was ironically underscored when lives were lost. One of the Indians drowned, others got sick, and a plane crash severely injured the pilot and five Indians who were being flown in. Herzog's rather literal approach to filmmaking reached the limit when he insisted on pulling his ship with pulleys and cables over a forty-degree slope at great risk to his extras, some of whom were in fact killed in the process. As Herzog put it, apparently without any hint of irony, "In this case we will probably have one of the last feature films with authentic natives in it. They are fading away very quickly. And it's a catastrophe and a tragedy that's going on and we are losing riches and riches and riches and riches. And we lose cultures and individualities and languages and mythologies and we'll be stark naked."[31]

The phrase "the last feature films with authentic natives in it" is an oxymoron. What is "authentic" about filmed natives when the very process of filming produces change? Herzog seems to have no awareness that his very words mimic in farcical fashion a whole history of colonial misrepresentation (the jungle brings out sexual urges, "fertility or whatever that's going on here in the jungle"). He even claims a benevolent interest in the indigenous peoples—he is helping the Indians get legal title to their lands so that "no settlers or no oil companies or no lumber people can exploit it and take it away from them." In his diary, Les Blank would write, "It feels so strange to be part of this old ritual warfare. I keep wondering if I'm not in a movie and find it scary to know that this film has no script."[32] The fact that this was a feature film and not a development project piles irony on irony: another adventurer arrives, dispenses rewards, and disappears leaving behind death and devastation but this time in the cause of cinematic illusion. At one point, Blank comments in his diary that they were going off "to shoot the destruction of nature going on with the building of a 12–15 degree slanted road with a bulldozer and dynamite" (p. 99); on another occasion he noted that they were off "to hunt for 'natives' to film" (p. 104).

Blank's assistant and film editor, Maureen Gosling, also kept a diary and proved to be one of the more perceptive observers. She was present at the confrontation between the filmmakers, the CIPA (a Peruvian indigenous advocate organization), and a group of Aguarunas who were hostile to the filming and who would eventually burn down the filmmaker's camp. Gosling wrote,

I was somewhat pleased that the natives had held their ground in the face of our 'white man's' pressure. But the fact that they were not following their own strategy and that their arguments adhered so closely to CIPA's rhetoric for dealing with troublesome outsiders, made me realize how vulnerable they were, and perhaps also how desperate they were for advice from those parties, such as CIPA, who were seemingly sympathetic to their cause. They were caught, as are all of the diminishing tribal peoples of the world, in a wrestling match with power plays. CIPA, with all its good intentions of defending native rights and issues, also held with a Marxist philosophy which regarded the natives as an underprivileged class in the context of a larger society, rather than as a separate culture. The built-in assumption in such a philosophy meant that the natives were lacking in what the other social strata in society had, so they should have all those things and provided for them apart from the larger society. (p. 169)

Whether one shares Gosling's overall viewpoint or not, she does at least make several perceptive points. What the film crews were doing, in fact, was incorporating the indigenous into market society while retaining the myth of traditional cultures. The contact with the film crews and the CIPA produced power struggles and new leaders within the indigenous group.

Amazonian culture and the environment seem to exist only as a passage for the madness of the white man, whom Herzog had already depicted in *Aguirre: The Wrath of God* (1972). *Fitzcarraldo* goes a step further, for now it is Herzog himself who makes the process of filming into a struggle against a nature that he sees basically as evil. In an outburst recorded by Les Blank in his documentary film and noted by yet another observer, Michael Goodwin, Herzog railed against the "obscene" Amazonian jungle: "I see fornication and asphyxiation and choking and fighting for survival and growing and just rotting away. The trees here are in misery and the birds are in misery. They don't sing, they just screech in pain."[34] Herzog's language recalls both an earlier German traveler, Count Keyserling,[33] and the Colombian novelist José Eustasio Rivera, whose novel *La vorágine (The Vortex)* was published in 1924 and also described the jungle as "vile and base." Decades before Herzog's rant, Rivera had his protagonist, Arturo Cova, lament, "No cooing nightingales here, no Versaillian garden or sentimental vistas. Instead the croaking of dropsical frogs, the tangled misanthropic undergrowth, the stagnant backwater and swamps. Here the aphrodisiac parasite that covers the ground with dead insects; the disgusting blooms that throb with sensual palpitation, their sticky smell as intoxicating as a drug."[35] Rivera is countering the romantic sentimentalization of nature, but in Herzog's fantasy world, nature conveniently figures as the alibi for the failure of modernization-as-mastery that Adorno and Horkheimer had seen as the remote principle of the Enlightenment itself, although this premise is never examined by the filmmaker.[36] The entire episode reminds us that what Europeans obsessively sought in the New World was a repetition of the Old, but in pristine circumstances. Onetti's and Mutis's novels are the disabused commentaries on this fact, for they reveal that the pristine cannot be recaptured and that individual enterprise, independent of any social formation, is an empty exercise.

CHAPTER SIX

The Magic of Alterity

It seemed that the only way to salvage the nation was with a blood transfusion from the primordial, from those indigenous and black cultures that had not been drained of spontaneity and vigor, that existed in the "depths" of the nation, in José María Arguedas's deep rivers, in the "deep" Mexico of Guillermo Bonfil Batalla, in the cellar of the Puerto Rican nation in José Luis González's *The Four Storeyed Country*.[1] These were the depths that were mined to discharge the specter of anachronism and exorcise the copycat ghost that haunted the Latin American intelligentsia, which always seemed to be thinking of what others had done.

The lure of "magical realism" was that it reenchanted the world by drawing into literature popular beliefs and practices as a form of dissent from post-Enlightenment rationalism. It was an invigorating bath in Latin American originality. On the negative side, magical realism was a form of cultural incorporation that collapsed literature into anthropology or made it into something of a raid on the rain forests in search of genetic samples. Although I depart from most critics in thinking of "magical realism" as an appropriation of racial difference, it is a reasonable assumption given the fact that race has been and continues to be one of the most persistent blind spots of Latin American politics and culture. This statement applies not only to countries such as Argentina and Chile, where indigenous populations are geographically marginalized, but also to Mexico with its many indigenous groups and languages.[2] And although Colombia is a country that includes many indigenous peoples as well as a substantial Afro-Colombian population, its major writer, Gabriel García Márquez, draws for the most part on the popular culture of Hispanic populations, although many of their beliefs—in animism and sympathetic magic—were appropriated from the indigenous and the black. The race card is a stronger suit when it is used to trump Eurocentrism, as it is in the enthnopoetics of Miguel Angel Asturias and José María Arguedas and in the writing of Alejo Carpentier. On the other hand, when magic was detached from indigenous and Afro-American practices and "deterritorialized," so to speak, it enabled certain writers—for instance, Jorge Luis Borges and Juan Carlos Onetti—to appropriate "magic" for secular narrative in order to destabilize the positivism on which post-Enlightenment thinking had been based. Magic secures belief even as it goes against common sense.

In cultural journalism in the United States, magical realism has become a handy if misleading rubric that stands for a common Latin American style. In a review of García Márquez's *Love in the Time of Cholera,* Edwin McDowell wrote, "Magical realism is the term used to describe the Latin literary penchant for intertwining fact and fantasy, reality and illusion, legend and superstition."[3] It is interesting that boundary crossing is here described as a "Latin literary penchant," as if it were some ingrained character fault. That the reviewer mentions magical realism at all given the fact that the novel in question is a meticulous and even laborious confrontation between nineteenth-century positivism and romanticism, both European imports, reveals how completely the term had become the yardstick for measuring all Latin American writing. "Rosario Ferré's novel is packed with magic, blood, sweat and tears," wrote Julia Álvarez for the book jacket of *The House on the Lagoon.*[4] When Bloomingdale ads began to mention magical realism, it was clear that the term had passed into the twilight zone of "idées reçues." Just as the term "exotic" became for an earlier generation a code word for darker-skinned nations, so "magical realism" has become linked to wayward fantasies of whatever kind and has been identified in U.S. and Canadian literatures[5] and in Indian and Chinese literatures, giving some credence to Gayatri Chakravorty Spivak's allegation that magical realism is taken to be "the paradigmatic style of the Third World."[6] When Latin

American novels do not conform to this stereotype, reviewers frequently express their disappointment. The reviewer of Manuel Puig's *Eternal Curse on the Reader of these Pages* contrasts its "pared down and displaced quality" with the writer's "passionate Latin early novels."[7]

Although not yet named as such, magical realism emerged in the late 1920s and early 1930s,[8] when writers were looking for ways to liberate narrative from the framework of positivist historiography that had underpinned the realist novels, and when several of them—Miguel Angel Ásturias, Alejo Carpentier, Darcy Ribeiro, José María Arguedas, Roa Bastos, Mario de Andrade—were engaged in ethnographic studies in their own backlands. Arguedas, who was a trained ethnographer, and Roa Bastos both compiled anthologies of indigenous literature. Haunted by the specter of anachronism, of being shadows of European culture, these writers based their claims of Latin American originality on the fragments and survivals of non-Western cultures in their societies and on the tradition of "wonders" that went back to the conquest and discovery. Latin American writers were acutely aware that metropolitan realism was a misfit in Latin America and, like James Joyce, they found the mythic on their doorstep. "Magic" and lore detached from religious roots were reterritorialized by the avant-garde. As Terry Eagleton wrote, referring to Ireland, "Languishing within a barren social reality, the colonized subject may beat the kind of retreat into fantasy and hallucination which lends itself more evidently to modernist than to realist literary practice."[9] But the claims of "magic" go further than this, involving everything from spirit possession to healing, from the use of hallucinatory drugs to inflicting injuries on enemies—in other words all that official scientific knowledge has brushed aside.

The genealogies of magical realism and "lo real maravilloso" are usually traced to the German critic Franz Roh as well as to the surrealist "marvelous" that flourished in Paris in the 1920s.[10] The performances of the Revue Nègre, the protests against the Moroccan War, the first popular exhibition of pre-Columbian art in France, the "profane illumination" of surrealism, and the exodus of French writers and ethnographers—Leiris, Valéry Larbaud, Michaux, and Artaud—to Africa and Latin America were indications that the axis of culture was shifting from its Eurocentric base, encouraged by a widespread belief in the decadence of Europe and the originality and dynamism of the Americas. Referring to the intellectual climate of France at that time, James Clifford observed that "reality, after the surrealist twenties, could never again be seen as simple or continuous, describable empirically or through induction."[11] Both the American "lost generation" and the Latin America émigré writers benefited from this turn. The Guatemalan Miguel Ángel Asturias and the Cuban Alejo Carpentier, both of whom lived in Paris during the 1920s and early 1930s, became ethnographic surrealists themselves, "representing" Afro-America and Indo-America for Europeans.

Magic was rooted in a racially distinct and predominantly rural world from which writers were separated, not only because their culture was primarily urban and international, but also because literacy was for them an index of modernity while orally transmitted cultures flourished in those backwaters that were untouched by modernity and were therefore, in Johannes Fabian's word, "downstream" from the developed world.[12] Literacy was held to be the great redeemer. In their youth, both the Peruvian José María Arguedas and the Mexican Rosario Castellanos participated in literacy campaigns among rural populations, campaigns that were meant to bring the undeveloped sectors of their societies into the modern world.

Fredric Jameson has argued that magical realism corresponds to a moment when "a mode of production (is) still locked in conflict with an older mode (if not the foreshadowing of a future one)." In García Márquez he discovers a turn to a more anthropological perspective: "[M]agic realism now comes to be understood as a kind of narrative raw material derived essentially from peasant society, and drawing in sophisticated ways on the world of village or even tribal myth."[13] Applying the term to "the realm of film," he further discovers that it can be grasped as a "possible alternative to the narrative logic of contemporary postmodernism" (whether there can be a "logic" of postmodern narrative is another matter) and contrasts postmodernism's nostalgic relation to the past with "the articulated superposition of whole layers of the past within the present," which is the precondition "for the emergence of this new narrative style" (p. 139). Though plausible, this account misses the fact that magic, insofar as it is an attempt to exercise control where science is inadequate or unavailable, resurfaces quite happily in postindustrial societies and thus is not necessarily locked into conflict with them. Advertisement constantly draws on magic. Shamanism flourishes in the Bronx and Brazilian candomble is practiced by the middle classes. Indeed, it can be argued that the crude design of capitalism, its lack of any ethical or spiritual dimension, would be exposed too harshly were it not able to harness and resignify traditional beliefs.

Jameson's argument also fails to include the essential element of race. The anthropologist Michael Taussig, on the other hand, has shown how deeply embedded race is in Latin American popular culture, where the inhabitants of the Andean lowlands, for example, constantly try to tap into the magic attributed to the highland Indian for healing. Taussig pointed out that, far from doing away with magic and shamanism, modernity tries to harness their power. "It is not just primitivism but Third World modernism, a neocolonial reworking of primitivism."[14] It is important to bear this in mind. Anthropologists played a dual role in this reevaluation of indigenous culture, depending on whether they were interested in the incorporation of tribes into modernity or whether they were searching for resistance to Western culture.

The obsession of the metropolitan world and especially of the anthropologist with indigenous magic is satirized in the 1982 film *On Top of the Whale,* directed by the Chilean-born Raúl Ruiz, who situates it in a postrevolutionary era when Holland is a communist republic and the Communist Party is allied with the Dutch Reformed Church. Thus it is not only capitalism that is shown to need the primitive but also the communist Left in so much as it shares the myths of modernization and progress. Filmed through red and yellow filters, *On Top of the Whale* satirizes every cliché of cultural difference. At one point there is a reading from Italo Calvino's *Invisible Cities* in which Marco Polo invents imaginary cities to entertain the Kubla Klan and which, as I show in Chapter 7, has become a favorite postmodern allegory. All this reinforces the absurdist framework of the "story," inasmuch as there is one.

A communist millionaire, appropriately named Narciso, invites an anthropologist, his wife Eva, and their child from the Communist Republic of Holland to visit his estates in Patagonia, where the anthropologist is to study the last two survivors of a native tribe on lands that were acquired after the slaughter of the Indians. Narciso seems to suffer from some vague guilt and at one point declares his intention of writing a novel as homage to "the noble race" his ancestors have exterminated. The predominant tropes of the film are shadow images, mirrors, and translation that show the essentially narcissistic nature of European expansion. What the Europeans search for is the mirror image of themselves; at one point the child even claims to be pregnant from the mirrors, underscoring the reproduction of the Same. The house the Europeans inhabit in Patagonia is an exact replica of Eva's house in Holland—a Dutch house on a canal.

When they first arrive, Narciso says the place is "full of shit" because the overseer has not looked after it. The countryside too is said to be "full of shit," and in one sequence Eva plays with shit. Objects excavated in the hope of finding the bones of massacred Indians turn out to be recently buried tins and bottles. A rabbit's skull is not evidence of sacrifice but the remains of a rabbit stew. The characters speak in English, French, Spanish, German, and Dutch yet they cannot understand the indigenous language. When the anthropologist attempts to learn it from the Indians—the appropriately named Adam and Eden—by holding up objects and asking "What is this?" they apply the word to totally different objects and concepts—"beating a child to death with a rock," "an eclipse of the sun, moon and stars," "menstruation," and "walking with no sense of direction." Alternatively when the anthropologist holds up the same object, the Indians keep offering different words for it. In exasperation, he finally writes in his journal that what they say and do has no meaning. The overseer, Luis explains that beating the Indians is not an act of cruelty because they like physical contact and Eva warns her child to keep away from the Indians although the child, having been brought up with progressive ideas, asks if that means that the proletariat are dangerous.

At the end of the film, the anthropologist still does not understand the indigenous language while the Indians have learned to speak German and English and talk of Hegel, Spinoza, Beethoven, and Mozart. Finally they ask the anthropologist, "What is it that you want to know about us?" "Are you going to do something with it (that is, the information)?" "I am leaving," the anthropologist replies. For, indeed, his job is done, for there is no outside to his world, at least none imaginable within his parameters. In the dreamlike atmosphere of the film, knowledge corresponds to fantasies; it is composed of narcissistic representations, the shadows in the cave from which the characters never emerge. They are indeed "full of shit."[15]

Ruiz's film can be taken as a humorous epilogue to the ethnographic surrealism that projected European avant-garde fantasy onto remote places and cultures. This cultural emigration in search of Europe's "other" had gathered momentum in the 1920s when Latin American writers found themselves in the surprising position of trolling their own countries for native forms of expression in order to claim the specificity of the Americas. Even the Mexican writer and classical scholar Alfonso Reyes participated in the cult of exoticism with a poem on the Tarahumara Indians, who "had leapt over the barrier of the five senses."[16] Both North and South American writers became apologists for an Americanism that was encouraged in Paris and more particularly in the pages of *transition,* a journal founded in 1927 and published in Paris by Shakespeare and Company. Edited by Eugene Jolas, the journal became a showcase both for the European avant-garde and for the new Americanism. It published ex-surrealists (Louis Aragon), dadaists (Arp), and experimental writing (Joyce's *Finnegan's Wake*). Its covers were designed by artists such as Miró, Kandinsky, and Picasso. But along with avant-garde experiment, the journal had an interest in "paramyths" and "interracial documents."

The Latin American contributors seized the platform offered by *transition* to claim privileged knowledge of non-European cultures and oral tradition. An essay by the Cuban anthropologist Fernando Ortíz explored the use of the sound riff known as "jitanjáfora," which Alfonso Reyes had defined as "the poetic form of the magical language, a literary survivor of the mysteriously liturgic black art of conjuration which is still alive and cherished by many who listen to it because of the irresistibly hypnotic, emotive force of the rhythm."[17] The jitanjáfora is "the independent aesthetic appraisal of words by the pure and simple value of their phonetic vibrations" (p. 175). Influential in Latin American scholarship, partly because of his invention of the term "transculturation,"[18] Ortiz compared the effect of jitanjáfora to that of a choirmaster "who has his singers sing a number of barbarous and untranslatable lyrics in order to give his audience the sound effect of the approach of a mob of wild, jungle people." Like the discord that black musicians introduce into European music in Alejo Carpentier's *Concierto barroco,*[19] the jitanjáfora disrupts the rationality of the dominant discourse but at the price of depriving the "mob of wild, jungle people" of any claims to rationality. Alliteration, onomatopoeia, and phonetic sounds with no signifying implications—that is with no *sense*—are racially marked. Noise from the margins clamors to be heard. And by arguing that one had to be Cuban to appreciate the jitanjáfora, Ortiz crosses a dangerous dividing line; for in claiming epistemological privilege on the grounds of his place of birth that metonymically gives him access to black culture, he implies that his potential non-Cuban readership will be excluded from understanding and appreciation.

The obsession with indigenous and black culture took a different turn in the 1960s as writers of the Americas looked to reenchant the fallen world by drawing on indigenous spirituality and forms of knowledge unknown to Europe. Looking for an alternative to the warrior society, young North Americans followed the peyote trail or visited María Sabines to eat her hallucinatory mushrooms or they imbibed the wisdom of Carlos Castañeda's yaqui guide.[20] In 1968, the poet Jerome Rothenberg published *Technicians of the Sacred,* a collection of "primitive poetry" from all areas of the world. In the "preface," Rothenberg wrote that the collection "shows some of the ways in which primitive poetry & thought are close to an impulse toward unity in our own time, of which the poets are forerunners."[21] He also contrasted "our world"—"open to multiple influences and data"—and theirs, which is mainly "self-contained." The commentaries that often stress oral techniques and comment on the monotony and the use of repetition are evidently intended to show that the poems deserve the attention normally given to high culture.

Mimesis and Alterity

The storyteller, the shaman, and popular mythology became ports of access to a sacred world as well as being identified with American originality, even as destruction of traditional societies seemed imminent. It is in this ambiguous terrain that *magical realism* and *lo real maravilloso* need to be situated as a form of reenchantment, as a challenge to European cultural hegemony, as a cultural resolution of racial difference but always in the threatening shadow of the imminent dissolution of their base.[22]

Alejo Carpentier's *Ecue-Yamba-o* and Miguel Ángel Asturias's *Leyendas de Guatemala (Legends of Guatemala)* were early symptoms of this anthropological phase out of which both authors later developed a more complex ethnopoetics. *Leyendas de Guatemala*

(Legends of Guatemala), first published in 1930 and translated into French by Francis de Miomandre, received the supreme accolade of praise from Paul Valéry, then the barometer of French high culture. After reading these "stories-dreams-poems," Valéry was struck by their heterogeneity. "What a mixture of torrid nature, of confused botany, of indigenous magic, theology of Salamanca in which the Volcano, the friars, the Sleep Man (Hombre Adormadera), the Merchant of Priceless Jewels, the flocks of dominical parrots, the master magicians that go to the villages to teach how to weave and the value of the Zero compose the most delirious of dreams."[23] For Valéry, the juxtaposition of such heterogeneous elements is what gave the book its originality.

In the preface to his novel *The Kingdom of this World,* Alejo Carpentier attributes the marvelous both to the history of the discovery of the Americas and to nature. "The fantastic is to be found at every stage in the lives of men who inscribed dates on the history of the Continent and who left names still borne to this day: from those who sought the Fountain of Eternal Youth, from the golden city of Manoa, to the first rebels or the modern heroes of the wars of independence . . . [B]ecause of its virginal landscape, its formation, its ontology, the Faustian presence of both Indian and Negro, the revelation represented by its recent discovery, and the fertile interbreeding it has fostered, America is far from having drained its well of mythologies."[24] Thus the "New World displays its magnificent plumage" in contrast to tired old Europe, a theme Carpentier tirelessly reiterates in *The Lost Steps.* His major novel, *El siglo de las luces (Explosion in a Cathedral),* brings together two miraculous forces—the infinite variety of primordial nature and the infinite variety of human cultures that forcibly cohabit because of conquest, miscegenation, and slavery. For although Carpentier still tends to draw sharp lines between the rationalism of Europe and the apparent disorder of the New World, he identifies mimesis (the butterflies of *The Lost Steps,* the great catalog of shells of *Explosion in a Cathedral*) as the dynamic source of creativity. So Esteban, one of the protagonists in *Explosion in a Cathedral,* reflects on the fact that the language of the Caribbean has had to adjust to the hybridity of natural phenomena. Certain trees are pineapple-porcelain or wood-rib while as far as marine life is concerned, "a fantastic bestiary had arisen of dog-fish, oxen-fish, tiger-fish, snorers, blowers, flying fish."[25] Nature, particularly Caribbean nature, seems to have inspired baroque ornamentation. The crossroads of empire and a natural wonderland of the Caribbean is where both mimesis and miscegenation display their creative potential, their productivity, hence the recurrent descriptions of islands, beaches, shells, fish, and plants. The symbiosis of nature and the human produces a burst of creative energy that defies habit and routine.[26]

In his essay "On the Mimetic Faculty," Walter Benjamin argued that man has an even higher capacity for mimesis than nature. "His gift of seeing resemblances is nothing other than a rudiment of the powerful compulsion in former times to become and behave like something else."[27] If this is the case, then Carpentier's fascination with mimesis can be read as the positive reversal of America as copy. Magic, which in *The Kingdom of this World* was still a curiosity, a superstition, is associated in *Explosion in a Cathedral* with the creativity of the mimetic.

Set in the late eighteenth and early nineteenth centuries, *Explosion in a Cathedral* explores the upheaval that followed the French Revolution and its repercussions in the Caribbean.[28] The title of the English translation suggests more explicitly than the Spanish title, *El siglo de luces (The Enlightenment),* the destructive force of the revolution that shattered the collective bond established by the church and empire and produced the explosion within the state religion itself. The revolution, witnessed by the cousins Esteban and Sofía in the Caribbean, France, and Spain, destroys the hierarchies imposed by European class and racial discrimination. But the Revolution that had initially embraced all kinds of heretical beliefs from freemasonry to spiritism and that had released unconscious forces, including the positive forces of "dis-order," was soon reined in and subjected to new controls by its leaders. Although it is the death of Sofía's father that initially leaves the family without paternal authority and frees them to live as if life were a theater of make believe, the arrival of the mysterious revolutionary Victor Hugues is the event that brings to an end their enclosed existence and thrusts them into the world. Sofia surrenders to the man, who is both friend and mentor, revolutionary and ultimately pragmatist and defender of the increasingly repressive postrevolutionary governments. Esteban, who during the years of the Convention lives in France before accompanying Victor Hugues to Guadalupe, becomes disillusioned with the reign of absolute reason and finds spiritual solace in the marvelous variety of the Caribbean. Sofía and Esteban come together again in Madrid and meet probable death in the repression of the Second of May uprising.

Summarized in this way, the novel may appear to be a story of disillusionment, though the destruction of the old (the death of the father, the revolt in Haiti, the uprising in Spain) provides the creative momentum that projects characters into another space, the space of freedom. The novel anticipates more recent writing that celebrates the multicultural societies of the Antilles, which had been fortuitously separated or brought into contact by colonialism, as a far richer cultural catalyst than Europe and the model for a new kind of universality.

The Ethnopoetics of Difference

The notion that there is a mythic substratum common to all cultures (the paramyths of *transition*) would be popularized by Joseph Campbell in his book *The Hero with a Thousand Faces*.[29] For Latin Americans writers, mythic characters—many of whom, like Jocasta, Antigone, Penelope, and Melusine, were feminine archetypes—provided handy structural skeletons on which to flesh out regional variations of the universal themes. Indeed, they were as much a part of the culture of the lettered in Latin America as in Europe, although, as Borges remarked, the Latin American writer could treat this repertoire with irreverence.[30] Penelope, for example, inspired the character in *Zona sagrada* based on María Félix, the Mexican film star, although like the Ulysses of Carpentier's *The Lost Steps* and like García Márquez's Erendira, she always betrays her immigrant status.

But there was also the untapped reserves of native culture and popular beliefs, whose value seemed to rise the more they were threatened by modernity. In Brazil, Guimarâes Rosa drew on the rural storytelling tradition in his novel *Grande Sertâo Veredas*. The Cuban Nicolás Guillén, the Puerto Rican Palés Matos, and the Ecuadorian Adalberto Ortíz appropriated santería and Afro-American language usage and rhythms,[31] as ethnography now gave writers access to those cultures that had been marginalized as "downstream."[32] Miguel Ángel Asturias (Guatemala), Augusto Roa Bastos (Paraguay), José María Arguedas (Peru), Darcy Ribeiro (Brazil), Mario de Andrade (Brazil), Adalberto Ortíz (Ecuador), Alejo Carpentier (Cuba), and Lydia Cabrera (Cuba) were all ethnographers or interested in ethnographic studies.[33] Roa Bastos, Arguedas, and Darcy Ribeiro compiled anthologies and wrote studies of indigenous cultures.[34] While "mestizaje" (racial mixing) had long constituted ideologies of Latin American and national differences, this valorization of the indigenous and Afro-American cultures provided grounds for an anticapitalist ethos and politics as well as a different point of entry into the universal.

Lévi-Strauss's monumental study *Mythologies* brought together in one great system the myths of the Americas, demonstrating the underlying unity of what had hitherto been considered a motley collection of native beliefs. Yet, as Derrida would point out, Lévi-Strauss's insistence that these indigenous peoples had no writing contributed to the idealization of oral cultures as communities of speech "in which all members are within earshot," and of writing as "the condition of social inauthenticity."[35] Gordon Brotherston argued further that evidence of script consciousness among the indigenous of the Americas was suppressed, a suppression that was perhaps motivated by the need to preserve "the overall model of oral America."[36] This having been said, for a generation of Latin American writers whose writing antedated that of Lévi-Strauss's *Mythologies,* the redemption of indigenous and black cultures and the valorization of oral culture as a bond of community amounted to an affirmation of values specific to the Americas that were an alternative to those of the dominant West.[37] That the indigenous were idealized for their communal values antithetical to modern individualism should be seen as part of the longstanding struggle to establish Latin American cultural and political worth, a concern that despite postmodernism never quite goes away.

Two influential novels of the Cold War period in Latin America— José María Arguedas's *Los ríos profundos (Deep Rivers)* and Miguel Ángel Asturias's *Hombres de maíz (Men of Maize)*—depict this search for indigenous alternatives to "savage capitalism" in the face of the modernization of rural society, in which the military often acted as the agents of change.[38] In contrast to the fallen world of modernity, produced by violence, there is another, feminized world, in which identities are formed not through an Oedipal narrative of rivalry with the father but as a surrender to the "feminine" and to a primordial sacred landscape not yet privately owned or exploited for profit.

Men of Maize recounts the painful but constantly renewed struggle against this fall into individualism. On the one hand there is the reduction of the community through classification, renaming, counting, and measuring (the empiricism of science) and on the other the striving for communal values maintained through oral tradition. The "magic" does not take the form of descriptions of ceremonies as in the indigenist novels, but as Gerald Martin observed, through poetics.[39] Asturias's prose style uses onomatopoeia, alliteration, rhythm, and repetition—all features of performance in oral cultures; these constitute signifying chains in a manner reminiscent of poetry establishing secret links that disrupt linear narrative. The apparently simple alliterative phrase, with the repetition of the "s" and the "o"—"Al sol le salió el pelo" ("the sun's hair grew"), for example, establishes links between the human, the natural, and the divine and ushers in an idyllic scene of the golden age before the army clears the communal lands to make way for private ownership. But there are also patriarchal (or at least hierarchical) resonances in this phrase, a hierarchy that seems to be overturned toward the end of the novel with the discovery of the stone in which hides the soul of María la Lluvia (María Rain), the reincarnation of the Piojosa Grande who had fled from the prior destruction.

> A sus espaldas de mujer de cuerpo de aire, de solo aire, y de pelo, mucho pelo, solo pelo, llevaba a su hijo, hijo también del Gaspar Ilóm, el hombre de Ilóm, llevaba a su hijo el maíz , el maíz de Ilóm, y erguida estará en el tiempo que está por venir, entre el cielo, la tierra y el vacío.
>
> [On the back of a woman whose body is of air, of air only, of hair, of much hair, only of hair, she carried her child, the child of Gaspar Ilóm, the man of Ilóm, she carried her maize child, the maize of Ilóm and she will stand upright in the time that is to come between heaven, earth, and emptiness.]

It is this woman of air and hair who articulates the past and the future, heaven, earth, and nothingness and thus overturns the scale of values that usually places the "sun" at the summit.

This utopian promise of regeneration incarnated in the feminine can only come about through the magical reenchantment of the land at the level of both production and reproduction. "Magic" in this sense is neither quaint superseded tradition nor New Age appropriation; rather it is what allows access to another form of rationality through values that have not yet been converted to exchange. As various critics have pointed out, Asturias often appends a rational explanation to apparently magical events, for literary narrative itself cannot wholly inhabit this other world.[40] Ethnopoetics is a form of translation that negotiates the meeting of disparate epistemologies and transforms their energies in the cause of justice and hence of political action. Asturias's son, a leader in the Guatemalan guerrilla movement appropriated the name Gaspar Ilóm from his father's novel. The Zapatista movement in Chiapas that emerged into visibility at the beginning of 1994 inaugurated their activities by addressing the public in indigenous languages, reversing the practice in which the indigenous had always been addressed in the dominant language. According to one commentator, a trace of that enchanted world had yet to totally disappear. "A still-not-lost looking towards the past opens the door to a still-not-arrived, towards the future."[41]

In the work of the Peruvian writer José María Arguedas, magic, especially the magic of sound, is "the ability to cross distances that are impossible to normal perception."[42] In his writing, there is almost a Pythagorian understanding of a cosmos bonded by sound. Speaking of the music of the *harawi,* an Andean rhythm, he wrote, "the vibration of the last note drills into the heart and transmits the evidence that there is no element in the celestial or earthly world that has not been reached and compromised by this final cry."[43] In an episode in his novel *Deep Rivers,* women who sell *chicha* (a fermented drink made from corn) are persecuted by the army; their defiance is underscored by the appearance of a harp player who performs satirical lyrics that bring "tradition" productively into a critical interpretation of the present. And in a well-known episode of the same novel, Arguedas discusses the etymology and sound of the spinning top *(zumbayllu),* with its power to break out of the walls of the college in which the protagonist is interned and to invoke the countryside beyond. Through onomatopoeia, which reaches a high degree of intensity in the quechua language, "the material essence of things" is preserved along with the traces of human interaction with them. It is sound above all that is the source of intensity and hence of illumination. Describing the quechua songs that resonate with the noise of the river, Arguedas writes "those who do not know quechua listen with great seriousness and divine the tragic and cruel in their content."[44]

In Chapter four, in reference to Juan Rulfo's *Pedro Páramo,* I pointed out the valorization of voice over sight. In the work of Asturias and Arguedas, magic is related to oral tradition, to the magic of voice, of songs and words that are physical carriers of memory that still resonates in print culture. This utopian moment before the global remapping of the urban and rural would, during the careers of both writers, be put into crisis, as registered in Arguedas's posthumously published *El zorro de arriba y el zorro de abajo* and Asturias's *Mulata de tal*. In their writing, the power of the indigenous derives from its territoriality, a territoriality that has sacred configurations.[45] This means that their styles were not readily exported to those areas of Latin America in which the indigenous were suppressed or exterminated. In this case "magic" is found elsewhere.

With the massive emigration into cities during the 1970s and early 1980s, indigenous and African magic were appropriated by new cults and religions, and incorporated into shamanistic ritual and the New Age spirituality of Carlos Castañeda and others. What Asturias and Arguedas had prized as the possible foundation of community could now be resignified in the individualistic ideology of advanced capitalism.

Magic Deterritorialized

Supposing that instead of appealing to some lost spirituality, the writer embraces secularization without necessarily subscribing to dull pragmatism. This is something like the projects of Juan Carlos Onetti and Jorge Luis Borges, both of whom "deterritorialized" magic, abstracting it from either religion or tradition. In his novel *Para una tumba sin nombre (For a Tomb without a Name),* Onetti "buries" the magic of oral culture though without the nostalgic cast that García Márquez often gives this transitional moment. The novel begins with a funeral ceremony attended only by the narrator and a goat. The identity of the buried and unhonored woman is in doubt since she is recalled only by survivors who may not necessarily be telling the truth. All we know from their stories is that a woman who might or might not be named Rosario is said to have made a living in bizarre fashion by standing outside the train station with a goat and begging train fare from travelers. Onetti has different characters tell and re-tell the story until no possible certainty remains. As Josefina Ludmer pointed out in an excellent analysis of how the novel constitutes its network of meanings and possible interpretations, the readings do not quite destroy the archaic substrata. Onetti describes the goat as having "the calm of an idol"; it exhibits such a "contempt for the tributes offered to its divine condition that it could not have expressed this even if it could speak." He thus quite explicitly stresses the symbolic significance of this animal that was associated with gods but also with the devil. As Ludmer observed, the goat had once figured in the phallic cult of Dionysius, and the Greek word for goat, *tragoi* (—in Spanish, "chivos," "cabrones") is the original nucleus of the word tragedy; goats are associated with various goddesses (Hera, Artemisa, Atenea). "The scapegoat bears the weight of social ostracism. But in the Middle Ages, the pagan gods were transformed into the devil that was represented as a goat, presiding over the orgiastic rituals of the witches' sabbath . . . The enemy of natural reproduction (and the family), the devil is the agent of cultural and artistic productivity."[46]

In his novel, Onetti uses the goat as a prop, as a device that defamiliarizes what would otherwise be a banal story. At the same time, its symbolic roles as "idol, god, priest, demon, phallus, scapegoat, offspring and product" leave traces in the social text, marking their transformation from religious and shamanistic symbols to a literary pretext.[47] As a survivor of some more ancient ritual, the goat provides Rosario with symbolic investment that can yield dividends in the telling. And it is put into circulation by the men who take over the narration of the story. In fact the voice of the female storyteller is never heard since she is already dead at the beginning of the novel and about to be buried in the tomb without a name. Her story is appropriated and reinvented by men, all of whom claim their places as protagonists in the tale. The novel buries a woman and with her the remains of shamanistic belief, while limiting secular narrative to the precincts of "masculine" exchange.

Jorge Luis Borges takes this burial of origins to another level. His 1932 essay "Narrative Art and Magic" is an agenda for his later "fictions."[48] In that essay, he reflects on William Morris's *Life and Death of Jason* (1867), a narrative in verse, probably not much read even in England, and Edgar Allan Poe's *Narrative of Arthur Gordon Pym*—two works that make believable the existence of mythical beings or uncanny places. Borges describes magic not in religious terms but as "that craft, or ambition, of early man." Citing what he terms "savage, or ridiculous, examples," he comes to the conclusion that "magic is not the contradiction of the law of cause and effect but its crowning nightmare." In other words, "to the superstitious mind" cause and effect refer not only to the laws of nature but also to imagination. In magic "every detail is an omen and a cause." But imagination is most actively employed when the spatial and temporal distances are greatest, when causal connection becomes strained. Hence Borges's global geography (China, Egypt, Spain, Britain, Scandinavia, Argentina, the United States) that distributes temporalities—medieval Spain, Anglo-Saxon Britain, Roman Egypt, nineteenth-century Argentina and the United States—on spatial lines. No longer a chronology of progress traced from a European center (France rarely appears on the Borgian map), all pasts are equally valued insofar as they can be activated in the present of reading. Reading is an art that requires polished skills which can be tutored by the very act in which the reader is coached as she goes along. She is coached to be skeptical of true accounts, of faithful reporting, of referentiality, to be wary of narratives that recreate our profile of reality as one more simulacrum, and to enjoy the illusory magic of cause and effect. I hardly need to mention "Death and the Compass," "The Garden of Forking Paths," and "Tlön, Uqbar and Orbis Tertius" to make the point that the reader is led from belief to a void. Indeed, Borges fulfills the secular project of literature at a moment when capitalism is beginning to erode traditional codes, to loosen traditional ties and ridicule existing disciplines (literary criticism in "Pierre Menard, Author of Don Quixote"; history in "Guayaquil"; anthropology in "Brodie's Report"; philosophy in "The Theologians").[49]

Not surprisingly, one of the great themes of Borges is treachery, or more particularly treachery to the person and faithfulness to the abstract. In "The Garden of Forking Paths," one of the protagonists is a Chinese who is spying for the Germans. He murders a specialist in Chinese culture, a certain Albert, in order to send a message to the Germans: when the report of the murder of the Chinese specialist appears in the papers, the nationality of the Chinese and the name of the murdered man, Albert, serve to inform the Germans that their Chinese spy has named the town Albert as the place they are to attack. The story marks the transformation of flesh and blood (Chinese as human being, Albert as a China specialist) into the virtuality of coded signs. As often occurs in Borges, death is a privileged moment of knowledge and consciousness. "He was in his act of magic when the blast obliterated him" are the final words of his story "The Waiting."

In his interviews and the many explanations of his work, Borges invariably insists that art has no relation to reality. Writing of "The Parable of the Palace," he stated that "It's a parable about art existing in its own plane but not being given to deal with reality . . . I mean if art is perfect, then the world is superfluous. I think that the poet never can cope with reality. So I think of art and nature, well, nature as the world, as being two different worlds."[50] Against the grain of these statements, Beatriz Sarlo has argued that "if the defense of the autonomy of art and of formal procedures is one of the pillars of Borges's poetics, the other, more conflictual, pillar is the philosophical and moral problem of the fate of human beings and the forms of their relation to society."[51] But what Borges's fictions rehearse again and again is the end of the social. Its logic is clearly stated in his story *The Utopia of the Tired Man,* in which a twentieth-century traveler comes upon a man of the distant future. In this future, there is no past. People produce in isolation the arts and sciences they need, and the paintings of the man of the future are an almost perfect white. There is no government since the subject has internalized the controls. In an ironic gesture the tired man gives a painting to the narrator before entering a crematorium to seek his voluntary death. What Borges projects into the far-off future is the society of imminence when individuals police themselves and when originality has come to seem as irrelevant as life itself. This ironic view of the libertarian future is worlds distant from the imagined communities of Arguedas and Asturias, but possibly closer to the world as we now find it.

PART THREE

A Cultural Revolution

CHAPTER SEVEN

Cultural Revolutions: Trouble in the City

Different time lines run through these chapters—the rapid time of modern communications, the frozen time of military dictatorships, the retrospective time of memory, and the strange temporalities of residues and remnants of the past. Yet in these different temporalities some events mark both the end of utopias and a cultural revolution— the military regimes in the Southern Cone, the civil wars and the repression in Central America, the economic crisis of the 1980s in Venezuela, the election of Fujimori in Peru. These were not only significant political changes that removed or weakened ideological opposition to neoliberal reform. They also changed the coordinates of people's lives, their expectations, their possibilities. That is what is meant by a cultural revolution. In a more narrow sense, the changes destabilized the literary intelligentsia, altering cultural institutions such as the book industry and forcing a reassessment of the intellectual's relationship to the new order.

This reassessment could not take place during periods of repression and civil war. In times such as these (the 1970s and early 1980s), it took all the ingenuity of writers and artists (as well as human rights workers and others) to break the silence of the media and of substantial sectors of civil society around the atrocities that were being committed.[1] I was privileged to see Catalina Parra's private scrapbook of the post-1973 period in Chile. In it were pasted fragmented news images, citations, a postcard of the notorious stadium where prisoners had been herded just after the coup. In Argentina, during the repression, the nearest that people came to talking about what was happening was in the highly coded references to repression in cartoons and in literary works. In Chile, in contrast, there was a significant revitalization of older avant-garde projects during the military regime. The art actions of Colectivo Acciones de Arte (CADA)—the Art Action Collective—against the institutionalization of art were tolerated because they were not perceived as political. In "Para no morir de Hambre en el Arte" ("Not to Die for Hunger in Art") the artists organized a parade of milk trucks that publicized milk distribution in poor areas. A white sheet was hung over a museum entrance "both as a symbolic closing down of the establishment and a metaphoric denunciation of continuing hunger."[2] In "Ay, Sudamérica," three airplanes dropped leaflets over poor sections of Santiago with the statement that "the work of improving the accepted standard of living is the only valid art form / the only exhibition / the only worthwhile work of art." To be sure, the old avant-garde gestures took on a new significance as the artists invaded the public space that the military had emptied of all opposition. And when the poet, Zurita, attempted to blind himself and Diamela Eltit cut and burned her arms, this focus on the body was a codified reference to other tortured bodies. Although these writers evoked a tradition of Catholic self-abnegation, they also drew attention to the disciplining of bodies by the military regime.

Out of the now anachronistic gestures of avant-garde revolt, there emerged a refractory aesthetic[3] that was powerfully registered by Diamela Eltit in her novel *Lumpérica (E. Luminata)*. Eltit had participated in CADA but she also performed a series of independent actions—for instance she read her novel in a brothel in a poor neighborhood of Santiago and made a video in which she kissed a homeless man, putting into practice a fantasy of social reconciliation.[4] Her novel takes place in the still uncharted territory "where history mingled with hysteria, crime coupled with sales," and where "[t]he signs of negative power fell mercilessly on Chilean bodies, producing disappearances, illegalities, indignities."[5] But *E. Luminata* is as much a staging as a narrative, "a scene not a story" wrote Ronald Christ.[6] Eltit describes her literary method as "working with bits of material, scraps of voices, exploring vaguely (I mean to say like a vagabond) genres, masquerades, simulacra and verbalized emotion."[7]

Set in a public square at night after curfew, when the daytime working people disappear into their homes and only the transgressors are abroad, its woman protagonist performs for a public of pale people—vagabonds who have reappropriated the vacated public space. The only illumination is the intermittent light of a neon sign, which determines what is visible at any moment: it is a sign "of negative power," setting up an interplay between the visual and the verbal, between the icon or fetish and the performative, between the virtual and the real. Photographic cuts, cinematic cuts, cuts in the text, cuts on the human body, on the arms call into question coherent narratives whether national, personal, or biological. The nighttime scenes are staged in an area that witnesses a baptism into the new technological society of control, a filming in which the woman adopts various poses in obedience to the camera work; there is an interrogation in which a witness is repeatedly asked to answer the same questions, a becoming animal, an operation on the woman's body, a series of variations on writing. In the closing scene of the novel, the woman dressed in grey, cuts her hair and turns herself into an anonymous bag lady. In Djelal Kadir's words "she becomes an unreadable text, a paradoxical national autobiography that goes unnoticed and, when perceived, remains unrecognizable except as alterior and aberrant (per)version of the master narrative's history and body politic."[8]

The text itself, as Ronald Christ noted, upsets literary decorum and destabilizes genre in a number of ways: "incursions by drama, verse, film, lyric, epic, fragment . . . violation by breached syntax (inversion of order again), illicit grammar, vulgar and foreign speech, bastard spellings (cacography for calligraphy), dismembered syntax and diction."[9] The critic Eugenia Brito, referring to not only Eltit's work but this new writing describes it as analogous to the repressed body deprived of its mother tongue: "raped, captured, reduced to a ghost, and finally in possession of the Other that administers, arranges its laws, exiles some of its terms and redistributes its body according to a new order that is written, inch by inch, over the nets, the bars imprinted on the captured, wounded and domesticated body.[10]

Lumpérica's protagonist dramatizes both the state's techniques for securing identification and a process of disidentification. Eltit's project is not to invert the male-female hierarchy but rather to maneuver within given space, which is precisely why the novel outlasts the historical moment of its composition. Lumpérica (the abject "lumpen" of the Americas) is not born again as a person but as a project, as a photographic negative of the image of the military. It also registers the exclusion of the "pale people," an exclusion that neoliberalism would reaffirm in a far more benevolent way by replacing overt repression by the subtler repressions of the free market.[11] The promotion of "free markets and democracy" in the 1980s and 1990s was both an economic and political project. Authoritarian governments "cannot manage the expanded social intercourse associated with the global economy" and gave way to new elites who "set out to modernize the state and society without any fundamental deconcentration of property and wealth, or any redistribution of political and economic power."[12]

An intelligentsia different from the humanistic or avant-garde were ensconced in state institutions and in universities, particularly private universities. These were the experts, the economists and specialists in business administration. New kinds of discourse began to circulate that stressed efficiency, transparency, and results but that made limited reference to the immediate past of repression and civil war. Book publication went through drastic changes as large conglomerates such as the Spanish-based Planeta nudged out smaller concerns whose owners had often been book lovers.[13] Artists were increasingly managed by a network of curators and private galleries.[14] It is the often painful readjustment of these "traditional intellectuals" that I discuss in these final chapters.

A Breach in the Lettered City

Early in 1971, the aging leftist José Revueltas, incarcerated in Lucumberri prison for his part in the student demonstrations of 1968, encountered the young writer José Agustín who had been imprisoned for drug possession.[15] The two of them became friends and Agustín would later adapt one of Revueltas's stories as a movie script. Though neither of the participants perceived it as such, the encounter was a passing of the torch from the old vanguard to what had become known as "La Onda" (the Wave). Though by no means apolitical— he had participated in the literacy campaign in Cuba in the early 1960s—Agustín claimed to have been liberated by rock music.[16] He belonged to a youth culture that had experimented with drugs and that shared the freer sexual mores of the hippy life-style. Indeed, by the early 1970s it was evident that rock music was forming the new avant-garde. Music had become the paradigmatic art of the age of mechanical production,[17] redrawing the boundaries between people along generational lines, which seem on the surface to be more egalitarian than class divisions, and using new media technologies of production and dissemination. Music crossed frontiers without much need for translation or adaptation and was thus seen both as a welcome guest but also as a vibrant challenge to national culture. Battle lines were drawn between those who eagerly embraced the rock revolution and those who prized the tradition of "folk" music, which often involved field work by performers such as Atahualpa Yupanqui, Mercedes Sosa, and Violeta Parra. The latter, in particular, was an indefatigable collector of indigenous music and an interpreter and composer of genius at a time when there was little or no interest in folk musical traditions among the intellectual community.[18]

But while Parra and others were interested in the inventiveness and dynamism of popular culture, others defended it as the true culture of the nation. The Brazilian samba singer Clementina de Jesús is described on a record sleeve as contributing to the rebrazilianization of Brazil. "For it cannot be denied that the indiscriminate and unregulated adoption of styles that are alien to our origins and which distort the development of our culture and promote denationalization of the one artistic form that is specific to the people—its music—is typical of underdeveloped cultures such as the Brazilian." The liner notes then launch into an appeal for a national culture less dependent on the marketplace. On the sleeve of a collection of Venezuelan traditional music, "Barlovento" collected by Luis T. Laffer, the work of the collector is described as exemplary given the fact that "many Venezuelans who ought to support this kind of work turn their eyes and ears to foreign groups and display open contempt for our own."

In Colombia, the *vallenato* is considered traditional and authentic even though it is a recent invention.[19] Although, as García Canclini and others have shown, "authentic" music was inevitably transformed as it migrated from villages and small communities to find national and international audiences,[20] the supposed authenticity of folk music was a crucial element in the invented tradition of national culture even when it was not the culture of the majority. A record cover of the music for the Ballet Folklórico Mexicano reads, "The Mexican Department of Tourism appreciates the company's value as a medium for projecting the beauty and riches of Mexico to people of other nations through music and dance." In her short novel, *La extraña muerte de Capitancito Candelario,* Rosario Ferré depicts the battle between Puerto Rican nationalists and statists as a Great Salsa War between *soneros* and *rockeros.*[21] Yet folk music readily adapted itself to the international market and soon "El cóndor pasa" was wailing from every loudspeaker. Industrialization and technical advances along with migration made possible the new hybrids and crossover styles. Even protest music was internationalized. The opposition between the nation (folk) and the foreign (rock) was soon eclipsed by the proliferation of fusions and hybrids that registered both the racial heterogeneity of the region and the technological advances of the record industry.[22]

The folk versus rock controversy was the surface manifestation of a far deeper problem: the issue of modernization that was increasingly measured by the outward signs of modernity—style, "modern" manners, and an emphasis on youth, transmitted by media that were far more difficult to control than print culture. When in 1960 Mexico passed the Federal Law of Radio and Television, its aim was to nullify the "noxious or disturbing influences on the harmonious development of children and youth"—which of course betrayed the presence of precisely those noxious influences; it also stated that radio and television was to "contribute to the cultural elevation of the population and to conserve its national characteristics, customs and traditions, the propriety of the language and to exalt the values of Mexican nationality."[23] In authoritarian Mexico, the music industry tried to modify rock's initial impact and convert it into a "nonthreatening vehicle for the expression of liberalism and leisure consumption,"[24] an image that became difficult to sustain once rock emigrated from the middle to the lower classes.

Thanks to its border with the United States, Mexico was particularly open to influences from the north, not only to rock music but to hippie counterculture. Thus the unintended consequence of the power of the U.S. music industry was that it also exported a youthful dissidence that was taken up by the writers of La Onda and chronicled in the writing of José Agustín, Gustavo Sainz, and García Saldaña.[25] Carlos Monsiváis described La Onda as "the school and university" of a youth culture which refused to belong to "the Great National Family."[26] Although in the 1950s and early 1960s rock music attracted mainly middle-class youths, many of whom had visited the

United States and who had the money to buy records and attend concerts, by the early 1970s rock festivals in Avándaro, Mexico and in Buenos Aires demonstrated its mass appeal. It had an anti-authoritarian ethos despite the fact that it raised fears in some circles that it was a tool of imperialism—a foreign influence, alien to "the nature of our lives and ideology."[27] Among the middle classes, the fluidity, style, and unconventionality of the counterculture was a welcome departure from rigid attitudes, formality, and "good" manners. Bodies became less disciplined, looser, unashamedly sensuous in contrast to all those disciplinary standards implied in words such as "recato" (modesty) and "viril" (virile). Hair was an especially controversial issue; unruly and long hair was emblematic of transgression and excess. The Chilean and Argentine military cropped the hair of hippies (or worse) as did the police in Mexico.

The rock festival at Avándaro in 1971, described as the Mexican Woodstock, constituted both the apocalyptic climax and "the ruined paradise of the Onda." "The young people there publicly liquidated traditional morality but were incapable of consolidating any visible alternatives to what they opposed," Carlos Monsiváis wrote.[28] At the other end of the continent, in Argentina, rock music's anti-authoritarianism became a form of youthful resistance to government oppression. Juxtaposing itself against "complacent music," Argentine rock tended with some exceptions to eschew the violence of the Left and Right, but its followers were continually hounded by police even before the military government took power. Temporarily eclipsed at the height of military repression, when rock music could not be transmitted by radio or television, it reemerged as a dissident voice.[29]

Youth cultures had their own language, an urban slang born out of drug and American counterculture, and the young writers of La Onda were savvy in street slang, the drug culture, and music. José Agustín, writer and rock aficionado, discovered that dance was an inventive form of nonverbal language that could liberate the body. Carlos Monsiváis contrasted the institutional language of officialdom "without vacillations, doubts, programmatic which is felt as a fortification of the class in power or the culmination of a repressive confidence" and "this language of yes and no, of 'simón' and 'nelazo.' . . . The lines are drawn. On the one hand transcendence, the language elaborated by a Mexican society which demands the attention of History, respect from other countries, the blessing of God and of the symbols of nationality and of the fellow citizens. On the other hand, immanence, that guarantee of Being, located in its epidermis by gods that can finally be grasped."[30] The words are extraordinarily prescient, marking as they do the postmodern shift from disciplining by parents and school to pleasurable acquiescence to the market.[31] The entire concept of the avant-garde had shifted from the literary tertulia to the hip.

By the 1990s, it was clear that Mexican society was no longer divided along class lines but segmented according to taste. "Whilst some follow Brahms, Sting and Carlos Fuentes, other prefer Julio Iglesias, Alejandra Guzmán and Venezuelan soap operas."[32] New rhythms not only dominated the air waves and television channels but synchronized with the rhythms of the new city that was emerging from the old, a city that was both material and virtual.

Rapid Transit

I left Mexico City in 1957 and returned in 1967 to a place that I hardly recognized. I left a city of clear air and breathtaking views of the volcanoes and the Ajusco mountain, a city where people traveled on public transport to the center to meet friends, to go to concerts, to shop. But 1957 was also the year Volkswagen began its assault on the city while Mayor Uruchurtu pushed his program of modernization. Soon there were cars everywhere; the middle-class population emigrated south toward the University City; freeways stretched across town, dividing barrios and enveloping nearby buildings in a constant traffic roar. What strikes me now is not so much the change itself that was happening everywhere but its rapidity. Within a generation, the Mexico enshrined in Elena Poniatowska's photographic essay *El último guajalote (The Last Turkey)* had almost gone.[33] That was the Mexico of street vendors, of uncrowded streets and unhurried pedestrians. It was also the Mexico depicted in José Emilio Pacheco's novel *Batallas en el desierto (Battles in the Desert)* as already in a state of subtle erosion.[34] It was not only the appearance of the city that had changed but its entire culture, as well as its language.

La Onda tapped into the nervous system of this rapidly changing Mexico City. In Gustavo Sainz's best-selling novel *Gazapo,* the city is already losing its familiar contours. A group of youths meet in Sanborns, patrol the city streets in their cars, tape-record one another, talk on the telephone, read comic strips. The very technologies at their disposal separate them from their parent's generation for they are freed from the spatial limitations of particular barrios and of familial control.[35]

Cities could no longer be narrativized in the old way as if, however chaotic, they still offered the possibility of community.[36] Fragmentary urban experience changed syntax and even the appearance of the words on the page as writers sought some correlative to the multiplicity of simultaneous perceptions. In 1962, a Chilean parodic "newspaper" *El Quebrantahuesos* resorted to a collage of fragments—cuttings of newspaper headlines, articles, and advertisements—to illustrate the new sensibility. In place of the older concerns with origins, originality, teleology, and identity, the editors substituted quotation (without an acknowledged source), simultaneity, and repetition.[37] In Brazil, advertisement influenced the layout of concrete poetry.[38] And throughout Latin America the new urban culture drastically altered the environment that had nourished literary culture.

In the posthumously published *The Lettered City,* the Uruguayan critic Ángel Rama traced the history of the lettered and their relation to power from the colonial period to the near present. Describing the intellectual environment in the early years of the twentieth century, he wrote that in order to identify the homes of intellectuals during this period—their workplaces, the universities, cafes, brothels, and bookstores they frequented—one need only to cover a few blocks of the old city.[39] Though this intimate environment did not altogether disappear with modernization, it was not long before literary cafes turned into historical landmarks or disappeared altogether.[40] The intellectual's relation to power also changed after the 1960s when literary celebrities began to lose some of their influence to professional economists, educators, and image makers.

Urban culture stratified the public in ways that were very different from the past. Instead of peasants and workers, there were now "rockeros" and "cocoleros." These youth cultures had a different look from the old national stereotypes, and their members were more interested in looking like their counterparts in other countries than in conforming to a national ideal. In the 1940s, Octavio Paz had been horrified by the hybrid Californian "pachuco" (the Mexican immigrant identifiable by his exaggerated clothes), describing him as a "clown," as a contradictory figure who invited persecution and yet wanted to belong, a strange creature who occupied an indeterminate space between the solitude of the Mexican and the solitude of the North American.[41] Yet even at this stage, the fractured language of the popular comedian Cantinflas reflected more accurately than anything in literature the instability of the marginalized immigrant to the city. By the late 1960s, thanks to radio, television, and the record industry, it was not easy to identify what was authentically national.

In 1970 a survey of eighteen Latin American cities revealed that about 31.4 percent of television programming was North American. A survey of 1973 listed 84 percent for Guatemala.[42] This can be attributed in part to the U.S. pioneer development of the technology, but there was also a flood of journals and magazines such as *Reader's Digest* and *Vogue* that were published in Spanish. Except for soap operas, which drew on a tradition of melodrama, the format of television programming was shaped from the north. In the early years, the gap between what was seen on the television and cinema screen and everyday life scandalized many intellectuals and fueled the debate over cultural imperialism that came to a head in Chile in 1972–73 during the media war that was being conducted against the Allende regime. Armand Mattelart and Ariel Dorfman's *How to Read Donald Duck*, which revealed the subliminal messages of Disney comics and warned of their insidious influence, was widely influential; the publication of its translation was banned in the United States.[43] The "free flow of information" advocated by the United States in international gatherings was therefore greeted with suspicion in many parts of the world, particularly in Latin America, because the technical superiority of the United States ensured that the free flow was predominantly from north to south. However, this defensiveness soon gave way to a more nuanced appreciation of the media and new forms of cultural literacy.

In their writing on mass and popular culture, critics such as Jesús Martín Barbero in Colombia and García Canclini in Mexico refused to adopt the divisions of high and low culture, placing literature within a spectrum that ranged from the orality of radio to the appropriation of older forms adapted to the extended public of television.[44] In a seminal book, *De los medios a las mediaciones (From Media to Mediations)*, Jesús Martín Barbero showed that while television in Latin America was in lockstep with theories of development that were introduced in the 1960s, it also required new forms of cultural competence. In its use of specific genres such as melodrama, now revitalized as soap opera, television represented, albeit in a diluted fashion, sectors of society that had hitherto been off the cultural map.

García Canclini emphasized the globalizing thrust of the media in the context of mass immigration to the cities and pointed out that Latin America had gone from being predominantly dispersed peasant societies that often had little contact with the rest of the nation to being a heterogeneous urban society bound together by local, national, and global networks.[45] Energies that had once flowed into national ceremonies and mass demonstrations are now dispersed among different communities and interests that map the city with their own invisible or visible itineraries. Though urban gangs still claim territories, these can be virtual: gangs mark their passage through the city with coded graffiti. The pathways of the women street vendors in Mexico City or of the gays cruising in São Paulo are both virtual and material. Most of all, and despite the gated communities that protect the rich, the city street is still the contact zone between cultures.[46]

The Unimaginable Community

The Latin American population explosion and immigration is of such magnitude that it is hard to imagine the megalopolis as a community. Bogotá, the "Athens of America," has grown in the past three decades from a city of 300,000 inhabitants to a city of 5 million. Mexico City is the most populated on the planet.[47] The *favelas* of Rio and the crowded hillsides of Caracas and Lima, where people do not even have water but must buy it or walk down the hillside to a spigot and then labor up again—such slums nestle by the freeways, the high-rise hotels and the shopping malls as visible threats that have sent the upper classes to refuges in gated communities. In 1982 in Caracas, riots and lootings turned threats into reality. The opening sentences of Vargas Llosa's novel *The Real Life of Alejandro Mayta* eloquently convey the middle class fear and loathing of the contamination that comes about when cities are no longer orderly. The once exclusive suburbs of Lima have been converted into a dung heap on which the lumpen struggle for survival. "If you live in Lima you have to get used to poverty and filth or go mad and commit suicide" the narrator concludes.[48] For a character in a novel by Fernando Vallejo, Medellín is "a capital of hate, heart of the vast kingdoms of Satan," in which the urge to kill competes with the rage to reproduce.[49]

The boundaries of the megalopolis are continually changing and the relationship to a hinterland is either blurred or, as in the case of the global city described by Saskia Sassen, its economy no longer has any relationship to its location.[50] New York, Tokyo, and London are global cities interconnected by electronic transactions while the infrastructures of goods and producers are scattered throughout the globe. This is, of course, true of sectors of many Third World cities that have rapidly shed custom and tradition in favor of corporate homogeneity. Examples are too numerous to mention but having observed the growth of Mexico City over the years, I found one such change particularly disconcerting. When I lived there in the 1950s, Mexico City was still a series of districts, the *"colonias"*—Roma, Narvarte, Doctores, Polanco—each one with its unique ambiance. When in the late 1950s highways were built through the city, many of these old *colonias* were split apart, divided from themselves. Life drained from the city's old center, which eventually was fashioned to be a "historic district" to attract tourists, while a freeway cut through *colonias* like Mixcoac stretching southward toward the crowning glory the Perisur shopping mall. But what touched me most of all was the removal of El Caballito, an equestrian statue on Mexico City's Reforma Avenue that had always served as a useful landmark between the Zona Rosa and the Alameda. The statue was replaced by a compromise monument—an abstract object that still retained something of the shape of a horse but was more in keeping with the corporate headquarters that now line the avenue.

This latter-day modernization is quite different from that of an early period when modernist literature and art took inspiration from the layout and sounds of the city. In her book *Una modernidad periférica*, Beatriz Sarlo argued that the paintings of Xul Solar, for instance, reflected modernity by depicting "modern chimerae-airplane men, with bird heads and chimneys for bodies."[51] But nowadays the signs of the modernist city have become completely scrambled; memories are insecure as city centers disappear or are remodeled and as populations move further into the suburbs. And since the megalopolis cannot be imagined as a totality, community, identity, and subjectivity have had to be rethought or refashioned from fragments and ruins. Not surprisingly in this situation there is a preoccupation with maps, lost landmarks, fragments of information, and, as I mention in Chapter 10, with the uncertainty of memory in the aftermath of historical trauma. Philosophers, urban planners, and social scientists contributing to prestigious journals such as *Punto de vista* (Buenos Aires), *Nueva sociedad* (Caracas), and *Revista de crítica cultural* (Chile) are obsessed not only with the baffling hermeneutics of the megalopolis but also with the difficulty of deriving any notion of *comunitas* from its pollution-ridden environment, its traffic-jammed streets, and the violence of everyday life.[52] In his book *Hybrid Cultures,* García Canclini approached Mexico City as a traveler whose journey takes him across different zones of cultural change.[53] What happens, he asked, to the lettered city when the literary pundit becomes the television talking head? What happens to monumental history when it is recast for the tourist trade? And what happens when information and culture flow along cable networks and telephone lines that connect distant places and link a city internationally?[54]

The ideal order that had made the city such a powerful symbol for the national community and for civic conduct, even if it never really coincided with the real city, is now impossible to reclaim. Indeed, one could argue that the vibrancy, the ephemeral encounters, the vertiginous changes, the infinite ruses of survival have made the city the trope of disorder, of spontaneity and chance though without (because of the international style of contemporary architecture) the fresh shock experienced by Benjamin's *flâneur* since everything seems familiar because it looks like everywhere else, so that even local color— a market, a mosque, whatever—is often the obligatory variation required by the tourist industry. And though cities are still administrative centers, real power is concentrated in the anonymous modern buildings that house high-tech communities, insurance firms, and banks or in the shopping malls.

What are the new images of the city? Ángel Rama as early as 1973 described Italo Calvino's *Invisible Cities* as a key work of our literary culture that takes into account the new social situations and myths of the contemporary world.[55] Published in 1970, *Invisible Cities* is a description of imaginary cities invented by young Marco Polo to entertain Kubla Khan, who is already old and contemplating the end of his empire.[56] Because, like Borges's fictions, Calvino's *Invisible Cities* have no particular referent in the real world nor are they utopian in the usual sense, they have encouraged speculation about subjects as varied as nomadic versus hierarchical thinking (Gerald Bruns),[57] the impossibility of the notion of the autonomy of literature (Timothy

Reiss),[58] and the foundation of society on the exclusion of women (De Lauretis).[59] Classified into cities and memory, cities and desire, cities and signs, thin cities, trading cities, cities and eyes, cities and the dead—all are enigmatic. The city of Zaira, for example, "does not tell its past, but contains it like the lines of a hand, written in the corners of the streets, the gratings of the windows, the banisters of the steps, the antennae of the lightning rods, the poles of the flags, every segment marked in turn with scratches, indentations, scrolls."

But what has proved seductive to many Latin Americans is that, while enigmatic, Calvino's cities evoke the mystery of living in a present in which the signposts have disappeared. "Cities, like dreams, are made of desires and fears, even if the thread of their discourse is secret, their rules are absurd, their perspectives deceitful, and everything conceals something else." But to what desires and fears do they correspond? José Joaquín Brunner, a social scientist who was minister of communication in Chile's government of "concertación" (which means harmony, adjustment, agreement), believes Calvino's city of Tamara to be a more accurate model for contemporary Latin America than García Márquez's city of Macondo.[60] Macondo, it will be recalled, was organized on the basis of the *oikos,* the domestic economy of the family of the Buendías who initially fled from the sea and hence from competitive global commerce. But Macondo is passé, for it "was nothing more than the nostalgic dream of the literary intelligentsia—a city of words—whose project of a Latin American alternative to Western capitalism never reached the masses. Tamara, on the other hand, is not a city of words but of signs, a "dance of signs," "signs that ceaselessly dance so that identities are made and unmade and constituted as the changing subjects of modernity." Tamara has definitely replaced the "ingenuous consciousness and the glorious natural state of Macondamérica. These are traditions that no longer exist for they are buried under the signs that dance in the conscience of Tamaramérica, communicating the discovery of its own modernity."[61] What Brunner ignores, writing after the end of the repressive Pinochet regime, is that the joyful dance of signs also includes tacit prohibitions. In Calvino's city, there are signs that indicate "what is forbidden in a given place (to enter the alley with wagons, to urinate behind the kiosk, to fish with your pole from the bridge) and signs that tell the inhabitants what is permitted (watering zebras, playing bowls, burning relatives' corpses)." If Tamara is the image of the contemporary city, what new prohibitions and exclusions does the dance of the signs conceal?[62]

No Respect

The megalopolis disorients the writer and the critic. Do I sink into the anonymity of the mass or am I carried to the height of celebrity? Is my Mont Blanc pen still a status symbol now that radio and television are in the ascendancy and cultural fashions are increasingly global? If I am no longer in the avant-garde, where do I stand? Knowing but distanced writers observe their own society as if it were an alien planet. Is the universal now global mass culture and the best-seller its literary manifestation? And if so, is there any room left for the public intellectual?

The Urban Chronicle

The urban chronicle published in daily newspapers has provided a provisional asylum. Originating in the nineteenth century when access to print culture set the writer apart, and as a by-product of journalism,[63] the urban chronicle had always been directly engaged with modernization and has now become a handy vehicle for registering change without resorting to the allegorical mode of the urban novels of the early 1960s *(La ciudad y los perros, La región más transparente),* in which the city was often a microcosm of the nation and the writer an all-seeing eye. The contemporary chronicler is on the streets, exposed to the risks and dangers of urban life, which he or she must negotiate like everybody else. In Edgardo Rodríguez Juliá's chronicle, *Cortijo's Funeral,* for example, the writer attends the wake and the burial of the popular *plena* musician Cortijo in a housing project in San Juan, Puerto Rico.[64] White-skinned and of Hispanic descent, he finds himself jostled in the crowd of blacks and mulattos in the Llorens Torres project which, as he points out, was incongruously baptized by the welfare state of Muñoz Marín and named after a romantic poet. No longer comfortably privileged as a detached observer, and armed with a Mont Blanc pen that only he recognizes as a status symbol, the writer finds that he has become the observed—and not only observed but judged as a "mamao," a jerk, a soft touch for whom the drug addict's slang is like a foreign tongue. All that the chronicler can record are surfaces—clothing styles, the messages on T-shirts, and the gestures of a group of men as they tell a joke that he cannot hear. But beneath the surface he detects the archaeological residues of a historical narrative of Puerto Rico: model for development, welfare state, a racially divided community in which black musicians had to make their reputation outside Puerto Rico. The chronicler must attend to the discontinuities, the fragments. But how does one read a crowd composed of singularities so pronounced that even individual subjects carry contradictory messages? Consider this description of a mulatto dockworker: "His shirt with its design of palm trees which he wears outside his pants, scarcely conceals the hard dock worker's muscles; the color of the exalted tropical twilight almost belies the work that has gone into his enormous torso. For the poor, fashion is not always an emblem of social condition. Perhaps he bought this shirt of palm trees and beaches in the sunset so that he could bask in the arcadia of his Beautiful Borinquén?" (pp. 18–19). A lot is packed into this description—the patent absurdity of the shirt's message of leisure in the life of a working man; a Third World that lives on bricolage, recycling, and the second hand; and the transformation of the Puerto Rican pastoral myth of Borinquén into a T-shirt design sold to tourists and then picked up in a sale by those excluded from the leisure activities it promises. Mass culture has produced a certain egalitarianism at least in attitudes if not in wealth, and this means that hierarchies—political or religious—are no longer respected. Even Rubén Blades who puts in an appearance at the funeral is not immune from the general disrespect and is mocked as a "pendejo" (a jerk).

This does not mean that mass society is more democratic, simply that it is volatile and unpredictable. When the crowds have dispersed, the sound of a few notes of Cortijo's music played on the guitar evokes the possibility of a kind of *permanencia* in the form of the musical phrase, which will be played, reinterpreted, transformed. While Rodríguez Juliá acknowledges that "tradition explodes into a thousand conflictive fragments," he also asks "how can we reconcile so much craziness with so much tenderness?" Affect can no longer be canalized into patriotism, socialism, official religion, or even literature, so that it is music—the same notes played by different people at different moments—that corresponds to something like Lyotard's "petit histoire," a form of temporality that he described as "simultaneously evanescent and immemorial."[65] The writer clings precariously to such fragments, his survival now depending on wit, rather than on any hope of "permanencia."

"Lo fugitivo permanece" (the ephemeral persists), which could apply to *Cortijo's Funeral,* is in fact the title of an anthology compiled by another urban chronicler, the Mexican Carlos Monsiváis, who did more than anyone to revive the genre. Aware that the pedagogical role of the lettered city and the utopianism of the city of words belong to the past, that the writer is now engaged in a game of survival that is also perhaps a struggle against anonymity, Monsiváis tirelessly monitors the urban scene and in particular the new protagonist—the multitude—"the multitude within the multitude," "the multitudes in the metro," "the multitudes (of students taking exams) in the University Stadium," "the whirlpool of traffic."[66] The writer's relation to that multitude has now changed. No longer set apart he occasionally dives into the mass, becoming one of the crowd, one of those who never stood out in the first place or who stood out for the wrong reasons—because of the color of skin or heterodox behavior. His only claim to difference is his wit.

Monsiváis's radio broadcasts and his witty articles made him a well-known figure in the student demonstrations of 1968, which were brought to an end October 2 with the massacre at Tlatelolco. In that year, Mexico had hosted the Olympic games, an event that poured money into the arts. An avenue of sculptures led to the new Olympic City and thousands of people, including writers, were employed in the preparations. But on July 26, the anniversary of the Cuban Revolution, police units attacked a preparatory school with bazookas, thus violating the autonomy of the university which had been a sacred principle of postrevolutionary governments. "Autonomy" theoretically meant that within the university there was free speech. The attack on the *Preparatoria* inaugurated weeks of protest demonstrations that the government of Díaz Ordaz immediately condemned as "[a] subversive movement that tends to create a hostile environment for our government and our country on the eve of the XIX Olympic Games." (Un movimiento subversivo que tiende a crear un ambiente de hostilidad para nuestro gobierno y nuestro país en vísperas de los juegos de la XIX Olimpiada).[67] When army tanks entered the university, a massive demonstration was organized on a historic site—the Plaza de Tres Cultures (The Plaza of Three Cultures), the site where the Aztecs put up their last fight against the Spaniards before the occupation of Tenochtitlán. The "three cultures" refer to the Aztec ruins, the colonial church, and the modern apartment buildings for middle-class residents; it is meant to symbolize the synthesis of different elements within the nation. Claiming that they had been fired on, the army launched an attack on the demonstrators, an unknown number of whom were killed. The violent suppression of the student movement in order to secure civic tranquility during the Olympic Games was a harbinger of things to come, as the government and the army colluded not only in occupying the university but in violently evicting the demonstrators from public space.

Though Tlatelolco was a minor incident when compared to the magnitude of the repression in the Southern Cone during the military governments, when thousands of people disappeared, it was devastating to the participants and a setback to democratization. The analysis of the incident would obsess several Mexican writers, among them Elena Poniatowska, Octavio Paz, and Carlos Monsiváis.[68] Each of these writers recognized that, however much the student demonstrations had followed the pattern of earlier protests, they represented something new—the emergence of an urban youth culture that was also a political culture. Elena Poniatowska's best-selling collage of eyewitness accounts and newspaper reports, *Massacre in Mexico,* hinted at government and army collusion in the massacre. It also pitted the voices of the younger generation against those of its more rigid and conventional elders. Octavio Paz, at that time the most renowned Mexican public intellectual, resigned as ambassador to India in protest over Tlatelolco, stating that the students aimed "to make public life truly public" through reform and not through revolution. Monsiváis's writing down to the present has been deeply affected by the event, and he has monitored the social and political consequences of Tlatelolco in the pages of *Siempre, Excelsior,* and *La Jornada,* acutely analyzing the often baffling spectacle of its aftermath.

While Paz stated that, with modernity, Mexicans had become contemporaries of the rest of the world, Monsiváis's sarcastic observation is that they aspire to be contemporaries of the nineteenth century.[69] "The alchemy of our country includes the transformation of the bar of gold into a copper ashtray." In an article entitled "Me and My friends," he explored the meaning that "friend" acquires in the politics of cronyism, the way that it papers over the cracks in national unity that the student demonstrators of 1968 had briefly opened up.

While Tlatelolco had exposed the myth of national unity, with the defeat of the student movement, divisions were once again sealed by myths of "friendship" and inclusion. "Unite, incorporate yourselves, join, assimilate. Don't lag behind. Come to the prize giving and the awards, come to the Great Game, to the Friendship Celebration. You are at home, consider yourself a member of the family."[70]

Instead of adopting a consistent voice, Monsiváis goes with the flow wherever that takes him, adapting his voice to the occasion. Thanks to a Protestant and provincial upbringing, he brings to the megalopolis the disabused eye of the outsider who can pass as an insider, writing in a style that is a mixture of sermon, sarcasm, and ventriloquism with echoes of the Bible, the cartoon, and ethnography. His project is encyclopedic: nothing less than a blow-by-blow account of Mexico's path to modernization explored in every fleeting manifestation of its culture, as well as the sparks of dissidence that briefly glowed in 1968 and that he continues to track in strikes, in new forms of political action, but also in mass culture itself. He uses the language of the Bible, advertisement, pop culture—citing popular songs and banal poetry. The distance from the masses, carefully preserved even by the populist intelligentsia, disappears in Monsiváis's writing, which turns the traditional concept of artistic value on its head. It is no surprise to find such protagonists of canonical Latin American literary texts as Doña Barbara and Arturo Cova rubbing shoulders with Eva Perón and the singer Jorge Negrete as examples of middle (and not high) camp, and he follows a recital by Berta Singerman, the last representative of the art of recitation, as avidly as a concert by the Doors.[71] His first book, *Días de guardar (Holy Days of Observance)*, is an example of cultural studies before they were labeled as such.

It is precisely the boundaries between the socially acceptable and the unacceptable that Monsiváis patrols. He was quick to understand that globalized urban culture had not only outstripped both the rigid political system and the hidebound morality of the Catholic Church but that faster travel, television, radio, and the record industry had introduced anti-authoritarian attitudes that were not necessarily channeled into politics. Cultural clashes were the overt manifestations of this juxtaposition of tradition and modernity. In two collections of urban chronicles, *Amor Perdido (Lost Love)* and *Escenas de pudor y liviandad (Scenes of Modesty and Frivolity),* he writes an unusual history of Mexico, tracking it through its popular celebrities and through its attitudes to sexuality. In these collections, there is no separation between high and low culture, between public figures and vaudeville artists. In *Amor Perdido,* for instance, the leader of the official trade union movement Fidel Velázquez shares a slot as "My Unforgettable Personality" with Miss Mexico, and the writer Salvador Novo figures in "This Is Really Scandalous" alongside the performance artists Irma Serrano and Isela Vega.

What Monsiváis identifies as a recurrent characteristic of Mexico is an incessant search for transcendence, however bizarre. As a secular intellectual he is acutely aware that desire and fear are more powerful than rational decisionmaking and that God is far from dead. In 1970, witnessing the convergence of young people on Oaxaca and Puerto Ensenada to observe the eclipse, he wrote an article, "God Never Dies," that proved to be prophetic. Years of secular education had failed to eradicate religious experience. "Centuries in which a rationalist minority failed to explain anything to a superstitious majority, decades of positivism implanted by means of an all-embracing pedagogical decision have neither taken fear into account nor dissipated it."

The titles of some of his collections, *Días de guardar (Holy Days of Observance), Nuevo Catequismo para indios remisos (New Cathecism for Lapsed Indians), Los rituales del caos (Rituals of Chaos)* are a tongue-in-cheek recognition of contemporary religiosity. For while in many countries of Latin America the church has reestablished its authority as arbiter of morals, leading campaigns against abortion and gay rights, religious experience also flows into the new spaces afforded by the megalopolis. In *Rituals of Chaos,* he describes a society in which patriotism, religion, morality, the private, the personal, and the sacred have all lost their aura, replaced by spectacles or ritual involving an endless recycling of whatever is at hand.[72] The availability of global cultures has loosened the grip of Catholic religion, traditional morality, and the national imaginary. People are free to seek other forms of faith, however extravagant—the ritual of a *lucha libre* match that pits good against evil (one of the Mexican fighters calls himself "The Saint"); the chauvinistic public at a boxing match; the rituals of pilgrims shuffling on their knees to the shrine of the Virgin of Guadalupe, and the heterogeneous celebrations at the shrine that mingle religion, nationalism, ethnicity, and pop culture.

People make sense of their lives, discover meaningful rituals and narratives, outside the structures provided by schooling or religion.

One of Monsiváis's most interesting conclusions is that individualism based on the integrity of the body is no longer possible in a mass society. The Mexican subway is so crowded that the limits of the body that had once defined the individual disappear in the mass so that even the sexual pleasure of bodily contact is diffused. The idea of private or individual life has become senseless in a city where the inside of the house is more crowded than the street and originality is nonsense when "we are so many that even the most eccentric thought is shared by millions" (p. 112). As for community, what holds the shifting crowd together may be nothing more than their fleeting copresence in the subway, at a conference, or attending a football match. Yet, far from adopting the apocalyptic tone of many of his contemporaries, Monsiváis celebrates all those movements and flows that exceed the disciplining limits imposed by the state.

In the megalopolis, then, the chronicler can no longer imitate Baudelaire's individualistic *flâneur* observing the crowd from the margins, but must survive by wit. Given the fact that "the most eccentric thought is shared by millions," wit *(ingenio)* and not originality is the mark of distinction, as it was (though for different reasons) in the seventeenth century. Monsiváis is the ventriloquist adopting the voice of adolescents, cultists, singers, defenders of morality, satire, and even the discourse of the sociologist, but always with that edgy hip take that makes him more than a mere chronicler. In a world that rhetorically values dialogue and the exchange of opinions, but processes these in the banality of the television interview, wit is the everyday ruse of survival adopted by the inhabitants of the modern city. Precisely because this particular wit has its origin in the Mexican tradition of the *albur* and *socarronería,* it is immediately recognized and celebrated across the national spectrum, though it is not necessarily exportable. Certainly his influence has been immense. During the 1997 Mexican elections, Monsiváis's satire of the morality codes of the conservative Partido de Acción Nacional (PAN) is said to have contributed to its third-place finish and to have helped Cuauhtémoc Cárdenas be elected mayor of Mexico City.

In choosing to intervene in this way, Monsiváis clears a road for letters where it is least expected—within the modern media and in the intersection between orality and print culture. Journalism, formerly relegated to a position below the literary, in however a limited manner, offers a place where the arms of the enemy can be turned against him. For decades, Monsiváis has used his column "Por mi madre, bohemios" ("A Toast to my Mother, Fellow-Bohemians") to reprint outrageous quotations from speeches by statesmen, politicians, and church officials. Thus, though the new urban culture may have sent literature to the margins, there is still a place in the press for the public intellectual.

CHAPTER EIGHT

The Seduction of Margins

Peter Stalleybrass and Allon White have argued that the low, internalized "under the sign of negation and disgust, consolidates and give sense to the high," and that "disgust always bears the imprint of desire."[1] What counted as "high culture" implied boundaries and margins that could only be crossed by imperiling the integrity they maintained. Yet tramps, outcasts, layabouts, the unspeakable, the "something" persistently haunt the portals of the literary institution as if they are the ghosts of a guilty conscience, demanding admittance. In Julio Cortázar's *Rayuela,* the signature Latin American novel of the 1960s, an encounter with a homeless tramp tests both the conventions of the genre and the conventions of gender. The protagonist Oliveira, though overcome by nausea and disgust, finds himself screwing the stinking clocharde Emmanuèle; and all the time he harbors the vague hope that he might discover the *kibbutz* (one of Cortázar's words for community) in the experience. True this descent into the lower depths has been a commonplace since Rimbaud tested literature's limits, but in the 1960s it was still a shock to the decorum of Latin American high culture in which the low and the racially other, when represented at all, were incorporated into a pedagogical or political scenario primarily as victims. But sentimental tears, as Gillian Rose wrote, "leave us politically and emotionally intact," as of course does any protest that does not involve risk.[2] Like Narciso in Raúl Ruiz's *On Top of the Whale,* which I mentioned in Chapter 6, the social protest writer knew that he lived on top of the bones of the conquered Indians but believed that writing a book about them absolved him from any responsibility for this past and answered any challenge to his status in the present.

But for many writers, particularly in the Caribbean, the racially other was erotically as well as politically charged. The *mulata,* in particular, had often represented "the desire for cultural synthesis," as had the *mestizo* in Indo-America, notwithstanding the awkwardness of claiming regional specificity based on sexual domination.[3] In the writing of Rosario Ferré of Puerto Rico, on the other hand, the black woman and the *mulata* have a potential for covert rebellion that has simmered for centuries thanks to colonialism's potent legacy.

Ferré grew up in the town of Ponce at a time when one of its worthiest citizens was a woman who, after working as a prostitute, had become the wealthy owner of a brothel. This well-known local personality, on whom she based the character Isabel la Negra in the story "When Women Love Men," led Ferré to believe that the victim of sexual exploitation could manage "to turn the exploitation around in her favor."[4] The women in her story still inhabit the structures set in place by Hispanic colonialism that had separated black from white, bad from good, inferior from superior, pure from impure. Whereas men could sometimes negotiate between these categories, women could not. Don Ambrosio had married the blond, upper-class Isabel Luberza but had taken Isabel la Negra as his lover. On his death, he left his house to be shared between the wife and the mistress, although their economic situations were now reversed. Isabel Luberza had become impoverished and Isabel la Negra, owner of a successful brothel, had grown rich. But as joint narrators of the story, their voices gradually blend as if each were an incomplete version of the other. When Isabel Luberza opens the door, "Isabel la Negra went weak at the knees. She was still so beautiful, I had to lower my eyes: I almost didn't dare look at her." For her part, Isabel Luberza imagines Isabel la Negra as "bewitchingly beautiful, her skin dark as night." Their symbiosis heals the breach created by the representation of women as temptress and saint in the context of patriarchal societies whose social fabric depended on favor, that is, on a masculine network of personal connections fortified by hierarchy. For Ferré, the exploitation of women binds them in a common cause irrespective of social inequality. It is precisely this utopian possibility that other writers cast in doubt.

The Scopic Regime

Power seduces. The penis is the instrument of phallic power, that which activates meaning and fantasy. In a series of vignettes entitled *Espejismos (Mirages)* by the Argentine writer Tununa Mercado, the male organ or its surrogate exercises a deadly fascination. A woman shopping in a busy marketplace, redolent with the scent of fruit and spices, becomes aware of a sound emerging

> from a crack in the ground, a subterranean prison that nobody ever knew existed from a hell that was assumed but never acknowledged by the powerful bustle outside; it emits a voiceless call, pure signal that turns out to come from a hook, the hook of somebody who has no hand and from that place, from this presumed tunnel underground, the hook appears and moves from one side to another, signals, with its sharp point takes hold of the edges and pulls, as if this tug would bring salvation, the promised rescue . . . The hook gropes, seeks, finds the firm point to grasp, trying to get the attention of a passer-by, trying to make someone notice his signal, and bend over to look into the darkness, inciting people to gaze into the hole from which it cries out though this cry is merely a grating sound, the squeal of the point of the hook on the edges, a petition submerged by the commotion outside, almost an inaudible whisper that, little by little, makes a transition from pointed steel to the bland material of flesh, deliberately flexible but without the force of conviction, without forte or pianissimo, a few feet from the tiny pyramids of chiles and mangos, at a few steps from the passers-by he is trying to attract and at a short distance from the eye which from its prison, the cripple's hook, the prosthesis of the dark subterranean inhabitant, slides, disappears and reappears and again recuperates for a few moments, the tension in the mouth of the floor, until it's nothing but a very fine tongue, whip, or snake that neither harms nor corrupts, but simple links and advances, trying out the possibilities of coming out, studying the situation outside.[5]

This minidrama of search, tension, and liberation rivets the protagonist precisely because the human actor is invisible, represented only by the prosthesis that is "tongue, whip, or snake," in other words language, domination and temptation. Notwithstanding his situation, the mutilated man still has the instruments of freedom while the woman-observer can only watch. Although never made explicit, the incident raises the question of whether the phallic power of the male antecedes the social.

Impossible Communion

In a fragment, "A Bela e a Fera" ("Beauty and the Beast"),[6] published after her death, the Brazilian writer Clarice Lispector not only shows the difficulty of equating two forms of oppression but also deploys the low in order to destabilize the sovereign subject as well as the limits of literature. Although apparently motivated by the modernist desire to represent and control dangerous material,[7] Lispector's encounter with the low is invariably shattering. In "Beauty and the Beast," Carla, an upper-class woman, is abruptly accosted by a beggar. Taken by surprise when her chauffeur fails to arrive to drive her home from her appointment with the hairdresser in the Copacabana Hotel, she finds she cannot fob him off with small change since she only has a five-hundred cruzeiro note—a quantity so large that it could only arouse the suspicion of the recipient. But the beggar's demand disconcerts Carla so completely that her world—the clocks and the traffic—seems to come to a stop. All kinds of odd thoughts invade her mind—thoughts about the economy of begging, about the differences between begging and earning, spending and hoarding. For no reason at all, except the confusion into which she is plunged, she asks the beggar if he speaks English. The beggar replies, "Falo sim. Pois nâo estou falando agora mesmo com a senhora? Porquê? A senhora é surda? Entâo vou gritar: FALO." (Yes, I am speaking. Aren't I now speaking to you? Why? Are you deaf? Then I'll shout I AM SPEAKING.)[8]

"Speaking" in this situation does not mean communicating. Nor is this a dialogue, for there is no compatibility between their two situations. Yet the beggar, despite his lowly status, still speaks from the masculine position that is all the more obvious since *falo* (I speak) also translates "phallus" in Portuguese. Yet because of his wound he is not fully a male either. The wound is the outward sign of his incapacity to participate in "normal" society. Although Carla bears no such outward stigma she knows that she too is a beggar in the sexual contract so that "[t]here are things that make us equal," thus defining their equality in terms of lack.

The story's title recalls the fairy tale "Beauty and the Beast," which from the seventeenth century has attracted women writers and in which the beauty accepts the beast and transforms him back into the handsome prince he once was.[9] In Lispector's story the transformation of the beast does not occur. The beggar's wound, the mark of his difference, is *grande demais* (too big) to be ignored. Yet Carla wants their unequal situation to be leveled in some way. She tries to find comparisons between herself and the beggar, and at one point sits on the ground to emphasize this equality. But the beggar then concludes that she must be some middle-class communist who, like all communists, must feel that she has a perfect right to her jewels and property. It would be legitimate to read this fragment as a parody of liberal guilt but it is more than that. For what draws Carla into the encounter is not the beggar so much as the wound, the wound which is "a reality," the visible symbol of his lack and of the inequality of their situations.

Yet by the time that Carla is rescued from the awkward situation, although not from its effects, by the arrival of her chauffeur, the beggar has become "a part of her alter ego." This is neither the symbiosis that Ferré suggests nor the symbolic identification with the ego ideal that had so far been the support of Carla's personality and that, in Slavoj Žižek's words, is an "identification with the very place *from where* we are being observed *from where* we look at ourselves so that we appear likeable, worthy of love."[10] Rather it is a recognition that the alien is now within.

The woman's carefully tended beauty is meant for the gaze of the other; it is a confirmation of her husband's status, which is the ground on which she is constituted as subject. The cosmetic glamor is a fantasy construct, an attempt to approximate what she believes to be desirable, but all of which is undermined by the encounter, along with her very subjectivity. Carla can longer un-self-consciously assume her status position as glamorous wife for there is a void where the "I" used to be. Nor is there a totalizing signifier that would allow the excluded on the grounds of gender and the excluded on the grounds of class to join in a common cause. In psychoanalytic terms, the beggar is a blockage or limit to the symbolic structure, a stain of ugliness and pain that cannot but destroy the fantasy self.

Lispector wrote two novels—*A Paixão segundo G.H.* *(The Passion According to G.H.)* and *A Hora da Estrela (The Hour of the Star)*—in which persons from the middle class find themselves confronting the low from a position of privilege.[11] Although the two novels are quite different in their positing of alterity, Lispector turns both confrontations into a questioning of the sovereign self and of authorship.

For middle-class women in Latin America, the closest relationship with people of a different class is that with the domestic servant. In

Brazil these were often illiterate or semiliterate women from peasant backgrounds who had emigrated to the city from the impoverished northeast. In *The Passion According to G.H.*, originally published in 1964, the maid who has just walked out of her job becomes a kind of absent presence, haunting the room she has vacated. On opening a wardrobe closet in her former maid's room, G.H. sees a cockroach that, in an automatic gesture of repulsion, she traps and wounds. The creature slowly dies in front of her eyes, prompting her agonized reflections. In her remorse she takes the cockroach (or thinks she takes it) into her mouth like a communion wafer. This is her "passion," initiated by this trivial event of walking into her maid's room to tidy it for the next occupant. Cockroach and maid are metonymically associated in household space.

For women, the boundedness of the house was traditionally both confinement and protection, a physical reminder of limits but also the space where they exercised power. It was linked to women's honor and bodily integrity, as is particularly clear in seventeenth-century Spanish drama, where the rogue male was always conspiring to get into the house, bringing with him disorder and possible contamination. In Lispector's novel the foreign body of the maid already suggests an encroachment on the protagonist's space.

The room turns out to be spotless and tidy, except for the cockroach that the woman, unexpectedly, because of the awkward placing of the wardrobe door, meets face to face; her initial emotion is a savage desire to kill, a reaction that changes to horror and fascination as she watches the creature slowly die, exuding a milky liquid. In the description of her changing reactions to the encounter, the narrator not only undergoes a radical change of heart from the desire to exterminate to a depersonalization, but in doing so she becomes aware of the prehuman history of this creature that existed from the time of the dinosaurs. The world loses its human face so that she begins to see herself, not in human form, but as a cave painting three hundred thousand years old or existing on a plain beneath a ruined city. What the encounter destabilizes is both temporal and spatial coordinates.

G.H. has a private income, dabbles in sculpture, and is self-sufficient. Until she steps into the maid's room, she lives in a state of sublime indifference to the vast infrastructure and the millenarian history that had supported her. But in the shock of her encounter, the world around her is estranged; the room high up in a block of flats becomes a "minaret" (the temple of an exotic religion) and also a machine constructed by hundreds of workers who had built the drains and water pipes "without realizing they were building that Egyptian ruin from which I looked now with the same look as in one of those beach photographs of mine." The security of her position as privileged onlooker is now precarious, for she is objectified in another's gaze (as in a beach photograph) and her apartment house has become the "Egyptian ruin." Construction and destruction, the remote past and the remote future, the observing and the observed can no longer be separated. Interestingly, her journey into this other space is narrated as a form of orientalism, for the East of fantasy, as Edward Said has shown, is the prop by means of which the enlightened West is constituted.[12]

The room is not only a minaret and an Egyptian ruin, but also a more primitive abode in which the maid is imagined as a kind of dark and opaque cave dweller. This image occurs to G.H. because the maid has left a crayon drawing on the walls of her room depicting the naked figures of a man and a woman and that of a dog. "The drawing was crude, made with the broken point of a crayon. In some places the edge was double as if one line was the tremor of the other. The rigidity of the lines impressed the gigantic figures on the wall as if they were three automata. Even the dog had a tame madness of something which does not move of its volition." The human figures are naked (not civilized), and do not appear to act of their own volition and thus are not sovereign subjects. Yet possibly these "primitive" paintings of the present are destined to be the archaeological trace of habitation in a remote future. Although the rigidity of figures, who do not seem to be aware of one another, reminds the protagonist of her own rigidity, the mural may also remind the readers of the man, woman, and dog who are the main characters of Graciliano Ramos's novel of the Brazilian northeast, *Barren Lives;* in this case, it would suggest a symbolic invasion into the middle-class home of the "low" and "primitive" region. But the traversal of space between her quarters and the maid's quarters has transported G.H. not only into the archaic but also into the prehuman (which she also describes as the demonic), and which she now, in the act of writing, tries to communicate using the human vehicle of language. For the cockroach gives her an insight into the premordial and into whatever preexisted the human. "If a person saw this reality, she would burn as if she had seen God. Prehuman life is a burning presence" (p. 65). To be sure, there is more than a trace of Heidegger in the narrator's meditations—after all, Lispector was well versed in philosophy—but Lispector is not writing philosophy but representing the existential situation that inaugurates a new level of consciousness.

The epigraph of the novel is a quotation from Bernard Berenson, "A complete life may be one ending in so full an identification with the non-self that there is no self to die." In *A Paixão,* the non-self belongs to another species entirely, a species whose capacity for survival is legendary and with which there can be no communication, except by ingestion. G.H. first brings the cockroach to her mouth (albeit unconsciously), as if engaging in the "melancholy cannibalism" described by Julia Kristeva that "accounts for the passion for holding within the mouth . . . the intolerable other that I crave to destroy so as to better possess it alive. Better fragmented, torn, cut up, swallowed, digested than lost . . . It manifests the anguish of losing the other through the survival of self, surely a deserted self but not separated from what still and ever nourishes it and becomes transformed into the self—which also resuscitates through such a devouring."[13] But this is only a first step in G.H.'s pilgrimage, for she then spits out the cockroach and rejects such saintly heroism in order to free herself of personhood and lose what she calls her "third leg," a leg that supported the "idea that I had of personhood."

The situation takes encounter with "the face of the other" to an extreme, for the face that summons her is not a human face and, in the encounter, G.H. is in danger of losing her human form.[14] Yet, as she looks out of her window, out of the room (her rock dwelling), she sees beyond the city roofs not only the desert of Asia Minor in the second millennium before Christ but also the *favelas,* and she imagines that in their place there could be another city, an Athens. She also imagines herself planning a city in the desert (the kibbutz again?), planting eucalyptus trees to fix the soil, perhaps referring to a different polis—that of Jerusalem.[15] G.H. also imagines two cockroaches making love in the Libyan desert. What is she imagining here if not an impossible polis, a community in which she could coexist with the maid or the cockroach with whom she shares the lowest denominator of commonality—sexual rutting. But physically trapped in the space beside the wardrobe, the boundaries of self become porous: her civilization has been invaded by barbarism, the human by the nonhuman. This is a shipwreck of the sovereign subject who is now conscious of her own lack, a lack that is constitutive, that is anterior to humanity, because it derives from that initial separation from nature. "The maternal bed which is human is anterior to the human."

I return later in the chapter to this presocial element that is so seductive. Indeed, Lispector describes the cockroach as "pure seduction. Eyelashes, eyelashes that by blinking call out." We might read this as an example of Lispector's humor that, according to Kristeva, shields us from crisis,[16] but it is also an invitation to cross a limit into self-destruction, or at any rate into a place the modern self cannot inhabit. Although some critics have remarked on Lispector's mystical language, what her narrator experiences, described as "the happiness of the shabat" or a taste for nothingness, is at the opposite pole to "the Christian-human-sentiment." In her descent into animality and the unclean, the narrator comes to understand that there is a demonic aspect to her journey that must end at a point beyond language and self, the point of wordless "adoration." The novel is a profane revelation, a journey through terror in which the reader is the ghostly companion and literature itself a conduit to a silence beyond.

In *The Hour of the Star* (1977), in contrast, there is a deliberate attempt on the part of the narrator to nullify the seductive power of the low. The male narrator's apparent obsession with an unremarkable and unattractive girl from northeast Brazil is an alibi for the poverty of his writing, which he prefaces with an account of his doubts and hesitations. The story is a writing in process, as it were, with the narrator's often self-deprecating comments and uncertainties in parenthesis. He claims not to belong to any social class and to be sensitizing himself by writing the story about an unremarkable girl. He argues that the story is a silent photograph, that he is compelled to write to defend himself against this woman who "accuses him," and that in order to write he must practice abstinence—"no sex and no soccer." Thus the low other is a product of guilt to which the response is self-mortification.

But Macabéa, the "girl from the North East" with the Old Testament name, is a loaded signifier. The poorest and most backward region of Brazil, the northeast was the scene of Graciliano Ramos's great novel, *Vidas sêcas (Barren Lives),* a masterpiece of minimalist fiction.[17] It is hard to escape the impression that Lispector has in mind this narrative of people fleeing from catastrophic drought. Or perhaps it is a sequel, for the only way for Ramos's protagonists to escape their barren lives was by way of emigration to the city, where another kind of barren life awaited them. Indeed, Macabea herself is envisioned as barren—as having dried ovaries—in contrast to her plump rival and coworker Gloria, who has the advantage not only of being white but of being a *carioca,* a native of Rio.

Of course the dice are already loaded and the story already told from the very instant that the narrator glimpses a girl on the street and imagines her life. Macabéa belongs to that scarcely visible mass of immigrants whose low state of consciousness cannot be romanticized. As imagined by the narrator, she is unwashed, smelly, spotty, careless about her appearance, always hungry, an incompetent typist who, even though she paints her nails for the Sunday excursion to the movies, cannot keep them clean. She is a person who, when she looks in the mirror, sees no reflection or only a deformed reflection. She lives "as if eating her own entrails," her only culture apart from the cinema is "Radio Reloj" (Radio Clock), which counts the seconds and, in between, broadcasts commercials and bits of information—for instance, that Charles the Great was known as Carolus. She even collects advertisements. She is a bundle of imperfections, a girl whose sense of being is reduced to "I am a typist, a virgin and I like Coca Cola." When she finally acquires a boyfriend, who has the grandiose name of Olímpico and a gold tooth, he turns out to be a born trickster. But it is also as if all of this demeaning description is needed in order to fortify the *bella figura* of the intellectual storyteller, who trembles at the thought that he might have been born in her place. What he contemplates is abjection, described by Kristeva as "(a) massive and sudden emergence of uncanniness, which, familiar as it is might have been in an opaque and forgotten life, now harries me as radically separate, loathsome. Not me. Not that. But not nothing, either. A 'something' that I do not recognize as a thing. A weight of meaninglessness, about which there is nothing insignificant and which crushes me. On the edge of non-existence and hallucination, of a reality that, if I acknowledge it, annihilates me."[18] Ab-jection is a thrusting aside in order that I might live. It is caused by what disturbs "identity, system, order."[19]

In this light, the narrative is precisely an attempt to cast aside, hence the many alibis, explanations, hesitancies with which the narrator approaches his "material." He complains that he is going through a minor hell with this story and that the girl is a truth he does not wish to know; he wonders if, by narrating it, he will be condemned to die as a violator of secrets. In the event, his story turns into melodrama. When Olímpico jilts Macabéa for her fellow-worker Gloria, she consults a clairvoyant who predicts that she will meet a blond and wealthy foreigner. Experiencing hope for the first time in her life, she walks into the street and is immediately knocked down by a speeding Mercedes with a blonde driver. For a time the narrator weighs the possibility of letting her live, but finally allows her to die.

The narrator knows that fantasy teaches us how to desire.[20] In Žižek's words, "desire 'takes off' when 'something' (its object-cause) embodies, gives positive existence to its 'nothing,' to its void." But the story is not finally about Macabéa's desire but about the narrator's, who realizes that it is in his power to kill or not to kill the fantasy that sustains his fiction. When Macabéa dies, his ego collapses and the story ends. "Macabéa killed me," he exclaims. We might ask why Macabéa haunts him when she is so deprived of attractive qualities, voice, agency, or anything resembling class consciousness unless it is that she is the guarantee of his mastery, of the precarious illusion of a sovereign self.

The Hour of the Star suggests that as long as authorship is identified with personal fantasy—with Vargas Llosa's "demons,"—it remains enclosed in the self-same, for in this particular kind of representation, the "low" is only there as a support for the high. Yet, for Lispector, the other alternative seems to be the drastic descent into the silent adoration that closes *The Passion according to G.H.* In the modernist text, these are the best alternatives for managing exclusion.

Claiming the Low Ground: *Testimonio*

The genre that best claimed privileged access to the underclass was the *testimonio,* although in doing so it upset genre boundaries and hence the secure place of the literary. Initially facilitated by the invention of the tape recorder, the *testimonio* opened the way to registering orality beyond the controlling mechanisms of the literary as well as to upsetting the idea of authorship. In his preface to *The Children of Sánchez,* Oscar Lewis made the claim that recorded testimonies of the underclass had superseded the realist novel.[21] Canonized by the *Casa de las Américas,* which began awarding prizes for *testimonio* in the early 1970s, its genealogy is traceable both to the theories by anthropologists and to Christian witness, although one of the first Latin American contributions to the genre, *Juan Pérez Jolote,* which was compiled by the Mexican anthropologist Ricardo Pozas, tended to support rather than challenge dominant opinions about the indigenous resistance to modernization.[22] Nevertheless, the tape-recorded interviews provided sociologists, anthropologists, and literary critics with an open window through which they could scrutinize guerrilla fighters, slum dwellers, the indigenous, and blacks, some of whom were looked to for love, solidarity, tactful understanding, and justification. *Testimonio* supplied the meat missing in postmodern discussions of otherness and abjection that had often elided the real "violence done to marginalized persons."[23] It also revealed a current of antiliterary *ressentimient.* As Alberto Moreiras pointed out, while *testimonio* is a literary act, it "already incorporates the abandonment of the literary. Testimonio provides the reader with the opportunity of entering what we might call a subdued sublime: the twilight region where the literary breaks off into something else, which is not so much the real as it is its unguarded possibility."[24]

The colossal amount of critical attention paid to *testimonio,* especially in the U.S. academy, is itself worthy of comment if only because of the heat and anxiety of the discussion that has focused largely on one particular testimonial, that of the Guatemalan Indian woman Rigoberta Menchú. The testimony, recorded by Elizabeth Burgos Debray and published in 1983, of her family struggle against military repression that led her to join the Guatemalan Army of the Poor was rapidly taken up as an inspirational document by solidarity movements, as an exemplary text for educating North American students, and as an ethical statement.[25] In the United States, right-wing critics understood it to be a step down the slippery slope that would lead to the devaluation of literature and of time-tested truths. To them it seemed like an outright insult to the Great Books tradition when Stanford University included the text in their curriculum, sending them scurrying for cover behind Western culture.[26]

Menchú's *testimonio* was criticized by the anthropologist David Stoll, who charged that "it served the ideological needs of the urban left and kept alive the grand old vision of Latin American revolution. It shaped the assumptions of foreign human rights activists and the new multicultural orthodoxy in North American universities."[27] Putting himself in the position of the one who is presumed to know, though apparently without sophisticated knowledge of the indigenous languages of the area, Stoll found factual discrepancies in Menchú's account and used these to castigate both the validity of armed struggle and U.S. solidarity movements in the United States. Stoll's main charge is that armed struggle "has strengthened rationales for repression, poisoned other political possibilities that might have been more successful and, repeatedly been fatal for the left itself, by dismaying lower-class constituents and guaranteeing a crushing response from the state."[28] This curious argument, which has the effect of placing the onus for violence on the oppressed, is not unlike the justification for torture satirized by Martha Rosler in her video *A Simple Case of Torture,*[29] in which she exposed the underlying reliance of the argument for torture on the grounds of "realism." That being said, Stoll's book also demonstrates the astonishing international impact in an increasingly globalized culture of *I, Rigoberta Menchú* and its repercussions within Latin American studies and cultural studies in the United States.[30] To describe all the responses to this *testimonio* would require a volume in itself, but I think at least it is worth emphasizing that not only did the book come to occupy the privileged place in the canon formerly held by realism, substantially crossing the division between fiction and documentary account, it also filled a political need when, with the end of the Vietnam War, opponents of U.S. foreign policy turned their attention to Central America and solidarity movements as a form of practical participation.[31]

That Rigoberta was a woman, a member of an insurrectionary indigenous group, and indeed a "subaltern" was unprecedented to say the least. The English translation un-self-consciously described the *testimonio* as "one of the few complete expressions of Indian self-knowledge since the Spanish conquest."[32] Its authenticity was guaranteed by the fact that it transcribed the *spoken* word: "that is why we have to listen to Rigoberta Menchú's appeal and allow ourselves to be guided by a voice whose inner cadences are so pregnant with meaning that we actually seem to hear her speaking and can almost hear her breathing. Her voice is so heart-rendingly beautiful because it speaks to us of every facet of the life of a people and their oppressed culture."[33] This is directed to the reader who, because she is in "an inhuman and artificial world," finds herself experiencing feelings that she thought "lost forever." There is no need to emphasize that here orality is made to stand for authenticity and close contact between people, nor that the relationship between transcriber and witness is fraught with communicative problems of intonation, irony, and all the varied strategies that even a faithful transcription of orality usually fails to capture.[34] It is precisely these strategies and the fact that the voice is mediated by a transcriber that make the *testimonio* uncommonly interesting as well as controversial, as different discourses overlap and comment on each other. For example, as the native informant Rigoberta is generic, while as narrator of her coming-of-age life story she is unique; as narrator of political struggles she represents the indigenous Maya, while her coming to consciousness is made possible by the community-based Catholic organizations. "I am a Christian," she wrote, "and I participate in the struggle as a Christian" (p. 133). The "witnessing" with its Christian connotations perturbs the secular and individualistic project of authorship.

The practice of the *catequistas* is to draw parallels between the Bible and the everyday life of oppressed peoples. This is a process that posits a universal—ecumenical Christianity—that transcends the state and subsumes the local and the particular while distancing itself from the worldly church that is manipulated by the state. In liberation theology, the poor are privileged—it is they who inherit the Kingdom of Heaven—so that the experience of oppression and suffering are sources of knowledge and transformation. "We believe that, when we started using the Bible, when we began studying it in terms of our reality, it was because we found in it a document to guide us. It's not that the document itself brings about the change, it's more that each one of us learns to understand his reality and wants to devote himself to others. More than anything else, it was a form of learning for us" (p. 135). Christianity could thus embrace both the uniqueness of the indigenous experience and its survival tactics (of which one is secrecy)[35] at a time when the Left had difficulty in creating "an expansive universal discourse, constructed out of, not against, the proliferation of particularisms of the last few decades."[36] That Menchú's text (and given all the usual reservations about its textuality and its potential public of nonindigenous people) posits a universal is what has made it both seductive and difficult for the U.S. secular academic. It reverses the relationship of knowledge–power by putting the academic on the side of ignorance. And it does so in the name of a Christian universalism that is generally filtered out in its U.S. reception in favor of readings that extract either a salutary ethics[37] or a promise of an alliance based on the commonality of interests between "subaltern subjects and intellectuals and professionals like ourselves who seek to represent them in some way."[38]

Yet the literary institution that seems to have been most affected by the book was that of the U.S. university, where literary studies were increasingly threatened by often vaguely defined cultural studies and the testimony disturbed accepted ways of reading.[39] Perhaps more crucially, it also raised a problem that had hitherto been dormant, namely, the institutionalized hegemony of the U.S. university in Latin American studies, especially in disciplines such as political science and anthropology that had often taken for granted the active agency of the north over the south.[40] The involvement of those disciplines in the Cold War had already tainted their objectivity; but in addition, post-modern criticism turned attention both to the discursive formations that supported domination and also to the assumptions and practices that structured those disciplines themselves. This was particularly acute in anthropology, where Latin America constituted a "field" for the outside observer. To take one of the most eloquent examples among many, Nancy Scheper-Hughes's *Death without Weeping,* which is strongly influenced by liberation theology and its base communities, is laced both with self-criticism and the kind of sanctioned ignorance encouraged by the relation of the U.S. to the Third World.[41] Her shock at meeting women for whom the death of a child by starvation is such a common occurrence that mourning is irrelevant led her to question not only her native assumptions but anthropology itself: "[Anthropology] concerns the way in which knowledge is generated, the interests it serves, and the challenge to make our discipline more relevant and nonoppressive to the people we study." She then rather desperately asked, "What prevents us from becoming 'organic' intellectuals, willing to cast our lots with, and cleave to, the oppressed in the small, hopefully not totally meaningless ways that we can?"

In a similar self-criticism, John Beverley registered subaltern studies both as "a conceptual instrument for retrieving and registering the presence of the subaltern" and as an attempt to work "against the grain of our own interests and prejudices by contesting the authority of the academy and knowledge centers at the same time that we continue to participate in them and to deploy that authority as teachers, researchers, administrators, and theorists."[42] In a similar vein and addressing the literary institution, Doris Sommer argued that the protocols of reading instilled by the U.S. academy encourage a desire to conquer textual differences. What she calls "particularist" texts such as *I, Rigoberta Menchu* should, she believes, invite "interpretive reticence" and constraint.[43]

While these represent healthy departures from the arrogant exclusions of the U.S. academy, they also manifest its power. On the other hand, the subaltern wants publicity, perhaps more than reticence, though on their own terms. That is why the neo-Zapatistas in Chiapas hold out locally for indigenous rights but publicize these on the Internet. As Mary Louise Pratt pointed out, *respect* is a key word for the indigenous, as is *dignity.*[44] Respect is an absolute requirement for indigenous peoples to act as equals and agents in the political forum. That this respect could only be gained by a show of armed strength was a tragic consequence of the drastic situation to which they had been reduced by government policies in both Guatemala and Mexico. Both *I, Rigoberta Menchú* and the communiqués of the Zapatista movement are political documents that draw on rhetorical devices and sometimes on strategies that are commonly used in literature. The communiqués, for example, use parody, storytelling, and irony, suggesting that the aesthetic is by no means confined to high culture.

The Aesthetic Turn

In the 1970s and 1980s, political agency was increasingly claimed by groups who had not before then been active in the public spheres—relatives of the disappeared, old-age pensioners, victims of violence, human rights and environmental activists, women mobilizing around demands for basic necessities. These nongovernmental organizations are not necessarily the unblemished voice of the people; more than anything they register the extension of politics into what had formerly been thought of as the private sphere, as well as into ethics. But not only politics but literature too lost its former contours and became absorbed either into entertainment or into a newly defined field of the aesthetic that drew its potency from the margins, from the rejected anachronisms and the socially anomalous. Margins, however, no longer suggest a territory into which the artist can escape but rather the subtle points of dissonance that disturb the world as it is presented to us and may come from anachronistic traces that well up in memory, from the disruption of surfaces that unexpectedly reveal the primordial, or from the performance of tacit prohibitions.

At the height of the Pinochet regime, Diamela Eltit filmed a video in which she was shown reading from her novel *Lumpérica* (1983) in a brothel in one of the poorest sectors of Santiago and another video in which she was shown kissing a homeless man. "Kissing the tramp" she said, "related sexuality and society and this has always interested me . . . I believe that there is a rather archaic erotic which in this sense is presocial so to speak in the sense of a society that is highly structured. I believe that the kiss, any physical contact, goes beyond a determined social class for example so my idea was effectively to obey those very primary functions and to kiss a marginal person, when codes dictate a stratification of classes, at least in this country."[45] What is important to stress here is that the "archaic erotic" cannot be identified with "backwardness" or "underdevelopment" but rather signals the traces of the presocial that cannot be processed by categories such as class.

The fragmentary style and the vernacular of Eltit's novels register those residues that modernization leaves in its wake and draw attention to what is overlooked by its cosmetic gaze. In an essay on "Nomadic Bodies," Eltit commented on the collective suicide of three Andean peasant women who, for unknown reasons (all reasons for suicide are unknown), had first killed all their livestock, then had hanged their dogs, and finally had hanged themselves. She described this as a "deliberate death achieved through a staging that like all stagings is charged with cyphers and metaphors."[46] In his book on the *Ideology of the Aesthetic,* Terry Eagleton refers to the "aestheticization of value" in postmodernism.[47] In the case of Eltit, I would argue that what occurs is rather the restoration of value to the aesthetic—in this case to the "composition" of the scene of death that mysteriously and enigmatically stalls the communicative act and any possibility of deciphering. The scandal of the Andean women is staging the "archaic" death scene in a way that could not be processed within the paradigm of modernity.

Eltit wrote two books that document marginal lives. *El padre Mío (My Father)* and *El infarto del alma (Soul Stroke). El padre Mío* is the tape-recorded speech of a schizophrenic tramp who calls himself "My Father" and lives in one of the favored locations of Eltit's novels, "the waste ground," the *erial,* a marginal area said to be a kind of negative—"[l]ike a photographic negative which is necessary in order to configure a positive—the rest of the city—thanks to a strong territorial exclusion and in order that the social system secured by strong and persistent hierarchizations might remain intact."[48] Although in her preface Eltit turns the tramp's paranoid railings against banks and politicians into an allegory for political discourse under repression, there is no comfortable political message of solidarity here, for there is no narrative except that of conspiracy and persecution. The critic Nelly Richard has pointed out that not only is the speech characterized by circular repetition that can have no purchase outside itself, but the vagabond has no identity because his humanity is reduced to remnants of speech. His discourse is sewn together from remnants of public discourse apparently culled from newspapers, radio reports, or street talk in which the only constant is the vast universal conspiracy. The text thus frustrates the expectations of a documentary truth and a witnessing that characterizes testimonial literature.[49]

The persecuting agencies the tramp rails against are political parties, societies, government offices, and the United Nations so that, even though the discourse is not coherent, agency is attributed to the legal, financial, and bureaucratic network that keeps society together and whose codes El Padre Mío scrambles. "The Badilla-Padilla family is my family; do you know who they were? Related to King George, one of them who is king of Spain, the earlier one is still alive, I can assure you. But Padre Mío lives on an illegal income because he cashed the insurance policy of my family and they never got the money" (p. 41). In describing the schizophrenic, Deleuze and Guatarri wrote: "It may be said that the schizophrenic passes from one code to another, that he deliberately *scrambles all the codes* by quickly shifting from one to another, according to the questions asked him, never giving the same explanation from one day to the next, never invoking the same genealogy, never recording the same event in the same way."[50] This is certainly applicable to Eltit's vagabond who is concealed rather than revealed in this scrambling of codes.

Eltit maintained that her idea was not to "attempt to change anything, to cure anything," nor was she interested in victim literature, since such literature robs the soul of its space and its inhabitants. Rather, she wrote, "my project was to restore the aesthetic that is proper to those spaces and which mobilizes them and to give a narrative stature to those voices traditionally oppressed by official culture and damaged by a redemptive narrative."[51]

Soul Stroke is a collaborative work. Along with the photographer Paz Errázuriz, Eltit visited a home for the mentally ill and the indigent. Housed in what had been a tuberculosis hospital at Putaendo, when the tuberculosis epidemic ended the building was converted into a state hospital for the poor and insane, many of whom had formed affective relations with one another. The photographs by Errázuriz are almost all of couples, often disparate in age or in looks, but all clearly of the underclass, their bodies ravaged and uncared for. The book, however, is not about establishing links with this underclass but about their need for each other, their "aesthetic" that takes them beyond the administered society. Eltit's record of the visit is a combination of diary, fictional first-person love letter, meditation on personhood and on romantic love (after Denis de Rougement, *L'Amour et l'Occident*), and a gloss on Errázuriz's photographs. The coupling of the mentally ill (they are all heterosexual couples) manifests the desire for a union of bodies traumatized by the initial separation from the mother. The maternal body transformed into a vehicle of the species also suffers a trauma as the generic function enters into conflict with individuation. "The mother has the odd sensation of not existing or half existing and as she opens a way in her contradictory thinking, she realizes at last, that she has only lent her body to this other body."[52] Because the other is formed by separation, love must always be a yearning over an absence; and those who yield unconditionally to love do not accept the disciplinary rules of society. Eltit's marginality is thus couched as an implicit or even involuntary refusal and defiance of common sense.

One theme of Eltit's texts, which I pursue in the following chapters, is that the historical trauma suffered by Chile and other Latin American countries has left unsuspected psychic depths exposed to view. This does not mean that historical change is irrelevant but rather that discourses of reform, of healing, and of human rights attend only to the surface. Once literature has refused to define itself in relation to a posited "low," it become free to reinvent itself as a floating "aesthetic" that may surface anywhere there are fissures in what is accepted as the real.

CHAPTER NINE

Bodies in Distress:
Narratives of Globalization

In a brilliant book on delinquency, Josefina Ludmer wrote that delinquency is "a mobile historical and changing frontier (crimes change with time) and not only serves to discriminate, separate and exclude but also to articulate the state, politics, society, subjects, culture and literature."[1] Nowadays when states have all but abandoned the attempt to ameliorate the lot of their citizens, relying on the market to create opportunities and safeguards, the delinquent is the lightning rod of all social ills and not surprisingly so, for statistics of violent deaths all over the continent are staggering.[2] Violence is epidemic. In Colombia, human rights workers have documented 47,000 cases of human rights violations.[3] In Brazil, which has the highest level of lethal police violence of democratic countries, police shot street children because they were a nuisance.[4] The everyday reality for most people in these countries is fear.

It is not that violence is anything new but that somehow, in the context of modernity, it seems inexplicable, a kind of throwback to a more primitive past despite the disruptions brought about by globalization: a million or so Colombian homeless peasants thrown off their lands because of warfare between drug lords, guerrilla, and the government; Ecuadorian Indians unable to subsist on their inherited lands; thousands of parentless street children. One could go on. Structures that maintained productivity, dignity, and *hombría* (manliness) based on the notion of patriarchal governance have collapsed. Behind the shiny surface of globalization lurks the primitive *lex talionis* that is practiced among those cast aside in the explosive conjunction of consumerism and poverty.

The rapid transmission of information and images, migration, and changes in the work place have exacted a heavy toll among the poorest sectors of society. Flexible production and the deployment of women as sweatshop workers together with the surplus of unemployed males have destabilized male–female relations in many communities. In the workplace, women's bodies are valued primarily for their flexibility although this has not necessarily improved their status and, at a time when women's issues—women in development, population control, violence against women—are at the forefront of debate in international organizations, it is a melodrama of fear that is enacted in the anecdotes, gossip, and rumor that circulate among the poor.[5]

It is in this undervalued area that we find the narratives and fantasies of the excluded and marginalized. As purveyed by the World Bank, by official circles in Europe and the United States, and by international organizations, globalization is often narrated as a migrant journey into the arms of a benevolent First World father, while at a ground level, below visibility on the world map, delinquency is perpetrated not by kids on the street but by voracious outsiders. Fantasies circulate—of the vampiric *chupacabras* (literally, goat-sucker), or the old story of the *robachicos* (the kidnapper of children) who now trades in organs for transplant. Whether such stories are true or not is irrelevant; what is significant is that people believe the stories and act on the basis of them. For instance in Lima, women took their children out of school because of rumors that the *sacaojos* (the bandit who robs eyes) was on the loose. These are archaic stories pressed into service as explanatory narratives that account for injustice and inequality. They correspond in a deterritorialized world to what Gilles Deleuze and Félix Guatarri described as "neo-territories that are often artificial, residual, archaic; but they are archaisms having a perfectly current function, our modern way of 'imbricating,' of sectioning off, of reintroducing code fragments, resuscitating old codes, inventing pseudo codes or jargons."[6]

Such reterritorializing fantasies of benevolent fathers and vampiric feeding can perhaps be understood as ways of registering the trauma of subjectivity within globalization, a trauma that is suffered above all upon the body of women, the women victims of the serial killer, the women and children whose bodies are used for transplant, the exploited girls in the sex trade in Central America, and the slain maquiladora girls whose bodies are found in the desert near Juárez. But these are not the crime stories that circulate in print culture where the "delinquent" is the surrogate for the collapse of civil society.

The *Costumbrismo* of Globalization

The life and death of delinquents has become a common theme of urban chronicles, newspaper articles, and the fiction I describe as the *costumbrismo* of globalization.[7] *Costumbrismo* was a nineteenth-century response to modernization. But whereas in the nineteenth century the old customs could be captured as quaint anachronisms on the verge of disappearance, the contemporary texts are postapocalyptic, reflecting the horror of the middle classes as their whole cultural world implodes. As the narrator of the novel *La virgen de los sicarios* tells it: "In the shipwreck of Colombia, and this loss of our identity, nothing is left for us."[8] Nineteenth-century *costumbrismo* was expressed in descriptive sketches of human residues left behind by progress; contemporary urban chronicles are descriptions of this process in reverse. Reading from the norm of post-Enlightenment citizenship, they are likely to appear beyond intelligibility. Thus Susan Rotker wrote of Alonso Salazar's *Born to Die in Medellín*, "Here there is no articulation, nor complaints or explanations: fatality occurs and that's where it ends, everything is corrupt and natural, one does not see alternatives or guilty parties."[9]

But the questions raised by these texts is not due simply to the apparent rejection of accepted ethical standards, for what they emphasize is an excess of violence that goes beyond self-interest. In *La ley de la calle: Crónicas de jovenes protagonistas de la violencia en Caracas (The Law of the Streets; Chronicles of Young Participants in Violence in Caracas),* based on interviews with juvenile delinquents in a correction center, and *Born to Die in Medellín,* based on first-person accounts of young boys involved in the drug culture, the protagonists lust after consumer goods while knowing they are likely to meet an early death. The boys are motivated by status that is defined by clothing styles, and they attain their ends by theft, murder, and selling drugs. "Sneakers are my image," according to one of the boys of *La ley de la calle,* who declares, "Chaveto (was killed) because of the damned Nike. He had seen me sometimes with my Charles Barkley, my Bull Jackson and my Black Point. I have always used designer shoes and I've never had any bother with that."[10] In *Born to Die in Medellín,* Alonso Salazar underscored the obsession with name brands: "The contract killers take the consumer society to its extreme; they turn life (their own and that of their victims) into a commodity to deal in, into a disposable object."[11] Whereas honor was once staked on female virtue, status has now migrated to clothing, motorcycles, and guns. Yet consumer society and a high rate of poverty cannot altogether account for this alliance of consumption and death.

Slavoj Žižek described the death drive as the subordination of the human psychic apparatus "to a blind automatism of repetition beyond pleasure-seeking, self preservation, accordance between man and milieu."[12] It is this "beyond self-preservation" that strikes the reader of these chronicles of violence, for the young killers are perfectly conscious that they will not survive beyond the age of twenty. This stands in stark contrast to the interests in survival at any cost and the postponement of death that is the obsession of Western societies, particularly the United States. It is precisely the "beyond self-preservation" that tests the limits of what is intelligible to us on the outside.

The word *sicario* comes from Latin and means a paid assassin. Its very antiquity, its Latinity, evokes a residue of premodern mentality, now reactivated by modern consumption. The *sicarios* are described as celebrating death with parties, music, and dance. A priest interviewed by Salazar commented, "While they are alive, they give instructions as to what ceremonies they want, and the records that are to be played. Those leaders like Flaco, are created by the lead of bullets, by their strength, by heroic deeds . . . These lads talk to their dead leader, they touch him, play the music he liked, and it affects them deeply." The *sicarios* use playful euphemisms—for instance, the dead body becomes *el muñeco* (the doll)—that deprive killing of any transcendental significance. In this repetitive cycle of vengeance, the honor code is thus translated into the new global conditions in which the body of the laborer is replaceable and his product is death. "They know they are 'disposable,'" Salazar wrote, "so that when they join a group they start to think of death as something completely natural." Yet we need to tread carefully here, for Alonso Salazar's *Born to Die in Medellín* is addressed to a public for whom the personal accounts of young killers, their associates, their women, and other members of the community may encourage the notion that they are conspiring in their own destruction, which perhaps in turn nourishes the wish fulfillment of the civilized who would be only too happy for them to self-destruct. A comforting thought. Meanwhile let's have some vicarious pleasure.

But it is the gendering of *sicario* culture that tells us something about the unholy alliance between the traffic in lives and the deathly logic of a masculinity that links an archaic *lex talionis* to consumer culture. Instead of a punitive God who instills feelings of guilt, the *sicarios* are devoted to the all-forgiving Virgin: in the words of Alonso Salazar, "they worship a female God who is tolerant and permissive." Mother's Day in Medellín "is the most violent day of all." Women in this narrative are the bearers, helpers, and facilitators. The priest interviewed by Salazar not unnaturally would like to see a return to the old order: "They need to find again the male god, the God who punishes and instills fear." In other words, the fascist state would be the perfect antidote.

In a study of rape cases in Brazil, which described how a similarly gendered narrative exonerated male violence, Lia Zanotta Machado argued that there was a "reinscription of that code (the code of masculinity) within the generally accepted values of an individualistic society" in which the idea of social success no longer has connection with work.[13] Removed from any loyalty to a national or family structure, or from any system of ethics, individualism is turned into indiscriminate violence and, in the case of the *sicarios,* into self-destruction.

In Fernando Vallejo's novel *La virgen de los sicarios (The Virgin of the Sicarios)* and in Paulo Lins's, *Cidade de Deus,* set in a *favela* of that name, the authors withhold moral judgment on killers. In one incident in *Cidade de Deus,* a jealous lover severs the arms and legs of a newborn infant as revenge on his unfaithful mistress, an event that is related without overt authorial comment. And although the middle-class and "lettered" narrator of *The Virgin of the Sicarios* often evokes horror on the reader's part, this is not from any moral concern for the victims. What concerns him is the opinion of those on the outside for whom Medellín has become the pit of barbarism. He frequently complains that the rule of law has broken down, that the women of the *colonias* (the slum areas) are a menace to society, and that the killers are therefore fulfilling a useful social function since the poor are better off dead. The fact that he is a homosexual hardly complicates matters, for he takes on the role of the permissive mother. In love with a green-eyed "angel," Alexis, who is a cold-blooded killer, a child killing machine, he subordinates everything to the erotic attraction of the boy and, like the mothers described by the priest in *Born to Die,* defends his angel who kills for any reason, or for none at all—because someone answers back, because they're in the way. He kills young and old, rivals, and people he sees on the street. Inevitably Alexis too is killed from the back of a motorcycle as is the narrator's next lover, Wilmar, who is Alexis's killer. In the narrator's view, it makes no sense to say "life is worthless" because there is no criterion of value and "there is nothing more ephemeral than yesterday's dead."

The narrator absolves his angel of guilt by attributing this deadly cycle to the corruption and the collapse of civil society, and to the women of the *colonias* and their frenetic reproduction, or to the "dark people" with whom they copulate. Unless we read irony into the account, the viewpoint is misogynist and racist.[14] It is as if the novel in exaggerated fashion places before us the ultimate absurdity— the disassociation of the female reproduction machine and the male death machine, both of which function blindly, the one to reproduce and the other to exterminate. The narrator accompanies his denunciations with frequent appeals to some "civilized outside" in whose eyes Colombia is a barbaric place. In this regime all values other than exchange value melt into air. Does the *desechable* (the garbage) simply extend the logic of globalization until it reaches the end of human history? Or does the collapse of law and civil society strip away the trappings of civilized man and woman, leaving the barbarous automata beneath? At best, we can read the denunciations ironically as a reflection on the narrator; but by our doing so, he becomes the most obscene character of the novel, the "invisible man," the one who gets an erotic charge and vicarious pleasure out of his killer-lovers, whilst absolving himself and those readers who fall into the same position of irresponsibility. As a *letrado,* he is "our" ally, "Mon semblable, mon frère." The question is whether he is deliberately forcing us to face the "fascist within" or whether he expects our complicity.[15]

Men without Masculinity

In Emilio Pérez Cruz's chronicles of Mexico City, *Borracho no vale (The Drunkard Doesn't Count),* the protagonist, faced with both state and random violence, also renounces responsibility. Unlike the chronicles of the *sicarios,* however, his are of survival at any cost, even at the risk of his own humiliation. The stories were originally published in the magazine *La Garrapata* in the 1980s when Mexico was entering the North American Free Trade Agreement (NAFTA) and was in transition from being a postrevolutionary welfare state to a state that facilitated globalization. Although the stories are written in the slang of the squatter settlement Netzahualcoyotl, the author also invents words and uses acronyms and foreign words to narrate the story of the good soldier Schweik of globalization. His language underscores the difference between the standard and the aberration, between the citizen and the marginal. An English translation cannot do justice to the inventiveness of the slang. After his girlfriend, Lipa, has been raped, he uses the word *"calmex"*—a carpetbag word that can be translated as "keep calm" or "cool it." The suffix "ex" is used for many commercial products and "mex" is a shorted form of Mexico, as in the name of the nationalized gas company Pemex. So *calmex* packs in a host of allusions. In other stories he uses drug culture language—*chemo, chido, andar chiva*—and a vocabulary—*carnal* (buddy), *simón* (an emphatic yes)—that have crossed the frontier from the chicano culture of California.[16]

The title is explained by the story of the cat and the mouse. The cat saves the mouse from drowning in a barrel of wine and makes it promise to do anything the cat says as soon as it has recovered from its intoxication. Instead of making good on its promise, the mouse hides in a cave and says to the cat, "How can I agree to a contract which condemns me to being eaten? Besides who takes any notice of a drunkard? The drunkard 'doesn't count.'" The literal translation from Spanish is "the drunkard is worthless" or "without value." He is outside any system of values, outside the contractual obligation that conceals the inequality of those who enter into it. In one of the stories, the drunkard tries to join the police force—known as "la tira" *(la tiranía):* "Why should I want to be a laborer? Isn't it better to be the friend of the citizen? Besides if you're a laborer there's no chance of you getting compensation; if your hand's cut off they sew it on again.

Social Security have already done it. These days, you can't make extra money out of your limbs" (p. 14).

The word for money in Mexican slang is *lana* (wool), a word that goes back to the colonial period when worth was expressed in terms of a product; its use underscores the contrast between older forms of production and the cannibalization of a person's body as a desperate way of earning cash. The drunkard believes that by joining the bank police (banks being a favorite target of armed gangs), he'll be given the chance to die like a hero during the inevitable holdup and "the manager will pass around the hat and so will private enterprise and your woman, kids and all will reap the benefit and have the chance to progress with what they're given for my bones" (pp. 14–15).

In this sentence Pérez Cruz summarizes an entire process of social transformation dominated by the privatized bank and its manager *(el regente)* who "echando una porra" gives his support *(porra* is not only passing round the hat but can also mean a club and a violent gang, which underlines that this support is enforced). Private enterprise is described as passing round the hat as if they were street entertainers looking for pennies, and the señora *(ñora)* and the kids *(los bodoques)* get their chance thanks to the surplus value derived from his bones. The logic of the death drive is, on this occasion, disguised as neoliberal "voluntary" welfare.

The drunkard never gets into the police and either sponges on others or finds temporary jobs in the informal economy. On the second of October, the anniversary of the 1968 massacre of students at Tlatelolco, he claims not revolution but *chupamaro* militancy (a pun on the Tupamaro guerrilla movement of Uruguay and on *chupar* (to drink)). He parodies the traditional proclamation of Mexican independence with his own salute: "Viva la briagoberta alegría, muera el mal gobierno" (Long live open fly happiness, down with bad government). He celebrates unbridled male pleasure—the *briagoberta* (with resonances of Rigoberta (Menchú?) and "bragueta abierta," the ever-open fly). The drunkard does not function as a citizen, as a father, or as a worker. Women sustain the household and though he briefly entertains the notion of marrying one of the women he lives with, it is only to reject the responsibility.

He cannot really sustain the illusion of machismo, however, because he is unable to respond to violence with violence. On a Sunday walk with his girlfriend, they meet up with members of the police who rape her. He is forced to stand by, unable to defend her. "I helped her get up and said to her keep calm kid, calm because we might come up against another patrol and if we do, we'll get it good. I took Lipa to Lomas (that is Lomas de Chapultepec, the wealthy suburb where she works as a maid)—but I was left with the question—was this a new tactic of the negro Durazo to increase the police force?" (p. 31). The reader needs to know that "el negro Durazo" was a notoriously corrupt police chief of Mexico whose biography became a best-seller;[17] the drunkard's bitter conclusion that rape is perhaps the way Durazo increases the police force underscores the subject's helplessness in the face of police violence and corruption. Unable to protect his woman, he is stripped of the essential attribute of traditional masculinity. The title of this story is "Recordar es volver a gatear" (To remember is to crawl like a baby again).

As I read these stories I was increasingly struck by their resemblance to the novels and stories of the Scottish writer James Kelman, suggesting that it may not be a Latin American phenomenon only, that one consequence of globalization is this human residue for whom the attributes of dominant masculinity are claimed but are no longer fully realizable, although they cannot embrace the feminine either. Both writers use nonstandard idioms. Kelman's novel *How late it was. How late* won the Booker prize, an award that was much criticized by the guardians of correct English. Like *Borracho no vale,* the novel is written in slang and the protagonist is a drunk. At the beginning of the story he is beaten by the police so severely that he is blinded and reflects, "It wasnay a case of blaming the sojers (the police), that was stupit, nay fucking point; it's the system; they just take their orders. Mind you there is the one fuckking order: batter fuck out the cunts so they know they're boss." "Cunt" becomes the term for men and women of the defeated classes. "Nay fucking point; it's the system" registers the helplessness, the lack of agency.[18]

In each of these narratives, national identity is a joke. In *La virgen de los sicarios,* Colombia exists only as a series of formalities that nobody takes seriously. This is also true of the Mexico of *Borracho no vale.* The city is mapped not as a civic center but as a wayward trajectory for men who are in search of death or oblivion through alcohol, which is surely another form of the death drive. In *La virgen de los sicarios,* the absolute narcissism of the *sicario* leads to death.[19] With every death the killing machine acknowledges the inevitable reciprocity. With every evasion the drunkard disavows his worth as a human being. Traditional masculinity as well as its disavowal cannot support responsible subjects and, in abdicating responsibility, these men empower the very system of which they are victims.

Disidentifications

Neither identifying nor counteridentifying with the dominant culture, the transvestite disidentifies—or, in Judith Butler's words, stands "under a sign to which one does and does not belong."[20] In Buenos Aires, the transvestite Lohana tore up his identity card outside Congress because she refused to be categorized as male, pointing out that transvestites refuse gender categories imposed by the state bureaucracy.[21]

In Chile, the transvestite performer, writer, and radio commentator Pedro Lemebel has argued that disidentification destabilizes not only gender but categories of race and class. During the military dictatorship, he and Francisco Casas performed as "Las Yeguas del Apocalipsis" (The mares of the apocalypse). "We reinvented ourself as a body, difference, morbidly sexed, and *lumpen,*" wrote Francisco Casas.[22] With the return to democracy, Lemebel's transvestism, his mestizo face, his camp performances, and his roots in the *poblaciones* situated him as an outsider in a society that traditionally represented itself as European-descended and respectful of traditional values. Even so, like Carlos Monsiváis he has acquired a popular as well as an elite audience because of his radio broadcasts on *Radio Tierra*. In his urban chronicles, he mixes "high" style with slang (the title of one of his books, *Loco Afán (Mad Urgency)* refers to a poem by the seventeenth-century Spanish writer Quevedo) but writes of the lowest strata of Santiago society—the rent boys, impoverished male prostitutes dying of AIDS, the adolescent slum inhabitants, and criminals. His style is deliberately excessive, mixing baroque metaphors with minority slang, overlaying the literary with the private dialect of the marginalized.[23]

The very disparity between Lemebel's use of ornate metaphor and of catachresis strains comparison beyond any limit, and the sordid scenes he describes are disconcerting, commingling tragedy and humor, melodrama and sentimentality. In "Poppies also Have Thorns," a *loca* (homosexual) picks up a stranger and has sex in a vacant lot. In the aftermath of the sex act, "the faded sphincter is a blind iris *(pupila)* that blinks between the buttocks"—an extraordinary metaphor that suggests a blinded gaze that draws attention to itself. The gaze that had aroused desire is now extinguished, yet the blind eye claims attention. Perhaps that is why the stranger in a rage of self-disgust stabs the *loca* to death, a stabbing that is described as if it were a performance. The *marica's* body contorted by the stab wounds adopts "the pose of Marilyn Monroe in front of the flash lights." "Almost casually the metal cuts as if it were a coincidence, a superficial scratch, a ladder in the stocking, a tear in the Christian Dior outfit that is styled in purple."[24] This dramatic defiance is described as if it were a fashion model's minor crisis on the runway, or as if the *loca* were a film star seeking the spotlight even in death.

For Lemebel the city is a theater of illicit desire. Rubbing against other bodies on crowded buses, in parks, in bathhouses, in empty lots, the unbridled desire of his marginal characters is as anonymous as it is communal. The transvestite, in particular, crosses dangerous boundaries, mocking the surveillance of the state but exposed to the dangers of random violence. There is a city of body parts—anus, penis, thighs—that emit sweat and smells, that feel pain and pleasure. In one of the most blistering of these chronicles, "Encajes de acero para una almohada penitencial" (Steel Lace for a Prison Pillow), Lemebel wrote of the initiatory rape of new male prisoners, catachrestically associating rape with liberation.[25] The backside of the raped prisoner is compared to the Andean cordillera and "the stony mountain passes through which horse thieves and escapees gallop to freedom." The rape scene becomes a children's game of hide and seek and a system of carnal excavations that is likened to a network of escape tunnels—in Lemebel's words, "a topology of desperation that drills its emancipation in rock." Sodomizing is a prison escape: "Penetrating the brick with surges of passion, with scratchings and tearings in the furrows of the back." Here the fantasy of freedom breaks out of confinement in the individual. These are "alliances of sex and death that are not domesticated in the cloister and which tear of their own accord the steel gauze of their confinement." The fantasy of a prison break works itself out on the body of the abjected prisoner who will in turn become a rapist.

Lemebel's "AIDS chronicles" are like the flash that captures the photographic image as well as being works of mourning for the victims. "The Last Supper of the Popular Unity Party" (Popular Unity was the party of Salvador Allende, whose government was over-thrown by the 1973 military coup) is at one and the same time mourning, counterhistory, and snapshot. On New Year's Eve of 1973, a group of wealthy transvestites go slumming; they arrive late for the feast prepared by their low-class counterparts, after the chickens have already been eaten. Somebody makes a funeral pyre of the discarded chicken bones in an uncanny foreshadowing of the ossuaries of the dead that would follow the military coup. Toward the end of the party, a photograph is taken. "Perhaps the only vestige of that time of social utopias when the 'locas' glimpsed the fluttering of their future emancipation." But hardly anyone in that group photograph is now alive. "The fly dirt left patches on the cheeks as a cosmetic forecast of sarcoma. All the faces appear spotted with this purulent drizzle. All the laughs that flutter on the balcony of the photograph are handker-chiefs that are saying farewell from an invisible prow." As in "Steel Lace for a Prison Pillow," Lemebel confronts his readers with the disjunction between sexual utopias and social divisions. The irony is that the class division that would bring the Popular Unity government to an end would be removed by the AIDS epidemic that decimated all social classes.

Disguise, masquerade, and nicknames are the transvestites' re-sources for evading given identities. In "Los dos mil nombres de María Camaleón" (The Two Thousand Names of María Chameleon), Lemebel wrote about the "collection of nicknames that hides the baptized face." The transvestite "covers with feathers, celebrates, tranvestizes, masks, stages identity by means of a nickname . . . names, adjectives and nouns that constantly rebaptize him according to his state of mind." In verbal snapshots of AIDS victims, Lemebel has also stressed that the denial of self-identity and of illness patients always go through is not negative, as in common psychoanalysis, but is a way of fighting terror. His character Loba Lamar could never un-derstand the negative meaning of positive in medical vocabulary until she was almost at her last gasp. Lemebel turns this potentially tragic situation to farce, as the dying Loba protests her inevitable fate and dies ludicrously with her mouth wide open: "There we were stupidly peering at the portal of her mouth, as yawning as an abyss, as open as a black well from which her talkative tongue scarcely peered out." Frozen in this unbecoming gesture, Loba's death face horrifies the *locas*. Rescue arrives in the person of the wrestler Tora, who reshapes

Loba's mouth into a kiss, a cosmetic improvement that pathetically underscores the horror.

There is no religious transcendence in Lemebel's writing. The AIDS epidemic is suffered, sometimes in grotesque fashion, by individuals whose only resource is a community of fellow sufferers. It is the negative that blanks out the human face of globalization.[26]

Laborers of Death

The male body is no longer the measure of the cosmos, yet sexual fantasies are more powerful than ever. Short-term gender politics, especially when they ignore the deeply rooted psychology of sexual difference, tend to come up against the persistence of male domination, as such theorists as Judith Butler, Kaja Silverman, and Pierre Bourdieu have noted.[27]

In Latin America, the Catholic Church has been a guardian of traditional morals, successfully blocking any projects of abortion and even, in some countries, divorce, despite the large percentage of illegal abortions and nonlegal families. Even the conversion of Chile into a showcase for neoliberal policies has had little effect on matters of sexual politics in that country. In this regard, the novels of the Chilean writer Diamela Eltit are particularly perceptive because they stage on the surface level what is usually repressed or concealed. In her novel El cuarto mundo (The Fourth World), the male fetus in the womb is already conscious, vying for space with a twin sister.[28]

The novel like the child cannot choose its time but comes into a world it has not made, with compulsions and urges that the subject does not necessarily control. Eltit's novel Los trabajadores de la muerte (Laborers of Death) explores the death drive.[29] Framed by chapters in which a girl with a mutilated arm enters into a wager with a male dreamer who wants the girl to interpret his dream, the novel is structured around an Oedipal narrative in three voices: a first-person narrative of a mother who is disgusted by mothering; a second-person narrative of a man en route to Concepción (that is, both to the Chilean city and to conception); and a first-person male narrative of the nighttime of this same man. The journey to Concepción is initiated as an act of revenge. A mother issues a command her son must obey by returning to Concepción, which is the site of the father's betrayal and the goal of the journey backward toward ancient times. There are references to a landscape devastated by drought and to a senile, toothless Pythian as a mocking oracle. In other words, the novel is constructed on the ruins of the Oedipal legend. In one of the mother's dreams she sees "una piedra milenaria, arcaica," (a millenary ancient stone) on which she places the firstborn twin to offer it as a sacrifice.

Repetition in the novel is related to the death drive. In the nighttime sections, the first-person narrator who declares himself freed from family history and describes himself as an autodidact, whose nightmare is the burning of the library at Alexandria (the destruction of the archive), needs a rival and love object in order to be himself. But the love object he finally comes upon in Concepción is his half-sister whom he will finally kill in order to execute the mother's vengeance. In this parodic retelling of Oedipus, male violence corresponds to female *ressentiment*. It offers a dark and primal view of human subjectivity suggesting that sexual difference and *ressentiment* are deeply embedded in a fantasy subject whose mythic support is already suspect.

A male dreamer telling an ancient tale thus confronts the mutilated female who, at the end of the novel, will be the one possessed of power, the power of the enigma. Like the Lacanian real, the girl generates fantasy but cannot be known.

In the long-standing discussions of feminism in Latin America, women were divided between the politics of equality (as developed in the United States) and the politics of difference (as developed in France). This was not a dispute over influences but between the social constructivists and those for whom difference was as old as civilization or, in the Lacanian version, anterior to subjectivity. What strikes us in the chronicles of violence is the articulation of old codes of behavior with consumerism, an articulation made necessary because of the gap in the social that Diamela Eltit's novel makes explicit.

CHAPTER TEN

Obstinate Memory:
Tainted History

From ancient history to pop culture, *This Week in History* gathers
together the triumphs, tragedies and trivia of one week into fast-
paced news of the past.

ADVERTISEMENT FOR THE HISTORY CHANNEL

There is no transcendental court of appeal for the contemporary tragedy. The period initiated by Dostoevsky's Grand Inquisitor is one in
which cruelty has no unearthly punishment and often no earthly reason. In Dostoevsky's account there is still an individual with whom to
empathize, a boy torn to death by dogs. In our time, only too often are
we given the image of the mass of bodies—the massacres of Rwanda
or Kosovo—out of which it is difficult for those of us watching the
television screen or looking at news photographs to construct a meaningful narrative. Yet another massacre, another mass grave. Yet another holocaust of anonymous dead and disappeared and yet again
the stumbling attempts of survivors or torture victims to describe
their experience. In Argentina and Chile, and in Guatemala and El
Salvador, this gruesome truth has yet another dimension, for bodies
are still being disinterred.

True, the interment of the past and its hauntings are an old story,
going back to the conquest; in popular culture that holocaust still accounts for evil winds that issue from the unhallowed indigenous bodies.[1] Contemporary atrocities, on the other hand, bear directly on
present-day politics, and memory and commemorations are contentious. In his book, *Twilight Memories* on post-Holocaust Germany,
Andreas Huyssen argued that "[t]he struggle for memory is also a
struggle for history and against high-tech amnesia."[2] But history has

come under suspicion insofar as it sutures events into an official narrative that relies on what is deemed to constitute a fact.

History on Trial

In Borges's story "Guayaquil," the narrator attempts to uncover the truth of a key historical moment in Latin America—the moment when the liberator, San Martín, for reasons that are obscure, bowed out of the independence struggle leaving Bolívar as its sole leader. In the story the narrator and his rival, Zimmerman, have discovered in Sulaco (the imaginary country of Conrad's *Nostromo*), a missing letter from Bolívar that will offer the clue to the mystery of San Martín's renunciation. In a gesture that duplicates that of San Martín, the narrator cedes his right to visit Sulaco and remains in his ancestral home where he burns the notes he has made on the incident. Historical fact in this account is a text whose gaps and omissions are fostered by caprice. The paradox of the story is that the narrator claims to have burned his only account of his meeting with Zimmerman and his renunciation of the coveted letter, yet we, the readers, are reading his account of the matter. His gesture of renunciation is a farcical reenactment, a sop to his own vanity, leaving the truth as elusive as ever. Not only is the factual fragile, prey to the vagaries of personal passion that dictates what will survive as historical record, but the testimony is doubly a fiction.[3]

Borges's story seems to foreshadow the radical contingency that rejects narrative and teleological history.[4] In Latin America such narratives were always difficult to accommodate to the untidy patterns and the patchiness of modernization, as the writers of the "boom" generation were quick to realize. Several of them turned to writing historical novels as they attempted to charter not only the waywardness of the continent, its nonconformity to the recipes of historicism, but also those subjective factors that the historical narrative overlooked. Mario Vargas Llosa's *The War of the End of the World*, Alejo Carpentier's *Explosion in the Cathedral*, Carlos Fuentes's *The Campaign*, and Gabriel García Márquez's *The General in his Labyrinth* put the subject back into history although without recovering subaltern voices.[5] Vargas Llosa's *The War of the End of the World*, for instance, is based on a historical rebellion of a religious sect in northeastern Brazil in the late nineteenth century. Led by Antonio Conselheiro, the rebels successfully fought a campaign against the Republican army before he and his followers were exterminated. In Vargas Llosa's account, both sides are driven by a fanaticism that leads to senseless devastation. The historical narrative in this case suggests a criticism of the guerrilla warfare of the 1960s and 1970s.

In the novels of this generation, history still has a lesson to teach while in more recent historical novels—César Aira's *Ema la cautiva (Emma the Captive)* and Carmen Boullosa's *Los cielos de la tierra (The Heavens of Earth)* and *Duerme (Sleep)*⁶—history is emancipated from documentary sources, even when these underpin the narrative, and gives way to myth.

Official history is a narrative of heroes who are not easily dethroned. In Mexico, when a group of intellectuals revised school textbooks by eliminating the more dubious incidents, the opposition was such that the new textbooks were soon dropped from the syllabus. In Chile, the artist Juan Dávila's portrayal of Bolívar as a transvestite became an international scandal.⁷ Such incidents illustrate how closely history is still implicated in national identity.

In an effort to counter official history, Eduardo Galeano, in the preface to his three-volume anthology *Memories of Fire,* stated emphatically that he is not a historian. "From the outset, it (Latin America) has been condemned to amnesia by those who have prevented it from being . . . I am not a historian. I am a writer who would like to contribute to the rescue of the kidnapped memory of all America, but above all of Latin America, that despised and beloved land. I would like to talk to her, share her secrets, ask her of what difficult clays she was born, from what acts of love and violation she comes."⁸ Here "America," anthropomorphized as female, is held to communicate through particular texts whose sources are listed at the end of each volume. But Galeano's claim to "rescue the kidnapped memory of America" turns out to be the rescue not of memory but of texts, mostly anecdotes of rebellion and resistance to oppression from pre-Columbian times to the near present, and drawn from a variety of sources (including historical narrative) and genres. Whatever their merits, Germán Arciniegas and Ernesto Cardenal, two of the authors cited by Galeano, are not necessarily to be relied on for the rigorous documentation that he claims. "Memory," in this case, is not oral tradition or personal recollection but a literary rendition of an already-written past. What has been ignored is the work of formerly marginalized groups of indigenous peoples and Afro-Americans who are revising the histories that have excluded them and reexamining oral tradition.

Oral tradition has a special relation to memory and to the past, which it both commemorates and reinvents. That is why memory is thought to be on the side of the angels, an unquestioned good, a calling forth of all that is lost in transcription and documentation. Oral communications and performances are revised as they pass from person to person, so that their variants tap particularities and local nuances that the universal project of history overlooks.[9] The thousands of Bolívar anecdotes that flourish in Colombia and Venezuela confound the monumentality of the national hero. In some of these versions, he is said to be the child of a black laundress and is rowed from his birthplace to La Guaira by a boatful of black oarsmen—a tale that tells us nothing of the historical Bolívar but accurately expresses black Venezuelans' attempt to put themselves back into a history from which they have been excluded.[10] The messianism of popular indigenous rebellions has been fueled by traditions, invented or otherwise. At the present time, indigenous groups seek to restore myths and festivities suppressed by the conquerors.

In his book *The Presence of the Word*, Walter Ong makes the spoken word the repository of knowledges that print culture blotted out.[11] Tapping the memory of subjects who had been absent from the historical record activates both a more vital subjective relation to the past and gives some access to underground or hidden collectivities—the remnants of Judaism, the scraps of indigenous beliefs, the culture of women and Afro-Americans. Memory also has a privileged relation to the constitution of the subject, for it gives a sense of continuity that by analogy has been extended to communities that have taken as their task the protection of traditions against an invasive colonial world. So now it is not just memory but *social* or *collective* memory that is seen as resistant to the dominant narrative, although this can also disappear if it is not preserved in some way.[12] Finally, there is a memory *work*, a productive activation of memory enabling it as a political weapon in traumatized societies.

In a critical account of postmodernism and memory, Kirwin Lee Klein observed that postmodern thinking often smuggles in semireligious language deployed in favored contemporary terms—"aura," "Jehnzeit," "messianic," "sublime," "apocalypse," "fragmentation"

—concluding that "this is not the vocabulary of secular critical practice."[13] But it is precisely the inability of "secular critical practice" to account for extremes of horror, for the amnesia brought on by trauma, and for what cannot be uttered in the language of pragmatism that accounts for this apparent backsliding. Hector Schmucler also pointed out that the word "memory" often acquires an exemplary and even a magical function "that stems from an opaque determinism." That is why there has to be critical reflection on the historical trauma that prompts social memory.[14] This is one of the tasks that literature has undertaken.

The Politics of Memory

In the countries of the Southern Cone the problem is not only how this critical reflection is to be sustained but also how to deal with the amnesia officially imposed by laws that prevent a settling of accounts with the past. In Argentine, the government of Alfonsín, which took over in 1983 after the military dictatorship, initially undertook to investigate human rights violations by the military. They formed an independent commission, CONADEP (Comisión Nacional sobre la Desaparición de Personas, or National Commission on the Disappearance of Persons), whose 1984 publication of victim testimonies, *Nunca Más (Never More)*, was based on 50,000 pages of evidence.[15] *Nunca Más* is not a dispassionate document but what is most striking is that the emotion is expressed far more strongly in the report of the commission than in the actual testimonies of victims, who often had difficulty describing the horror. Indeed, during the trials of members of the military junta, the proceedings were stopped whenever witnesses became too emotional.[16] The *Nunca Más* report itself uses strongly emotional language to impress on the readers "the enormity of what had happened, the transgression of the very foundation of the species."[17]

The trial and sentencing of members of the military junta were halted after five months by the government, which placed a sixty-day limit on new criminal summons, in other words a *punto final* (a full stop). This was followed by the Ley de Obediencia Debida (Law of Due Obedience) that gave amnesty to most members of the armed forces, which in turn was followed in 1989 and 1990 by presidential pardons for those still in jail, including members of the junta.

In Chile, there was a similar freezing of the process. The Aylwin government—the *Concertación de Partidos por la Democracia,* or Accord of Parties for Democracy—began its regime in 1990 by publishing a list of detained and disappeared persons, putting up a monument to the victims of the military government in the General Cemetery, and creating a Comisión de Verdad y Reconciliación (Commission of Truth and Reconciliation) without judicial powers, whose aim was to "contribute to the global clarification of the truth about the most serious violations of rights committed in recent years." Its report analyzed the causes of human rights violations and the behavior of the armed forces and the judiciary and proposed a series of measures to prevent any repetition. "In a televised address, President Aylwin asked for pardon for the victims and requested that those responsible for violations recognize the pain they had caused." Amnesty was then given for human rights crimes committed between 1973 and 1978, effectively halting any proceedings until the arrest of Pinochet in London in 1998, an arrest that had worldwide repercussions.[18]

In all countries of the Southern Cone, courts continue to deal in some way or another with death and disappearance, nearly thirty years after the events that caused them. In Guatemala and El Salvador peace processes prompt public revelations of what had always been locally known and remembered.[19]

The power of the media, on the other hand, has supported the official versions of events. In Chile, the story goes, a nation dangerously divided went through periods of chaos and internal strife; order was restored by the military and this allowed the eventual transition to democracy and a policy of reconciliation. Torture, exile and death, the wreckage of the Left, the overturning of a democratically elected government, and the dirty wars that destroyed innocent as well as guilty lives are folded in to an upbeat narrative.

But for relatives of the dead and disappeared and many others, there is a less palatable story that cannot be suppressed. In Argentina, on the twentieth anniversary of the military coup that took place on March 25, 1996, thousands of people demonstrated in different parts of Buenos Aires, including at the sites of former death camps. Among the organizations that participated in this commemoration were the Mothers of the Plaza de Mayo (now split into two factions), the *Abuelitas* (Grandmothers) of the Plaza de Mayo, human rights organizations, and the Children of the Disappeared—that is to say, those organizations and civilian groups that had taken on the task of investigating the fate of the children of the disappeared and identifying the torturers. Through ritual and performance, these groups have turned their subjective memories into collective memories; and they have used personal testimonies to challenge the management of memory in the service of the state. There are other modest but insistent reminders like the necrologies published in the daily papers in commemoration of the disappeared, whose individual fates are detailed under their photograph.

What gave a powerful inflection to the official policy of amnesia, however, was the fact that it occurred during a period of transition to a free market economy, with all that implies in the way of bombarding the society with images and "information." As Walter Benjamin noted, the eyes of the modern city dweller are "overburdened with protective functions" because of the proliferation of images.[20] To similar effect has been the proliferation of other forms of communication—printed signs, handouts, newspapers, magazines, e-mail messages and notices—designed for such rapid scanning that they scarcely make an imprint on consciousness. The media operate like a vast shredding machine that reduces even the most significant events to confetti. When, in Argentina, the photographs of the disinterred bodies of the victims of the military appeared on bookstands alongside pinups, images of horror were assimilated into entertainment.

Collective or social memory has traditionally been activated by place, by specific sites. The relative permanence of certain places resists the rapid flow of time and permits sedimentation. That is why particular places—the sites of death camps, for example—have become places of commemoration although there are major contentions over how those who died should be remembered, revealing in part the depth of division in societies between those who supported the military and those who want them to be brought to justice. Such contentions are of major importance for they bring issues of memory, justice, and history into civic debate.[21]

Modernization and urban planning, too, contribute to the erasure of historical memory. Beatriz Sarlo has characterized the shopping mall as a machine of amnesia. "In the shopping centers," she wrote, "which are conservationist, history is paradoxically treated as *souvenir* and not as a material support of an identity and temporality that always stand in conflict with the present."[22] Perhaps the most egregious example is the Punto Carretas shopping mall in Montevideo that was built on the site of a notorious prison where, during the recent military regime, dissidents and revolutionaries were kept in solitary confinement and where some were shot. The thick walls that surrounded the prison have been left standing on one side of the mall, and the old prison entrance now serves as the entrance to the mall—a three-story kaleidoscope of stores and eateries such as Burger King. Here postmodern citation (the remains of the prison walls) lends a playful aspect to the shopping center, marking the difference between the grim "before" and the joyful shopping spree of the "after." That the prison was the site of a spectacular escape by Tupamaro guerrillas, who tunneled under the wall into a house opposite the prison, is allowed to be forgotten; unless you already know about it, there is nothing to indicate that it ever happened. One is struck above all by the sheer impudence of the architects who reduced the violence of the past to a citation, emptying the stones of any association with dread and repression. In some ways it stands as a parody of recent history, and the clearing of space by the military so that the development of a global market economy would not be hindered.

Given this will to forget, it is civic organizations—the Mothers of the Disappeared, the Grandmothers of the Disappeared, the Children of the Disappeared in Argentina, and the Families of the Disappeared in Chile—that have undertaken the work of detection, forensic research, identification of remains, the tracing of children, and the accumulation of evidence in order to bring the perpetrators to justice. In Argentina, the Children of the Disappeared marked the houses of torturers. Human rights organizations identified loopholes in the amnesty law that permitted torturers to be tried for the abduction of children and the murder of foreigners. In such circumstances in which the sifting of data and expertise in law are of primary importance, in which the historical trauma shows up the poverty of language, literature and art are in a delicate position; for it is all too easy to exploit sensationalism or to fill with words what is not altogether utterable.

Is Torture a Literary Matter?

As is well known from Elaine Scarry's study, *The Body in Pain,* pain eludes memory and verbal articulation.[23] The laconic statements of victims published by human rights organizations underscore the inexpressibility of torture. "Twice I was taken blindfolded to another annex and there they forced me to strip beside a wall and roughly with aggressive words they lay me on flexible metal bed, they tied me down as on a stake and then 'shocked' *(picanear)* on the lower abdomen and the vulva while they interrogated me," goes one statement in *Nunca Más*.[24] Victims grope for a language that fails them, so that their narrative of horror is often banal.

Memoirs promise the truth but also often founder on the poverty of language. Those memoirs that recount the dictatorship in Argentina, such as Jacobo Timerman's *Prisoner without a Name, Cell without a Number*[25] and Alicia Partnoy's *Little School*,[26] have the force of revelation even though their authors struggled to articulate their experience. It is a rare memoir—for instance, Partnoy's *Little School* or Hernán Váldez's *Tejas verdes*—that manages to convey the effect of pain and abjection.[27] In both these memoirs, the body is a repository of somatic rather than verbal memory, which manifests itself in attempts to avoid further pain. In Partnoy's memoir, "The Little School" is the euphemistic name given to the prison in which the military carried on their obscene activities. A prisoner was "a package," and those who had given information were *chupados* (sucked dry). While she was being tortured, Partnoy tried to displace the pain by repeating a children's rhyme about a rabbit that she had recited to her daughter. When she recited this to herself in baby talk, it was both an act of defiance but also a tragic infantilization.[28]

In experiences reported at second hand, there is a fine line between banality and voyeurism. After reading a report on torture in the *Times Literary Supplement,* the Argentine poet Juan Gelman wrote:

> los genitales se disiparon en la niebla de Londres
> envueltos en las hojas amarillas del times literary supplement
> la tinta los excitó
> la tinta convirtió su rabia en hechos somáticos eróticos
>
> acá lo somático es así:
> aplican la picana eléctrica en los genitales
> queman golpean el cuerpo tendido y vuelven a aplicar la picana
>   eléctrica en los genitales
>
> varados en el sur[29]
>
> [The genitals have disappeared in London fog
> Wrapped in the yellow pages of the times literary supplement

> The ink excited them
> The ink converted their rage into erotic somatic facts
> Here the somatic goes thus:
> They apply the electric prod to the genitals
> They burn and beat the prone body and again apply the electric
>   prod to the genitals
> Aground in the south]

"They apply the electric prod to the genitals" foregrounds the distance of words from the experience; the power of words to circulate, to convey information across distance is ineffective here and the affectless language of journalism ensures that torture will soon become old news as far as the metropolis is concerned: as for the "south," it is now "aground," a dehumanized experimental body that cannot articulate its suffering.

One of the most powerful fictional representations of the effects of torture is Luisa Valenzuela's "Cambio de armas" ("Weapon Exchange"), the story of a woman who has no memory of the immediate past.[30] Confined to an apartment where she waits the visits of a lover, she slowly reconstructs her recent history through a process of induction by observing the behavior of her apparent lover or husband while fearing the surfacing of a true memory. The lover is a member of the secret police who has tortured and broken her; and when they have sex they are watched by two men in the corridor. The "lover" wants to bring back memory because, without her remembrance of torture, his triumph over her is incomplete. What makes her resist abjection is somatic memory and the association of the keyhole of the apartment (the witness to her imprisonment) with the sights of an assault rifle. This "void" or hole is a recurrent trope of the story; it is the void of the past that the staging of a "normal life" is intended to cover over; it is the lack in herself that the sexual act is supposed to fill; it is also the blocked passage to the outside world to which she does not have the key and the blocked consciousness that can only be liberated when she finally remembers how to destroy the blockage—that is, her lover.

Valenzuela's story shows how fine a line there is between the literary representation of rape and torture and pornography and between sadomasochism and torture, both of which offer voyeuristic pleasure. The market is indiscriminate—what for some is a moral outrage may well be titillating to others. If there is no sensitivity to the problems of expression, a narrative or a memoir may well end up responding to the demand of the market for sensationalism.

But if Valenzuela examines this risky borderline between sadomasochism and torture, other less skillful writers do not. I am thinking in particular of the novel by Lawrence Thornton, *Imagining Argentina,* and Omar Ribadella's *Requiem for a Woman's Soul,* both of which use torture and disappearance to add piquancy and sensation to their texts.[31] Thornton's novel, praised by J. M. Coetzee on the book's jacket as "brave, inventive and powerful," has as its protagonist a theater director who is able to imagine what happens to the disappeared. But the descriptions of torture cannot escape the banal: "When live wires were applied to his testicles, he felt as if a hot vise had been clamped to the tenderest part of his body," or "she felt hands on her breasts which reached inside her brassiere, and then there was intense pain as her nipples were crushed." Ribadella's *Requiem for a Woman's Soul* is straightforwardly voyeuristic. Purported to be based on papers found by a priest, it details the sexual indignities committed on a woman prisoner. What makes the book problematic, however, is that the descriptions of torture are suspiciously close to the prose style of soft porn: "The first guard to enter my cell during what I believe to be the night hours was the pervert who, after the usual fondling and obscenities, ejaculated again all over my breasts." This not only represents a favorite fantasy of porn literature and film but by emphasizing "pervert" and "obscenity" the description underscores the intention of the text and crosses the line between information and titillation.

It is difficult for literature to question these mixed emotions when it un-self-consciously uses the narrative devices of crime fiction.[32] The same may be said for true confessions like the memoir *El infierno* by Luz Arce, who, after a period of militant leftist activity, went over to the DINA (the Chilean secret police).[33] Luz Arce had been an athlete who joined the Socialist Party and rose rapidly in the ranks to become a bodyguard working in the Moneda during the presidency of Allende. After the military coup, she went underground for a short time, was captured and repeatedly raped and tortured with the electric prod while watching her companions go to their death. She finally broke when her brother was brought in by the DINA and when her child was threatened. The sergeant who was supposed to help her bathe sodomized her. But in common with many victims, Luz Arce's description of pain under torture is laconic: "He beat and burned me. I cannot describe that moment. As soon as I recovered consciousness I lost it again." At other times, she uses commonplace metaphors—it was "as if a thousand needles had entered me . . . Strong pains in the stomach made me groan . . ."

Once broken, Arce was kept for a year in a limbo, after which she began to integrate herself into the military intelligence corps thanks to her affairs with high DINA officials. Luz Arce rose rapidly from a post as secretary to become a high-level official of the DINA. She drew up intelligence reports, gave names, and was present at some torture sessions. She explains that she was able to do this because she managed to disassociate herself from her surroundings. She professes anguish for fellow prisoners condemned to death but is also attracted to the high-level officers with whom she had affairs. Her disgust is largely reserved for the lower ranks. She describes herself as having been starved for family affection as a child, and this too becomes a useful alibi since her affairs with the military, like those with members of the underground, can be attributed to her need for affection.

What strikes a jarring note in this recounting is not so much the account of torture but the narrative framework of confession and Christian forgiveness that makes of Luz Arce a successful survivor rather than a guilty participant, conforming to Paulo Virno's description of the contemporary cynic.[34] Her story is prefaced by a priest, her religious conversion serving as a guarantee of her social redemption. She repeatedly mentions her testimony to the Truth Comission and the information she had given about the disappeared in order to stress her usefulness to the redemocratization process. In the words of the critic Nelly Richard, memoirs such as Arce's "naturalize obedience to a higher authority of the Church allowing these women who have occupied places generally thought to be 'masculine,' because they are associated with power, to retain their feminine identity, and once again uphold the family, motherhood and responsibility from which position they then plead for pardon."[35] Diamela Eltit argued that such narratives privilege the flexible and adaptable subject that is promoted by late capitalism. "What is broken, what is fragmented in these memories," Eltit wrote, "is the rupture of the very thing that defines the subject's identity as belonging to an ideological core, a political backbone, leaving it exposed to the void, to its own nothingness, and to the ideological price of self-disembodiment." What disturbs Eltit, however, is not that women like Luz Arce are broken, since few readers are in a position to judge the situation of those who were raped, tortured, and imprisoned, but rather the telling of the story in a way that trivializes treachery by making it a recurrent aspect of their character. Treachery becomes synonymous with adaptability. Such nomadic subjects devoid of ethics and dedicated to survival at any cost have become intelligible in the era of savage capitalism and neoliberalism.[36]

Luce Arce's book was published by the Spanish publishing house, Planeta, now one of the privileged institutions of the culture industry. As Nelly Richard pointed out, "The memory of the dictatorship that is disseminated by the market enters into that play of signs that are rapidly recycled in the flux of the market and there is no time to do more than mention history in passing: references to the past must not present any rough edges nor communicative harshness so as not to alter the light rhythm of variations and diversion that characterizes the aesthetics of redemocratization." Where, Richard asks, "is that reflexive and analytic density of memory; it is precisely the conflictive and interrupted memory whose meanings, intentions, styles, passions and calculations are not debated." She thus questions the staging of memory as true memories and asks, "[I]s it enough to know about the past for it to acquire active meaning? Can we believe the memory has been activated just because certain discourses evoke it?" She argues that memory is more than what has gone before; the politics of amnesia make it necessary to reintegrate fragments of the past into new interpretive structures, making the past say what was not known before or what was silenced and producing reconceptualizations of what has happened in order to salvage and to make note of omissions. "Memory must be made into a productive complex *(nudo)* that gathers together the traces of historical signification and narratives in the present."

In her 1986 novel *Por la patria (For the Fatherland)* Eltit uses fractured language to speak of torture:

> Me ven, me toman, me temen,
> Me cercan, me pescan, me cuelgan.
> L'ostil
> gresan
> gresan
> GRESAN
>
> Romuert
> Estoy

By scrambling words—*sangre* (blood) becomes "gresan"; *muerto* (dead) becomes "romuert"—the novelist underscores the fact that torture fragments the very process of articulation so that what might be communicated as *estoy muerta* (I am dead) becomes a private language.

Disappearance

The massive disappearances in Argentina has made the work of mourning particularly agonizing. On the one hand there is the contentious battlefield in which the politics of memory are waged and, on the other, the slower and more painful work of mourning that often cannot be completed.[37] Addressing both the representation of death in Western culture and the anonymity of modern death exemplified in the media's treatment of massacres and epidemics, Nelly Snaith wrote of the need to find forms other than those enthroned by the aesthetic or documentary traditions to deal with material "on which it is as difficult to speak as to be silent, a matter that surely weighs on the unconscious of social feeling and ought to weigh on the active consciousness of a society that is none other than its members."[38] After seeing the Argentine film *The Official Story,* which chronicled the fate of the children of the disappeared and became an international success, she was repelled by its use of melodrama and the fact that the film concentrates on the individual and is unable to deal with the unnamed dead of the common graves. For Snaith, films and literature that disidentify—that is, that interrupt the process of identification—are more effective in disturbing the spectator or reader. One work she cites is Griselda Gambarro's play *El campo (The Camp),* which, though written before the military coup, staged the culture of fear.[39] But she also could have mentioned Gambarro's play *Atando cabos (Loose Ends),* a dialogue between a man (possibly a former army officer) and a woman who are shipwrecked together on an island. The woman cannot travel by air because of the haunting memory of the body of her fifteen-year-old daughter being thrown from a plane during the repression. The officer, Martín, tries to flirt with the woman but becomes irritated when she insists on talking of her daughter, about whose death he feels no guilt for he is not a survivor but the victor. He tells her, "I don't need to imagine. I wrote the book. I wrote every story you ever heard. And the people who write the stories are the only ones that can be free and proud. We don't need absolution." The woman, however, has the last word, promising that "you'll drown on land because you won't be able to wipe out my memory.

You can never live in this world that I'm passing through. You can never swim in the same water."

The Argentine poet Juan Gelman drew on the language of the mystics to speak of the pain and guilt he felt after the disappearance of his son. Gelman had been sent to Rome during the worst of the terror in Argentina to act as the spokesperson of the *montoneros*. In 1976, his son Marcelo Ariel, aged twenty, and his son's pregnant wife Claudia disappeared. Marcelo Ariel was executed, his body placed in an oil drum filled with sand and cement and thrown into the San Fernando River where it was found thirteen years later. Claudia was transferred to Montevideo and never seen again. Gelman spent years tracing the whereabouts of their child who was born in captivity and put up for adoption.

The poems addressed to his son deploy Gelman's unusual punctuation—the slash dividing phrases. In them, Gelman often assumes the place of what has generally been considered the "feminine" and addresses his son as if he were still a baby or a child that he is nursing or comforting before going to sleep.

> ¿tan me desfuiste que ya no veré
> crepuscularte suave como hijo
> compañándome a pulso? / ¿delantales
>
> que la mañana mañanó de sol? /
> ¿bacas que te paceiron la dulzura? /
> cuaderno de la vez que despertabas
> como calor que nunca iba a morir?[40]

The son who is addressed as *niña* (girl) cries out against *la padre* (father with the feminine article). Gelman plays on the similarities between the word for father—*padre*—and the word for suffering—*padecimiento*—creating the neologism *padrecimiento* (father suffering). His pain affects the tongue—*lengua padecida* (suffered tongue)—yet he also questions whether bodily pain can be commuted into mental pain: "¿Cómo no son de mi cabeza . . . estos padeceres?" (How are these sufferings not of my head?). Joan Lindgren's fine translations of Gelman's poems in *Unthinkable Tenderness* does not include this poem, so I offer my own version of the last lines:

> Little soul do you fly from me? you un-went so far that I will not
>   longer see
> you softly and twilighting like a son

accompanying me, step by step
aprons that morning morninged in sunlight?
cows that sweetly grazed? notebook of the time that you woke
    like warmth that was never going to die?

The questions in the final lines refer back to an irrecoverable moment of domestic and pastoral bliss, but memory is a deceptive notebook, "notebook of the time that you woke like warmth that was never going to die." I translate *desfuiste* as "unwent" rather than diswent because I was reminded of the "undead"—those who are not properly buried and so continue to haunt. His son went away but he also disappeared. He unwent—and there are the little pieces that are left. Putting together the pieces is not picking up and carrying on for there are connotations of exhumation and bodily remains. In the final verse introduced by the domesticity of the apron and the childish misspelling "bacas" (for *vacas* (cows)), he goes back to childhood when the boy (feminized as *niña*) used to wake in the night, "like a warmth that was never going to die." Why the feminization? In fact it is only by altering the attribution of particular qualities to men and women that the poet can express grief that has undone the supposedly strong armor of the masculine.

In many poems of the series, Gelman uses the prefixes "des," "un," or "dis" to turn a positive into a negative in a process of derealization. In poem VII he speaks of *"deshijándote"*—"unsoning you," "unsoning me." In poem VIII the son is *"desmadrado"*—unmothered—but *desmadre* is also slang for chaos. The son "ungirls," "unsuffers," the father "gelmans him." The suffix "dis" is not only a negative but suggests a reversal of the process of birth and creation. Finally, memory has nothing to hang on to but loss:

> no quiero otra noticia sino vos /
> cualquiera otra es migajita donde
> se muere de hambre la memoria / cava
> para seguir buscándote / se vuelve
>
> loca de oscuridad / fuega su perra /
> arde a pedazos / mira tu mirar
> ausente / espejo donde no me veo /
> azogás esta sombra / crepitás
>
> sudo de frío cuando creo oírte /
> helado de amor yago en la mitad
> mía de vos / no acabo de acabar /

> es claramente entiendo que no entiendo
> (I want no other news except of you / any other
> would be feeding crumbs to the memory
> that is dying of hunger / that digs and digs
> to keep on looking for you/ goes
> crazy with darkness / sets its own fury on fire /
> burns to pieces / looks at your absent gaze /
> mirror where I can't see myself /
> you silver this shadow / a rustling of you
> cold sweat when I think I hear /
> you / frozen with love I lie with my half
> of you / always unable to come /
> clearly I understand that I don't understand.)[41]

Memory is a constant process of frustrated agony, a burning, the absence of an image. "It dies of hunger," "digs to go on searching," "returns mad with darkness." The digging recalls the grave dug in the air in the well-known poem by Paul Celan, "Todesfuge." Although Gelman has the memory of the son as a child, he cannot remember the pain of his dying because it is outside his own experience. And if memory balks then the work of mourning cannot be completed. "No acabo de acabar." Here Lindgren's translation "always unable to come" makes too explicit the suggestion of physical love. The Spanish "no acabo de acabar" ("I do not finish finishing") is more appropriate to the incompleteness of the work of mourning.

While many of Gelman's poems are epitaphs for lost causes and lost comrades on the Left, these poems and a remarkable prose poem to his mother upset traditional representations of masculine and feminine. In the poem-letter to his mother, he evokes the plenitude of the womb, reproaches her for expelling him, and asks, "¿Por eso escribo versos? / ¿Para volver al vientre donde toda palabra va a nacer? / ¿por hilo tenue? / ¿la poesía es simulacro de vos? / ¿tus penas y tus goces? / ¿te destruís conmigo como palabra en la palabra? / ¿por eso escribo versos? / ¿te destruyo así pues? / ¿nunca me nacerás? / ¿las palabras son estas cenizas de adunarnos?" ("Why do I write poems? To return to the womb where every word is born / because of a tenuous thread? Is poetry your simulacrum? Your suffering and pleasure? Are you destroyed with me as word in the word? Is that why I write? Do I destroy you then? Will you never give birth to me? Are words these ashes of our uniting?")[42]

Obstinate Memory

How is memory to be nurtured, maintained, or activated among generations who did not experience the trauma? To ask this is to pose the question of much post-Holocaust writing on representation.[43] In shooting the film *Obstinate Memory*, Patricio Guzmán attempted to intervene against amnesia by filming a Chilean audience while they watched parts of his seven-hour documentary *The Battle of Chile*, which had been filmed in 1973 but never released for public screening in that country. The three-part 1973 film had recorded the unrest and violence of the last months of the Allende government, the bombing of the Moneda palace, and the beginnings of repression. Returning to Chile after nearly a quarter of a century, Guzmán showed videos of *The Battle of Chile* to groups of students who would have been too young to experience the events as well as to others who had lived through them, and filmed their reactions.

In the second documentary, Guzmán included clips from *The Battle of Chile* and interviews with viewers. He also staged representations that brought the slogans of the past incongruously into the present. A clip from his 1973 film that shows President Allende "saluting crowds of supporters during a parade from a slow-moving car surrounded by personal body guards is juxtaposed with a reenactment of the scene with the same bodyguards, now visibly older, marching beside an empty car on a silent and empty street watched by a stunned handful of spectators." As Marcial Godoy points out in a review of the film, "this staged juxtaposition between past and present performs the act of remembrance itself while simultaneously exposing a locality that has been emptied of all referents for collective remembrance."[44] In her discussion of the film, Nelly Richard distinguishes between recollection and memory; the film activates recollection "making it vibrate biographically in the individual confrontation with the past and emphasizing the emotive link between recollection and memory." Yet, in her opinion, the film does not answer the question of how individual memory can be linked to some form of social inscription.[45] One of the final images of the film is of a student overcome by emotion after the showing of the *Battle of Chile*. His inability to utter even the most minimal sound exposes not only the problem of memory but of language itself.

The visual image records an absence, a loss. As Roland Barthes wrote in *Camera Lucida,* when we look at a photograph of ourselves we anticipate our death.[46] In the politics of memory in Argentina and Chile, photographs of the disappeared held up in demonstrations or placed along the streets were eloquent reminders not only that the person had been there but also of the virtuality of memory and the irrecoverability of the past. This was brought home clearly in a *New York Times* article on Charles Harmon, whose disappearance in Chile was concealed by U.S. officials who were privy to his fate. A photograph of the young hippy and his wife juxtaposed with one of his middle-aged wife at the present time illustrated the immense gulf between then and now. With the passage of time, the outmoded hair styles and the clothing seem anachronistic, estranged, no longer part of our world. In the exhibition entitled "Buena Memoria," or the good memory, the Argentine artist Marcelo Brodsky reproduced photographs from the 1968 yearbook of the National Lycée. Crosses covered the faces of two disappeared pupils. The others were depicted in photographs showing them as having grown up, launched their careers, and had families. The final photograph in the exhibition showed the currents of the river into which many bodies of the disappeared were thrown. As witness to the fact that "I was here" but am no longer here, the photograph is a haunting as much as a memory. It is the passage of time that was recorded, a passage of time that does not diminish the urgency of a demand for justice but brings to the fore new perspectives, nuanced perceptions that transcend the binary oppositions of the past.

Writing of an exhibition of the work of Carlos Altamirano in the Fine Arts Museum of Santiago, in which framed portraits of the disappeared were interspersed with a variety of other images, Nelly Richard pointed out that the "fixity and suspension of these photographic portraits are in contrast with the changing rapidity of the electronic flow suggested by the sequence formed by the other images." She went on to comment that "Altamirano's work suggests the conflict between the photographic trace of the disappeared (a trace that is always at risk of disappearing) and the multiple technologies of forgetting that occupy the act of seeing, clearing the gaze until memory loses any significance and its knot of violence is left without weight or gravity of significance."[47]

Critics like to cite Walter Benjamin's assertion that "[t]o articulate the past historically does not mean to recognise it 'the way it really was.' It means to seize hold of a memory as it flashes up at a moment of danger." "Only the historian will have the gift of fanning the spark of hope in the past who is firmly convinced that even the dead will not be safe from the enemy if he wins."[48] By stretching it a bit one can see how the house arrest of Pinochet represented such a moment of crisis, though in a world that can no longer be thought in the oppositional terms that Benjamin suggested. The arrest of Pinochet made history once again possible by forcing open the archives. Legal loopholes allowed lawyers to revive cases after the immense archaeological work of discovering and identifying bodies. While obstinate memory initiates the task, it cannot but be allied to justice and restitution as these are reinscribed in the social text.

Literature in a State of Memory

In his book *The Untimely Present,* the Brazilian critic Idelber Avelar wrote that Tununa Mercado's novel, *En estado de memoria (In a State of Memory)* "narrates the conditions of possibility for writing after catastrophe."[49] Written as a first-person narrative of exile and return, it is both memoir and novel—a text that is difficult to classify because, although the protagonist is clearly identifiable as Mercado herself, a referential reading is the least illuminating approach.[50] It is a deeply philosophical not to say ethical work that examines subtle states of consciousness in a way that is unusual in Latin American literature. And it is a sustained account of mental and physical symptoms beyond the immediate reality of exile in order to lay bare the very condition of personhood. It might even be described as "counter-memory," which for Foucault is similar to what Nietzsche called true history—that is a "history that severs its connection to memory, its metaphysical and anthropological model, and constructs a counter-memory—a transformation of history into a totally different form of time."[51]

In the opening pages of the novel, the anonymous narrator is waiting for her turn at the psychiatric clinic when a man called Cindal bursts into the waiting room in great distress from an ulcer, howling with pain and pleading to be committed. "The patients assembled in the waiting-room for problems that were quite minor compared to Cindal's terminal situation, were frozen, gripped by his shrieks and howls." The psychoanalyst refuses to change the schedule, however, and Cindal hangs himself: "Cindal whose name returns with regularity, always with the stress on the letter i, whose twisted posture appears over and over, was left to die because his demands could not be answered, and because demands of that nature do nothing but interfere with the lives of others and undermine the plenitude to which everyone has a right." It is these demands "that could not be answered" that are engaged by the novel. It is as if the skin of fantasy that protects most of us from recognition of the real, that is of death and mortality, is missing, leaving the protagonist permanently exposed to the horror of everyday life. By "real" I meant that fundamental human condition for which there is no cure and that many institutions seek to cover over with the veil of normalcy. Psychiatry with its promise of a cure is the principle offender, and the fact that Argentina is a country that probably has more psychiatrists per capita than any other country in the world, makes the many misencounters with promised cures all the more poignant.

In the course of the novel, the narrator extracts some bitter humor from her various unsuccessful visits to psychiatrists as well as other healers—dentists, gynecologists, and faith healers, even witch doctors, shamans and "masters." In one of her psychiatric sessions she is unable to utter a word, and "not one manifestation of the unconscious slipped out, not one dram." In another session with a friend who combined Freudian psychoanalysis, Zen Buddhism, and the way of Tao, she finally confesses that she wants to write but is baffled when the psychiatrist suggests taking a course in copy writing. From such frustrated encounters the narrator often emerges with physical symptoms that her psychiatrists vainly attempt to interpret, and when no explanation is forthcoming they refer her "from one set of hands to another, from the couch to the chair, with fluctuating interpretations of the symptoms, mistaking rigidity for hysteria, neurological disorder for returning to the womb, incontinence for attention-winning strategies and so on." This is a woman for whom the given world is intolerable, a woman who cannot deal with competition, tests, evaluations, and the countless ways in which one individual is pitted against another to measure his or her social worth. Her defense when she is forced into one of these situations is evasion, self-effacement, and refusal. It is not that she is antisocial but rather that the "social"—interpellating, as it does, a sovereign subject—is quite alien to her. Everything in her life suggests a flight from individuation. Her work as a ghost writer—correcting other people's prose, infiltrating her own ideas into another's writing—is anonymous, never publicly acknowledged. Her clothing and furniture are second-hand as if she cannot exercise those privileges of individualism—choice and taste. Indeed this condition of self-effacement applies to the published novel itself, with its grey and black color that fades into the background beside the bold red, orange, and blue favored by the book trade.

Exile does not altogether account for this extreme state of alienation. On a return visit to Argentina at the end of the military dictatorship, she revisits her old school and encounters a schoolteacher who is exactly as she remembers her. But the encounter brings back the memory of her first day at school when she discovered that she was not on the rolls. Even in those days, she felt that she was not inscribed in the social text.

Exile exacerbates a condition that is already latent, the more so because it is a period of suspense outside the normal flow of time. Reports of death and disappearance are inescapable; there are daily telephone calls, newspaper reports, the atrocity stories of new arrivals. "We almost always dream of death," she writes, using the collective pronoun while casting doubts on the possibility of a collective experience of exile. True, there are common experiences. Exiles live at second-hand. "We lived by proxy, through third parties, struggling with the memory of a country that was a thousand kilometers away and transporting it to the *barrios* of Águilas and Tlacopac." But the collective "we" turns out to be as illusory as those endless meetings and discussions, for she and her comrades merely construct a "political cathedral without territorial foundations," a structure that disappears as soon as the military government falls and the exiles return. What might for others have constituted a community among exiles is for her an expenditure of energy that cannot be the foundation for the future.

Nor can the narrator take refuge in memory as if it offered some translatable lesson or meaning. Memory for her is so intimately bound up with particularities—a gesture, a casual remark that sticks in the mind, some seemingly unimportant everyday activity like grilling a steak—that it becomes inscribed as *habitus* but, on no account, can it be commuted into social or collective memory. Thus the novel raises the crucial question of the possibility of a common or shared memory among those who have not lived the experience. In an attempt to understand what the return from exile might eventually mean for her, the narrator visits the village in Asturias, Spain, where her friend the exiled Ovidio Gondi was raised and finally tracks down a woman who remembers his father. She is shown a photograph of a field and a cross that marks the site where the father had been executed three years after Franco took power. But this experience that she carefully stores in her memory cannot be passed on to Gondi himself, who declares, "Everything is unreal and that's how it remains in one's memory." Even history when commuted into memory becomes private. On Sundays with her family she ritualistically visits the house, now a museum, in which Trotsky was murdered. The visits do not clarify the historical event nor convert her to Trotsky's political cause, but rather have the effect of absorbing this public figure into private family mythology.

On her return to Buenos Aires, she revisits the streets and buildings of her earlier life often without recognizing them, fictionalizing scenes that had never happened. Visiting her old apartment, she has a paranoid fantasy rather than a memory. The memory of her father walking down the streets of her native Córdoba is overlaid by the actual presence of one of the generals who still walks with impunity through the city. Feeling like a stranger whose psyche and body have acquired a membrane that separates her from the world, reality itself is affected: "things no longer have their former, normal weight and density, and they keep their distance from the subject in question, the mutant element in the structure" (p. 105). Still seeking some collective experience, she joins the Mothers of the Plaza de Mayo in their Thursday demonstrations, meeting women who have lost entire families in the repression. But she is not one of them, and as the days pass, so does the concept of community and of the polis as the place of achievable justice.

While some writers aspire to invent a new language, Mercado wants a new image of consciousness. At one point, she describes a "cellular chamber," "a secret factory, a compartment outside the flow of the five senses but spanning and subsuming them all through condensations still lacking nomenclature" (p. 69). It is this supplementary compartment that is both the place of terror, as she faces the possible destruction of the self, and the place that nourishes the imagination. What she discovers when she dares to penetrate "the forbidden zones of my memory" is not the memory of herself but an old photograph of concentration camps with mass anonymous bodies, open graves, a Nazi parade. For what is deeply recessed in memory is a holocaust and the shared responsibility of all humanity in the atrocity. And this photograph is, in its way, an image of community, "a collectivity" in which the individual (whether buried in a mass grave or in the ranks of the military) has been obliterated. Thus Mercado seems in quest of the "excluded middle" as Gillian Rose called it, between the libertarian or individualistic society and the totalitarian community.[52]

Mercado's narrator can only make tentative efforts from her own solitude to establish some minimal contact with others. In the first week of her return to Argentina, she becomes obsessed by a homeless man lying on a park bench exposed to the weather. He is said to have suffered a trauma that makes him shun the normal props of everyday life—the daily news, shelter, friendship. She tries to make contact with him only to realize that, though his condition seems to reflect her own "exposure," there is no commonality in their different solitudes.

Retreating into her study, she sits facing a high wall that blots out the view of the city and on which she begins to write. But she will not emerge from this Platonic cave with absolute knowledge, nor is it the kind of self-discovery that we often encounter in women's writing in which, after the trials of growing up, the girl finally puts pen to paper and arrives at consciousness of her own personhood. Still less does it lead to the self-forgetfulness that occurs when she is weaving. Writing is a far less benevolent experience; in it "one only encounters misfortune; and not misfortune as a personal sentiment, but as an expression of fundamental nakedness: not knowing, the inability to fill the void or approach the universal." The "void" is greater than the historical trauma. It is not something with which one comes to terms or that can be healed. Indeed, the months she had spent in a reading group in Mexico pouring over Hegel's *Phenomenology of Mind* without attaining some final grasp of the material is symptomatic, for, if we are to believe Slavoj Žižek, "Hegel knows very well that every attempt at rational totalization ultimately fails, this failure is the very impetus of the 'dialectical progress.'"[53]

The narrator's wall—"her doom and incitement," her "witness wall," a "hurdle" between herself and her "descent back to earth"—is an accident of construction that blocks her view while reflecting light before sinking into darkness. On its surface are traces like hieroglyphs that beg to be deciphered. And it is on this surface that she finally begins to write, not in a linear progression, but by forming small nuclei of writing with overlapping texts until, overloaded with writing, the wall slips down "like a sheet of paper sliding vertically into a slot." The destiny of writing is always this unknown and the message can only be sent when the wall of personal and collective memory is transformed into writing. The ending is both enigmatic and visionary, neither cure nor solution, and like all major works of fiction it raises questions rather than proposing solutions. But those questions are more pertinent today than ever before: they relate both to the crippling individualism of contemporary society and to the attempts to imagine community in something other than the framework of the national and an activity that is not work. Its politics are those of refusal.[54]

But memory can also be a cyborg affair—invented, reworked, and vertiginously reproduced by machines. Putting a positive aspect on things, Donna Haraway wrote, "The machine is not an *it* to be animated, worshipped, and dominated. The machine is us, our processes, an aspect of our embodiment."[55] Such is the proposition of Ricardo Piglia's novel *La ciudad ausente (The Absent City),* which confronts the problem of the social in the age of technology.[56] The novel is loosely structured by the travels of a journalist, Junior, descendant of British travelers, through Buenos Aires in a quest to preserve the "museum" of Macedonio Fernández, the eccentric anarchist writer for whom the museum was not a monument but a memory machine for his dead wife, for "la eterna."[57] Although the reader can assume that the novel is set in postdictatorship times, the entire city is under surveillance, peopled by informants and by batteries of cameras. People are elusive and "something had happened to the sense of reality." In a clinic, a certain Dr. Araña operates on memory, on "the white knots" or myths that "define the grammar of experience," transforming people from psychotics into addicts—that is into the postmodern abject. Since there is no longer an outside, resistance has to be rethought to avoid the pathetic fate of Julia Gandini, who goes from being a militant to become the voice of common sense. In his travels, Junior meets Russo, a disciple of Macedonio, who explains that "Macedonio clearly grasped the sense of this new situation. One must influence reality and use the methods of science to invent a world in which a soldier who has spent thirty years in the jungle obeying orders is impossible." (The reference is to a news story of a Japanese soldier who spent thirty years on a Pacific island and did not know that the Second World War was over). Russo believes that everything is controlled.

The new state is a mental state and all that remains of resistance is Macedonio's memory machine.

But memory is no longer Proustian since nobody any longer has memories of their own so it is Macedonio's Elena, now a memory machine, who is the source of stories that proliferate from a nuclei of white knots, or figures engraved on the banks of tortoises, the longest living creatures. Both white knots and the tortoise shell figures are the deep structures of storytelling that can link human beings in a virtual community that escapes the vigilance of the state. The novel ends with Piglia's Elena seeking the old lost voices in the desert, dragging herself towards the oasis and like Molly Bloom uttering her "yes" to the world.

In a seminal essay on "Postdictatorship and the Reform of Thinking," Alberto Moreiras, referring particularly to Chile, argued that political rethinking in the postdictatorship regime is done in the condition of mourning. "Marked by the loss of an object, thinking in postdictatorship thinks from depression and even thinks, above all, that very depression."[58] The Brazilian critic Ildeber Avelar also drawing on the Freudian description of the work of mourning and on Benjamin's discussion of allegory, situates a number of contemporary works of fiction in what he calls "the untimely present." He contrasts passive forgetting, "that brand of oblivion that ignores itself as such, not suspecting that it is the product of a powerful repressive operation," with the work of mourning.[59] He believes that literature reasserts its value as it undertakes the work of mourning that society itself tries to drown in the cacophony of triumphant celebration and argues that the new hegemony imposed by the military "reproduced itself by relentlessly annihilating the aura of the literary, unveiling that aura as a remnant of a moment still incomplete in the unfolding of capital." This new hegemony came into being with "the fall of the great alternative social project to emerge in Latin America at that moment: Salvador Allende's Popular Unity." What emerges from the terror is a topology of defeat of "the political practices that could have offered an alternative to the military regimes." At a time of "the epochal crisis of storytelling and the decline of the transmissibility of experience," literature can still hold out the possibility if not of alternatives, of the possibility of thinking beyond mourning.[60]

At the same time, as I argue in the last chapter, "literature" itself has become an uncertain category.

CHAPTER ELEVEN

Inside the Empire

Nothing escapes the neoliberal. Art and literature are not excluded. They are included.

DIAMELA ELTIT[1]

Ricardo Piglia's "yes" uttered in the desert and Diamela Eltit's mother and son baying like dogs at the very limits of the city at the end of her novel *Los vigilantes* are both situations on the edge. From each of them the view is not of triumphant capitalism but of the slender possibility of the recovery from catastrophic disaster that had swept away many of the assumptions that structured rebellion and opposition to the given world.[2] The desert and the moon are figures for a vanished space outside of the existing order that had been the place of the utopian imaginings I examined in the first three chapters of the book.

What many describe as the end of the utopian is a mild way of describing what has been lived in much of Latin America as historical traumas, in the aftermath of which both politics and culture have been irrevocably dislocated.[3] Each nation, however, had entered this new phase differently: in El Salvador and Guatemala, after repression and civil war that killed thousands; in Colombia civil society continues to coexist with civil war. In Peru, the campaign against the Shining Path guerrilla movement furthered the authoritarianism of the Fujimori regime. In the countries of the Southern Cone—Argentina, Brazil, Chile, and Uruguay—the military governments of the 1970s and early 1980s left a devastating legacy while eventually passing on the governmental torch to a democracy that is "complementary to and supportive of the transition to market-oriented economies."[4] Given the "intensified fusion of cultural, political, and financial interests" that, as Román de la Campa wrote, "closely correlates with postmodern constructs in the cultural terrain and neoliberalism in the

political sphere," art, music, and book publishing are increasingly influenced by market demands that, in turn, have radically altered literary culture.[5] Not only has the neoliberal nation state more to gain by
exporting soap operas than by encouraging literature, but the market
far from being a *free* market exercises its own exclusions.

Although there is still state support in most Latin America countries in the way of prizes, honors, and subsidies for artists and writers,
private enterprise has now stepped in as a major patron. One of the
most lucrative literary prizes is given by the publishing house Planeta,
and often goes to novels which can be assured of a public.[6] Corporate
sponsorship of this kind is a form of repressive selectivity since certain
kinds of literature and art are judged too marginal to reach the mass
public and there are not enough independent publishers and galleries
to serve as a counterbalance.

These days, culture is overwhelmingly the province of entertainment and of comfort activities that in turn generate "lite" criticism
that never challenges the *doxa*. "Lite" invades the novel and poetry as
well as popular music, while political dissidence may be more directly
and forcefully expressed in rock music and rap than in the arts, even
though the music industry is thoroughly commercialized. As state patronage weakens or disappears and corporate patronage takes over,
the enemy of artistic endeavor is no longer an overtly repressive state
but the standardizing effects of commercialization and the market
that have effectively driven poetry and avant-garde fiction to the
margins of culture, to the shelter of little magazines and artisan publications, and nowadays to the particularity of web sites. There are,
however, still pockets of avant-garde and bohemian dissidence, although these are fast disappearing. And what counts as literature has
changed, for it is no longer confined to categories that separate fiction
from reality. Hybrids of fiction and "real life," of true and invented
history, of travel literature and novel blur such boundaries. There are
new possibilities and constraints.

It can be argued that access to world literature through translation
lifts writers out of their provincialism. One symptom of this is that
contemporary Latin American novels and short stories take the world
as their scenario and are set in Europe, Africa or Asia.[7] Whereas in the
old days, culture flowed in one direction only between Paris, London,
and New York to Latin America, it is now two-way traffic in a world
that has no one cultural center. Translation that was always a road

out of provincialism is now recognized as more than a secondary exercise, a practice that is essential to emancipation and an "opening towards alternative versions of universality that are wrought from the work of translation itself."[8] This kind of translation confronts the international market that demands easy translatability, which of course constitutes another form of discrimination and selection.

Here the question of value resurfaces with a vengeance, especially when writers court an international public based on the "Latin" quality of their work. Laura Esquivel's *Like Water for Chocolate* is an interesting example of the "lite" literature since it entertains the notion of rebellion and offers a representation of Mexico that is not patriarchal but women dominated.[9] Both the novel and the film that is based on it question an already superceded tradition, represented by the repressive mother who is head of the household, although it is clear that the values she represents (the absurd tradition of not allowing one of her daughters to marry) belong to the distant past. The novel evokes tradition that is already dead (if it ever existed) in order to endorse a new order marked by the reconciliation of north and south through the marriage of the good doctor John's son and Rosario's daughter, Esperanza. In passing, it's interesting to note that *Like Water for Chocolate* can be classified as a "food" film of which there is an increasing number of examples (*Babbette's Feast* and *Chocolat,* to name two obvious examples). Such films allegorize eating as an idealized form of a consumption that knits communities together. In *Like Water for Chocolate,* food is both remedy and poison, separating the weak digestion from the robust. The novel is a more sophisticated version of the consumer side of the literary spectrum, where one finds the *novelas semanales* and *novelas rosas* with their invariable structures and their happy closure. Interestingly, the majority of the Mexican public enjoyed precisely those aspects of the film I have just criticized—for instance, the archaic customs that afforded them nostalgic pleasure, although this does not prove much except for the effectiveness of the *doxa.*[10]

Isabel Allende's recent novels suggest a more complex adjustment to the international market and to the presence of a Latino public in the United States, although their relentless chronologies suggest a kind of voiding of history's impact. Confronting this kind of translatability, Gayatri Chakravorty Spivak has stressed the importance of cultural literacy and of responsible translation especially as "[d]emocracy changes into the law of force in the case of translation from the third world."[11]

In the academic study of literature, there is a breakdown of older criteria of evaluation and the once clear divisions between high and popular art, between "what stood the test of time" and what was ephemeral. New forms of regionalization (Cono Sur studies, Andean studies, Caribbean studies) have redrawn the literary map following the geopolitical lines that are replacing national categories. Cultural studies that are not bound to the evaluative criteria of traditional literary studies have, from their institutional base in the United States, contributed to global homogenizing while ignoring "the significant density and the operative materiality of their corresponding enunciative contexts."[12] Paradoxically, it is in the academy and particularly in the U.S. academy, where Latin American studies deploy considerably more resources than in Latin American itself, that experimental art and difficult fiction still find a readership.[13]

The Argentine critic Beatriz Sarlo and the Brazilian writer and critic Silviano Santiago have different responses to this crisis of value. In *Escenas de la vida posmoderna,* Sarlo monitored the possible effects on politics, art, and intellectual life of the culture industry and argued that different brain functions are brought into play with channel surfing, the viewing of video clips, and the kind of problem solving that occurs in video games; she contrasts this with the intellectual involvement required by reading. Castigating the "cultural neopopulism" of many critics who celebrate the relativism of taste and the disappearance of artistic value, she reminds her readers that it was the avantgarde that produced the best of twentieth-century culture.[14] "All cultural manifestations are not equal," she wrote. "There is something in the experience of art that makes it into a moment of semantic and formal intensity different from that of cultural practices, sport or television's continuum." In order to restore a critical edge to thinking and productive dissidence to the arts, she proposed more state patronage and the nurturing of cultural criticism "freed both from neopopulist celebration of existing culture and from the elitist prejudices that undermine the possibilities of articulating a democratic perspective."[15] While her analysis of new technologies is not different from that of many other critics, her remedies are no more convincing because past practices are not necessarily viable models. As one critic put it, "If in the past communication was organized fundamentally by means of

language and the institutions of ideological and literary/artistic production, today, because it is invested with industrial production, communication is reproduced by means of specific technological schemes
(knowledge, thought, image, sound, and language reproduction technologies) and by means of forms of organization and 'management'
that are bearers of a new mode of production."[16] If this is the case,
something more than deep reading seems to be indicated.

In contrast to Sarlo, Silviano Santiago argued that, in a country like
Brazil, literacy training is fruitless and it would be more effective to
tutor people in the sophisticated reception of television and video.

> [Reading] should be understood as an activity that transcends the expe-
> rience of knowledge, transmitted by phonetic writing. In a mass society
> of peripheral capitalism such as Brazil, we should look for the ways to
> improve the interpretation of both spectacle and simulacra by ordinary
> citizens. This means that the production of meaning ceases to be a mo-
> nopoly of restricted minorities who are, in conditions of inequality, bet-
> ter trained and thus more sophisticated. With that change, the singular,
> or authoritarian interpretation made by a legitimizing group (tradition-
> ally professional critics or experts) disappears. Meaning in symbolic
> and/or cultural production becomes plural and unattainable in its plu-
> rality.[17]

This recommendation reasserts the pedagogical function of the intellectual and extends the concept of critical reading to the media. But it
does not take into account the severely impoverished nature of the
media themselves, an impoverishment that has everything to do with
ratings.

Lines of Flight

In search of new ways of thinking about late capitalism and its cultures, many critics have drawn on the writing of Gilles Deleuze and
Félix Guattari, whose concepts—"lines of flight," "deterritorialization," "minority writing," "becoming-animal"—are common cur-
rency in Latin American intellectual debates as well as in left political
thinking in Europe.[18] Published in 1972, Anti-Oedipus, the first volume of their collaborative work Capitalism and Schizophrenia, was
not only a frontal attack on the institution of psychoanalysis but a
new configuration that broke down the separation of the individual
and the social and offered a typology of different societal and subjec-

tive regimes—from the primitive socius and the despotic and imperial machines to late capitalism's deterritorialization or abstraction of
value and affect. Capitalism, in their view, is the ultimate global
movement, functioning axiomatically rather than to a code; in other
words, it is indifferent to content and functions as an immanence
rather than in obedience to outside control.[19] Although, in their view,
deterritorialization (or abstraction) is not exclusive to capitalism but
is a process that begins with the simplest gesture—eating, for example[20]—it is a particularly powerful way of rethinking the fetishism
of the commodity, the money form, and the contemporary global
financialization. Concept-images such as the war machine and becoming-animal defy the separation of the human from the machine
and "nature" (if such a thing still exists). The globe is not divided into
oppositional blocks, one of which is destined to triumph over the
other, but into flows, coagulations, escapes. Resistance is not putting
up a fight to the death but the detection and intensification of "lines of
flight" that transform individuals. A new vocabulary of resistance val-
orizes margins, the minor, defections from the state, and active experimentation rather than global revolution.[21] It is not hard to understand, therefore, why their shift of emphasis from the state-controlled
subject to potentiality should be so appealing, for they give the intellectual a critical, though not a pedagogical or representative, role.

The influence of their thinking extends from the gay poet and activist Nestor Perlongher, for whom "becoming-woman" was a response
to patriarchal society, to the ethnographer Nestor García Canclini,
grappling with the cultural changes brought about by globalization.
In a chapter of his book *Hybrid Cultures,* García Canclini explains
hybridization as "the breakdown and mixing of the assemblages that
organized cultural systems, the deterritorialization of symbolic processes and the expansion of impure genres."[22] The novelty is that artistic practices no longer have any consistent paradigms and given the
ubiquity of hybridization, "all cultures today are border cultures."
Why then do some cultural practices transform meanings and situations and others do not?

No critic has been more inventive in grasping the need for a new
imaginary space for Latin America than the Chilean critic Nelly Richard, who, while making selective use of some of the same terms as
Deleuze and Guattari, has marshaled these into a broad critique of
neoliberalism as well as an evaluation of refractory cultural practices

in whatever form they take. Although she writes almost exclusively of Chile, her language reflects the global shift from the vertical (hierarchical) to the lateral, from the center to borders, from strong to weak or insubstantial, from primary to secondary, from the integrated to the unintegrated, from whole to fragments and shreds, from the complete and finished to the incomplete.

In *Residuos y metáforas (Residues and Metaphors)* Richard focuses on the particular historical trauma of postdictatorship Chile, a trauma whose origin is now in danger of slipping into oblivion. Using a geological metaphor, she sets out to identify "residual zones of unstable formations of cultural-symbolic deposits and sedimentations where the shredded meanings accumulate that tend to be omitted or set aside by social reason." These may be fragments of discourses "judged insubstantial" by the strong categories of academic discourse, but, though secondary and unintegrated, they "are able to displace the power of signification toward the most neglected limits of the scales of social and cultural value, in order to question discursive hierarchies from lateral positions and hybrid decentering."[23] The simple, direct, and transparent that is valued by the communications industry, and the practical, the pragmatic, the commonsensical valued by cynical reason may both be subverted by the artifice of staging and masking and by exploiting the ambiguities and slippages of language. There is no longer some absolute distinction that separates the cultural and the political. The aesthetic (defined as the will to form), the cultural (symbolic figurations), and the political (codifications of power and struggles over meaning) overlap and interact in the same space. Although she uses the terms "periphery" and "center," these are not necessarily geographical but virtual. The center is the place where hegemonic meaning is established and from which it is disseminated; the periphery is where the borders of intelligibility become friable.

Thus all kinds of cultural practices can be brought into Richard's analysis, even a news item like the 1996 escape by helicopter of several members of the guerrilla group Frente Patriótico Manuel Rodríguez from the maximum security prison in Santiago. The group had engaged in armed struggle against the dictatorship but their flight took place during the "transition," in which the dominant discourse stressed the consensus around the center that guaranteed political, social, and economic stability as against the chaos and danger represented by the "extremes," generally associated with the Allende regime and hence with groups like the Frente Patriótico. The preparations for the flight were meticulously coordinated both inside and outside the prison; a helicopter, whose pilot was not in on the plot, was rented and the group made their successful flight to freedom. Described as "spectacular" in the press, the escape resignified the two symbols of Chilean repression—the maximum security prison and the helicopter—and revitalized in the Chilean public the utopian dream of emancipation that had long been buried by the military and by the government of the transition. "Taking Heaven by Assault," the escapees confounded the *doxa* and reopened the utopian possibilities that the military dictatorship had foreclosed. In Richard's words, both the escape and the subsequent accounts of it published by the group constituted "the poetics of the event that altered the controlling syntax of everyday life, and enabled the opening of the lines of flight between zones of censure and inhibition in order to deterritorialize the everyday towards unsuspected margins of rebellion and contradiction" (p. 234, my translation). In common with other contemporary radical thinkers, Richard stresses that "deterritorialization" is not a negative separation from roots and authenticity, but rather a release of energies that would otherwise be bound to institutions such as the patriarchal family, the nation, and the work ethic.

Richard's writing reflects the changing place of literature in the spectrum of culture, for while she includes certain literary texts in her discussion of refractory practices, these are dispersed among different genres and activities. They are as likely to surface in memoirs, photographs, clothing style, transvestite performance, and art as much as in literature as such. This raises the question of what distinguishes refractory practices from the *doxa* and what possible repercussions they might have. Did the spectacular escape have long-term effects or was it merely a transient disturbance?[24]

The Glass House of Neoliberalism

Nelly Richard and other Chilean critics have nevertheless contributed to the redefinition of the public intellectual as a culture critic, and Richard gives space in the journal she founded, the *Revista de crítica cultural*, to those who like herself are engaged in an examination of the present, a reexamination of the past, and a redefinition of political and cultural alternatives. That this kind of redefinition should occur so vigorously in Chile is not hard to explain, for Chile had represented itself as the exemplary neoliberal state.[25] The government of the transition carried on the social change that the "Chicago boys" had begun under the military, changes that involved privatization and "making abundant natural resources available to transnational capital."[26] This, of course, involved a different national image, one that was put on display at the Seville World's Fair in the form of an iceberg. In her essay, "El modelaje gráfico de una identidad publicitaria," ("A Graphic Model of Advertisement Identity"), Richard argues that the iceberg was a way of marking a cool distance from any association with the murk of underdevelopment or the heated politics of the Popular Unity government of Allende. The Chilean organizers of the exhibit put on display the image of an efficient and attractive society whose two guiding concepts were Chile as a supermarket and the iceberg as national monument. The organizers had the iceberg towed from the Chilean Antarctic in order to create a kind of magical realist spectacle.[27] This natural marvel was intended to erase any reference to historical Chile—to disorder or insurrection—as well as to hide from view the internal conflicts over tradition/modernity, periphery/metropolis, and so on. Its pure whiteness decontaminated Chile of all former ideological references.

Richard's attention to the visual and the iconic registers the overwhelming importance of vision and the gaze in contemporary life. That everything is now on view is reinforced by the constant references to "transparency" in the new hegemonic discourse, a transparency that supposedly establishes the difference between the clear present and the dark corruption and secrecy of the past. Transparency is the seal of good conduct for presidents and generals in Chile, Argentina, Central America, and indeed the world, implying that now that the free market is in place, everything is on view, nothing is hidden any more, in contrast to the murky secrecy of the military regimes and the underground plotting of the guerrilla movements. But it also means that everything is on view like commodities in a showcase, a comparison that was inevitable when a transparent house was erected by artists in the center of Santiago. Funded by an official organization, the transparent house was designed so that viewers could watch the everyday activities of the inhabitant, an attractive woman, as she did household chores, showered, and went about her daily business.

Privacy was abolished. Private life had now become transparent, available for viewing, no longer hidden behind walls. But transparency was unexpectedly shown to be problematic when a woman who physically resembled the actress-inhabitant was chased down the street by a horde of excited men. The spectators seem to have taken transparency for availability, the woman for commodity, illustrating once again that technological modernity does not imply more enlightened attitudes.

The incident revealed the power of the gaze in a society of spectacle that regulates what is to be seen and what is invisible. Because of the ubiquity of television, video screens, and advertising, a blizzard of images overloads the eye. The consequences were vividly illustrated in an exhibition by the Chilean artist Catalina Parra that addressed the indiscriminate proliferation of images that are unavoidable in any modern urban setting.[28] Stitching together torn fragments from illustrated magazines, photographs, newsprint, and headlines, she put together several series whose titles (taken from the newspaper headlines and ads) proclaim the new common sense: "It's Indisputable." "It's Incomparable." These headlines assert themselves over a surface of fragmented images that are at once familiar and difficult to identify with any certainty—often sutured with bold stitches. Images of nature are juxtaposed with news photographs of war, perhaps of Kosovo though it could be any war. Who are these Asians waiting in a hangar? Who is that crowd running from gunfire? It is doubtful whether the spectator can match them up to any particular event. Indeed, the very fact that they are no longer identifiable shows how rapidly they are shuffled off into some twilight zone where one Third World crisis looks very much like another and this month's ad erases the memory of last month's.

The titles "It's Indisputable," "It's Uncontestable," and "If you Can't See much of a Difference" are newspaper headlines that evaluate while blocking out any other opinions. The emphasis on the negative acquires the force of the repression that is also emphasized in the recurrent images of police, soldiers, and guns. What we are seeing is the iron fist behind the freedom, and the incompatibility of elements of a global narrative that are visibly stitched together. The drabness of many of the news photographs depicting poverty and violence contrasts with the brightly colored pieces torn from advertisements that show clothes or furniture or sometimes nothing at all, just color. Nor can we escape from this world of commodities into nature since nature too is packaged and sold. The highly colored images of mountains and lush natural scenery are, after all, the images we construct of nature as a selling point. Parra's exhibition is one example of how political art is being realized in a globalized world in which vast populations and vast areas are "grey" and unspecified, like the "pale people" in Diamela Eltit's novel *Lumpérica*. It also reminds us that the visual is always already constructed, never innocent.[29]

Transparency is one term in a global discourse that claims universality (while practicing exclusions) and is by no means democratic in the full sense of the word. Given the difficulty of acting from an "outside," how can the limited democracies be transformed? Although this is a question most likely to be addressed by political theorists, it impinges on a cultural field in which the visibility of actors is made possible by their particularities, by difference.

Difference

In contemporary societies, culture is always political or perhaps the political is more and more cultural, as societies deploy and stage difference—gender difference and ethnic difference—as marketing devices. Political performance has, of course, always been staged by charismatic leaders. Former President Fujimori of Peru used a trademark karate chop to claim attention. President Vicente Fox of Mexico wears cowboy boots and a big hat to fortify his rural macho image.

Under what circumstances, then, does the performance of identity become transgressive? Judith Butler's widely discussed theory of "performance" emphasizes the constructed sexual and gender identities that self-reflexive performativity brings to the fore. In "Subversive Bodily Acts," the final chapter of her book *Gender Trouble,* Butler proposes "a set of parodic practices based in a performative theory of gender acts that disrupt the categories of the body, sex, gender, and sexuality and occasion their subversive resignification and proliferation beyond the binary frame."[30] Taking the case of drag, which "plays upon the distinction between the anatomy of the performer and the gender that is being performed," she argued that "[i]n imitating gender, drag implicitly reveals the imitative nature of gender itself—as well as its contingency," thus depriving "hegemonic culture and its critics of the claim to naturalized or essentialist gender identities."[31] In a discussion with Slavoj Žižek and Ernesto Laclau, she further explores the difficulties of claiming both particularity and universalism.[32]

In Latin America, however, the transformative performance of gender took place under particularly tragic circumstances and in a drastically divided situation. Best known is the example of the Mothers of the Plaza de Mayo of Argentina, who walked round the Plaza de Mayo every Thursday both during the military regime and after, showing photographs of their disappeared children. They transformed motherhood into a new kind of political agency that altered its traditional associations with domesticity and subordination. The epithet "mad" applied to these women by the military measured the extent of their transgression of what officially defined motherhood and the family. That the mothers reinscribed women into the social text was itself an exact illustration of what Deleuze and Guattari mean by "lines of flight." Yet the mothers have subsequently split into two groups, one of which, under the leadership of Hebe Bonafini, is more inclined to a hard line, resisting what they see as easy negotiation, so that the concept "mother" can no longer mobilize all those it earlier had around the same demands. In another well-known example of transformative performance, the Zapatista movement in Chiapas staged ethnicity when, in taking over municipalities in January 1994, they spoke in the indigenous tongues of the region. Both these movements used traditional categories of difference (mothers, Indians) while subtly changing their attributes. The mothers came out of the home and occupied public space at a time when it had been emptied of public activity and were able to articulate their struggle with the international human rights organizations, although they also retained their particularity. The indigenous groups and former guerrillas transformed the image of the submissive, tradition-bound Indian and now make demands on behalf of civil society.[33]

Masks are significant in Mexican culture. Until the year 2000, the candidate for presidency was "unmasked" *(destapado)* just before the election campaign that the government always won. But the ski masks worn by the Zapatista leaders and by subcomandante Marcos, who is not indigenous, were intended to ensure anonymity for the male and female representatives of the group so there would be no danger of identifying the leaders or creating the cult of personality. On the other hand they accused neoliberalism of imposing the masks of anonymity and individualism on the masses.³⁴ Superbarrio, an activist on behalf of neighborhood groups in Mexico City is yet another example of politically expedient masking and performance. He disguised himself as a wrestler who donned the costume of Superman—thus effecting a double disguise as comic-book hero and wrestler. But while the Superbarrio was a local character, the Zapatistas have made claims to be something more—to represent and make universal the utopian hope of a multicultural and radically democratic Mexico from the particularity of indigenous Chiapas.

The ideology of feminist, gay and lesbian, indigenous, and Afro-American movements in the 1980s and early 1990s was based on the history of past exclusions, and their subsequent emergence onto the cultural and political scene signaled a period of extraordinary literary and artistic creativity as well as of women-centered grassroots movements. In his book *Journeys through the Labyrinth,* Gerald Martin forecast that "there can be little doubt that the great age of women's writing in Latin America is still to come."³⁵ The indigenous demonstrations in 1992 on the five-hundredth anniversary of the "discovery" of America similarly rehearsed for the public sphere the historical exclusion of the indigenous but put on view the multilingual cultures of the Americas, destabilizing the very idea of Spanish or Latin America. During the same decade, gay and lesbian movements dared to demonstrate openly. Yet the great democratic opening for women, gays, transvestites, and ethnicities also occurred at a time when difference had become marketable. Politically feminism became divided between those who chose to work within existing institutions, including government institutions, and those who wanted to retain autonomy.³⁶ While there are still common causes among feminists—for instance, the right to choose to have an abortion—substantial political change has been slow to come for them as it has for gay and indigenous activists. Indeed, one of the characteristics of neoliberalism in many countries of Latin America has been its ability to initiate economic change while limiting popular demands in the political field. Hence the paradox that there is a growing number of women, gay, and indigenous intellectuals who find themselves grappling with the same old problems of violence, limits on reproductive rights, inequality, and abuse. Raquel Olea wrote that in postdictatorship Chile, feminism "as a social movement and space of negotiation has lost its subversive power which formerly enabled it to bring to public notice the themes and the needs of women."[37] Divisions have occurred among feminists, gay activists, and among the indigenous as institutionalization works against the more radical elements.

It is, however, the transvestite body that has come to represent a powerful site of resistance because it is a visible indication of the arbitrary imposition of gender categories. In Buenos Aires, the transvestite Lohana tore up her identity card outside the government office after being told to dress as a man in order for a photograph to be acceptable to the authorities. In an interview she explained, "We are the living proof that one can be something different from man or woman, one can be a transvestite for example. So we who construct the transvestite we are those who are born with certain genitals and they give us a sex, a gender and socialize us and we then say it doesn't suit me; what I want is to construct my identity, autoconstruct my identity in a different gender."[38] Lohana's action struck at the state's gender classification and at compulsory heterosexuality, demonstrating that the individual and not the state nor the church were now the privileged arbiters of identity. But although Lohana's demonstration showed the fraying borders of state power, in its voluntarism it reflected the ideology of free choice.

This is a danger of which the transvestite performer Pedro Lemebel is perfectly aware. He addresses both the exclusionism of the past and the inclusionism of the present. Thus his manifesto "Hablo por mi diferencia" ("I speak from my difference") read at a left-wing meeting in Santiago was a reproach to the old leftists who had failed to understand that their machismo had allied them to reaction. The manliness *(hombría)* of the militant may not, Lemebel argued, be superior to the "manliness" of the gay men and transvestites who confront mockery and aggression everyday on the city streets. At the same time, he underscored the new problems posed by the neoliberal state—for instance the facile citation by rock music performers such as Michael Jackson of bisexuality in their dress and behavior, as they market a version of gender difference that depoliticizes its refractory potential.[39]

Nevertheless, the celebratory phase of gay and transvestite difference ended abruptly with the AIDS crisis that also put a new face on globalization. The nomadic transvestites of Severo Sarduy's novel *Cobra* published in 1972 are supplanted in *Pájaros de la playa (Beach Birds)* by tropes of confinement, hospitalization with its litany of attempted cures and medicines. Lemebel's chronicles of gay cruising in *La esquina es mi corazón* published in 1995 were followed by his chronicles of the AIDS crisis, *Loco afán*. Mario Bellatín's ironically named *Salón de belleza (Beauty Parlor),* in which the parlor is a hospice and the protagonist looks after his patients and his tropical fish, is a melancholy coda to liberation. Epidemic and death are now also revealed to be global.

What's Left of Literature?

There are no taboo subjects left in contemporary publishing and there is not much that really matters. Ricardo Piglia claims that Borges would have difficulty finding a publisher for his *Fictions* at the present time and that the market or mass culture now sets the standards of what is published.[40] The critical minority, those who see complexities beyond the formulaic, is either forced into artisan forms of publishing, into readings (that return orality to literature), or into the academy—although the academy is no longer necessarily a shelter for creativity, being torn by the same forces and the same demand for performativity as the rest of society.

Giorgio Agamben wrote that "the society of the spectacle is not only aimed at the expropriation of productive activity, but also, and above all, at the alienation of language itself, of the linguistic and communicative nature of human beings, of that *logos* in which Heraclitus identifies the Common. The extreme form of the expropriation of the Common is the spectacle, in other words, the politics in which we live."[41] Yet poetry, possibly the most marginalized of genres, is directly engaged with language; given the new forms of orality made possible by radio, television, and cell phones and the new forms of literacy made possible by the Internet, it is necessarily engaged with its alienation. In a thoughtful book on modern Latin American poetry, William Rowe suggested that some poets "use the poem as a way of thinking," though he did not mean, by this, that they should draw on preexisting thoughts. He argued that "if we are talking about poetry as a capability for that degree of transformation, as opposed to an ordinary or conformist experience, then the language it works with will not be some specialized jargon, preserving its meaning by sealing itself off from the unending flow of speech."[42]

That the subtitle of Rowe's book is *History and the Inner Life* may seem surprising given the emptying of personhood in postmodernism. But here "inner life" means perception stripped of all support of the *doxa*. Thus in a discussion of Parra he wrote, "The ordinary, that powerful force of social modeling, starts to disappear because there is nothing for it to latch on to, nothing to make sense of; other possibilities are released. These are not easy to name, because they arise inside and against that everyday social use of language. Parra gives us the language of the everyday but without the ideological, religious and sentimental glue that makes it hang together and fill up whatever space there is" (p. 43).

Many of the poets discussed by Rowe—among them Nicanor Parra, Gonzalo Rojas, Jorge Eduardo Eilson, and Carmen Ollé—belong to a generation who lived through the collapse of belief in utopia and in literature with a capital "L," a collapse whose various moments this book has recorded. He regards each of the poets to be linked by their refusal of guarantees and by their awareness of the collapse of belief structures.[43] "Making sense requires concordance between rhetoric and belief. That is, the language of conviction needs to be backed by security of belief; otherwise, the voice of authority mocks itself and belief-structures collapse through lack of any discourse capable of sustaining them" (p. 45). Rowe's notion of "inner life" acquires power in these circumstances as long as it is not thought of as a refuge or shelter, nor as an avant-garde gesture, but rather as a refusal of the constructed network of the social. Thus writing of the poetry of Carmen Ollé, he stated that "the need is to make a place between noise and symbol, in other words between the unformed and a tradition that imprisons" (p. 25).

It makes no sense in Rowe's terms to speak of effectiveness, popularity, or marketability. The poets discussed by him are staging a kind of interior exodus, although it is not clear whether this anticipates the formation of a different kind of collectivity or constitutes a withdrawal from the social. If the latter, then, their ascesis would be perilously close to libertarianism.[44]

It is fitting that this book comes to rest on the shoals of present difficulties. It has been mainly concerned with the many versions of utopia that have foundered over the last forty years and above all with the abandonment of "the lettered city." This is far from being only a negative scenario, for something is still alive among the rubble if only an effort of will. And the stirrings are, after all, now planetary.

Notes
Index

Notes

Introduction

1. Michael Hardt and Antonio Negri, *Empire* (Cambridge, Mass.: Harvard University Press, 2000), p. 183.
2. Fredric Jameson, *The Seeds of Time* (New York: Columbia University Press, 1994), p. 118.
3. Serge Guilbaut, *How New York Stole the Idea of the Avant-Garde: Abstract Expressionism, Freedom and the Cold War,* trans. Arthur Goldhammer (Chicago: Chicago University Press, 1993).
4. For an account of the misreadings of Marx's distinction between use and exchange value, see Gayatri Chakravorty Spivak, "From Haverstock Hill Flat to U.S. Classroom: What's Left of Theory," in Judith Butler, John Guillory, and Kendall Thomas, eds., *What's Left of Theory: New Work on the Politics of Literary Theory* (New York: Routledge, 2000), pp. 1–39.
5. Carlos Fuentes, *La nueva novela hispanoamericana* (Mexico: Joaquín Mortíz, 1969).
6. Carlos Fuentes, *Don Quixote or the Critique of Reading* (Austin: Hackett Memorial Lecture Series, 1976), p. 49.
7. Mario Vargas Llosa, *García Márquez: Historia de un deicidio* (Barcelona: Seix Barral, 1971).
8. The literary theories of the character Morelli who appears in *Rayuela* were published in Julio Ortega, ed., Julio Cortázar, *La casilla de los morelli* (Barcelona: Tusquets Editor, 1973).
9. Octavio Paz, *Children of the Mire,* trans. Rachel Phillips (Cambridge: Harvard University Press, 1974). Rubén Medina, *Autor, autoridad y autorización: Escritura y poética de Octavio Paz* (Mexico: El Colegio de México,

1999), has studied the relationship between Paz's poetry, his essays, and the revisions that Paz made over the years to his poetic theory.

10. On Argentina, see Oscar Terán, *Nuestros años sesentas: La formación de la nueva izquierda intelectual argentina 1956–66,* 3rd ed. (Buenos Aires: Imago Mundi, 1993).

11. Ibid., p. 79. On the Di Tella Institute, see John King, *El Di Tella y el desarrollo cultural argentino en la década del sesenta* (Buenos Aires: Gaglianone, 1985).

12. René Wellek and Austin Warren, *Theory of Literature,* 3rd ed. (London: Penguin Books, 1963), p. 27.

13. Enrique Anderson Imbert, "Prólogo a la primera edición," *Historia de la literatura hispanoamericana,* 3rd ed. (Mexico: Fondo de Cultura Económica, 1961), pp. 7–11.

14. Julio Cortázar, *La casilla de los morelli* (Barcelona: Tusquets, 1973), p. 47.

15. Jorge Castañeda, *Utopia Unarmed: The Latin American Left after the Cold War* (New York: Knopf, 1993), p. 277.

16. Nicola Miller, *In the Shadow of the State: Intellectuals and the Quest for National Identity in Twentieth Century Spanish America* (London: Verso, 1999), p. 6.

17. Neil Larsen, *Reading North by South: On Latin American Literature, Culture and Politics* (Minneapolis: University of Minnesota Press, 1995), p. 66.

18. Carlos Fuentes, *La nueva novela hispanoamericana* (Mexico: Joaquín Mortíz, 1969), p. 23.

19. For a discussion of the modernism of modern Latin American fiction, see Gerald Martin, *Journeys through the Labyrinth: Latin American Fiction in the Twentieth Century* (London: Verso, 1989).

20. Rama was himself a victim of the Cold War. He had been appointed to a position at the University of Maryland and was teaching and lecturing in the United States when a deportation order came from the Immigration and Naturalization Service. He was then forced to defend himself against absurd charges—for instance, that the Uruguayan journal *Marcha,* of which he had been editor, had frequently published "the work of communist writers." The source of the rumors is hardly mysterious. At that time Uruguay was ruled by a military junta that zealously pursued a "war on communism," extended to include all dissidents. In the middle of writing "an essay that explores the relation of the intelligentsia to power and argues for the broad democratization of intellectual functions," Rama found himself engaged in this phantasmagoric and eventually losing battle. When I saw him in Paris in 1974 just before his last trip to Colombia at the invitation of President Betancourt, he was still at work on his interrupted book *La ciudad letrada (The Lettered City).* The essays he published in the journal *Marcha* offered what he termed a "social democratic" position on political and cultural questions. Like many of his contemporaries Rama viewed Latin American culture (as well as its economy and politics) as a work in progress, powered by a dream of democratic emancipation. But he was also

well aware that neither he nor other members of the literary intelligentsia were playing on a level field. Throughout the 1960s, when he was literary editor of *Marcha,* that journal had consistently taken issue with Cold War cultural policies.

21. John Beverley, *Subalternity and Representation: Arguments in Cultural Theory* (Durham: Duke University Press, 1999) p. 47.

22. Carlos Monsiváis, José Emilio Pacheco, Elena Poniatowska, *El derecho a la lectura* (published by all the major Mexican publishing houses, 1984).

23. Marvin E. Gettleman et al. eds., *El Salvador: Central America in the New Cold War* (New York: Grove Press, 1981).

24. Jean François Lyotard, *The Postmodern Condition: A Report on Knowledge,* trans. Geoff Bennington and Brian Massumi (Minneapolis: University of Minnesota Press, 1984), p. 5.

25. Giorgio Agamben, *Homo Sacer: Sovereign Power and Bare Life,* trans. Daniel Heller-Roazen (Stanford: Stanford University Press, 1998).

26. Andreas Huyssen, *Twilight Memories: Marking Time in a Culture of Amnesia* (New York: Routledge, 1995), p. 92.

27. Hardt and Negri, *Empire,* p. 308.

28. Gillian Rose, *Mourning Becomes the Law: Philosophy and Representation* (Cambridge: Cambridge University Press, 1996), especially pp. 74–76.

29. William I. Robinson, "Polyarchy: Coercion's New Face in Latin America," *NACLA Report on the Americas* 34, no. 3 (Nov./Dec. 2000), p. 48.

30. See, for example, Román de la Campa, *Latin Americanism* (Minneapolis: University of Minnesota Press, 1990).

31. Quoted by Ellen Spielman, "El estado de la cuestión," in Ellen Spielman, ed., *L@s rel@ciones cultur@les entre @meric@ L@tin@ y Est@dos Unidos después de l@ guerr@ frí@* (Berlin: Wissenschafterlicher Verlag, 2000), p. 11.

32. Lia Zanotta Machado, "Masculinidade, sexualidade e estupro: As construções da virilidade," *Cadernos Pagú* 11 (1998), pp. 231–273.

33. Martin, *Journeys through the Labyrinth,* p. 24.

34. Emilie L. Bergmann and Paul Julian Smith, eds., *Entiendes? Queer Readings, Hispanic Writings* (Durham: Duke University Press, 1995).

35. On the legal demands of the indigenous movements, see Guillermo Delgado, "La ley al paso de la tortuga," *Ojarasca* 31–32 (April/May, 1994), pp. 34–36.

36. Robinson, "Polyarchy," p. 48.

37. Judith Butler, "Restaging the Universal," in Judith Butler, Ernesto Laclau, and Slavoj Žižek, *Contingency, Hegemony, Universality* (London: Verso, 2000), p. 174.

1. Killing Them Softly

1. Frances Stoner Saunders, *The Cultural Cold War: The CIA and the World of Arts and Letters* (New York: New Press, 2000).

2. Thomas Braden, quoted by Christopher Lasch, "The Cultural Cold War," in *The Agony of the American Left* (New York: Knopf, 1969), p. 111.

3. Stephen G. Rabe, *Eisenhower and Latin America: The Foreign Policy of Anticommunism* (Chapel Hill: University of North Carolina Press, 1988), p. 11.

4. John Dos Passos, *Brazil on the Move* (New York: Doubleday, 1963), p. 45. Although published in 1963, this book is based on a number of visits to Brazil beginning in 1948. The threat of communism is its underlying theme. A year after its publication, the U.S. navy "encouraged" a military coup in Brazil by its presence off the coast.

5. Jorge G. Castañeda, "In the Beginning: Communists and Populists," in *Utopia Unarmed: The Latin American Left after the Cold War* (New York: Knopf, 1993), pp. 23–50.

6. Jeane Kirkpatrick, *Dictatorship and Double Standards* (New York: Simon and Schuster, 1982).

7. Elizabeth Anne Cobbs, *The Rich Neighbor Policy: Rockefeller and Kaiser in Brazil* (New Haven: Yale University Press, 1992), p. 34.

8. Cary Reich, *The Life of Nelson Rockefeller: Worlds to Conquer 1908–1958* (New York: Doubleday, 1996), p. 240. As Reich also points out, intelligence gathering was also part of the operation. For a searching account of Rockefeller's combination of Latin American political policy, business interests, support of missionary activities, and the use of culture as propaganda, see Gerard Colby with Charlotte Dennett, *Thy Will Be Done. The Conquest of the Amazon: Nelson Rockefeller and Evangelism in the Age of Oil* (New York: Harper Collins, 1995).

9. Arthur Pincus, "New Imperialism in Latin America" *Politics* 1, no. 3 (April 1944), pp. 74–80, especially p. 79.

10. Colby and Dennett, *Thy Will Be Done,* p. 112.

11. For the extent of Rockefeller's interests and ambitions in Latin America, see Reich, *The Life of Nelson Rockefeller,* and Colby and Dennett, *Thy Will Be Done.*

12. Reich, *The Life of Nelson Rockefeller,* pp. 214–222.

13. Irene Herner, Gabriel Larra, and Rafael Ángel Herrerias, *Diego Rivera: Paraíso Perdido en Rockefeller Center* (Mexico: Ediciones Edicupes, 1986). The mural was reportedly removed because it offended Rockefeller's father. See Reich, *The Life of Nelson Rockefeller,* p. 111.

14. Serge Guilbaut, *How New York Stole the Idea of the Avant-Garde: Abstract Expressionism, Freedom and the Cold War,* trans. Arthur Goldhammer (Chicago: University of Chicago Press, 1993), p. 173. On CIA funding of exhibitions, see Stoner Saunders, "Yanqui Doodles," in *The Cultural Cold War,* ch. 16.

15. Eva Cockcroft, "Abstract Expressionism: Weapon of the Cold War," *Artforum* 12, no. 10 (June 1974), p. 127. For a well-documented account of the effect of the Cold War on art institutions, especially in Argentina, see

Andrea Giunta, *Vanguardia, Internacionalismo y política: Arte argentino en la década de los '60* (Buenos Aires: Paidos, 2001).

16. *The Gringo in Mañanaland,* a documentary film compiled by Deedee Hallek, shows how blatantly Hollywood portrayed "south of the border" in these years as an unruly area that was in need of North American efficiency.
17. *Politics* 2, no. 6 (July 1946), pp. 211–212. The memo purportedly was passed on by a friend of the journal.
18. Gaizka S. de Usabel, *The High Noon of American Films in Latin America* (Ann Arbor: University of Michigan Research Press, 1982), p. 160.
19. Julianne Burton, "Don (Juanito) Duck and the Imperial-Patriarchal Unconscious: Disney Studios, the Good Neighbor Policy, and the Packaging of Latin America," in Andrew Parker et al., eds., *Nationalisms and Sexualities* (New York: Routledge, 1992), pp. 21–41.
20. On tourism and the Third World, see Cynthia Enloe, *Bananas, Beaches and Bases. Making Feminist Sense of International Politics* (Berkeley: University of California Press, 1990).
21. Julianne Burton, in *Partisan Review* 12, no. 1 (Spring 1945), p. 226, commented, "What we can learn of Latin America from *The Three Caballeros* is less than little. But what we learn of where *we* live is a good deal."
22. Quoted by Allen L. Woll, *The Latin American Image in American Film* (Los Angeles: UCLA, Latin American Center Publications, 1977), p. 58.
23. Nestor García Canclini, *Las culturas populares en el capitalismo* (Havana: Casa de las Américas, 1982); *Transforming Modernity: Popular Culture in Mexico,* trans. Lidia Lozano (Austin: University of Texas Press, 1993).
24. Marc Eliot, *Walt Disney. Hollywood's Dark Prince* (New York: Birch Lane Press, 1993), p. 180.
25. Burton, "Don (Juanito) Duck and the Imperial-Patriarchal Unconscious," p. 31.
26. Eliot, *Walt Disney,* p. 245.
27. On animation, see Eric Lorin Smoodin, *Animating Culture: Hollywood Cartoons from the Sound Era* (New Brunswick: Rutgers University Press, 1993).
28. Seth Fein, "Everyday Forms of Transnational Collaboration: U.S. Film Propaganda in Cold War Mexico," in Gilbert M. Joseph, Catherine C. Legrand, and Ricardo D. Salvatore, eds., *Close Encounters of Empire: Writing the Cultural History of U.S.–Latin American Relations* (Durham: Duke University Press, 1998), pp. 400–450.
29. Fein, "Everyday Forms," p. 413, documents the collaboration of industrialists and unionists in the exhibition of films "intended to offset radical organizing."
30. S. de Usabel, *The High Noon of American Films,* p. 171.
31. Warren Dean, "The USIA Book Program: Latin America," *Point of Contact* 3 (Sept.–Oct., 1976), pp. 4–14.

32. Joanne P. Sharp, *Condensing the Cold War. Reader's Digest and American Identity* (Minneapolis: University of Minnesota Press, 2000).

33. Stoner Saunders, "Candy," in *The Cultural Cold War,* pp. 105–128; Peter Coleman, *The Liberal Conspiracy: The Congress for Cultural Freedom and the Struggle for the Mind of Postwar Europe* (New York: Free Press, 1989); Lasch, "The Cultural Cold War," p. 64.

34. The first peace congress was held in 1948 in Wroclaw, Poland. See Donald Drew Egbert, *Social Radicalism and the Arts—Western Europe: A Cultural History from the French Revolution to 1968* (New York: Knopf, 1970). For Latin American participation, see Pablo Neruda, *Memoirs,* trans. Hardie St. Martin (New York: Farrar, Straus, and Giroux, 1976), p. 187.

35. Lasch, "The Cultural Cold War," pp. 63–114, especially pp. 64–65.

36. Coleman, *The Liberal Conspiracy,* p. 56; Stoner Saunders, *The Cultural Cold War,* p. 119.

37. The organization was funded through the Farfield Foundation (incorporated in 1952) and various other front organizations. See Coleman, *The Liberal Conspiracy,* especially 46–49. Stoner Saunders details the way funding was arranged. See *The Cultural Cold War,* pp. 128–156. See also María Eugenia Mudrovcic, *Mundo Nuevo: Cultura y Guerra Fría en la década del 60* (Buenos Aires: Beatriz Viterbo, 1997), p. 28. Both Coleman and Mudrovcic emphasize changes in Congress policy first in 1958 when fervent anticommunism gave way to "thaw" and the "end of ideologies," and again in 1964 when the first hints of CIA financing began to force defensive positions.

38. Coleman, *The Liberal Conspiracy,* p. 46.

39. For the disciplines during the Cold War, see Noam Chomsky et al., *The Cold War and the University: Toward an Intellectual History of the Postwar Years* (New York: New Press, 1997). For literature, see Tobin Siever, *Cold War Criticism and the Politics of Skepticism* (Oxford: Oxford University Press, 1993). Siever, to my mind, makes too much of a leap from Cold War suspicion to "critical scepticism." But his thesis that the Cold War affected the use of language and vocabulary is worth pursuing.

40. Mark Jancowich, *The Cultural Politics of the New Criticism* (Cambridge: Cambridge University Press, 1993), p. 100.

41. Allen Tate, "To Whom is the Poet Responsible?" in *The Man of Letters in the Modern World: Selected Essays 1928–1955* (New York: Meridian Books, 1955), pp. 23–33, especially p. 31.

42. Ibid. There have been several post hoc reflections by writers on the period. See Stephen Spender, *The Thirties and After: Poetry, Politics and People 1933–75* (London: Fontana, 1978), especially pp. 161–164. See also John Goldsmith, ed., *Journals, 1939–1983* (London: Faber and Faber, 1985).

43. Frank Kermode, *Not Entitled* (New York: Farrar, Straus, and Giroux, 1995).

44. Coleman, *The Liberal Conspiracy,* p. 85. See also Mudrovcic, *Mundo Nuevo,* pp. 21–23.

45. This was written before recent revelations that Silone, even while in the Communist Party, was spying for the fascists.

46. "La experiencia de Guatemala: Por una política de la libertad en Latinamérica," *Cuadernos* 9 (Nov.–Dec. 1954), pp. 88–93.See p. 90. Translations of quotations from *Cuadernos* and *Mundo Nuevo* are my own.

47. Coleman, *The Liberal Conspiracy,* pp. 153–155.

48. Reported for *Cuadernos* by Jaime Castillo, "El congreso continental de la cultura de Santiago de Chile," *Cuadernos* 2 (June–Aug. 1953), pp. 84–87.

49. Ibid., p. 87.

50. David Dubinsky, "McCarthy y la verdadera defensa de la libertad," *Cuadernos* 5 (March–April 1954), pp. 69–74.

51. Jorge Mañach, "El drama de Cuba," *Cuadernos* 26 (May–June 1958), p. 63.

52. *Cuadernos* 35 (March–April 1959), p. 61.

53. René Wellek and Austin Warren, *Theory of Literature* (London: Penguin Books, 1963). For the ideological import of their theories, see Timothy Reiss, "Autonomy, Nostalgia and Writing for the Aesthetic: Notes on Cultures and Exchange," *Centennial Review* 39, no. 3 (Fall 1995).

54. Michel Collinet, "La unidad latina y los nacionalismos," *Cuadernos* 13 (July—Aug. 1955), pp. 25–31, especially p. 31.

55. Castañeda, "In the Beginning," p. 42.

56. For an exhaustive discussion of such recipes, see Mark T. Berger, *Under Northern Eyes: Latin American Studies and U.S. Hegemony in the Americas 1898–1990* (Bloomington: Indiana University Press, 1995).

57. Julian Gorkin, "El Congreso por la Libertad de la Cultura en Iberoamérica," *Cuadernos* 3 (Sept.–Dec. 1953), pp. 96–100.

58. *Cuadernos* 1 (March–May 1953), p. 4.

59. Gorkin, "El Congreso por la Libertad de la Cultura en Iberoamérica," p. 97.

60. Natalicio González, "Trayectoria y misión de América," *Cuadernos* 1 (March–May, 1953), p. 5.

61. Salvador de Madariaga, "Europa y América," *Cuadernos* 1 (March–May, 1953), p. 17.

62. Roberto Giusti, "Influencia occidental y obra de creación latinoamericana," *Cuadernos* 19 (July–Aug., 1956), pp. 30–36.

63. For instance, it included an essay by Manuel Gamio, "Diálogo sobre cuestiones indígenas," *Cuadernos* 6 (May–June 1954), pp. 91–93.

64. Luis Monguió, "Nacionalismo y protesta social en la literatura hispanoamericana," *Cuadernos* 58 (March 1962), pp. 41–48.

65. On the influence of the Bandung conference, see Aijaz Ahmad, "Three Worlds Theory," in *In Theory: Classes, Nations, Literatures* (London: Verso, 1992), pp. 287–318.

66. Carlos Fuentes, "Entrevista con el Presidente Dorticos," *Política* 2, no. 35 (Oct. 1961), p. 22 (my translation). "Con su acción de vanguardia, la

Revolución Cubana ha abierto aquí el camino para que en el futuro nuestros paises superen la presión unilateral que los EU ejercen a través del sistema panamericano."

67. John Mander, *Static Society: The Paradox of Latin America* (London: Gollancz, 1969); John Mander, *The Unrevolutionary Society: The Power of Latin American Conservatism in a Changing World* (New York: Knopf, 1969).

68. John Mander, "Mexico City to Buenos Aires," *Encounter* 25, no. 3 (Sept. 1965), pp. 5–14.

69. Nelson A. Rockefeller, *The Rockefeller Report on the Americas: The Official Report of a United States Presidential Mission for the Western Hemisphere* (1969).

70. Guilbaut, *How New York Stole the Idea of the Avant-Garde,* p. 274.

71. Ibid., p. 74.

72. Lawrence Alloway, "The International Style," *Encounter* 25, no. 3 (Sept. 1965), pp. 71–74, especially p. 74. As Andrea Giunta made clear in *Vanguardia, Internacionalismo y política,* Alloway had not always embraced this position.

73. David Alfaro Siqueiros, "Mexican Art in Paris," in *Art and Revolution* (London: Lawrence and Wishart, 1975), pp. 145–175.

74. "La cortina de Nopal" was first published in 1956 in the "México en la cultura" supplement of the newspaper *Novedades,* and was reprinted in *Cuevas por Cuevas: Notas autobiográficas* (Mexico: Era, 1965).

75. Alaíde Foppa, *Confesiones de José Luis Cuevas* (Mexico: Fondo de Cultura Económica, 1975), p. 86.

76. Shifra M. Goldman, *Contemporary Mexican Painting in a Time of Change* (Austin: University of Texas Press, 1977), chs. 2 and 3.

77. See especially Carlos Monsiváis, "Notas sobre la cultura mexicana en el siglo xx," in *Historia General de México,* vol. 2 (Mexico: El Colegio de México, 1981), p. 1491. See also Nestor García Canclini, *Culturas híbridas: Estrategias para entrar y salir de la modernidad* (Mexico: Grijalbo, 1989), pp. 86–93; *Hybrid Cultures: Strategies for Entering and Leaving Modernity,* trans. Christopher L. Chiparri and Silvia L. López (Minneapolis: University of Minnesota Press, 1995), pp. 58–65.

78. Marta Traba, *Arte Latinoamericana Actual* (Caracas: Universidad Central de Venezuela, 1972), p. 67.

79. Jorge Luis Borges, "The Argentine Writer and Tradition," trans. James I. Irby, in *Labyrinths: Selected Stories and Other Writings* (New York: New Directions, 1962), pp. 177–185.

80. "Octavio Paz en Cornell," *Mundo Nuevo* 3 (Sept. 1966), p. 73.

81. José Donoso, *The Boom in Spanish-American Literature: A Personal History* (New York: Columbia University Press, 1977), p. 11.

82. Mario Vargas Llosa, "La literatura es fuego," *Contra viento y marea* 1 (Barcelona: Seix Barral, 1983), p. 133.

83. Carlos Fuentes, *La nueva novela hispanoamericana* (Mexico: Joaquín Mortíz, 1969), p. 23.

84. As María Eugenia Mudrovcic pointed out (*Mundo Nuevo*, p. 25), ILARI inherited the sites, equipment, and personnel of the Congress centers in Argentina, Brasil, Chile, Peru, and Uruguay; it opened new centers in Paraguay and Bolivia and closed those in Mexico and Colombia.

85. For a more extensive discussion of the funding of *Mundo Nuevo* and ILARI, the role of the Ford Foundation, the links with the CIA, and the revelation by the *New York Times* of those links, see Mudrovcic, *Mundo Nuevo*, pp. 24–38. This well-documented account draws on Emir Rodríguez Monegal's documentation at Princeton and on the records of the Ford Foundation and the Congress for Cultural Freedom in Chicago. For additional information from a Cuban perspective, see Ernesto Sierra, "Requiem para *Mundo Nuevo*," *Casa de las Américas* 213 (Oct.–Dec. 1998), pp. 135–139.

86. Pablo Rocca, *35 años en Marcha (Crítica y Literatura en Marcha y en el Uruguay 1939–1974)* (Montevideo: Intendencia Municipal, 1992).

87. "Presentación," *Mundo Nuevo* 1 (July 1966), p. 4.

88. Mudrovcic, *Mundo Nuevo*, p. 67, wrote about this use of anecdotal information in the journal as a way of furthering its message—that the Cold War was over and that Latin American literature was in its ascendancy.

89. "Presentación," *Mundo Nuevo* 1, (July 1966), p. 4.

90. Severo Sarduy, "Las estructuras de la narración," *Mundo Nuevo* 2 (Aug., 1966), p. 18 (discussion with Emir Rodríguez Monegal).

91. *Mundo Nuevo* 19 (Jan. 1968), p. 94.

92. "México: Congreso de escritores," *Mundo Nuevo* 13 (July 1967), p. 77.

93. "El congreso del P.E.N. club," *Mundo Nuevo* 5 (Nov. 1966), pp. 85–90.

94. "Harto de los laberintos," *Mundo Nuevo* 18, (Dec. 1967), pp. 5–6.

95. See Beatriz Sarlo, *Jorge Luis Borges: A Writer on the Edge* (London: Verso 1993); Jean Franco, "The Utopia of a Tired Man," in *Critical Passions* (Durham: Duke University Press, 1999), pp. 327–365.

96. "La CIA y los intelectuales," *Mundo Nuevo* 13 (July 1967) (editorial).

97. Thomas Braden, "I'm Glad the CIA Is 'Immoral,'" *Saturday Evening Post* (20 May 1967). On the scandal caused by the article, see Stoner Saunders, *The Cultural Cold War*, pp. 398–406.

98. "Al lector," *Mundo Nuevo* 11 (May 1967), p. 4.

99. Rodríguez Monegal, "La CIA y los intelectuales," *Mundo Nuevo* 14 (Aug. 1967), pp. 11–20.

100. Rodríguez Monegal, "Una tarea cumplida," *Mundo Nuevo* 25 (July, 1968), p. 4.

101. Diario de Caracas," *Mundo Nuevo* 17 (Nov. 1967), p. 20.

102. Ibid., p. 23.

103. Mudrovcic, *Mundo Nuevo*, pp. 65–66.

104. The influential Uruguayan journal *Marcha*, on the other hand, whose liter-

ary editor was Ángel Rama, closely monitored both subsidizing of journals and CIA influence. See Rocca, *35 años en Marcha.*

105. Clarival do Prado Valladares, "Negritud o mundo negro," *Mundo Nuevo* (Oct. 1966), pp. 64–70.

106. Carlos Fuentes, *Cambio de piel* (Mexico: Joaquín Mortíz, 1967); *A Change of Skin,* trans. Sam Hileman (London: Jonathan Cape, 1968). The original title before publication was *El sueño.*

107. Carlos Fuentes, "La situación del escritor en América Latina," *Mundo Nuevo* 1, (July 1966), p. 5.

108. Alan M.Wald, *The New York Intellectuals: The Rise and Decline of the Anti-Stalinist Left from the 1930s to the 1980s* (Chapel Hill: University of North Caroline Press, 1987).

109. García Canclini, *Culturas híbridas,* pp. 96–106, discusses the contradictory attitudes of Paz and Borges toward television.

110. Rubén Medina, *Autor, autoridad y autorización: Escritura y poética de Octavio Paz* (Mexico: El Colegio de México, 1999), p. 40. Medina's book is an excellent analysis of Paz's poetic and political trajectory. See also Jorge Águilar Mora, *La divina pareja: Historia y mito en Octavio Paz* (Mexico: Era, 1978); Jason Wilson, *Octavio Paz: A Study of his Poetics* (London: Cambridge University Press, 1979).

111. Mario Vargas Llosa, *Contra viento y marea (1962–82)* (Barcelona: Seix Barral, 1983); Octavio Paz, *Tiempo nublado* (Barcelona: Seix Barral, 1983). In 1986 Seix Barral published a two-volume edition of Vargas Llosa's work, this and a third volume (1964–1988) was published in 1990. Some of the essays are translated into English in John King, ed., *Making Waves* (New York: Farrar, Straus, and Giroux, 1996).

112. "Respuesta a un consul," *Letras de México* 7 (1943), p. 5, quoted by Medina, *Autor, autoridad y autorización,* p. 138.

113. These revisions are examined by Ruben Medina in *Autor, autoridad y autorización.*

114. Octavio Paz, *Children of the Mire: Modern Poetry from Romanticism to the Avant-Garde,* trans. Rachel Phillips (Cambridge, Mass.: Harvard University Press, 1974), p. 157.

115. Octavio Paz, "Himno entre ruinas," *Libertad bajo palabra,* 2nd ed. (Mexico: Fondo de Cultura Económica, 1968), pp. 211–213.

116. Octavio Paz, "Poesía de soledad y poesía de comunión," in *Primeras letras (1931–43),* ed. Enrico Mario Santí (Mexico: Vuelta, 1988), pp. 294–295.

117. Ibid., p. 298.

118. Octavio Paz, *El arco y la lira* (Mexico: Fondo de Cultura Económica, 1956), pp. 36–37.

119. Octavio Paz, "El verbo desencarnado," in *El arco y la lira,* pp. 229–248. In later editions, the final chapter "El verbo desencarnado" was replaced by one with the title "Los signos en rotación," which is also the title of a book of essays: Carlos Fuentes, ed., *Los signos en rotación y otros ensayos* (Madrid: Alianza Editorial, 1971).

120. Octavio Paz, *El laberinto de la soledad* (Mexico: Fondo de Cultura Económica, 1959); *The Labyrinth of Solitude: Life and Thought in Mexico,* trans. Lysander Kemp (New York: Grove Press, 1961).

121. Quoted by Hugo Verani in the prologue to Octavio Paz, *Pasión crítica* (Barcelona: Seix Barral, 1985).

122. Octavio Paz, *El ogro filantrópico: historia y pólitica 1971–78* (Barcelona: Seix Barral, 1979), p. 333. For a discussion of Paz's position as independent intellectual, see Nicola Miller, *In the Shadow of the State: Intellectuals and the Quest for National Identity in Twentieth Century Spanish America* (London: Verso, 1999), pp. 130–131.

123. Octavio Paz, prefatory note to *The Other Mexico: Critique of the Pyramid,* trans. Lysander Kemp (New York: Grove Press, 1972), pp. vii–viii.

124. "Will to Form," *Mexico: Splendors of Thirty Centuries* (New York: Metropolitan Museum of Art, 1990), pp. 5–38.

125. For example, Jaguar in *The Time of the Heroes* and Fuschía in *The Green House.* He did sign a manifesto in 1965 supporting the armed struggle of the Movimiento de Izquierda Revolucionaria (MIR) in Peru, though a year later was arguing for a socialism that would allow writers free expression even if they were hostile to socialism. See "Toma de posición" and "Una insurreción permanente," in Vargas Llosa, *Contra viento y marea,* pp. 75–76 and pp. 85–88.

126. Mario Vargas Llosa, *García Márquez: Historia de un deicidio* (Barcelona: Seix Barral, 1971).

127. Mario Vargas Llosa, "Luzbel, Europa y otras conspiraciones," in Vargas Llosa, *Contra viento y marea,* pp. 150–159, especially p. 155. This was a reply to Oscar Collazos who had published a criticism of the boom novelists (see Chap. 3). See also "La literatura es fuego," in ibid., pp. 132–137.

128. On lies, see Mario Vargas Llosa, *Historia de Mayta* (Barcelona: Seix Barral, 1984); *The Real Life of Alejandro Mayta,* trans. Alfred MacAdam (New York: Farrar, Straus, and Giroux, 1986).

129. For instance, Mario Vargas Llosa, *La tia Julia y el escribidor* (Barcelona: Seix Barral, 1977); *Aunt Julie and the Scriptwriter,* trans. Helen Lane (New York: Farrar, Straus, and Giroux, 1982).

130. Mario Vargas Llosa, "In defense of the black market," *New York Times Magazine,* 22 February, 1987. The article expounds the ideas of Hernando de Soto from whom he later became estranged.

131. *El pez en el agua* (Barcelona: Seix Barral, 1993); *A Fish in the Water,* trans. Helen Lane (New York: Farrar, Straus, and Giroux, 1994). For his critique of cultural nationalism, see, for example, "El elefante y la cultura," in Vargas Llosa, *Contra viento y marea,* pp. 438–447.

132. Mario Vargas Llosa, *Lituma en los Andes* (Barcelona: Planeta, 1993); *Death in the Andes,* trans. Edith Grossman (New York: Farrar, Straus, and Giroux, 1996). For a discussion of this novel, see Efrain Kristal, *Temptation of the Word: The Novels of Mario Vargas Llosa* (Nashville: Vanderbilt University Press, 1998); Misha Kokotovic, "Vargas Llosa en los Andes: The Ra-

cial Discourse of Neoliberalism," *Confluencias* 15, no. 2 (Spring 2000), pp. 156–167.

133. Mario Vargas Llosa, "The Truth of Lies," in *Making Waves,* ed. John King (New York: Farrar, Straus, and Giroux, 1996), p. 327.

2. Communist Manifestos

1. José Donoso, *Curfew,* trans. Alfred MacAdam (New York: Weidenfeld and Nicholson, 1988), p. 3.

2. Antonio Skármeta, *Burning Patience,* trans. Katherine Silver (New York: Pantheon Books, 1987).

3. Julieta Kirkwood, *Ser política en Chile: las feministas y los partidos* (Santiago: Flacso, 1986).

4. Matilde Urrutia, *Mi vida junto a Pablo Neruda* (Barcelona: Seix Barral, 1986).

5. Stuart Hall, "Cultural Studies and its Theoretical Legacy," in *Cultural Studies* ed. Lawrence Grossberg, Cary Nelson, and Paula A. Treichler (New York: Routledge, 1992), p. 279.

6. Jorge Castañeda, *Utopia Unarmed: The Latin American Left after the Cold War* (New York: Knopf, 1993), p. 25. One of the founders of Mexico's Communist Party was the Indian Menabendranath Bhatachayra Rao.

7. Frida Kahlo, *Diario: Autorretrato íntimo* (Mexico: La Vaca Independiente, 1995), p. 225.

8. Hayden Herrera, *Frida: A Biography of Frida Kahlo* (New York: Harper and Row, 1983), pp. 434–439.

9. Samir Amin, *Re-Reading the Postwar Period: An Intellectual Itinerary* (New York: Monthly Review Press, 1994), p. 37.

10. Introduction to Kahlo, *Diario,* p. 21.

11. Pablo Neruda, "Viaje al norte de Chile," in *Obras completas,* vol. 2, (Buenos Aires: Losada, 1957), pp. 52–70.

12. Castañeda, *Utopia Unarmed,* p. 30.

13. See Álvaro Ruiz Abreu's biography, *José Revueltas: Los muros de la utopía* (Mexico: UAM-Xochimilco; Cal y Arena, 1992). There are a number of interesting memoirs and testimonials by working-class members of the party.

14. Ibid., p. 83.

15. José Revueltas, "Prológo al lector," *Obra literaria,* vol. 1 (Mexico: Empresas Editoriales, 1967), p. 12.

16. Carlos Monsiváis, "Mártires, militantes y memoriosos," *Amor Perdido* (Mexico: Era, 1977), pp. 126–152, especially p. 127. "Memoriosos" is literally "thoughtful," but there may be a sly reference to Borges's, "Funes, el memorioso," whose detailed memory becomes a nightmare.

17. Roque Dalton, ed., *Miguel Mármol: Los sucesos de 1932 en El Salvador* (San Salvador: Editorial Universitaria Centroamericana, 1982); Roque Dal-

ton, ed., *Miguel Mármol,* trans. Kathleen Ross and Richard Schaaf (New York: Curbstone Press, 1987). On Dalton, see Gabriel Zaid, "Colegas enemigos: una lectura de la tragedia salvadoreña," *De los libros al poder* (Mexico: Grijalbo, 1988), pp. 157–213.

18. Dalton, ed., *Miguel Mármol,* trans. Ross and Schaaf, p. 29. See also Benita Galeana, *Benita,* trans. Amy Diane Prince (Pittsburgh: Latin American Review Press, 1994).

19. José Revueltas, "Los errores," *Obra literaria,* vol. 2 (Mexico: Empresas Editoriales, 1967), pp. 83–365.

20. This separation of head and body, intellectual and lumpen, takes a grotesquely comic turn in the story "Hegel y yo" in which a legless student nicknamed Hegel shares the same prison cell with a violent "instinctive" murderer. See José Revueltas, "Hegel y yo," *El apando y otros relatos* (Mexico: Era, 1985), pp. 127–137.

21. José Revueltas, *Dialéctica de la conciencia* (Mexico: Era, 1982), p. 82.

22. Elena Poniatowska, *Tinísima* (Mexico: Era, 1992).

23. Galeana, *Benita,* pp. 130–1.

24. Isidoro Gilbert, *El oro de Moscú: La historia secreta de las relaciones argentinas-soviéticas* (Buenos Aires: Planeta, 1994). Although this book concentrates on Argentina, it gives a detailed account of Communist Party politics at this time.

25. Shifra M. Goldman, *Dimensions of the Americas: Art and Social Change in Latin America and the United States* (Chicago: Univesity of Chicago Press, 1994).

26. David Alfaro Siqueiros, "El movimiento pictórico mexicano, nueva vía del realismo," in Adolfo Sánchez Vázquez, ed., *Estética Marxista,* vol. 2 (Mexico: Era, 1970), pp. 74–84.

27. Ibid., p. 83.

28. Ibid.

29. The Mexican state, since the revolution of 1910–1917, has been an important patron of the arts. Even today, several prominent writers receive lifetime fellowships from the state, although patronage has increasingly been privatized. See Nestor García Canclini, *Hybrid Cultures: Strategies for Entering and Leaving Modernity,* trans. Christopher L. Chiparri and Silvia L. López (Minneapolis: University of Minnesota Press, 1995).

30. Nicola Miller, *In the Shadow of the State: Intellectuals and the Quest for National Identification in Twentieth Century Spanish America* (London: Verso, 1999), pp. 44–55.

31. The manifesto was drawn up by Siqueiros. See David A. Siqueiros, *Art & Revolution* (London: Lawrence and Wishart, 1975), pp. 24–25.

32. Carlos Monsiváis, *Amor Perdido,* 3rd ed. (Mexico: Era, 1978), p. 113 (my translation).

33. Ibid., p. 114.

34. For a list of private galleries in the 1950s, see Alejandro Ugalde Ramírez,

José Luis Cuevas y la renovación plástica de México: 1950–1968 (Mexico: Universidad Iberoamericana, Tesis de Licenciatura, 1993), p. 23.

35. José Luis Cuevas, "La cortina de nopal," *Cuevas por Cuevas: Notas autobiográficas* (Mexico: Era, 1965).

36. Germán Arciniegas, ed., *The Green Continent* (New York: Knopf, 1944), p. vii.

37. Bernard Traven, *The Rebellion of the Hanged* (Chicago: I. R. Dee, 1994); *The Treasure of the Sierra Madre,* trans. James Naremore (Madison: University of Wisconsin Press, 1979).

38. My translation from an essay included in *O Partido Comunista e a liberdade de criaçâo* (1946), and cited by Alfredo Wagner Berno de Almeida, *Jorge Amado. Politica e literatura: Uin estudo sobre a trajetoria intelectual de Jorge Amado* (Rio de Janeiro: Editora Campus, 1979), p. 202.

39. A reconstruction of the film was made by Richard Wilson, Myron Meisel, and Bill Krohn and was released by Paramount pictures in 1993 with the title *It's All True.*

40. Berno de Almeida, *Jorge Amado,* p. 213. He attended the World Congress of Writers and Artists for Peace in Wroclav, Poland in August 1948 and the Paris Peace Congress of 1949.

41. Ibid., p. 242.

42. Jorge Amado, *Gabriela, Clove and Cinnamon,* trans. James L. Taylor and William L. Grossman (New York: Knopf, 1962). For a discussion of this novel as a symptom of Amado's turn away from political engagement, see Neil Larsen, "The 'Boom' Novel and the Cold War," *Reading North by South, On Latin American Literature, Culture, and Politics* (Minneapolis: University of Minnesota Press, 1995), pp. 74–78.

43. Jorge Amado, *Dona Flor e seus dois maridos* (Sâo Paulo, Martins, 1966); *Dona Flor and Her Two Husbands,* trans. Harriet de Onis (New York: Knopf, 1969).

44. Pedro Mir, *Hay un país en el mundo y otros poemas de Pedro Mir* (Santo Domingo: Taller, 1982), pp. 33–63; *Counter Song for Walt Whitman and Other Poems,* trans. Jonathan Cohen and Donald Walsh (Washington, D.C.: Azul Editions, 1993); Pablo Neruda, *Canto General,* included in *Obras completas,* vol. 1, pp. 319–722. References are to the English translation by Jack Schmitt, *Canto General* (Berkeley: University of California Press, 1991).

45. Ernesto Cardenal, *El estrecho dudoso* (Buenos Aires: Ediciones Carlos Lohle, 1972).

46. Nicolás Guillén, *El diario que a diario* '(Havana: Unión de Escritores y Artistas de Cuba, 1972) *The Daily Daily,* trans. Vera M. Kutzinsky (Berkeley: University of California Press, 1989).

47. Volodia Teitelboim, a leading Chilean communist writes in his biography— *Neruda: An Intimate Biography,* trans. Beverley J. Delong Tonelli (Austin: University of Texas Press, 1991), p. 274—that when Neruda joined the party in 1945 many other intellectuals joined with him.

48. Enrique Mario Santí, *Pablo Neruda: The Poetics of Prophecy* (Ithaca: Cornell University Press, 1982), especially pp. 179–187.

49. Jean Franco, "Orfeo en Utopía: el poeta y la colectividad en el *Canto General*," in Isaak Jack Levy and Juan Loveluck, eds., *Actas: Simposio Pablo Neruda* (Columbia: University of South Carolina Press, 1975), pp. 267–289.

50. Aimé Césaire, *Cahiers d'un retour au pays natal* (Paris: Présence Africaine, 1983).

51. Gilles Deleuze and Felix Guattari, *Anti-Oedipus: Capitalism and Schizophrenia,* trans. Robert Hurley, Mark Seem, and Helen R. Lane (New York: Viking Press, 1977) pp. 198–199.

52. Included in the collection *Estravagario,* in *Obras completas,* vol.2, pp. 147–149.

53. From a speech given by Neruda in 1954 and included in *Obras completas,* vol. 1, p. 30.

54. Number 25 of *Cien sonetos de amor,* in *Obras completas,* vol. 2, pp. 301–302.

55. Emir Rodríguez Monegal, *Neruda, el viajero inmóvil,* 2nd rev. ed. (Caracas: Monte Ávila, 1977).

56. Pablo Neruda, *Memoirs,* trans. Hardie St. Martin (New York: Farrar, Straus, and Giroux, 1976), p. 154.

57. Isidoro Gilbert, *El oro de Moscú: La historia secreta de las relaciones argentino-sovieticas* (Buenos Aires: Planeta, 1994).

58. Frances Stoner Saunders, *The Cultural Cold War: The CIA and the World of Arts and Letters* (New York: New Press, 2000), p. 350. He did, of course, eventually receive the Nobel prize in 1971.

59. Berno de Almeida, *Jorge Amado,* p. 203.

60. Ibid.

61. Neruda, *Memoirs.*

62. Donoso, *Curfew.*

63. Neruda, *Memoirs,* p. 332.

64. Adolfo Sánchez Vázquez, "Los problemas de la estética marxista," in Sánchez Vázquez, ed., *Estética y Marxismo,* vol. 1, p. 11. The *Canto General* had, of course already broken this mold.

65. For a different view of Amado's realism, see Larsen, "The 'Boom' Novel and the Cold War," pp. 64–78.

66. Sánchez Vázquez, ed., *Estética y marxismo,* vol. 1, p. 31.

3. Liberated Territories

1. Karl Marx, "Money, or the Circulation of Commodities," in *Capital,* (trans. Samuel Moore and Edward Aveling, vol. 1 (New York: International Publishers, 1967), pp. 94–145. For a discussion of Engels's distortion of Marx's definition of use and exchange value, see Gayatri Spivak, "From Haverstock Hill Flat to the U.S. Classroom: What's Left of Theory?" in Ju-

dith Butler, John Guillory, and Kendall Thomas, eds., *What's Left of Theory: New Work on the Politics of Literary Theory* (New York: Routledge, 2000), pp. 1–39.

2. An exception to this negative evaluation is the collection *Cultura y política en los años '60* (Universidad de Buenos Aires: Instituto de Investigaciones "Gino Germani," 1997).

3. For a discussion of the film's nostalgia as well as of photographic representation of "The Special Period," see Ana Dopico, "Disappearing City: Havana, History, and Vision" (paper presented at the Juan Carlos Center, New York University, 2000).

4. Jorge Castañeda, *Utopia Unarmed: The Latin American Left after the Cold War* (New York: Knopf. 1993), pp. 70–73.

5. Oscar Terán, *Nuestros años sesenta: La formación de la nueva izquierda intelectual en la Argentina, 1956–1966* (Buenos Aires: Ediciones El Cielo por Asalto, 1993), pp. 112–113.

6. Jorge G. Castañeda, *Utopia Unarmed,* p. 78. See also Jorge G. Castañeda, *Compañero. The Life and Death of Che Guevara* (New York: Knopf, 1998).

7. Che Guevara, "El socialismo, el hombre y el arte," in Adolfo Sánchez Vázquez, ed., *Estética y Marxismo,* vol. 2 (Mexico: Era, 1970), p. 414. See also Jon Lee Anderson, *Che Guevara: A Revolutionary Life* (New York: Grove Press, 1997), for Che's repeatedly stated views on the militant.

8. Daniel James, ed., *The Complete Bolivian Diaries of Che Guevara and Other Captured Documents* (New York: Stein and Day, 1968).

9. See Edgardo Anguita and Martin Caparrós, *La voluntad: Una historia de la militancia revolucionaria en la Argentina 1966–73* (Buenos Aires: Norma, 1997). The book is a detailed compilation of case studies and reporting of the period.

10. "Responsabilidad del intelectual ante los problemas del mundo subdesarrollado," Declaración general de la comisión número tres del Congreso," *Casa de las Américas* 8, no. 47 (March–April 1968), pp. 102–105, especially p. 103.

11. Mario Benedetti, "Sobre las relaciones entre el hombre de acción y el intelectual," *Revolución y Cultura* 4 (15 Feb. 1968), p. 30.

12. Quoted in "Sumario," *Casa de las Américas* 8, no. 47 (March–April 1968), p. 3.

13. Gonzalo Aguilar, "Rodolfo Walsh, mas allá de la literatura," *Punto de vista* 67 (Aug. 2000), pp. 10–14.

14. Antonio Cisneros, "Paris, 5è," *Canto ceremonial contra el oso hormiguero* (Havana: Casa de las Américas, 1968), pp. 57–59. The English translation, bearing the title "Loneliness," is included in Antonio Cisneros, *The Spider Hangs Too Far from the Ground,* trans. Maureen Ahern, William Rowe, and David Tipton (London: Cape Goliard, 1970), pages unnumbered.

15. See Van Gosse, *Where the Boys Are: Cuba, Cold War America and the Making of a New Left* (London: Verso, 1993).

16. Anderson, *Che Guevara,* p. 468, quoting Simone de Beauvoir. The Sartre quotation may be apochryphal as it was related to me by Alejo Carpentier, who was anything but a reliable source.

17. In an interesting article on the writing by women about their experience in the literacy campaign, Luisa Campuzano argued that the scarce encouragement given to memoirs and testimonials channeled the records of this experience into the novel and may account for the scarcity of women writers in postrevolutionary Cuba. See Luisa Campuzano, "Cuba 1961: Los textos narrativos de las alfabetizadoras. Conflictos de género, clase y canon," *Unión* 9, no. 26 (Jan.–March 1997), pp. 52–58.

18. Pamela Maria Smorkaloff, *La cultura literaria y el proceso social en Cuba* (Havana: Editorial Letras Cubanas, 1987), gives a brief overview of publishing before the revolution and an exhaustive description of cultural institutions and publishing in postrevolutionary Cuba.

19. It is important to stress that censorship was prevalent in Latin America at this time. See, for instance, the case of Argentina as described in Andrés Avellaneda, *Censura, autoritarismo y cultura: Argentina 1960–83* (Buenos Aires: Centro Editor de América Latina, 1986).

20. Roberto González Echeverría, *La ruta de Severo Sarduy* (New Hampshire: Ediciones del Norte, 1987), especially p. 30.

21. For a discussion of literature in the first decade of the Cuban Revolution, see Lourdes Casal, "Literature and Society," in Carmelo Mesa Lago, ed., *Revolutionary Change in Cuba* (Pittsburgh: University of Pittsburgh Press, 1971), pp. 447–469.

22. Roberto Fernández Retamar, "Hacia una intelectualidad revolucionaria en Cuba," in Francisco Fernández-Santos and José Martínez, eds., *Cuba: una revolución en marcha* (Paris: Ruedo Ibérico, 1967), pp. 292–293.

23. Guillermo Cabrera Infante, *Mea Cuba* (Barcelona: Plaza y Janes, 1992).

24. Quoted by Anderson, *Che Guevara,* p. 483.

25. Dasso Saldívar, *García Márquez: El viaje a la semilla* (Madrid: Alfaguara, 1997). This criticism did not extend to Fidel himself, whom García Márquez continued to support. See Plinio Apuleyo Mendoza, *El olor a la guayaba,* 2nd ed. (Barcelona: Bruguera, 1983), pp. 140–146.

26. Casal, "Literature and Society," pp. 457–458.

27. Lisando Otero, "El escritor en la revolución cubana," included in Fernández-Santos and Martínez, eds., *Cuba,* p. 305. The letter is dated March 30, 1966.

28. Lisandro Otero, "Cuba: Literatura y Revolución," first published in the Mexican journal *Siempre* in June 1966 and reprinted in Sánchez Vázquez, ed., *Estética y Marxismo,* vol. 2, pp. 343–353. Otero has revised his opinions since this time.

29. Anderson, *Che Guevara,* p. 376.

30. Guillermo Cabrera Infante, *Tres Tristes Tigres* (Barcelona: Seix Barral, 1965); *Three Trapped Tigers,* trans. Donald Gardner and Suzanne Jill Levine in collaboration with the author (New York: Harper and Row, 1971).

31. Lumsden Ian, *Machos, Maricones and Gays: Cuba and Homosexuality* (Philadelphia: Temple University Press, 1996).

32. Randy Martin, *Socialist Ensembles: Theater and State in Cuba and Nicaragua* (Minneapolis: University of Minnesota Press, 1994), p. 117.

33. See, for instance, Gordon Brotherston and Ed Dorn, eds., *Con Cuba* (London: Cape Goliard, 1969); J. M. Cohen, ed., *New Cuban Writing* (London: Penguin Books, 1970).

34. Susan Sontag, introduction to Stermer Dugald, *The Art of Revolution* (New York: McGraw Hill, 1970).

35. Mario Vargas Llosa, "Crónica de Cuba," in Fernández-Santos and Martínez, eds., *Cuba,* p. 510.

36. "Tres preguntas a Lisandro Otero," *R-C* 1, no. 2 (1967), pp. 95–96.

37. *R-C* 1, no. 1 (1967), p. 5.

38. Carlos Rafael Rodríguez, "Problemas del arte en la Revolución," *R-C* 1, no. 1 (1967), pp. 6–15, especially p. 11.

39. Ibid., p. 13.

40. Carlos Rafael Rodríguez, "Preguntas y respuestas," *R-C* 1, no. 1 (1967) p. 29. (my translation). In a discussion of the ballet, he returned to his obsession with homosexuality and forecast that, in the future, all young revolutionaries would be "energetic," and cut cane as well as dance.

41. J. M. Cohen, ed., *Writers in the New Cuba* (Baltimore: Penguin, 1967), p. 11.

42. For Padilla's account of his imprisonment, see his memoir *Self-portrait of the Other,* trans. Alexander Coleman (New York: Farrar, Straus, and Giroux, 1990). See also Jorge Edwards, *Persona non grata* (Barcelona: Seix Barral, 1974); *Persona non Grata: A Memoir of Disenchantment with the Cuban Revolution,* trans. Andrew Hurley (New York: Paragon House, 1993).

43. Claudia Gilman, "La situación del escritor latinoamericano: La voluntad de politización," in Enrique Oteiza, ed., *Cultura y política en los años '60* (Universidad de Buenos Aires, 1997), pp. 171–186.

44. Angel Rama, "Las malandanzas de Reinaldo Arenas," *El Universal* (Caracas), 12 September 1982. The dispute arose because Rama had published an article in the New York journal *Review* about exiles from the Southern Cone without mentioning Cuban exiles. That it was an issue at all is astonishing.

45. Reinaldo Arenas, *El mundo alucinante* (Mexico: Diogenes, 1969); *Hallucinations, Being an Account of the Life and Adventures of the Friar Servando Teresa de Mier,* trans. Gordon Brotherston (London: Jonathan Cape, 1971).

46. Reinaldo Arenas, "Literatura y revolución." *Casa de las Américas* 31–32 (Nov.–Feb. 1968–1969), p. 164.

47. Reinaldo Arenas, *Antes que anochezca* (Barcelona: Tusquets, 1992); *Before Night Falls,* trans. Dolores M. Koch (New York: Viking, 1993).

48. Brad Epps, "Proper Conduct: Reinaldo Arenas, Fidel Castro, and the Poli-

tics of Homosexuality," *Journal of the History of Sexuality* 6, no. 2 (1995), pp. 231–283.

49. Virgilio Piñera, *La carne de René* (Madrid: Alfaguara, 1985); *Rene's Flesh,* trans. Mark Schafer (Boston: Eridanos Press, 1989); José Quiroga, "Fleshing out Virgilio Piñera from the Cuban Closet," in Emilie L. Bergmann and Paul Julian Smith, eds., *Entiendes? Queer Readings, Hispanic Writings* (Durham: Duke University Press, 1995), pp. 168–180.

50. José Lezama Lima, *Paradiso* (Mexico: Era, 1968); *Paradise,* trans. Gregory Rabassa (Austin: University of Texas Press, 1988).

51. José Lezama Lima, *Las Eras Imaginarias* (Caracas: Fundamentos, 1971).

52. Paul Julian Smith, "The Language of Strawberry," *Sight and Sound* 4 (1994), pp. 31–33; José Quiroga, "Revolution: Strawberry and Chocolate," in *Tropics of Desire* (New York: New York University Press, 2000), pp. 124–144.

53. I was present at a meeting of the jury of Casa de las Américas in January of that year when she criticized intellectuals who lived outside their own countries.

54. Castañeda, *Utopia Unarmed,* pp. 184–185.

55. Irwin Silber, ed., *Voices of National Liberation: The Revolutionary Ideology of the "Third World" as Expressed by Intellectuals and Artists at the Cultural Congress of Havana January 1968* (Brooklyn: Central Book Company, 1970), see Appendix 3, "Reports of the Cultural Congress of Havana," esp. p. 300 for guidelines for intellectuals.

56. "Responsabilidad de los intelectuales de los paises subdesarrollantes," *Casa de las Américas* 47 (March–April 1968), pp. 121–123.

57. Jesús Díaz, "El fin de otra ilusión. A propósito de la quiebra de *El Caimán Barbudo* y la clausura de *Pensamiento Crítico,*" *Encuentro de la cultura cubana* 16–17 (Spring–Summer 2000), pp. 106–119.

58. Lourdes Casal, *El caso Padilla: Literatura y revolución en Cuba. Documentos* (Miami: Ediciones Universal, 1971); Heberto Padilla, *Fuera del juego* (Havana: Casa de las Américas, 1968). Three of Padilla's poems were published in *R-C* 3 (Nov. 1967), pp. 65–67.

59. Mario Vargas Llosa, "El socialismo y los tanques," in Vargas Llosa, *Contra viento y marea* (Barcelona: Seix Barral, 1983), pp. 160–163.

60. Vargas Llosa, "Carta a Haydée Santamaría," in ibid., 164–165.

61. Vargas Llosa, "Carta a Fidel Castro," in ibid., 166–168 (my translation).

62. Oscar Collazos, Julio Cortázar, Mario Vargas Llosa, *Literatura en la revolución y revolución en la literatura,* (Mexico: Siglo xxi, 1970). Vargas Llosa also published the reply as "Luzbel, Europa y otras conspiraciones" in *Contra viento y marea,* pp. 150–159.

63. Fidel Castro, "Palabras a los intelectuales," in Raul Martínez, ed., *Revolución, Letras, Arte* (Havana: Editorial Letras Cubanas, 1980), p. 14.

64. For theater in the period of rectification, see Randy Martin, "Cuban Theater under Rectification," in *Socialist Ensembles: Theater and State in Cuba*

and Nicaragua (Minneapolis: University of Minnesota Press, 1994), pp. 158–189.

65. Jesús Díaz left Cuba and founded *Encuentro de la cultura cubana* in 1996. This scholarly journal, published in Madrid, avoids both uncritical admiration and uncritical hostility toward Cuba.

66. The journal *Areito* was an early attempt at *raprochement,* edited by Cubans living in the United States. For a brief summary of exile literature, see Lourdes Gil, "La apropiación de la lejanía," *Encuentro de la cultura cubana* 15 (Winter 1999–2000), pp. 61–69.

67. Marta Harnecker, "Democracia y socialismo," *Temas* 16–17 (Oct. 1998–June 1999), pp. 120–135. This issue is a survey of forty years of revolution which has the subtitle, "Sociedad Civil en Debate." For the views of artists working in the 1980s, see Coco Fusco and Robert Knafo "Interviews with Cuban Artists," *Social Text* 15 (Fall 1986). And for the Mariel generation, see Jesús J. Barquet, "La generación de Mariel," *Encuentro de la cultura cubana* 8–9 (Spring–Summer 1998), pp. 110–125.

68. Ambrosio Fornet, introduction to "Bridging Enigma: Cubans on Cuba," in *South Atlantic Quarterly* 96, no. 1 (Winter 1997), p. 7.

69. Brian Eppes, "Proper Conduct: Reinaldo Arenas, Fidel Castro and the Politics of Homosexuality," *Journal of the History of Sexuality* 6, no. 21 (1995), pp. 231–283.

70. Osvaldo Sánchez, *La isla posible* (Barcelona: Destino, 1995), quoted by Kevin Power, "Cuba: One Story after Another," in *While Cuba Waits: Art from the Nineties* (Santa Monica: Smart Art Press, 1999), p. 44.

71. For a more extensive discussion of Cuban theater, see Martin, *Socialist Ensembles;* Rine Leal, *Teatro Escambray* (Havana: Letras Cubanas, 1975).

72. "El cine y la cultura," *Alea: Una retrospectiva crítica* (Havana: Letras Cubanas, 1987), pp. 273–283.

73. Julio García Espinosa, *Por un cine imperfecto* (Madrid: Miguel Castellote, 1976).

74. Edmundo Desnoes, *Memorias del subdesarrollo* (Mexico: Joaquín Mortíz, 1977); *Inconsolable Memories,* trans. the author (New York: American Library, 1967).

75. Julianne Burton, "*Memorias del subdesarrollo* en tierras del superdesarrollo," in *Alea: Una retrospectiva crítica* (Havana: Letras Cubanas, 1987), pp. 111–121.

76. Tomás Gutiérrez Alea, *Dialéctica del espectador* (Havana: Cuadernos de la Revista Unión, 1982), especially pp. 69–70.

77. This point is made by Aijaz Ahmed, *In Theory: Classes, Nations, Literatures* (London: Verso, 1992), pp. 287–318.

78. William Gálvez, *Che in Africa: Che Guevara's Congo Diary,* trans. Mary Todd (New York: Ocean Press, 1999).

79. Roberto Fernández Retamar, *Calibán: Apuntes sobre la cultura de nuestra América* (Mexico: Diogenes, 1974); *Caliban and Other Essays,* trans. Ed-

ward Baker, foreword by Fredric Jameson (Minneapolis: University of Minnesota Press, 1989).

80. Carlos Fuentes, *Paris. La Revolución de Mayo* (Mexico: Era, 1968), p. 32.

81. Edward W. Said, *Culture and Imperialism* (New York: Knopf, 1993), p. 213.

82. Gayatri Chakravorty Spivak, *Outside in the Teaching Machine* (New York: Routledge, 1993), p. 13.

83. Van Gosse, *Where the Boys Are: Cuba, Cold War America and the Making of the New Left* (London: Verso, 1993).

84. Fredric Jameson, foreword to Fernández Retamar, *Caliban and other Essays,* pp. xi–xii.

85. Román de la Campa, "Postmodernism and Revolution: Borges, Che, and Other Slippages," in *Latin Americanism* (Minneapolis: University of Minnesota Press, 1999), pp. 31–56.

86. John Berger, "Che Guevara," in *The Look of Things,* ed. Nikos Stangos (New York: Viking Press, 1971), pp. 42–53.

87. This is clear from an interview in Leandro Katz's documentary film *El día que me quieras.*

88. I discuss the biographies in my essay "Baile de fantasmas en los campos de la guerra fría," in Mabel Moraña, ed., *Nuevas Perspectivas desde/sobre América Latina: El desafío de los estudios culturales* (Santiago: Cuarto Propio, 2000). The three biographies I refer to are Jorge Castañeda, *Compañero: The Life and Death of Che Guevara* (New York: Knopf, 1998); Paco Taibo II , *Guevara: Otherwise Known as Che,* trans. Martin Michael Roberts (New York: St. Martin's Press, 1997); John Lee Anderson, *Che Guevara: A Revolutionary Life* (New York: Grove Press, 1997).

89. For other "sympathetic" Hollywood versions of the war in Central America, see Oliver Stone's *Salvador* and John Sayle's more allegorical treatment of the theme in *Men with Guns.*

90. Liliana Porter, "A Vague Chance or Precise Laws," interview with Ana Tiscornia, *Atlantica* 13 (Winter 1995–1996).

91. Castañeda, *Compañero,* p. 497.

92. Quoted by Martin, *Socialist Ensembles,* p. 205.

93. John Beverley and Marc Zimmerman, *Literature and Politics in the Central American Revolutions* (Austin: University of Texas Press, 1990), p. xiii. In a rather curious later assessment, Beverley would write that the "failure" of the book was "not only conjectural but theoretical." John Beverley, *Subalternity and Representation: Arguments in Cultural Theory* (Durham: Duke University Press, 1999), p. 4.

94. Ibid., p. 78. For a substantial criticism of this view, see Greg Dawes, *Aesthetics and Revolution: Nicaraguan Poetry 1979–1990* (Minneapolis: University of Minnesota Press, 1993), pp. x–xv.

95. For the influence of the Teatro Escambray on the Nicaraguan Nixtayolero, see Martin, *Socialist Ensembles,* pp. 98–99.

96. Ernesto Cardenal, "Economía de Tahuantinsuyu," in *Homenaje a los indios americanos* (Buenos Aires: Ediciones Carlos Lohlé, 1972), p. 39.

97. Ernesto Cardenal, "Apocalipsis," in *El estrecho dudoso* (Buenos Aires: Ediciones Carlos Lohlé, 1972), pp. 106–110.

98. Many of these poets, including Cardenal, contributed letters to the bilingual magazine *El corno emplumado (The Plumed Horn)*, edited by Margaret Randall and Sergio Mondragón.

99. Jaime Quezada, *Un viaje por Solentiname* (Santiago: Sin Fronteras, 1987), p. 48.

100. Ibid., p. 27.

101. Ibid., p. 46.

102. Dawes, *Aesthetics and Revolution*, pp. 77–78.

103. Quezada, *Un viaje por Solentiname*, p. 89.

104. Mayra Jiménez, ed., *Talleres de poesía* (Managua: Ministerio de Cultura, 1983), p. 13.

105. Mayra Jiménez, ed., *Poesía campesina de Solentiname* (Managua: Ministerio de Cultura, 1980), p. 37.

106. Ignacio Elacurría, *Freedom Made Flesh*, tr. John Drury (Maryknoll, N.Y.: Orbis Books, 1976), pp. 108–112.

107. Ernesto Cardenal, *Gospel in Solentiname*, trans. Donald Walsh, vol. 3 (Maryknoll, N.Y.: Orbis Books, 1976–82), pp. 61–62.

108. Cardenal, *Gospel in Solentiname*, vol. 1, p. 87.

109. Martin, *Socialist Ensembles*, pp. 97–101.

110. Peter Burger, *Theory of the Avant-Garde*, trans. Michael Shaw (Minneapolis: University of Minnesota Press, 1984), p. 83.

111. For example, the collection *Artefactos* (1973), which offended many Allende supporters. See William Rowe, *Poets of Contemporary Latin America: History and the Inner Life* (Oxford: Oxford University Press, 2000), pp. 70–77.

112. Luis Camnitzer, "Art and Politics: The Aesthetics of Resistance," *NACLA Report on the Americas* 28, no. 2 (Sept.–Oct. 1994), p. 41.

113. Quoted in ibid., p. 40.

114. Omar Prego, *La fascinación de las palabras: Conversaciones con Julio Cortázar* (Barcelona: Muchnik Editores, 1985), p. 133.

115. Julio Cortázar, *Libro de Manuel* (Buenos Aires: Sudamericana, 1973); *A Manual for Manuel*, trans. Gregory Rabassa (New York: Pantheon Books, 1978), p. 8.

116. Manuel Puig, *El beso de la mujer araña* (Barcelona: Seix Barral, 1976); *Kiss of the Spider Woman*, trans. Thomas Colchie (New York: Knopf, 1979).

4. Antistates

1. Flores Galindo, *Buscando un inca : identidad y utopía en los Andes* (Mexico: Grijalbo, 1993).

2. Tomas Eloy Martínez, *Santa Evita* (Barcelona: Seix Barral, 1995); for a photographic record, see Matilde Sánchez, *Evita: Imagenes de una pasión* (Buenos Aires: Planeta, 1997).

3. Michel Foucault, "Of Other Spaces," *Diacritics* 16 (Spring 1986), pp. 22–27.

4. William Rowe and Vivian Schelling, *Memory and Modernity: Popular Culture in Latin America* (London: Verso, 1991).

5. Josefina Ludmer, *El cuerpo del delito: Un manual* (Buenos Aires: Libros Perfil, 1999), studies the figuration of the delinquent in both literary and nonliterary works to mark the frontier of the state's system of signification.

6. Edgardo Rodríguez Juliá, *La noche oscura del niño Avilés* (Rio Piedras: Huracán, 1984); José Luis González, *Puerto Rico: The Four Storyed Country and Other Essays,* trans. Gerald Guiness (Mapplewood, N.J.: Waterfront Press, 1990).

7. Gilles Deleuze and Felix Guattari, "How to Make Yourself a Body without Organs," in *A Thousand Plateaus: Capitalism and Schizophrenia* trans. Brian Massumi (Minneapolis: University of Minnesota Press, 1987), pp. 149–166. The notion is derived from Artaud and refers to the egoless and nontotalized body.

8. Gabriel García Márquez, "La Sierpe (Un país en la Costa Atlántica)," first published in *El Heraldo* (Baranquilla) and reprinted in Jaques Gilard, ed., *Textos costeños,* vol 2 (Buenos Aires: Sudamericana, 1987), p. 512.

9. Gabriel García Márquez, "La increible y triste historia de la cándida Eréndira y de su abuela desalmada" (1972), in *Cuentos 1947–92* (Barcelona: Norma, 1996), pp. 307–372; *Innocent Erendira and Other Stories,* trans. Gregory Rabassa (New York: Harper and Row, 1978), pp. 1–59.

10. Gabriel García Márquez, "Los funerales de la Mamá Grande" (1962), in *Cuentos 1947–92,* pp. 216–235; *No One Writes to the Colonel and Other Stories,* trans. J. S. Bernstein (New York: Harper and Row, 1968).

11. Gilles Deleuze and Felix Guattari, *Anti-Oedipus,* vol. 1 of *Capitalism and Schizophrenia,* trans. Robert Hurley, Mark Seem, and Helen R. Lane (New York: Viking Press, 1977), pp. 140–142.

12. "Blacamán el Bueno, vendedor de milagros" (1972), in *Cuentos 1947–92,* pp. 295–306; "Blacaman the Good: Vendor of Miracles," in Gabriel García Márquez, *Collected Stories,* trans. Gregory Rabassa (New York: Harper and Row, 1984), pp. 252–261.

13. Fernando Coronil, "The Nation's Two Bodies," in *The Magical State: Nature, Money and Modernity in Venezuela* (Chicago: University of Chicago Press, 1997).

14. Gabriel García Márquez, *El otoño del patriarca* (Barcelona: Plaza y Janes, 1975); *The Autumn of the Patriarch,* trans. Gregory Rabassa (New York: Avon Books, 1975). The translation in the text is mine.

15. See Mary Louise Pratt, *Imperial Eyes: Travel Writing and Transculturation* (London: Routledge, 1993).

16. For a discussion of modernity as a lost object in Latin American writing, see Carlos J. Alonso, *The Burden of Modernity* (New York: Oxford University Press, 1998), pp. 162–166.

17. Gabriel García Márquez, *Del amor y otros demonios* (Mexico: Diana, 1994); *Of Love and Other Demons,* trans. Edith Grossman (New York: Knopf, 1995).

18. Gabriel García Márquez, *El general en su laberinto* (Madrid: Mondadori, 1989); *The General in His Labyrinth,* trans. Edith Grossman (New York: Knopf, 1990).

19. Augusto Roa Bastos, *Yo el Supremo* (Buenos Aires: Siglo xxi, 1974); *I The Supreme,* trans. Helen Lane (New York: Knopf, 1987).

20. J. P and W. P. Robertson, *Letters on South America, Comprising Travels on the Banks of the Parana and Rio de la Plata* (London: J. Murray, 1843).

21. Thomas Carlyle, *Critical and Miscellaneous Essays* vol. 4 (New York, 1899), pp. 261–321.

22. "Misplaced ideas" is the phrase used by Roberto Schwartz. See "Beware of Alien Ideologies: An Interview with *Movimento,*" in John Gledson, ed., *Misplaced Ideas: Essays on Brazilian Culture* (London: Verso, 1992), pp. 33–40.

23. Deleuze and Guattari, *Anti-Oedipus,* p. 205.

24. Klaus Theweleit, *"Women Floods Bodies History,"* in *Male Fantasies,* vol. 1, trans. Stephen Conway in collaboration with Erica Carter and Chris Turner (Minneapolis: University of Minnesota Press, 1987), p. 391.

25. Julio Ortega, *"Pedro Páramo:* A Metaphor for the End of the World," *Studies in Twentieth Century Literature* vol. 14, no. 1 (Winter 1990), pp. 21–26.

26. Joseph Sommers, "Los muertos no tienen tiempo ni espacio (un diálogo con Juan Rulfo," in Joseph Sommers, ed., *La narrativa de Juan Rulfo: Interpretaciones críticas* (Mexico: Sepsetentas, 1974), p. 21.

27. Jim Tuck, *The Holy War in Los Altos* (Tucson: University of Arizona Press, 1982), p. 5.

28. Ibid., p. 25.

29. Although there seems no reason for using a French word where an English word exists, *ressentiment* has acquired a conceptual baggage thanks to Nietzsche. For a note on Nietzsche's use of the word, see Walter Kaufman's introduction to Friedrich Nietzsche, *On the Genealogy of Morals* (New York: Vintage Books, 1969), p. 5.

30. Fredric Jameson, *The Political Unconscious: Narrative as a Socially Symbolic Act* (Ithaca, N.Y.: Cornell University Press, 1981), p. 205.

31. I discuss the disassociation of the senses more fully in an essay, "El viaje al país de los muertos," in Sommers, ed., *La narrativa de Juan Rulfo,* pp. 117–140.

32. Gilles Deleuze, *Différence et répétition* (Paris: Presses Universitaires de France, 1976), pp. 108–109.

33. Walter Benjamin, "Theses on the Philosophy of History," *Illuminations,* trans Harry Zohn (London: Jonathan Cape, 1970), pp. 255–266.
34. Juan Rulfo, *El llano en llamas* (Mexico: Fondo de Cultura Económica, 1954); *The Burning Plain and Other Stories,* trans. George D. Schade (Austin: University of Texas Press, 1967).
35. This invites comparison with the Mothers of the Plaza de Mayo in Argentina who wanted the disappeared sons and daughters to be restored to them "with life."

5. The Black Angel of Lost Time

1. Pablo Neruda, "El fantasma del buque de carga," *Obras completas,* 3rd ed., vol. 1 (Buenos Aires: Losada, 1957), pp. 199–200.
2. Carlos Fuentes, *La nueva novela hispanoamericana* (Mexico: Joaquín Mortíz, 1969), p. 23.
3. On dependency theory as advanced in the 1970s, see Osvaldo Sunkel and Pedro Paz, *El subdesarrollo latinoamericano y la teoría del desarrollo* (Mexico: Siglo xxi, 1970).
4. Arturo Escobar, *Encountering Development: The Making and Unmaking of the Third World* (Princeton: Princeton University Press, 1995), p. 44.
5. Ibid., pp. 53–54.
6. Neil Larsen, *Modernism and Hegemony: A Materialist Critique of Aesthetic Agencies* (Minneapolis: University of Minnesota Press, 1990), pp. xiv.
7. Ildeber Avelar, *The Untimely Present: Post-Dictatorial Latin American Fiction and the Task of Mourning* (Durham: Duke University Press, 1999), p. 12.
8. Gabriel García Márquez, *Love in the Time of Cholera,* trans. Edith Grossman, (London: Penguin Books, 1989).
9. Mario Vargas Llosa, *La casa verde* (Barcelona: Seix Barral, 1976); *The Green House,* trans. Gregory Rabassa (New York: Harper and Row, 1968), p. 238.
10. Juan Carlos Onetti, *El astillero* (Buenos Aires: Fabril Editora, 1961); *The Shipyard,* trans. Rachel Caffyn (New York: Scribners, 1968).
11. On fantasy, see Slavoj Žižek, *The Plague of Fantasies* (London: Verso, 1997); Kaja Silverman, *Male Subjectivity at the Margins* (New York: Routledge, 1992).
12. Onetti paid homage in "Requiem por Faulkner ("Padre y maestro mágico"), in *Requiem por Faulkner y otros artículos* (Montevideo: Arca, 1975), pp. 164–167.
13. Thomas Mann, *Buddenbrooks,* trans. H. T. Lowe-Porter (London: Secker and Warburg, 1930), p. 13.
14. Charles Olson, *Call Me Ishmael* (San Francisco: City Lights, 1947), p. 12.
15. Emir Rodríguez Monegal "Conversación con Juan Carlos Onetti," in Jorge Ruffinelli, ed., *Onetti* (Montevideo: Biblioteca de Marcha, 1973), pp. 256–

257. It is possible that his view of allegory was of something dry and super-imposed.

16. Walter Benjamin, *The Origin of German Baroque Drama,* trans. John Osborne (London: Verso, 1977), p. 233.

17. Larsen appeared in *La vida breve* and in the novel, *Juntacadáveres* published after *The Shipyard.* See Rodríguez Monegal, "Conversación con Juan Carlos Onetti," pp. 248–257.

18. In this case I have made a more literal translation than the published version Larsen is trying to give his speech a professional tone. Page references in the text refer to the published translation by Rachel Caffyn cited in note 10.

19. Escobar, *Encountering Development,* p. 5.

20. Silverman, *Male Subjectivity at the Margins* p. 41.

21. Slavoj Žižek, *The Sublime Object of Ideology* (London: Verso, 1989), p. 33.

22. Louis Althusser, "Ideology and Ideological State Apparatuses," in *Lenin and Philosophy and Other Essays,* trans. Ben Brewster (New York: Monthly Review Press, 1971).

23. Arthur Schopenhauer, *The World as Will and Idea,* vol. 1, trans. R. B. Haldane and J. Kemp, 4th ed. (London: Kegan Paul, Trench, Trubner, 1896), p. 402.

24. Ibid., p. 401.

25. Álvaro Mutis, *Maqroll: Three Novellas,* trans. Edith Grossman (New York: Harper Collins, 1986). This selection includes *La nieve del Almirante (The Snow of the Admiral), Ilona llega con la lluvia (Ilona Comes with the Rain),* and *Un bel morir (A Beautiful Dying).*

26. Sigmund Freud, *Beyond the Pleasure Principle,* trans. James Strachey (New York: Liveright, 1969), p. 58.

27. Silverman, *Male Subjectivity at the Margins,* p. 58.

28. *The Seminar of Jacques Lacan,* ed. Jacques-Alain Miller, book 2 (New York: Norton, 1991), p. 100.

29. "Imperial nostalgia" is a term coined by Renato Rosaldo. See chapter 3 of *Culture and Truth: The Remaking of Social Analysis* (Boston: Beacon Press, 1989), pp. 68–87.

30. Les Blank and James Bogan, eds., *Burden of Dreams: Screenplay, Journals, Reviews, Photographs* (Berkeley: North Atlantic Books, 1984).

31. From the documentary film *Burden of Dreams.*

32. Blank and Bogan, *Burden of Dreams,* p. 90.

33. Count Keyserling, *South American Meditations on Hell and Heaven in the Soul of Man,* trans. Teresa Duerr (New York: Harper Brothers, 1932).

34. Michael Goodwin, "Up the River with Werner Herzog," in Blank and Bogan, eds., *Burden of Dreams,* p. 225.

35. José Eustasio Rivera, *La vorágine* (Madrid: Catedra, 1990); *The Vortex,* trans. Earle K. James (New York: G. P. Putnam, 1935) p. 231.

36. Theodor W. Adorno and Max Horkheimer, *Dialectic of Enlightenment,* trans. John Cumming (New York: Herder and Herder, 1972).

6. *The Magic of Alterity*

1. José María Arguedas, *Los rios profundos* (Buenos Aires: Losada, 1958); *Deep Rivers,* trans. John V. Murra (Austin: University of Texas Press, 1978); Guillermo Bonfil Batalla, *Mexico profundo: Una civilización negada* (Mexico: Grijalbo, 1994); José Luis González, *El país de cuatro pisos y otros ensayos* (Rio Piedras: Huracán, 1980); *The Four Storeyed Country and Other Essays,* trans. Gerald Guiness (Princeton: Markus Wiener, 1993).

2. Sonia Montecinos, *Madres y huachos: Alegorías del mestizaje chileno* (Santiago: Cuarto Propio, 1991).

3. Edwin McDowell, "Boom in U.S. for Latin Writers," *New York Times,* 4 January 1988, section C, p. 13.

4. Rosario Ferré, *The House on the Lagoon* (New York: Farrar, Straus, and Giroux, 1995).

5. See Amaryll Chanady, "La influencia del realismo hispanoamericano en el discurso norteamericano, europeo y africano," in Pamela Bacarisse, ed., *Tradición y actualidad de la literatura iberoamericana,* Actas del xxx Congreso del Instituto Internacional de Literatura Iberoamericana, vol. 2 (Pittsburgh: University of Pittsburgh Press, 1995), pp. 301–305. The author reviews the application of the term "magical realism" to non–Latin American writing.

6. Gayatri Chakravorty Spivak, *Outside in the Teaching Machine* (New York: Routledge, 1993), p. 13.

7. Allen Josephs, "Negative Symbiosis," *New York Times,* 4 July 1982, section 7, p. 9.

8. As critics have pointed out, the term "magical realism" was used in Europe in the 1920s. See Ilemar Chiampi, *O realismo maravilhoso: Forma e ideologia no romance hispanoamericano* (Sâo Paulo: Editora Perspectiva, 1980). I refer here only to Latin America.

9. Terry Eagleton, *The Ideology of the Aesthetic* (London: Basil Blackwell, 1990), p. 322.

10. Irlemar Chiampi, *O realismo maravilhso,* in Lois Parkinson Zamora and Wendy Faris, eds., *Magical Realism: Theory, History, Community* (Durham: Duke University Press, 1995). For a neo–avant-garde comment, see Kamau Brathwaite, "El RM como aspecto del cosmos dislocado," *Casa de las Américas* 39, no. 213 (Oct.–Dec. 1998), pp. 37–40.

11. James Clifford, "On Ethnographic Surrealism," in *The Predicament of Culture: Twentieth-Century Ethnography, Literature, and Art* (Cambridge: Harvard University Press, 1988), p. 120. On ethnography and Latin

América literature, see Robert Gónzalez Echeverría, *Myth and Archive: A Theory of Latin American Narrative* (Cambridge: Cambridge University Press, 1990); Amy Fass Emery, *The Anthropological Imagination in Latin American Literature* (Columbia, Missouri: University of Missouri Press, 1996).

12. Johannes Fabian, *Time and the Other: How Anthropology Makes Its Object* (New York: Columbia University Press, 1983).

13. Fredric Jameson, "On Magic Realism in Film," *Signatures of the Visible* (New York: Routledge, 1992), pp. 128–152, especially 128–129.

14. Michael Taussig, *Shamanism and Colonialism, A Study in Terror and Healing and the Wild Man* (Chicago: University of Chicago Press: 1987), p. 172.

15. Raúl Ruiz, *On top of the whale* (The Netherlands, 1982).

16. Alfonso Reyes, "Yerbas de Tarahumara," *transition* 25 (Fall 1936), p. 16.

17. Fernando Ortiz, "Jitanjáforas en Cuba," *transition* 25 (Fall 1936), p. 178.

18. Ortiz was initially led to the study of Afro-Cuban culture by the preface to his book on criminology, *Hampa afrocubana: Los negros brujos* (1906), by Lombroso. His major work, *Contrapunto de tabaco y azúcar* (Havana: Consejo Nacional de la Culture, 1963), was a significant contribution to the study of Afro-Cuban culture. See Román de la Campa, *Latin Americanism* (Minneapolis: University of Minnesota Press 1999). See especially pp. 64–66 and 74–79 for Ortiz's use of the term and its appropriation by the Uruguayan critic Angel Rama. See also John Beverley, *Subalternity and Representation: Arguments in Cultural Theory* (Durham: Duke University Press, 1999).

19. Alejo Carpentier, *Concierto barroco* (Mexico: Siglo xxi, 1974).

20. Carlos Castañeda, *Journey to Ixtlan* (New York: Simon and Schuster, 1973).

21. Jerome Rothenberg, ed., *Technicians of the Sacred: A Range of Poetries from Africa, America, Asia & Oceania* (New York: Doubleday, 1968), p. xxii.

22. For a critical overview of this topics, see Angel Flores, "Magical Realism in Latin American Fiction," *Hispania* 38 (May 1955), pp. 187–192; Erik Camayd-Freitas, *Realismo mágico y primitivismo: Relecturas de Carpentier, Asturias, Rulfo y García Márquez* (New York: University Press of America, 1998) pp. 303–325, gives a useful outline.

23. Alejo Carpentier, *Ecue-Yamba-O: Novela afrocubana* (Buenos Aires: Editorial Xanandu, 1968); Miguel Ángel Asturias, *Leyendas de Guatemala,* vol. 1 (Madrid: Águilar, 1967). The edition includes Valéry's letter to Francis de Miomandre (pp. 17–18), thanking him for the *Leyendas* and commenting on them.

24. Alejo Carpentier, *El reino de este mundo* (Buenos Aires: Editorial América Nueva, 1974); *The Kingdom of this World,* trans. Harriet de Onis (London: Andre Deutsch, 1990).

25. Alejo Carpentier, *El siglo de las luces* (Barcelona: Seix Barral, 1962), p. 182; *Explosion in the Cathedral,* trans. John Sturrock (London: Minerva, 1991), p. 178.

26. Michael Taussig, *Mimesis and Alterity* (New York: Routledge, 1993), p. 111.

27. Walter Benjamin, "On the Mimetic Faculty," *Reflections,* trans. E. Jephcott (New York: Harcourt Brace Jovanovich, 1979), p. 333.

28. Roberto González Echeverría, *The Pilgrim at Home* (Ithica, N.Y.: Cornell University Press, 1977), identifies a cabbalistic substratum in this novel.

29. Joseph Campbell, *The Hero with a Thousand Faces* (New York: Pantheon Books, 1949). See also Claude Lévi-Strauss, *The Savage Mind* (London: Weidenfeld and Nicholson 1966); Northrop Frye, "Archetypal Criticism: Theory of Myths," *Anatomy of Criticism* (Princeton: Princeton University Press, 1971), pp. 121–239.

30. Jorge Luis Borges, "The Argentine Writer and Tradition," in *Labyrinths: Selected Stories and Other Writing,* ed. Donald A. Yates and James Irby (New York: New Directions, 1962), p. 184.

31. Guimarâes Rosa, *Grande Sertâo Veredas* (Rio de Janeiro: José Olimpio Editores, 1963); *The Devil to Pay in the Backlands,* trans. James L. Taylor and Harriet de Onis (New York: Knopf, 1963); Adalberto Ortiz, *Juyungo: Historia de un negro, una isla y otros negros* (Buenos Aires: Editorial Americalee, 1943); Nicolás Guillén, *Songoro cosongo: Poemas mulatos* (1931), in *Songoro cosongo motivos de son* (Buenos Aires: Losada, 1967); Luis Pales Matos, *Tun Tun de pasa y griferia: Poemas afroantillanos* (San Juan: Biblioteca de Autores, 1974).

32. Johannes Fabian, *Time and the Other: How Anthropology Makes Its Object* (New York: Columbia University Press, 1983).

33. Amy Emory, *The Anthropological Imagination in Latin American Literature* (Columbia, Mo.: University of Missouri Press, 1996); Roberto González Echeverría, *Myth and Archive: A Theory of Latin American Narrative* (Cambridge: Cambridge University Press, 1990).

34. Augusto Roa Bastos, *Las culturas condenadas* (Mexico: Siglo xxi, 1978); José María Arguedas, *Mitos, leyendas y cuentos peruanos,* 2nd ed. (Lima: Casa de la Cultura del Peru, 1970); Darcy Ribeiro, *Kadiweu: Ensaios etnológicos sobre o saber, o azar e a beleza* (Rio de Janeiro: Petropolis, 1980).

35. Jacques Derrida, *Of Grammatology,* trans. Gayatri Chakrovorty Spivak (Baltimore: Johns Hopkins University Press, 1976).

36. Gordon Brotherston, *Book of the Fourth World: Reading the Native Americas through their Literature* (Cambridge: Cambridge University Press, 1992), pp. 40–45.

37. José María Arguedas, "El monstruoso contrasentido," *Señores e indios: Acerca de la cultura quechua* (Montevideo: Arca, 1976).

38. Arguedas, *Los ríos profundos; Deep Rivers,* trans. John V. Murra; Miguel

Ángel Asturias, *Hombres de maíz* (Mexico: Fondo de Cultura Económica, 1981); *Men of Maize,* trans. Gerald Martin (New York: Delacorte Press, 1975).

39. Gerald Martin, "Estudio general," in Asturias, *Hombres de maíz,* pp. xciv, cviii–cix.

40. Camayd-Freitas, *Realismo mágico y primitivismo,* pp. 202–203.

41. Adolfo Gilly, *Chiapas la razón ardiente* (Mexico: Era, 1997), p. 111.

42. William Rowe, "La música como espacio sonoro," in *Ensayos arguedianos* (Lima: Sur, 1996), pp. 35–57.

43. Quoted in ibid., p. 44. See also the discussion of the sounds of nature in Arguedas's final novel, *El zorro de arriba y el zorro de abajo,* in Martin Lienhard, *Cultura popular andina y forma novelesca: Zorros y danzantes en la última novela de Arguedas* (Lima: Tarea, 1981), pp. 47–52.

44. José María Arguedas, "El carnaval de Tambobamba," in Rama, ed., *Señores e indios* (Buenos Aires: Calicanto, 1976).

45. Gordon Brotherston, "Configurations of Space," in *Book of the Fourth World,* pp. 82–102.

46. Josefina Ludmer, "Estudio preliminar," in Juan Carlos Onetti, *Para una tumba sin nombre* (Barcelona: EDHASA, 1978), pp. 47–48.

47. Ibid.

48. Jorge Luis Borges, "Narrative Art and Magic," trans. Norman Thomas di Giovanni, in "Prose for Borges," *Triquarterly* 25 (Fall 1972), pp. 209–215.

49. See Beatriz Sarlo, *Jorge Luis Borges: A Writer on the Edge* (London: Verso, 1993), p. 5.

50. Richard Burgin, *Conversations with Jorge Luis Borges* (New York: Avon Books, 1969), p. 94.

51. Sarlo, *Jorge Luis Borges.*

7. Cultural Revolutions

1. Kathleen Newman, "Cultural Redemocratization: Argentina, 1978–89," in Juan Flores, Jean Franco, and George Yudice, eds., *On Edge: The Crisis of Contemporary Latin American Culture* (Minneapolis: Minnesota University Press, 1992) pp. 161–187.

2. Nelly Richard, "Performances of the Chilean Avanzada," *Margins and Institutions: Art in Chile since 1973* (Sydney: Art and Text, 1986). I consulted a reprint of this article in Coco Fusco, ed., *Corpus Delecti: Performance Art of the Americas* (London: Routledge, 2000), pp. 203–17.

3. The word is Nelly Richard's.

4. For her participation in CADA and her independent actions, see Leonidas Morales, *Conversaciones con Diamela Eltit* (Santiago: Cuarto Propio, 1998), pp. 157–171.

5. Diamela Eltit, "Errant, Erratic," preface to *E. Luminata,* trans. Ronald Christ (Santa Fe: Lumen Press, 1997), p. 4.

6. Ronald Christ, Extravag(r)ant and Un/erring Spirit," in ibid., p. 206.

7. Eltit, "Errant, Erratic," p. 7.

8. Djelal Kadir, *The Other Writing: Postcolonial Essays in Latin America's Writing Culture* (West Lafayette: Purdue University Press, 1993), p. 192. See also Raquel Olea, *Lengua víbora: Producciones de lo femenino en la escritura de mujeres chilenas* (Santiago: Cuarto Propio, 1998), pp. 47–62.

9. Christ, "Extravag(r)ant and Un/erring Spirit," pp. 208–209.

10. Eugenia Brito, *Campos minados: Literatura post-golpe en Chile,* 2nd ed. (Santiago: Cuarto Propio, 1994), p. 11.

11. For a detailed discussion of the novel, see Eugenio Brito, "La narrativa de Diamela Eltit: Un nuevo paradigma socio-literario de lectura," in *ibid.,* pp. 111–132.

12. William I. Robinson, "Polyarchy: Coercion's New Face in Latin America, *NACLA Report on the Americas* 34, no. 3 (Nov.–Dec. 2000), pp. 42–48.

13. Joaquín Mortíz, for instance, the Mexican publishing house founded by exiled republican Spaniards, encouraged young writers in the 1960s but eventually became a subsidiary of Planeta.

14. Luis Camnitzer and Mari Carmen Ramírez, *Beyond Identity: Globalization and Latin American Art* (forthcoming, Minnesota University Press).

15. José Agustín, *El rock de la cárcel* (Mexico: Editores Mexicanos Unidos, 1986), pp. 91–132.

16. *El rock de la cárcel* is an autobiographical account of the music and drug culture of the 1960s. See also his book *La contracultura en México: La historia y el significado de los rebeldes sin causa, los jipitecas, los punks y las bandas* (Mexico: Grijalbo, 1996).

17. Angel G. Quintero Rivera, *Salsa, sabor y control: sociología de la música "tropical"* (Mexico: Siglo xxi, 1999).

18. Leonidas Morales, "Violeta Parra: La génesis de su arte," in *Figuras literarias: Rupturas culturales* (Santiago, Peluén, 1993), pp. 127–144; Jaime Londoño and Bernardo Subercaseaux, *Gracias a la vida: Violeta Parra* (Buenos Aires, Galerna, 1976).

19. Peter Wade, *Music, Race and Nation: Música Tropical in Colombia* (Chicago: University of Chicago Press, 2000), pp. 176–188. Gabriel García Márquez was a patron of the *vallenato*-songs accompanied by accordion music from Colombia's coastal region.

20. Nestor García Canclini, *Transforming Modernity: Popular Culture in Mexico,* trans. Lidia Lozano (Austin: University of Texas Press, 1993).

21. Rosario Ferré, "La extraña muerte del capitancito Candelario," in *Maldito Amor,* (Mexico: Joaquín Mortíz, 1986), pp. 167–201.

22. For a discussion of music in relation to latino identity, see Juan Flores, *From Bomba to Hip-Hop: Puerto Rican Culture and Latino Identity* (New York: Columbia University Press, 2000).

23. Eric Zolov, *Refried Elvis: The Rise of the Mexican Counterculture* (Berkeley: University of California, 1999), p. 59. For the case of Chile both before

and after the Pinochet dictatorship, see "La censura en Chile," a dossier included in *Nomadías* 4, no. 4 (Dec. 1999), pp. 79–97.

24. Zolov, *Refried Elvis,* p. 91.

25. A key essay on the movement is Margo Glantz, *Onda y escritura en México: Jóvenes de 10 a 23* (Mexico: Siglo xxi, 1971). José Agustín objected to his inclusion in the movement, see *Onda y Beyond* (Columbia: University of Missouri Press, 1968).

26. Carlos Monsiváis, "No queremos el eclipse, queremos revolución," in *Dias de guardar* (Mexico: Era, 1970), pp. 101–104.

27. Zolov, *Refried Elvis,* p. 40.

28. Carlos Monsiváis, "La nación de Avándaro," in *Amor Perdido* (Mexico: Era, 1978), pp. 247–255.

29. Alberto Beltrán Fuentes, *La ideología anti autoritaria del rock nacional* (Buenos Aires: Centro Editor de América Latina, 1989).

30. Carlos Monsiváis, "Dios nunca muere (Crónica de un eclipse)" in *Días de guardar,* p. 104.

31. For imminence and modernity, see Michael Hardt and Antonio Negri, *Empire* (Cambridge: Harvard University Press, 2000), pp. 71–74.

32. Nestor García Canclini, *Consumidores y ciudadanos: Conflictos multiculturales de la globalización* (Mexico: Grijalbo, 1995), p. 51.

33. Elena Poniatowksa, *El último guajalote* (Mexico: Cultura/Sep, 1982).

34. José Emilio Pacheco, *Las batallas en el desierto* (Mexico: Era, 1981).

35. Gustavo Sainz, *Gazapo* (Mexico: Joaquin Mortíz, 1965); *Gazapo,* trans. Hardie St. Martin (New York: Farrar, Straus, and Giroux, 1968).

36. For instance in the city novels of the 1960s such as Carlos Fuentes, *La región mas transparente,* Julio Cortázar's *Rayuela,* and Mario Vargas Llosa's *Conversación en la Catedral.* For the new city, see Nestor García Canclini, *Consumidores y ciudadanos,* p. 96.

37. Ronald Kay, "Rewriting," *Manuscritos* 1 (1975) pp. 5–31.

38. See Augusto de Campos, Haroldo de Campos, and Decio Pignatari, *Teoria da poesía concreta: Textos críticos e manifestos 1950–60* (São Paulo: Livraria Duas Cidades, 1975).

39. Angel Rama, *La ciudad letrada* (Hanover, N.H.: Ediciones del Norte, 1984), pp. 156–157.

40. A novel by the Mexican writer Gonzalo Celorio, *Y retiemble en sus centros la tierra* (Mexico: Tusquets, 1999), which describes the last bar crawl of a university professor around the center of Mexico City, charts the loss of the city of the lettered.

41. Octavio Paz, "El pachuco y otro extremos," in *The Labyrinth of Solitude: Life and Thought in Mexico,* trans. Lysander Kemp (New York: Grove Press, 1961).

42. Luis Ramiro Beltrán and Elizabeth Fox de Cardona, *Comunicación dominada: Estados Unidos en los medios de América Latina* (Mexico: Nueva Imagen, 1980), pp. 65–66.

43. Ariel Dorfman and Armand Mattelart, *Para leer al Pato Donald* (Santiago: Edictiones Universitarias de Valaparaiso, 1971).

44. Martín Barbero, *De los medios a las mediaciones: Comunicación, cultura y hegemonía* (Barcelona: G. Gili, 1987).

45. Nestor García Canclini, *Culturas híbridas: Estrategias para entrar y salir de la modernidad* (Mexico: Grijalbo, 1989), p. 265.

46. Rossana Reguillo Cruz, *En la calle otra vez: las bandas: identidad urbana y usos de la comunicación,* 2nd ed. (Tlaquepaque, Jalisco: ITESO, 1995).

47. The figures are taken from a special issue of *Nueva Sociedad* no. 12 (July–Aug. 1992) "Que tal, América Latina?" The special issue includes articles on all the capital cities of Latin America. Interestingly, despite the title "How is it going, Latin America?," it is by way of cities that the state of the hemisphere is assessed.

48. Mario Vargas Llosa, *The Real Life of Alejandro Mayta,* trans. Alfred MacAdam (New York: Farrar, Straus, and Giroux, 1986).

49. Fernando Vallejo, *La Virgen de los sicarios* (Bogotá: Afaguara, 1994), pp. 96–97.

50. Saskia Sassen, *The Global City: New York, London, Tokyo* (Princeton: Princeton University Press, 1991).

51. Beatriz Sarlo, *Una modernidad periférica: Buenos Aires 1920 y 1930* (Buenos Aires: Nueva Visión, 1988), p. 13–14.

52. There is an ambitious study by Nestor García Canclini, Alejandro Castellanos, and Ana Rosas Mantecón on Mexico City, *La ciudad de los viajeros: Travesías e imaginarios urbanos: México, 1940–2000* (Mexico: Universidad Autónoma Metropolitana, 1995). The research used photographic and filmic archives and ten different groups registered the reaction of city dwellers to the images of the city.

53. Nestor García Canclini, *Hybrid Cultures: Strategies for Entering and Leaving Modernity,* trans. Christopher L. Chippari and Silvia L. Lopez (Minneapolis: Minnesota University Press, 1995), p. 4.

54. Nestor García Canclini, "Capitales de la cultura y ciudades globales," in *La globalización imaginada* (Mexico: Paidos, 1999), pp. 164–178.

55. Angel Rama, "Italo Calvino: La semiología del relato," *Plural* 23 (Aug. 1973), pp. 8–12.

56. Italo Calvino, *Invisible Cities,* trans. William Weaver (New York: Harcourt Brace, 1974).

57. Gerald Bruns, "Cain: Or, the Metaphorical Construction of Cities," *Salmagundi* no. 74–77 (1987), pp. 70–85.

58. Timothy J. Reiss, "Autonomy, Nostalgia, and Writing for the Aesthetic: Notes on Culture and Exchange," *Centennial Review* 39, no. 3 (Fall 1995), pp. 513–536.

59. Teresa de Lauretis, "Through the Looking-Glass: Woman, Cinema and Language," in *Alice Doesn't: Feminism Semiotics Cinema* (Bloomington: Indiana University Press, 1984), pp. 12–36.

60. José Joaquín Brunner, "Tradicionalismo y modernidad en la cultura," in *Rosa María Alfaro* et al., eds., *Communicación y cultura política: Entre públicos y ciudadanos* (Lima: Calandria, 1996), pp. 35–72.

61. Ibid., p. 72.

62. García Canclini, *Consumidores y ciudadanos,* pp. 72–73.

63. Julio Ramos, *Desencuentros de la modernidad en América Latina: Literatura y políitica en el siglo xix* (Mexico: Fondo de Cultura Económica, 1989).

64. Edgardo Rodríguez Juliá, *El entierro de Cortijo (6 de octubre de 1982),* 3rd ed. (Rio Piedras: Huracán, 1985); see Juan Flores, "La venganza de Cortijo: Nuevos traqzos de la cultural puertoriqueña," in *La venganza de Cortijo y otros ensayos* (Rio Piedras: Huracán, 1997).

65. Jean-Francois Lyotard, *The Postmodern Condition: A Report on Knowledge,* trans. Geoff Bennington and Brian Massumi (Minneapolis: University of Minnesota Press, 1984), p. 22.

66. García Canclini, *La ciudad de los viajeros,* p. 111.

67. Quoted by Carlos Monsiváis in the essay "La manifestación del Rector," *Días de guardar* (Mexico: Era, 1970), p. 215.

68. Elena Poniatowska, *La noche de Tlatelolco: Testimonios de historia oral* (Mexico: Era, 1971); *Massacre in Mexico,* trans. Helen Lane (New York: Viking Press, 1975); Octavio Paz, *Postdata,* 4th ed. (Mexico: Siglo xxi, 1974); *The Other Mexico. Critique of the Pyramid,* trans. Lysander Kemp (New York: Grove Press, 1972); Carlos Monsiváis, *Días de guardar* (Mexico: Era, 1970). For novels that are based on the massacre, see Cynthia Steele, *Politics, Gender, and the Mexican Novel, 1968–1988: Beyond the Pyramid* (Austin: University of Texas Press, 1992).

69. Monsiváis, *Días de guardar,* p. 68. For a selection of Monsiváis's writing in English, see, Carlos Monsiváis, *Mexican Postcards,* trans. John Kraniauskas (London: Verso, 1997).

70. Carlos Monsiváis, "Yo y mis amigos," in *Días de guardar* pp. 65–77.

71. Carlos Monsiváis, "El hastío es pavo real que se aburre de luz en la tarde: Notas del Camp en México," in *Días de Guardar,* pp. 171–197.

72. Carlos Monsiváis, *Los rituales del caos* (Mexico: Era, 1995).

8. *The Seduction of Margins*

1. Peter Stalleybrass and Allon White, *The Politics and Poetics of Transgression* (Ithaca: Cornell University Press, 1986), p. 191.

2. Gillian Rose, *Mourning Becomes the Law: Philosophy and Representation* (Cambridge: Cambridge University Press, 1996), p. 54.

3. Vera M. Kutzinski, *Sugar's Secrets: Race and the Erotics of Cuban Nationalism* (Charlottesville: University of Virginia Press, 1993), p. 165.

4. Rosario Ferré, "How I wrote 'When Women Love Men,'" trans. Rosario Ferré, *The Youngest Doll"* (Lincoln: University of Nebraska Press, 1991). A translation of the story is included in ibid., pp. 133–145.

5. Tununa Mercado, *Espejismos: Canon de alcoba* (Buenos Aires: Ada Korn, 1988), p. 22–23.
6. Clarice Lispector, "A Bela e a Fera o a Ferida Grande Demais," ("Beauty and the Beast or the Wound that was too Big"), included in the edition of *A Paixâo Segundo G.H.* (Florianópolis: Universidad de Santa Catarina Press, 1988), pp. 151–157.
7. Andreas Huyssen, "Mass Culture as Woman: Modernism's Other," *After the Great Divide: Modernism, Mass Culture, Postmodernism* (Bloomington: Indiana University Press, 1986), pp. 44–62.
8. Lispector, "A Bela e a Fera," p. 155.
9. Marina Warner, *From the Beast to the Blonde: On Fairy Tales and Their Tellers* (New York: Farrar, Straus, and Giroux, 1994).
10. Slavoj Žižek, *The Sublime Object of Ideology* (London: Verso, 1989), p. 105. See also Slavoj Žižek, *The Plague of Fantasies* (London: Verso, 1997).
11. Clarice Lispector, *The Passion according to G.H.,* trans. Ronald Sousa (Minneapolis: University of Minnesota Press, 1988); *The Hour of the Star,* trans. Giovanni Pontiero (Manchester: Carcanet, 1986).
12. Edward Said, *Orientalism* (New York: Pantheon Books, 1978).
13. Julia Kristeva, *Black Sun: Depression and Melancholia,* trans. Louis S. Roudiez (New York: Columbia University Press, 1989), p. 12.
14. For the "face" of the other as a summons to responsibility, see Emmanuel Levinas, "Ethics as First Philosophy," in *The Levinas Reader,* ed. Seán Hand (Oxford: Blackwell, 1989), pp. 75–87.
15. For Athens and Jerusalem as contrasting ideals of the polis, see Rose, *Mourning Becomes the Law,* pp. 15–39.
16. Kristeva, *Black Sun,* pp. 228–229. Kristeva contrasts Lispector's *Apple in the Dark* with Duras's writing. Lispector's writing has attracted many prominant women critics. See Hélène Cixous, "L'approche de Clarice Lispector," in *Entre l'Écriture* (Paris: Des Femmes, 1986), pp. 115–199; Rosi Braidotti, *Nomadic Subjects: Embodiment and Sexual Difference in Contemporary Feminist Theory* (New York: Columbia University Press, 1994), pp. 191–195.
17. Graciano Ramos, *Barren Lives,* trans. Ralph Edward Dimmick (Austin: University of Texas Press, 1965).
18. Julia Kristeva, *Powers of Horror: An Essay on Abjection* (New York: Columbia University Press, 1982), p. 2.
19. Ibid., p. 4.
20. Slavoj Žižek, *Looking Awry: An Introduction to Jacques Lacan through Popular Culture* (Cambridge: Massachusetts Institute of Technology, 1991), p. 12.
21. See my discussion in "Oedipus Modernized," in *Plotting Women* (New York: Columbia University Press, 1998) pp. 147–174.
22. Fredric Jameson recognized this genealogy in "On Literary and Cultural Import-Substitution in the Third World," in George M. Gugelberger, ed.,

The Real Thing: Testimonial Discourse and Latin America (Durham: Duke University Press, 1996), pp. 172–191, especially pp. 187–188. See also John Beverley and Marc Zimmerman, "Testimonial Narrative," in *Literature and Politics in Central American Revolutions* (Austin: University of Texas Press, 1990), pp. 173–211.

23. George Yúdice, "Testimonio and Postmodernism," in Gugelberger, ed., *The Real Thing,* pp. 42–69, especially p. 51.
24. Alberto Moreiras, "The Aura of Testimonio," in Gugelberger, ed., *The Real Thing,* pp. 192–224, especially p. 195.
25. Allen Carey-Webb and Stephen Benz, eds., *Teaching and Testimony: Rigoberta Menchú and the North American Classroom* (Albany: New York State University Press, 1996).
26. Mary Louise Pratt has extensively documented these reactions in "*I, Rigoberta Menchú* and the 'Culture Wars,'" in Arturo Arias, ed., *The Rigoberta Menchú Controversy* (Minneapolis: University of Minnesota Press, 2001), pp. 29–48.
27. David Stoll, *Rigoberta Menchú and the Story of all Poor Guatemalans* (Boulder: Westview Press, 1999). The quotation is from the book jacket but it is a fair summary of the argument that became its chief selling point. Various responses to Stoll are collected in Arias, ed., *The Rigoberta Menchú Controversy.* See also John Beverley, "Our Rigoberta? *I, Rigoberta Menchú,* Cultural Authority and the Problem of Subaltern Agency," in *Subalternity and Representation: Arguments in Cultural Theory* (Durham: Duke University Press, 1999), pp. 65–84).
28. Stoll, *Rigoberta Menchú,* p. 282.
29. Martha Rosler, *A Simple Case for Torture, or How to Sleep at Night* (1983).
30. Elizabeth Burgos Debray, ed., *Me llamo Rigoberta Menchú y así me nació la conciencia* (Barcelona: Argus Vergara, 1983); *I, Rigoberta Menchú: An Indian Woman in Guatemala,* trans. Ann Wright (London: Verso, 1984).
31. See the essays in Carey-Webb and Benz, eds., *Teaching and Testimony.*
32. Burgos Debray, ed., *I, Rigoberta Menchú.*
33. Elizabeth Burgos Debray, introduction to ibid., p. xii.
34. Elzbieta Sklodowska, *Testimonio hispanoamericano: historia, teoría, poética* (New York: Peter Lang, 1992), has explored the various accounts of the genealogy of *testimonio,* the multiple and contradictory definitions, and the "poetics of mediation" in the case of *I, Rigoberta Menchú.* For a discussion of the privileging of the book to the detriment of indigenous forms of script and communication, see Walter Mignolo, *The Darker Side of the Renaissance: Literacy, Territoriality and Colonization* (Ann Arbor: University of Michigan Press, 1995). Mignolo also has a valuable discussion of the interventionalist role of the scholar. For discussions of other *testimonios,* see René Jara and Hernán Vidal, eds., *Testimonio y literatura* (Minneapolis: Institute for the Study of Ideologies and Literature, 1986).

35. Doris Sommer sees this secrecy as directed toward the reader. See her "No Secrets for Rigoberta," in *Proceed with Caution When Engaged by Minority Writing* (Cambridge: Harvard University Press, 1999), pp. 115–137.
36. Ernesto Laclau in Judith Butler, Ernesto Laclau, and Slavoj Žižek *Contingency, Hegemony, Universality: Contemporary Dialogues on the Left* (London: Verso, 2000), p. 306.
37. George Yúdice, "Testimonio y concientización," *Revista de crítica literaria latinoamericana* 36 (1992), pp. 207–227; Doris Sommer, "Not Just a Personal Story: Women's *Testimonios* and the Plural Self," in Bella Brodsky and Celeste Schenck, eds., *Life/Lines: Theorizing Women's Autobiography* (Ithaca: Cornell University Press, 1988) pp. 107–130. Doris Sommer, "Sin secretos," *Revista de crítica literaria latino americana* 36 (1992), pp. 135–153.
38. Beverley, "Our Rigoberta?" p. 83.
39. See Mary Louise Pratt, "*Me llamo Rigoberta Menchú:* Autoethnography and the Recoding of Citizenship, in Carey-Webb and Benz, eds., *Teaching and Testimony*, pp. 57–72. See also Sommer, "No Secrets for Rigoberta."
40. Jean Franco, "Diálogo de sordos," in Ellen Spielman, ed., *L@s Rel@ciones cultur@les entre @meric@ L@tin@ después de l@ guerr@ frí@* (Berlin: Wissenschaftlicher Verlag, 2000) pp. 234–241.
41. Nancy Scheper-Hughes, *Death without Weeping: The Violence of Everyday Life in Brazil* (Berkeley and Los Angeles: California University Press, 1991).
42. John Beverley, *Subalternity and Representation: Arguments in Cultural Theory* (Durham: Duke University Press, 1999), p. 31.
43. Doris Sommer, "No Secrets for Rigoberta."
44. Adolfo Gilly, *Chiapas. La razón ardiente* (Mexico: Era, 1997) p. 104.
45. Leonidas Morales, *Conversaciones con Diamela Eltit* (Santiago: Cuarto Propio, 1998), pp. 168–170.
46. Nelly Richard, Francesca Lombardo, Diamela Eltit, "Lo que brilla por su ausencia," *Revista de Crítica Cultural* 11 (Nov. 1995), p. 43.
47. Terry Eagleton, *The Ideology of the Aesthetic* (Oxford: Basil Blackwell, 1990) pp. 382–383.
48. Diamela Eltit, preface to *El Padre Mío* (Santiago: Francisco Zeghers, 1989), p. 11.
49. Nelly Richard, "Bordes, diseminación, postmodernismo: una metáfora latinoamericana de fin de siglo," in Josefina Ludmer, ed., *Las culturas de fin de siglo* (Buenos Aires: Beatriz Viterbo, 1994), pp. 240–248.
50. Gilles Deleuze and Félix Guattari, *Anti-Oedipus,* vol. 1 of *Capitalism and Schizophrenia,* trans. Robert Hurley, Mark Seem, and Helen R. Lane (New York: Viking Press, 1977), p. 17.
51. Eltit, preface to *El Padre Mio.*
52. Diamela Eltit and Paz Errázuriz, *El infarto del alma* (Santiago: Francisco Zeghers, 1994), pages unnumbered.

9. Bodies in Distress

1. Josefina Ludmer, *El cuerpo del delito: Un manual* (Buenos Aires: Perfil, 1999).
2. See Susana Rotker, "Ciudades escritas por la violencia," in *Ciudadanías del miedo,* ed. Susana Rotker (Caracas: Nueva Sociedad, 2000).
3. "Colombia: Memory and Accountability," *NACLA Report on the Americas* 34, no. 1 (New York: July–Aug. 2000), pp. 42.
4. Paulo Sérgio Pinheiro, "Navigating in Uncharted Waters: Human Rights Advocacy in Brazil's "New Democracy." *NACLA Report on the Americas,* vol. xxxiv, num. 1 pp. 47–51.
5. See Rotker, "Ciudades escritas por la violencia."
6. Gilles Deleuze and Félix Guattari, *Anti-Oedipus,* vol. 1 of *Capitalism and Schizophrenia,* trans. Robert Hurley, Mark Seem, and Helen Lane (New York: Viking Press, 1977), p. 357.
7. *Costumbrismo* is a description of archaic and disappearing customs and traditions as represented in chronicles, novels, paintings, and engravings.
8. Fernando Vallejo, *La virgen de los sicarios* (Bogotá: Alfaguara, 1994), p. 40 (my translation). See also Boris Muñoz and José Roberto Duque, *La ley de la calle: Testimonios de jóvenes protagonistas de la violencia en Caracas* (Caracas: Fundarte, 1995); Alonso Salazar, *No nacimos pa' semilla* (Colombia: CINEP, 1990); *Born to Die in Medellín,* trans. Nick Caistor (London: Latin American Bureau, n.d.); Paulo Lins, *Cidade de Deus* (São Paulo: Schwarcz, 1997).
9. Susana Rotker, unpublished paper.
10. Muñoz and Duque, *La ley de la calle,* p. 40.
11. Salazar, *Born to Die in Medellín,* p. 120.
12. Slavoj Žižek, *The Sublime Object of Ideology* (London: Verso, 1989), p. 4.
13. Lia Zanotta Machado, "Masculinidade, sexualidade e estupro. As construcôes da virilidade," *Cadernos Pagú* 11 (1998), pp. 231–273.
14. Mary Louise Pratt, "Tres incendios y dos mujeres extraviadas: El imaginario novelístico frente al nuevo contrato social" unpublished paper.
15. For the "fascist within," see Gillian Rose, *Mourning Becomes the Law: Philosophy and Representation* (Cambridge: Cambridge University Press, 1996).
16. Emilio Pérez Cruz, *Borracho no vale* (Mexico: Plaza y Janes, 1988).
17. Carlos Monsiváis, "The Crime Page in Mexico," in *Mexican Postcards,* trans. John Kraniauskas (London: Verso, 1997), pp. 155–157.
18. James Kelman, *How Late It Was, How Late* (London: Minerva, 1994) pp. 63–4.
19. Richard Price, *Clockers* (New York: Avon Books, 1993), makes an interesting contrast. Here the game of the protagonist, Strike, is survival.
20. Judith Butler, *Bodies that Matter: On the Discursive Limits of "Sex"* (New

York: Routledge, 1995), p. 219. See José Esteban Muñoz, *Disidentifications: Queers of Color and the Performance of Politics* (Minneapolis: University of Minnesota Press, 1999), pp. 11–13.

21. Interview with Lohana in Irina Mendieta, "Identidades huidizas. Fisuras de un mecanismo de identificacion" unpublished paper.

22. Francisco Casas, "Las Yeguas del Apocalípsis (The Mares of the Apocalypse): The Equine Lips of Exile," in Coco Fusco, ed., *Corpus Delecti: Performance Art of the Americas* (London: Routledge, 2000), pp. 220–222.

23. Lemebel often uses the language of gay subculture, like *tusa* and *boa,* two slang words for penis.

24. Pedro Lemebel, "Las amapolas también tienen espinas," in *La esquina es mi corazón* (Santiago, Cuarto Propio, 1995), pp. 123–129. The translation in the text is mine. Lemebel has also published *Loco afán: Crónicas del sidario* (Santiago: Lom, 1996); *De Perlas y cicatrices* (Santiago: Lom, 1996).

25. Pedro Lemebel, "Encajes de acero para una almohada penitencial," in *La esquina es mi corazón,* pp. 45–49.

26. For other novels of the AIDS epidemic, see Severo Sarduy, *Pájaros en la playa* (Barcelona: Tusquets, 1993); Mario Bellatín, *Salón de belleza* (Barcelona: Tusquets, 1994).

27. Judith Butler, *Bodies that Matter;* Kaja Silverman, *Male Subjectivity at the Margins* (New York: Routledge, 1992); Pierre Bourdieu, *La domination masculine* (Paris: Seuil, 1998).

28. Diamela Eltit, *El cuarto mundo* (Santiago: Planeta, 1988); *The Fourth World,* trans. Dick Gerdes (University of Nebraska Press, 1995).

29. Diamela Eltit, *Los trabajadores de la muerte* (Santiago: Planeta, 1999).

10. Obstinate Memory

1. Michael Taussig, *Shamanism and Colonialism: A Study in Terror and Healing and the Wild Man* (Chicago: University of Chicago Press, 1987), p. 373.

2. Andreas Huyssen, *Twilight Memories: Marking Time in the Culture of Amnesia* (New York: Routledge, 1995), pp. 3–5.

3. Jorge Luis Borges, "Guayaquil," in *El informe de Brodie* (Buenos Aires: Emecé, 1970), pp. 111–124.

4. Judith Butler, Ernesto Laclau, and Slavoj Žižek, *Contingency, Hegemony, Universality: Contemporary Dialogues on the Left* (London: Verso, 2000).

5. Alejo Carpentier, *El siglo de las luces* (Barcelona: Seix Barral, 1962); *Explosion in the Cathedral,* trans. John Sturrock (London: Minerva, 1991); Carlos Fuentes, *La campaña* (Madrid: Mondadori, 1990); *The Campaign,* trans. Alfred MacAdam (New York: Farrar, Straus, and Giroux, 1991); Gabriel García Márquez, *El general en su laberinto* (Madrid: Mondadori, 1989); *The General in His Labyrinth,* trans. Edith Grossman (New York:

Knopf, 1990); Mario Vargas Llosa, *La guerra del fin del mundo* (Barcelona: Seix Barral, 1981); *The War of the End of the World,* trans. Helen R. Lane (New York: Avon Books, 1985).

6. César Aira, *Ema la cautiva* (Buenos Aires: Editorial Belgrano, 1981): Carmen Boullosa, *Cielos de la tierra* (Mexico: Águilar, 1997): *Duerme* (Mexico: Alfaguara, 1994).

7. Diamela Eltit and Nivia Palma, "El caso 'Simón Bolívar' y la polémica del Fondart," *Revista de crítica cultural* 9 (Nov. 1994), pp. 25–35.

8. Eduardo Galeano, *Memory of Fire,* vol. 1, *Genesis,* trans. Cedric Belfrage (London: Quartet Books, 1985), p. xv.

9. William Rowe and Vivian Schelling, *Memory and Modernity: Popular Culture in Latin America* (London: Verso, 1991).

10. Yolande Salas de Lecuna, *Bolívar y la historia en la cultura popular* (Caracas: Universidad Simón Bolívar, 1987).

11. Walter J. Ong, *The Presence of the Word: Some Prolegomena for Cultural and Religious History* (New York: Simon and Schuster, 1967).

12. In "Las exigencias de la memoria," *Punto de vista* 68 (Dec. 2000), Hector Schmucler reminds us that Maurice Halbwachs, who first studied social memory, died miserably in the Buchenwald concentration camp, where his name and identity were removed postmortem. His pupil Jorge Semprún, who was also in the camp, gave an account of this in *La escritura o la vida* (Barcelona: Tusquets, 1995), pp. 5–9. See Maurice Halbwachs, *Les cadres sociaux de la mémoire* (Paris: F. Alcan, 1925); Paul Connerton, *How Societies Remember* (Cambridge: Cambridge University Press, 1989).

13. Kirwin Lee Klein, "On the Emergence of *Memory* in Historical Discourse," *Representations* 69 (Winter 2000), pp. 127–150.

14. Schmucler, "Las exigencias de la memoria," p. 7.

15. *Nunca Mas: Informe de la Comisión Nacional sobre la desaparición de personas* (Buenos Aires: Editorial Universitaria, 1984). There was also a television documentary.

16. Elizabeth Jelin, "The Minefields of Memory," *NACLA Report on the Americas* 33, no. 2 (Sept.–Oct. 1998), pp. 23–29. Elizabeth Jelin "La política de la memoria: El movimiento de derechos humanos y la construcción democrática en Argentina," in Carlos Acuña et al., eds., *Juicio, castigo y memorias: Derechos humanos y justicia en la política argentina* (Buenos Aires: Nueva Visión, 1995).

17. *Nunca Mas,* p. 15.

18. Tina Rosenberg, "In Chile, the Balance Tips Towards the Victims," *New York Times,* 22 August 2000, p. A20.

19. Susan Jonas, *Centaurs and Doves: Guaemala's Peace Process* (Boulder: Westfield Press, 2000).

20. Walter Benjamin, "On Some Motifs in Baudelaire," *Illuminations: Essays and Reflections* (London: Jonathan Cape, 1970), p. 193.

21. For the debate surrounding Memory Park in Buenos Aires, see Graciela

Silvestri, "El arte en los límites de la representación," and Andreas Huyssen, "El parque de la Memoria: Una glosa desde lejos," in *Punto de vista* 68 (Dec. 2000), pp. 18–28.

22. Beatriz Sarlo, *Escenas de la vida posmoderna: Intelectuales, arte y video-cultura en la Argentina* (Buenos Aires: Ariel, 1994), p. 19.

23. Elaine Scarry, *The Body in Pain: The Making and Unmaking of the World* (New York: Oxford University Press, 1985).

24. *Nunca Mas*, p. 49.

25. Jacobo Timerman *Prisoner without a Name, Cell without a Number* (New York: Vintage Books, 1982).

26. Alicia Partnoy, *The Little School: Tales of Disappearance and Survival*, trans. Alicia Partnoy with Lois Athey and Sandra Braustein (San Francisco: Cleis Press, 1998).

27. Hernán Valdés, *Tejas verdes: Diario de un campo de concentración en Chile* (Esplughes de Llobregat: Ariel, 1974); *Diary of a Chilean Concentration Camp*, trans. Jo Labanyi (London: Gollancz, 1975).

28. The difficulty of describing what actually went on in the camps is discussed by Hugo Vezzetti, "Representaciones de los campos de concentración en la Argentina," *Punto de vista* 68 (Dec. 2000), pp. 13–17.

29. Juan Gelman, "Somas," *Interrupciones*, vol. 1 (Buenos Aires: Libros de Tierra Firme, 1988), p. 21.

30. Luisa Valenzuela, "Cambio de armas," in *Cambio de armas* (Hanover, N.H.: Ediciones del Norte, 1985); *Other Weapons*, trans. Deborah Bonner (Hanover, N.H.: Ediciones del Norte, 1985).

31. Lawrence Thornton, *Imagining Argentina* (New York: Doubleday, 1987).

32. Miguel Bonasso, *Recuerdos de la muerte* (Buenos Aires: Bruguera, 1984), follows many of the conventions of Cold War crime fiction.

33. Luz Arce, *El infierno* (Santiago: Planeta, 1993).

34. Paolo Virno, "The Ambivalence of Disenchantment," in Michael Hardt and Paulo Virno, eds., *Radical Thought in Italy* (Minneapolis: University of Minnesota Press, 1996), pp. 13–32.

35. Nelly Richard, Francesca Lombardo, and Diamela Eltit, "Lo que brilla por su ausencia," *Revista de crítica cultural* 11 (Nov. 1995), pp. 28–43.

36. Ibid.

37. Ildeber Avelar, *The Untimely Present: Postdictatorial Latin American Fiction and the Work of Mourning* (Durham: Duke University Press, 1999).

38. Nelly Snaith, "La muerte sin escena," *Debate feminista* 11, no. 21 (April 2000), pp. 3–41.

39. Griselda Gambarro, *El campo* (Buenos Aires: Ediciones Insurrexit, 1967).

40. Juan Gelman, "A mi hijo," in *de palabra* (Madrid: Visor, 1994), pp. 120–155. The poem referred to is on p. 132.

41. Juan Gelman, *Unthinkable Tenderness*, trans. Joan Lindgren (Berkeley: University of California Press, 1997) p. 34.

42. Juan Gelman, "A Teodora," in *de palabra*, pp. 619–629.

43. See, for instance, Eric L. Santner, "History beyond the Pleasure Principle: Some Thoughts on the Representation of Trauma," in Saul Friedlander, ed., *Probing the Limits of Representation: Nazism and the "Final Solution"* (Cambridge: Harvard University Press, 1992), pp. 143–154.

44. Marcial Anativia Godoy, "Chile, Obstinate Memory," *NACLA Report on the Americas* 32, no. 2 (Sept.–Oct. 1998), p. 21.

45. Nelly Richard, "Con motivo del 11 de septiembre: Notas sobre "La memoria obstinada" de Patricio Guzmán," *Revista de crítica cultural* 15 (Nov. 1997), pp. 54–61.

46. Roland Barthes, *Camera Lucida: Reflections on Photography,* trans. Richard Howard (New York: Farrar, Straus, and Giroux, 1981), p. 96.

47. Nelly Richard, "Memoria, fotografía: drama y tramas," *Punto de vista* 68 (Dec. 2000), p. 31.

48. Walter Benjamin, "Theses on the Philosophy of History," in *Illuminations,* trans. Harry Zohn (London: Jonathan Cape, 1970), p. 257.

49. Avelar, *The Untimely Present,* p. 228.

50. Tununa Mercado, *En estado de memoria* (Buenos Aires: Ada Korn, 1990). Quotations in English are from *In a State of Memory,* trans. Peter Kahn (Lincoln: University of Nebraska Press, 2001).

51. Michel Foucault, "Nietzsche, Genealogy, History," *Language, Counter-Memory, Practice: Selected Essays and Interviews* (Ithaca: Cornell University Press, 1977), p. 161.

52. Gillian Rose, *Mourning Becomes the Law: Philosophy and Representation* (Cambridge: Cambridge University Press, 1996).

53. Slavoj Žižek, *For They Know Not What They Do: Enjoyment as a Political Factor* (London: Verso, 1991), p. 99.

54. For the difference between "activity" and "wage labor," see Virno, "The Ambivalence of Disenchantment."

55. Donna Haraway, "A Cyborg Manifesto," *Simians, Cyborgs, and Women: The Reinvention of Nature* (New York: Routledge, 1991), p. 180.

56. Ricardo Piglia, *La ciudad ausente* (Buenos Aires: Sudamericana, 1992).

57. There is an extensive discussion of Piglia's novel in Avelar, *The Untimely Present,* pp. 86–107. See also his discussion of Macedonio Fernández in ibid., pp. 101–110.

58. Alberto Moreiras, "Postdictadura y reforma de pensamiento," in *Revista de crítica cultural* 7 (Nov. 1993), pp. 26–35.

59. Avelar, *The Untimely Present,* p. 2.

60. Ibid., pp. 1–21.

11. Inside the Empire

1. Interview with Diamela Eltit, *El Mensajero* (Santiago), 16 July 2000.

2. This refers to the ending of Diamela Eltit's novel *Los vigilantes* (Buenos Aires: Sudamericana, 1994).

3. Ernesto Laclau, *New Reflections on the Revolution of Our Time* (London: Verso, 1990).

4. Agency for International Development, "The Democratic Initiative," quoted by William I. Robinson, "Polyarchy: Coercion's New Face in Latin America," *NACLA Report on the Americas* 34, no. 3 (Nov.–Dec. 2000), p. 45.

5. Román de la Campa, *Latin Americanism* (Minneapolis: University of Minnesota Press, 1999), p. 149.

6. Nestor García Canclini discusses this in *Culturas híbridas: Estrategias para entrar y salir de la modernidad* (Mexico: Grijalbo, 1989).

7. See, for example, the anthology of short stories edited by David Miklos, *Una ciudad mejor que esta: Antología de nuevos narradores mexicanos* (Barcelona: Tusquets, 1999).

8. This point is forcibly made by Judith Butler, "Competing Universalities," in Judith Butler, Ernesto Laclau, and Slavoj Žižek, *Contingency, Hegemony, Universality: Contemporary Dialogues on the Left* (London: Verso, 2000), p. 179, and see also Gayatri Chakravorty Spivak, translator's preface and afterword in Mahasweta Devi, *Imaginary Maps* (New York: Routledge, 1995).

9. Laura Esquivel, *Like Water for Chocolate: A Novel in Monthly Installments, With Recipes, Romances, and Home Remedies,* trans. Carol Christensen and Thomas Christensen (New York: Doubleday, 1992).

10. Nestor García Canclini, *Consumidores y ciudadanos: Conflictos multiculturales de la globalización* (Mexico: Grijalbo, 1995).

11. Gayatri Chakravorty Spivak, "The Politics of Translation," *Outside/In the Teaching Machine* (New York: Routledge, 1993), pp. 179–200, esp. p. 190.

12. Nelly Richard, "Academic Globalization, Cultural Studies and Critical Intellectual Practice: New Challenges" (unpublished paper).

13. Nelly Richard, "Antidisciplina, transdisciplina y redisciplinamientos del saber," *Residuos y metáforas,* pp. 141–160.

14. Beatriz Sarlo, "Intelectuales," *Escenas de la vida posmoderna: Intelectuales, arte y videocultura en la Argentina* (Buenos Aires: Ariel, 1994), pp. 172–198.

15. Ibid., pp. 197–198.

16. Maurizio Lazzarato, "Immaterial Labor," in Paulo Virno and Michael Hardt, eds., *Radical Thought in Italy* (Minneapolis: University of Minnesota Press, 1996), pp. 132–146, especially p. 143.

17. Silviano Santiago, "Reading and Discursive Intensities: On the Situation of Postmodern Reception in Brazil," *The Postmodern Debate in Latin America,* special issue of *Boundary* 2, (1993), p. 201.

18. Although I cite Deleuze and Guattari, in fact Deleuze provides the philosophical framework. See Paul Patton, *Deleuze and the Political* (New York: Routledge, 2000).

19. Gilles Deleuze and Félix Guattari, *Anti-Oedipus,* vol. 1 of *Capitalism and*

Schizophrenia, trans. Robert Hurley, Mark Seem, and Helen Lane (New York: Viking Press, 1977), especially pp. 259–261.

20. Gilles Deleuze, "Minor Literature: Kafka," in *The Deleuze Reader,* ed. Constantin V. Boundas (New York: Columbia University Press, 1993), p. 156.
21. Paolo Virno, "Virtuosity and Revolution: The Political Theory of Exodus," in Hardt and Virno, eds., *Radical Thought in Italy,* pp. 188–209.
22. Nestor García Canclini, *Culturas híbridas,* p. 264.
23. Richard, introduction to *Residuos y metáforas,* pp. 11–23, esp. p. 11.
24. The limitations of the cultural critique are addressed by John Beasley-Murray, "'El arte de la fuga,': Cultural Critique, Metaphor and History," *Journal of Latin American Cultural Studies* 9 (Dec. 2000), pp. 259–272.
25. Tomas Moulian, *Chile actual: Anatomía de un mito* (Santiago: Lom/Arcis, 1997).
26. Robinson, "Polyarchy," p. 46.
27. Nelly Richard, "El modelaje gráfico de una identidad publicitaria," in *Residuos y metáforas,* pp. 163–177. The reference to "magical realism" alludes to the "discovery of ice" at the beginning of García Márquez's *One Hundred Years of Solitude.*
28. Catalina Parra, Exhibition at the New Jersey Museum, 2001.
29. See Eduardo Sabrovsky, "Políticas del espacio y la mirada," in *Revista de crítica cultural 19* (Nov. 1999), pp. 14–21.
30. Judith Butler, *Gender Trouble: Feminism and the Subversion of Identity* (New York: Routledge, 1998), p. x.
31. Ibid., p. 138.
32. Judith Butler, "Restaging the Universal," in Butler, Laclau, and Žižek, *Contingency, Hegemony, Universality,* pp. 11–43.
33. See John Womack, ed., *Rebellion in Chiapas: An Historical Reader* (New York: New Press, 1999).
34. Subcomandante Marcos, "México 1998: Arriba y abajo—Máscaras y silencio," in ibid., pp. 356–362.
35. Gerald Martin, *Journeys through the Labyrinth: Latin American Fiction in the Twentieth Century* (London: Verso, 1989), p. 24.
36. For a discussion of these points see Francine Masiello, *The Art of the Transition: Latin American Culture and Neoliberal Crisis* (Durham: Duke University Press, 2001).
37. Raquel Olea, "Femenino y feminismo en transición," in Raquel Olea, ed., *Escrituras de la diferencia sexual* (Santiago:Lom / La Morada, 2000) pp. 53–60.
38. Unpublished interview of Lohana by Irina Mendieta.
39. Lesbians have in turn claimed a privileged role in challenging gender categories. See Norma Mogrovejo, *Un amor que se atrevió a decir su nombre* (Mexico: CDAHI y Plaza y Valdés, 2000).
40. Arcadio Díaz-Quiñones/Ricardo Piglia, "Conversación en Princeton," in

Ellen Spielman, ed., *L@s Rel@ciones Cultur@les entre @méric@ L@tina y Est@dos Unidos: después de l@ guerr@ frí@* (Berlin: Wissenschafterlicher Verlag, 2000), pp. 104–115.

41. Giorgio Agamben, *Means Without End: Notes on Politics"* (Minneapolis: University of Minnesota Press, 2000), p. 81.
42. William Rowe, *Poets of Contemporary Latin America: History and Inner Life* (New York: Oxford University Press, 2000), pp. 16–17.
43. The list is not exclusive and at the end of the book he lists many other poets who could have been included.
44. For a more extensive discussion, see Rowe, *Poets of Contemporary Latin America*; Masiello, *The Art of Transition.*

Acknowledgments

I have had this book in mind for several years, and so a considerable number of people have contributed in some way to my thinking. Of the many people who have helped me, I owe special thanks to Edward Said for his support and encouragement. I thank Patrick Deere, who helped edit the manuscript, and Ana Dopico, who read and commented on it. I am very grateful to Gayatri Chakravorty Spivak, Diamela Eltit, Licia Fiol Matta, Juan Flores, Josefina Ludmer, Francine Masiello, Tununa Mercado, Myriam Jiménez, Catalina Parra, Mary Pratt, Osvaldo Tcherkaski, and George Yudice for their conversations and comments. And a special thanks to graduate and undergraduate students who, in the course of my teaching career, have always posed the challenging questions.

Index

violence in, 220; gender roles in, 224; military regime in, 260; crisis of value in, 263–264

Brecht, Bertolt, 103

Breton, André, 42, 51

Brito, Eugenia, 181

Brodsky, Marcelo, 252

Brotherston, Gordon, 170

Brunner, José Joaquín, 192

Bruns, Gerald, 191

Buenos Aires, Argentina, 5, 39, 44, 191, 257–258; avant-garde in, 116; and Eva Perón's body, 121–122; rock music in, 185; transvestites in, 229, 273; Memory Park, 239, 256

Burger, Peter, 115

Burma, 82–83

Burnham, James, 30

Burroughs, William, 45

Burton, Julianne, 28, 103

Butler, Judith, 18, 229, 232; *Gender Trouble,* 270

Byron, Lord, 139

Cabrera, Lydia, 169

Cabrera Infante, Guillermo, 44, 49, 91–92, 100; *Tres tristes tigres,* 92

Caimán barbudo, 91, 98–99

Calles, Plutarco, 133

Calvino, Italo: *Invisible Cities,* 163, 191–193

Camisea, 155

Camnitzer, Luis, 116

Campa, Román de la, 260–261

Campas, 155

Campbell, Joseph: *The Hero with a Thousand Faces,* 169

Cantinflas, 188

Capitalism, 2, 17, 139, 147, 175, 192; and communism, 3, 11, 14, 71, 88, 163; and neoliberalism, 13–14, 54, 56, 182, 246, 261; reformed, 22–23; and humanism, 40; in Mexico, 68; in Cuba, 86–87; in Nicaragua, 112, 115; in Paraguay, 131; and nature, 141; and indigenous peoples, 170, 173; and globalization, 182, 264–265; in Chile, 245–246, 260; contemporary, 260–262, 268

Caracas, Venezuela, 39, 49, 95, 191

Cardenal, Ernesto, 3, 16, 86, 112–116, 236; *El estrecho dudoso,* 72, 112–114;

Homenaje a los indios americanos, 112–113; *Canto nacional,* 113

Cárdenas, Cuauhtémoc, 199

Cárdenas, Lázaro, 63

Caribbean Sea, 92, 167–169, 202

Carlyle, Thomas, 130–131

Carnival, 71, 92–93

Carpentier, Alejo, 5, 49, 89, 96, 100, 160–162, 169; *Concierto barroco,* 165; *Ecue-Yamba-o,* 166; *El reino de este mundo,* 167–168; *El siglo de las luces,* 167–169, 235

Carril, Delia del, 58

Carvajal, Ángel, 29

Casa de las Américas, 45–46, 52, 85, 90–91, 93–94, 96–97, 99, 211

Casas, Francisco, 229

Casey, Calvert, 91

Castañeda, Carlos, 166, 173

Castañeda, Jorge, 36, 59–60, 88, 110–111

Castellanos, Rosario, 162

Castillo Armas, Carlos, 33

Castro, Fidel, 1, 32, 85, 88–91, 93, 99–100, 111

Castro Cid, Enrique, 41

Catholicism, 96, 180; and capitalism, 3, 87, 112; and shamanism, 75; and communism, 84, 87; and indigenous peoples, 87, 214; in Nicaragua, 111–113; in Mexico, 133, 197–198; and globalization, 198; and abortion, 198, 232; and women, 245

Caudillismo, 33

Celan, Paul, 250

Censorship, 1, 12, 23, 33, 44–45, 90, 101

Central Intelligence Agency, 2, 22, 30–32, 34, 44–45, 47–49, 60, 80, 106

Cervantes, Miguel de: *Don Quixote,* 4, 90

Césaire, Aimé, 75

Chávez, Hugo, 110

Chiapas, Mexico, 7, 87, 172, 216, 271–272

Chicanos, 67, 187–188, 226

Children. *See* Youth

Chile, 26, 33, 43, 57–58, 62, 66, 86, 97, 107, 123, 163, 187, 191–192; military regime in, 11–12, 83–84, 179–180, 185, 229, 231, 239, 244–245, 251–253, 260, 266–267; lower class in, 14–15, 60; Continental Congress of Culture in, 34, 80; Communist Party in, 36, 57–58, 66, 73,